"ADIEU TO DEAR OLD POCK"

A tribute to the Pocklington and district men
who served in the Great War 1914-1918

A publication of
Pocklington and District Local History Group and Pocklington Town Council
Edited by Andrew Sefton

Dedication

This book is dedicated to the brave soldiers and volunteers of the Pocklington district who gave their lives to the cause of freedom for their King and Country, and all the brave soldiers who returned home and often stayed silent to their friends and families about the severe trauma they suffered during those dark days of war in very testing conditions. The book is published for the centenary of the end of the conflict with all participants now departed.

East Riding Yeomanry soldiers manning a Vickers-Maxim machine gun
Copyright York Museums Trust (York Castle Museum). (YORCM : 2009.107.27)
This postcard had a Pocklington postmark dated 19th Sept. 1914
and is believed to have been photographed at Ousethorpe Camp.

Addressed to R. Dunn, Ellerby, Skirlaugh, Hull. , Dear Amy,
Thanks for the socks they are fine. ...We have had some rotten weather here rain & wind.
This was taken in our Maxim gun kit we dug opposite the place where I sleep. 150 more recruits came from depot today.
My mare is alright yet. Love Frank (No news of moving).

1st Edition

Copyright © 2018

Printed by: Book Empire, PMM Group (UK) Ltd., Unit 7, Lotherton Way, Garforth, Leeds. LS25 2JY.

Pocklington and District Local History Group

Acknowledgements

The Pocklington and District Local History Group is a non-profit making organisation whose aim is to preserve and record the heritage and local history of Pocklington and the surrounding villages. Pocklington has always been a hub for the local area, being a market town, administrative centre with large parish. It is therefore appropriate that the group collects memories, information and photographs from Pocklington as well as nearby parishes and preserves them for future generations.

In World War One, Pocklington had a recruitment centre and had a long standing tradition of being a muster point for troops and soldiers going right back to the Scottish Wars of the 14th Century. Ousethorpe Military Camp at Millington was situated near to the town where it could access the resources of the town for supplies and the railway station for the transportation of soldiers. It had been used as a training camp in Edwardian times and for a large military exercise in the area in 1908. It may also have been utilised from the late eighteenth century by the Pocklington corps of volunteer infantry under the command of Robert Denison. A record of such a muster exists from 1805. Relics and badges from the period have also been found in the local fields by metal detector enthusiasts.

This research has been carried out using online tools, record offices and other sources including family feedback from holding two large exhibitions in the Oak House Arts Centre in 2014 and 2016. Always cross check the information provided here with your own research and family information. Please feedback any mistakes and if reprints are made, the information will be updated.

From a population of just under 3000 for Pocklington to see 300 men go off to fight in a war and to lose 53 out of those that were sent, shows the great sacrifice the town made to the cause. Their bravery is recognised by the medals awarded for their gallantry in action including the DCM, DFC, Military Cross and several Military Medals and Croix de Guerre. Even the rural East Riding's only Great War Victoria Cross was won by a native of Newton-on-Derwent.

I am indebted to Phil Gilbank, who has proof-read and given encouragement for the publication of this book and also to Jo and Peter Green for their help and support on the committee of the Pocklington and District Local History Group. Acknowledgement as well to the late Ken Durkin for his contributions and tireless enthusiasm for all aspects of Pocklington history. Thanks also to Martin Cooper and Graham Perry for starting the WW1 remembrance project on behalf of the town council over 10 years ago, and Martin's original substantial work and research on the fallen heroes on the Great War monument near the Post Office for the first exhibition held in the town in 2008. This was followed by further exhibitions and research by members of The Pocklington and District Local History Group in 2014 and 2016.

The title "ADIEU TO DEAR OLD POCK" comes from a letter written from the front by J.R. Campbell to the Howdenshire Chronicle and Pocklington Weekly News and published 28th April 1917. See Page 133.

Andrew Sefton

Pocklington and District Local History Group
http://www.pocklingtonhistory.com
September 2018

Table of Contents

North Facing

Grateful thanks to the following people for help with providing photographs, information and assistance for the production of this book:

Martin Cooper, Graham Perry, Phil Gilbank, Jo Green, Peter Green, Paul Frank, Caroline Hanna, Jim Ainscough, Trevor Brigham, Heather Buttle, John Derrick and the family of the late Ralph Johnson, Janet Gray, John Nottingham, Annie Beattie, Mike Silburn, Peter Halkon, Andrew Hart, David Savage, Graham Winteringham, Gillian Brooks, Stephen Elliot, Lynne Steel, Amanda Nicholls, Perry Hardy, Marcus Ramshaw, Paul Bennett, Jan Robertson, Roger Bellingham, Kevin Warcup of the Royal British Legion Pocklington Branch, the late Ken Durkin and the late Denis Moor, The British Library Board giving permission to use extracts from the 'Howdenshire Chronicle, Pocklington Weekly News and Market Weighton Advertiser' (known simply at the time as the Pocklington Weekly News and printed and published in Pocklington), East Riding of Yorkshire Council Archives, York Museums Trust, Canon Valerie Hewetson who has researched Barmby Moor, Fangfoss, Spital, Bolton, Allerthorpe, Thornton, Melbourne and Storwood soldiers, Angie Edwards Pocklington School Archivist. Chris Cosgrove kindly took specific gravestone photographs from my request on his visit to France in July 2018. Thank you to Daniel Sefton for the design of the front and back cover; and also to the Pocklington Town Council who initiated this Great War research project and have provided financial support for the publication of this book.

Pocklington Memorial

The Pocklington Weekly News dated Saturday, November 26th, 1921, carried the following news of the ceremony:

On Sunday last, a War Memorial was unveiled at Pocklington in memory of the local men who had fallen in the Great War. The raising of the money to carry out such a project was left entirely to the surviving Comrades who are to be congratulated on carrying the scheme to completion. The memorial is erected on a triangular piece of ground known as Smithy Hill, near Messrs R. M. English and Son's offices, and will in due course be surrounded by a palisading in order to give it greater preservation.

The Comrades under comrade Walter Barker (chairman of the committee) and headed by Pocklington Coronation Band, under the conductorship of Mr H. U. Buttle L. V. C. M. marched in procession from the club to the monument. Several members of Pocklington District Urban Council were also present. The Rev. A. F. Pentney M. C. (Wesleyan) conducted the proceedings, the vicar (the Rev I. McN. Smith) dedicating the memorial and the Rev L. Robinson (Primitive Methodists) delivering an address, the unveiling ceremony being performed by the mothers of the first and last boys from the town that fell in the war, these being Mrs C. Hotham (Pavement) and Mrs A. Skinner (Wold View).

Rev. A.F. Pentney said they were about to unveil a memorial for the boys, who fought with many who stood around that afternoon. The proceedings opened with the singing of the hymn " Oh God our help in ages past" followed by prayer by Rev. A. F. Pentney, in which he said many young men found themselves in a wonderful fellowship, and they not even counted their own lives that they might serve others, but actually gave their lives so that we might live.

The memorial, a splendid piece of work by Mr J. Richardson, New Street, Pocklington, is 13ft high, and is an octagonal column fixed on a stone base, both being of Yorkshire white hard stone, and surmounted by an ornamental cross of Yorkshire brown hard stone. Upon the memorial is inscribed: -

To the Glory of God.
and in Memory of our Comrades
who fell in the Great War,
1914-1918

ROLAND BROWN
FRANCIS C BUTTLE
ROBERT W BUTTLE
HENRY I CATTLE
JOHN COOPER
WALTER J CRISP
JOHN CROSS
JOSEPH EAGAN
FRED EASTON
JAMES ELLIOTT
ROBERT C ENGLISH
THOMAS W FISHER
CHARLES FLINT
FRED FOSTER
GEORGE GILYEAD
JIM GILES
GEORGE S GRAINGER
STANLEY HALL
JAMES HARRISON
CLIFFORD HAYTON

HENRY HOLMES
HERBERT HOLMES
ALFRED HOPPER
CHARLES HOTHAM
GEORGE M JAVERLEY
HERBERT JESSOP
ARTHUR JESSOP
HAROLD JOHNSON
HENRY JOHNSON
EDWIN KIRBY
GEORGE KEMP
JOHN LEE
JOHN PLUMB
ROBERT PRATT
THOMAS W RIPPON
FREDERICK W ROBSON
EDWARD M ROBSON
ARTHUR ROWNTREE
HERBERT SAVAGE
SYDNEY SCAIFE
GEORGE J SCOTT
GEORGE SKELTON
THOMAS R SKINNER
JOHN W SMITH
FREDERICK S SMITH
ARCHIE SPENCER
RICHARD M STUBBS
ARTHUR J TAYLEURE
JOHN W THOMPSON
RICHARD TIMBS
THOMAS R THORPE
WILLIAM WALKER

Many beautiful floral tributes were then placed against the memorial amongst them were the following: -

"In loving memory of our dear pals, who fell during the Great War, 1914-1918 from the Pocklington Comrades."
"In loving remembrance, from Harry and Cicely"
"In loving memory of our dear son and brother George Henry Grainger, killed in action April 24th 1917 `Gone but not forgotten' From Jonathan and family"
"In memory of those dear lads who fell for us 1914-1918"
"To my dear boy, who gave his life that others might live. `Peace perfect peace' From Mother and family-Mrs Thompson"
"Not forgotten, from Mr R. L. English, Smylett Hall"
"In ever loving memory, from A. and M. Skinner, E. B. Skinner and Eleanor and Beatty"
"From W. and A. Rowley and family, in affectionate remembrance"
"In memory of those dear lads who gave their lives for King and Country"
"In memory of a dear brother – Sergt Arthur Rowntree. To memory ever dear. From his loving sisters Rose and Elsie"
"In remembrance, from Mr and Mrs T. English and Mr Tim English"
"In loving memory of our dear son and brother, Private J. Harrison H.L.T killed in France 24th March 1914-R.I.P."
"In proud and loving memory of Private George Gilyead, 10th East Yorks' Reg'. From father, mother, sister and brothers."
"To the memory of my dear boy, Charles and to the Officers and men who gave theirs lives in the Great War, 1914-1918 M C Hotham."
"In loving remembrance of Rifleman F. C. Buttle, who gave his life for his country, 5th April 1917. `To memory ever dear'. From his father, mother and brothers."

THE UNVEILING OF THE MEMORIAL

Mrs Hotham and Mrs Skinner then pulled the cords, which released the flags. The Rev. McN. Smith, vicar, dedicated the memorial and offered prayer. Comrade Walter Barker read the names inscribed on the memorial, which had been erected in memory of their fallen pals. The Rev. L Robinson then delivered an address in which he said he counted it a privilege indeed to take part in that solemn service, yet it was with emotions strangely stirred and feelings singularly mingled that he attempted to speak.

It was an hour wherein deep pathos and yet proud glory were closely interwoven, and he felt that so, too, those present must have come with hearts pulsing with tenderness towards those whose sorrows were there carved in stone, and yet thrilling with wonder as they considered the exalted meaning to the town.

God grant that that stone might be more to the town than merely a public memorial, upon which to gaze with careless interest. From that hour let that place be sanctified in their hearts as hallowed ground. That memorial standing perpetually before their eyes had a high service to perform for everyone, for its ministry was to keep before their mind and soul the vision of sacrifice.

It was easy to forget or at least grow headless or thoughtless, and the memorial was to remind them of the pathos of it all, grim unseemliness of the passing of their manhood. When old people died it was like the gathering of the ripe sheaves of corn ready for the garner. When death befell the young, in whom the physical pulse so strong beat, who after the long preparation of childhood and youth stood at the meridian of their powers, whose future was so full of high hopes, glowing expectations and great possibilities of living and serving-that death was so pathetically different.

It was the sun going down while it was yet day, it was the bud broken of as it was opening to reveal its beauty and fragrance. This they were all called to remember as they gazed upon that memorial, which made the sacrifice so colossal, and the grief so poignant.

Let them never fail to appreciate the immensity of the sacrifice which had meant the almost clean out of a generation of the world, and which had bereft the world of a generation's toil and endeavour.

In all the glory of men there was never known so vast a sacrifice, but when they called to mind the stupendous sacrifice it recorded it was not a vision of futility they saw, it could not be either futile or useless. Every instinct of the human heart cried out against the supposition.

A journalist wrote during the late conflict that "Europe was a shambles". No! it was not a shambles. Human love and tears were too sacred to the great God of life, it was an altar on which were laid sacrificial gifts. From that gift should come to the race of men-nay was coming already-a mighty recompense.

Vast as was the claim of death, vaster was the glories that should to life ensue, the liquid drops of tears that had been shed should come again transformed to oriental pearl, advantaging their loan with interest of ten times double gain of happiness.

For four years ran the river of blood, but for generations to come it would nourish the now growing beauty of the dawning age. In the vision of faith, out of death sprang life abundant, and the very depth of the darkness was the dawn's own herald. The roots of the future nourished deep in the blood-bathed past, should expand into a beauty only dimly conceived by the most optimistic of them.

Let their hope be steadfast and their faith sure, in the imperious call to God, and to every God like faculty in man, in the vision that memorial brought they must make their hearts strong and their hands ready to welcome the dawning of a new day that they may play their part and take their place in the great forward march.

Let sorrow and the tears of which the monument recorded be to them the wine of a new sacrament, them to an undying allegiance to the greater hopes of their race. The memorial stood a challenge to them all to embark upon that right-thinking which was militant, and that would not cease in its endeavour until it had changed for ever those evil fashions of the day that were passing. As they gazed upon the cross surmounting it they who sorrowed would see the vision of infinite comfort, and immortal hope-the blessed consciousness that God knew.

They heard again the word of the book "I know their sorrows" for the Lord was a strong-hold in the day of trouble and tenderly regardeth them that were his, there was tender comfort in the graciousness of him who was the God of all comfort, and they in their heart of sorrows might enter that blessedness that only came to the eyes that wept, and like the Psalmist they would be able to assert in gladness "In the multitude of the sorrows I had in my heart thy comforts refresh'st my soul" and above all was the promise of immortality, the hope that maketh not ashamed for "In him shall be all made alive, for he is the first fruits of them asleep"

The Rev A. F. Pentney read the following letter from Mr J. W. Laister J.P, chairman of the Pocklington Urban District Council.

The Comrades of the Great War (Pocklington branch) I congratulate you on your efforts and success in the erection of a memorial to one and all of your comrades who, at the call of King and country, fought and made the supreme sacrifice in the Great War. The noble self sacrifice, untiring zeal, and deeds of heroism which marked their conduct in the time of fierce conflict, is emblazoned on the memory, and will never be erased therefrom.

I wish to bear my tribute to the illustrious dead, and to those who are bereft my sincere sympathy extends.

I regret my inability through indisposition, to be present with you at the unveiling thereof, which marks an epoch in the history of our native town. I trust that the time is not far distant when war will be impossible; when he, who came to bring peace on earth and good will to men, shall dwell in all hearts.

During the singing of the hymn "Abide with me" a collection was taken in aid of the fund to provide palisading round the memorial.

The Rev. A. F. Pentney announced the Benediction, and comrade J. Waters sounded "The Reveille" and the "Last Post" which brought to a close a most impressive and soul-stirring service.

Phil Gilbank wrote:- *War memorials across the country are well known for omissions and errors, and Pocklington is no exception. Inclusion in the book of everyone who served and on the war memorial to the fallen was decided by a local committee of 'Comrades of the Great War' which met a couple of years after the war ended.*

The confusion of who should be included is amply demonstrated by the town's two main memorials - the one outside the Post Office contains 53, while the one in All Saints church has just 46 names, and on closer inspection you can clearly see that some were added at the bottom after it had originally been carved.

Several men who died in the war that are not on Pocklington memorials are listed in various places as from or born Pocklington. Matters are further complicated by Pocklington's status as the district's registration centre, so those born in nearby villages had their births registered and recorded at Pocklington.

A notable example is the only WWI Victoria Cross winner born in the rural East Riding, Harry Wood, who was born at Newton upon Derwent in 1882 and had his birth registered at Pocklington, but who subsequently appeared in several publications as 'born at Pocklington'.

Pocklington and District Local History Group

Left : The War Memorial just after demolition of English's Mill and prior to building the Post office.
Above: The war memorial about the 1930's.
Below: Lord Halifax at the Pocklington British Legion Memorial Service in 1936

VISCOUNT HALIFAX, K.G., G.C.S.I., G.C.I.E., P.C., MAJOR W. H. CARVER, M.P., and COL. E. W. PICKERING, D.S.O., T.D., J.P., AT A BRITISH LEGION MEMORIAL SERVICE AT POCKLINGTON

VISCOUNT HALIFAX, K.G., INSPECTING BRITISH LEGION PARADE AT POCKLINGTON

Left: Pocklington School Great War Memorial in the school's chapel. At least 272 former pupils and ten masters served across all three services, and 63 died including six head prefects. All of the members of the 1914 cricket 1st XI served and several died. The first known old boy casualty in April 1915 was Capt. Gerald Kirk, a footballer with Bradford City and Leeds City (the forerunner of Leeds United). There is also a memorial book in All Saints church listing the school's former pupils killed in both world wars. (Thanks to Paul Bennett & Phil Gilbank for the information and photograph.)

Pocklington and District Local History Group

Top: A remembrance parade around the 1950's.

Above and Left: Recent remembrance parades in Pocklington. (Photos by kind permission of Roger Pattison & Phil Gilbank)

Pocklington and District Local History Group

Pocklington Memorial Heroes

Roland Brown - 2nd Lieutenant Reg. No. 4378, 201977 (H01)

Born:	Castleford 1897
Date and age on death:	Reported Missing 13th July 1918, aged 21
Enlisted:	West Yorkshire Regiment
Regiment on Death:	Alexandra Princess of Wales Own 4th Battalion Yorkshire Regiment or Kings Royal Rifles
Buried:	Perth Cemetery (China Wall), Ypres.
Occupation:	Unknown
Father:	Joseph Hill Brown, coal agent on railway
Mother:	Mary Brown
Brothers:	Harry
Sisters:	Eliza Anne Fawbert, Elsie
Address pre-enlistment:	Railway Houses, Coal Depot, Balk Road at Pocklington Railway Station

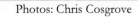

Photos: Chris Cosgrove

Roland Brown was born in Castleford in 1897, the son of Joseph Hill Brown and his wife Mary. His father worked for the North Eastern Railway Company and in 1911 the family still lived in Castleford, but they then moved to Pocklington where Joseph Hill Brown took over running the coal depot in the railway goods yard and appears in the 1918 Pocklington Register of Electors.

Roland enlisted as Pte 4378 in the West Yorkshire Regiment. He was posted to France on 6th January 1917, and just two weeks later he was commissioned as a 2nd Lieutenant with the 4th Battalion Yorkshire Regiment. The Book of Remembrance in All Saints Church listing all the Pocklington men who went to war records him as also being in the Kings Royal Rifles (see p. 193).

Germany launched a last desperate attempt to win the war in spring 1918. The allies suffered heavy losses and several northern battalions were decimated, causing them to be amalgamated into the 150th (York and Durham) Brigade. The reformed brigade remained in action until further casualties saw it withdrawn from the front on 15th July 1918. Brown was posted missing on July 13th and his memorial can be seen today in Perth China Wall Cemetery just to the east of Ypres.

Francis C. Buttle - Private Reg. No. 12244 (H02)

Born:	Pocklington in 1897
Date and age on death:	5th April 1917, aged 19
Enlisted:	Helmsley
Regiment on Death:	21st Battalion Kings Own Royal Rifles
Buried:	Bray Cemetery (Somme)
Occupation:	Joiner & grocers errand boy in 1911 age 14
Father:	George T Buttle (tailor)
Mother:	Dinah Buttle (bonnet maker)
Brothers:	Herbert W, George Harold
Address pre-enlistment:	30 London St., Pocklington

In the 1901 census the Buttle family lived on St. Helensgate, but by the time of Francis's death the family had moved to 34 Union street with Francis's grandparents, where in 1901 Charles and Mary Buttle ran a butchers shop and grocers. Charles died in 1909, perhaps George and his family moved in to help with the business on Charles death. Mary died in February 1917, she was a member of the Primitive Methodist Church also a member of the Pocklington and District Women's Liberal Association, which she represented as delegate at the central conference in London. In the 1918 Elector Register, at 34 Union Street was living George Thomas Buttle, Dinah Buttle and Herbert Ullathorne Buttle.

Frank, as he apparently liked to be known, was employed as a joiner by Mr Thomas J Lamb, who had premises at 20 Railway Street and also Church Lane, Pocklington.

Frank enlisted at Helmsley aged 19 years and 4 months in the 21st Battalion Kings Own Royal Rifles 9th Yeomanry on 5th Nov 1915. After receiving training as a rifleman he became a Bugler.

His record shows that he was stationed at Helmsley arriving on 15th Nov 1915, and was vaccinated on 18th Feb 1916; he left Sheerness for France on 26th Sept 1916.

Frank was wounded and admitted to the 48th clearing station France where he died from stomach wounds that evening. Fortunately Frank's brother George (also in the Kings Own Royal Rifles) got to see Frank before his death. He is buried at Bray Cemetery on the Somme.

Robert Wellage Buttle - Private Reg. No. 8438 (H03)

Born:	1889 at Greenwick (nr. Fridaythorpe)
Date and age on death:	18th June 1916 aged 28
Enlisted:	Pocklington
Regiment on Death:	8th Battalion East Yorks. Regiment
Buried:	Elzenwalle Brasserie Cemetery
Occupation:	Professional soldier
Mother:	Sarah Elizabeth Buttle
	(later Mrs T Huck)
Brothers:	James W
Sisters:	Hilda
Address pre-enlistment:	With the East Yorkshire Regiment

There seems to be no record of his father. In 1891 Robert lived with his grandfather on London Street, in the 1901 census he lived on Grape Lane with his mother, sister Hilda and brother James William. In the "In Memoriam" section of the Pocklington Weekly News the dedication is from Mother, Father, Brothers and Sisters. As recorded under his picture in the 25th December 1915 Pocklington Weekly News, Robert was a career soldier. He served in India for six years and transferred to France, at that time serving in the 2nd East Yorkshire regiment.

In the 27th May 1916 edition of the Pocklington Weekly News it records that Robert had been wounded on the 2nd May 1916. His mother is now Mrs T Huck of 65 Chapmangate. Mr Thomas Butler Huck had married Sarah Elizabeth Buttle late in 1901 in Pocklington.

Robert died, killed in action on the 18th June 1916, serving in the 8th Battalion East Yorkshire Regiment and is buried at Elzenwalle Brasserie Cemetery.

Henry Irving Cattle R.E. - Sapper Reg. No. 21662 (H04)

Born:	26th Sept 1891 at Pocklington
Date and age on death:	14th Aug 1917 aged 25
Enlisted:	7th December 1915 in Pocklington
Regiment on Death:	12th Battalion East Yorks. Regiment attached to 257th Coy Royal Eng.
Buried:	Coxyde Military Cemetery
Occupation:	Brewers clerk / acting manager
Father:	Henry Ward Cattle (brewer, spirit merchant)
Mother:	Annie Cattle
Brothers:	Robert Norman, Ronald M
Address pre-enlistment:	Panel House, Percy Road with the brewery in Chapmangate

The white house on the left is the brewery house. The entrance to the brewery was between the house and chapel and from the back in Kirkland Street.

Henry Irving (known as Irving) enlisted into the Army reserve at Pocklington on the 7th December 1915 and was mobilised and posted to the 9th East Yorkshire Regiment on the same day 8th February 1916. Later that year Irving was transferred to the 7th East Yorkshire Regiment on the 26th May 1916 after embarking for the front the day before. Irving joined the 12th Battalion East Yorkshire Regiment on 10th June 1916 at Etaples, joining them in the field on the 16th June 1916. Irving qualified as a bomber and was attached to the 257th Company Royal Engineers.

The Cattle family ran the Old Brewery in Chapmangate, and during the war lived at Panel House, Percy Road, Pocklington. In 1901 they lived on Chapmangate near The Manse and employed a servant Sophia Goodwill. Irving's brother Norman was in the Flying Corps, whilst Ronald was a wireless operator for the Marconi Company. Irving was gassed and returned home on sick leave. When he recovered there was a family re-union until the 8th August 1917 when Irving returned to the front, being killed five days later. He was killed instantly from enemy shellfire. When Irving's belongings were returned to the family they included, a purse, S & F book, letters, photos, a pouch, a diary, a book, big case, holder, watch chain, discs. Irving is commemorated on the family grave in Pocklington Cemetery. Irving had started to run the family business before he enlisted, with his father taking more of a back seat, but his death meant the family had to sell the brewery in 1921.

John William Cooper - Private Reg. No. 8425 (H05)

Born:	Circa 1888 at Bugthorpe
Date and age on death:	1st July 1916 aged 38 (CWGC), actually 28.
Enlisted:	Pocklington
Regiment on Death:	1st Battalion East Yorkshire Regiment
Buried:	Thiepval Memorial
Occupation:	Soldier
Father:	Charles (died 1888)
Mother:	Sarah Jane Cooper (a widow in 1891)
Brothers:	Alfred
Sisters:	Annie
Address pre-enlistment:	India with the 2nd East Yorkshire Regiment.

John William Cooper was born at Bugthorpe in 1888 but his family suffered early tragedy and poverty when father Charles Cooper died in Sep. 1888 at age 45 leaving his mother Sarah Jane as head of household. In the 1891 Census Sarah Jane had no occupation and was living at Bugthorpe with her young family of Alfred (12), John William (3) and Annie (11 months). By the 1901 Census he appears as William Cooper (pauper) age 13 with his sister Annie age 11 (pauper) in Pocklington Workhouse. He went to school in Pocklington, attending the National School in New Street. Annie got a job in the workhouse as a general domestic servant as recorded in the 1911 Census. In 1911 John Cooper appears in India with the 2nd Btn. East Yorkshire Regiment.

Annie married Walter Plumb in Pocklington in December 1914 but for poor Annie she lost both her brother in July 1916 and her husband Walter Plumb (who was in the Northumberland Fusiliers) a week later in August 1916, aged 27. The Commonwealth War Graves Commission gives John William Cooper's age as 38 when he died on 1st July 1916, but actually he was 28.

John Cooper's medal card shows he embarked for France with his battalion in January 1915. 1st July 1916 was the first day of the battle of the Somme, and the offensive began with an all night artillery bombardment. The 1st East Yorks. assembled in the trenches at 3.30 am, and attacked at 7.30 am, they suffered heavy losses from enemy machine guns but did make some territorial gains, John Cooper was killed in the attack.

Walter Joseph Crisp - Private Reg. No.14260 (H06)

Born:	1891 Bridlington
Date and age on death:	23 April 1917 aged 25
Enlisted:	Sept. 1914 in York
Regiment on Death:	8th Service Station South Staffordshire Reg.
Buried:	Arras Memorial Pas de Calais, France
Occupation:	Bank clerk (Barclays, York)
Father:	Joseph Crisp (Superintendent of Police in Pocklington)
Mother:	Louisa Anne Crisp
Brothers:	George
Sisters:	Jane
Address pre-enlistment:	Police Station, Pocklington.

The South Staffordshire's in the trenches in France

Walter was a clerk at Barclays Bank in York, born in Bridlington in 1901. The family lived in Water Fulford, York, and father Joseph was a Police Sergeant. The family later moved to Pocklington where Joseph became superintendent. Joseph and Louisa Anne later moved on to 126 Norwood, Beverley. From the Barclays Bank Register of Staff on active service, in the section for York local head office, is the name W J Crisp, with branch given as York. His rank/regiment was recorded as Corporal, 8th South Staffordshire. He was described as being single, his normal full salary was £100 per annum, his Army pay per annum was £18 5s, and his net salary paid by the bank was £81 15s. An annotation records him as killed in action. He lived in Pocklington on enlisting and enlisted at York in September 1914. On his death he was with the 8th Service Station South Staffordshire Regiment, he was killed on 23rd April 1917 aged 25. After the war, Barclays erected memorial panels in the London Head Office at 54 Lombard Street, which read "In honoured memory of the members of Barclays Bank Limited who gave their lives for King and country during the war A. D. 1914-1919". They include the name W J Crisp. His father Joseph Crisp went on to become deputy chief constable of East Yorkshire and was awarded the King's Police Medal in the 1921 new year's honours.

John Cross - Gunner Reg. No. 800886 (H07)

Born:	Pocklington in 1887.
Date and age on death:	25th August 1917, aged 30
Enlisted:	Bradford
Regiment on Death:	"A" Battery. 295th Brigade, Royal Field Artillery Territorial Force
Buried:	Templeux-le-Guerard Communal Cemetery Extension
Occupation:	Footman
Father:	
Mother:	Hannah
Sisters:	Sarah
Address pre-enlistment:	7 Southwick Crescent, Hyde Park, London

John Cross was born in Pocklington about 1887. In the 1891 census he is living with his mother Hannah and sister Sarah in Chapmangate, both also born in Pocklington. Hannah appears to be a single parent and working as a charwoman, their next door neighbours were the Kirby and Javerley families who both lost members in the conflict. The tenements in 19th century Chapmangate were some of Pocklington's most deprived housing. Hannah died in 1900 aged 43. Curiously, a John George Cross was also born about the same time in Dec. 1886 in Pocklington and is living with widower father Robert in Union St., in 1891. It seems mother Mary Hannah may have died in childbirth aged 29 in Dec. 1886, giving birth to John George.

In the 1911 census John Cross is in rather more upmarket surroundings. He is the footman in the London home overlooking Hyde Park of John Haworth Massey, a wealthy Lancashire brewery and mill owner.

John Cross enlisted in Bradford as a gunner in the 295th Brigade of the Royal Field Artillery, territorials who provided horse draw gun units to the front line infantry.

The 295th Brigade was formed in 1915 and went to France in February 1917. The brigade was involved in the third battle of Ypres/Passchendaele in late summer 1917 and John Cross was killed in action on 25th August. The allies suffered 240,000 casualties in the three month offensive.

Joseph Eagan - Private Reg. No. 44581 (H08)

Born:	1893 at Pocklington
Date and age on death:	14th May 1917 aged 26
Enlisted:	Hull
Regiment on Death:	9th Battalion Northumberland Fusiliers
Buried:	Arras Memorial
Occupation:	Factory Worker (confectionary labourer)
Father:	Luke Eagan, (bricklayers labourer)
Mother:	Sarah
Brothers:	H Eagan, Luke, Dan, John, James
Sisters:	Maggie, Sarah
Address pre-enlistment:	3 Poplar Grove, Derby St., Beverley Rd., Hull (living with brother Hugh a brewers labourer)

Joseph (Joe) was born into a large family. His mother is recorded as living on Church Lane. In the 1901 census the family lived on Grape Lane, unfortunately it appears his father died in 1906. Three of his brothers also served their country; H Eagan a farrier sergeant based at Salonika, Private Luke Eagan was employed as a joiners apprentice before the war, Private Dan Eagan who was discharged from service as being medically unfit after nine months.

Joe was employed in the Pocklington Cooperative stores for several years before leaving and living in Hull where he lived at 2 Aberdeen Avenue, Kimberley Street and worked at the Needler's sweet factory. He was married to Ellen. Joe originally enlisted in the East Yorkshire Regiment but was later transferred to the Northumberland Fusiliers.

53. THE "FIGHTING FIFTH" (NORTHUMBERLAND FUSILIERS) AFTER THE BATTLE OF ST. ELOI.

Private Joe Eagan wrote home to Pocklington in January 1917 thanking his friends for the Christmas parcel he received whilst convalescing in hospital from illness. Joe was killed in action during the attack of Greenland Hill at Arras by the 9th Btn. Northumberland Fusiliers and the 10th Lancs. Btn. Fusiliers who led the assault with 12th Btn. Manchester Regiment in support.

Fred Easton - Shoeing Smith Reg. No. 101896 (H09)

Born:	Pocklington in 1881
Date and age on death:	6th January 1916 aged 34
Enlisted:	Woolwich
Buried:	Pocklington Cemetery
Father:	James Easton, (blacksmith)
Mother:	Mary
Brothers:	John William (William), Henry (Harry), Arthur
Sisters:	Sarah E, Mary A, Margaret S (Maggie)
Occupation:	Blacksmith
Regiment on Death:	"P" Battery Royal Horse Artillery
Address pre-enlistment:	50 Chapmangate, Pocklington.

James ("Jim") Easton's blacksmith business was in Church Lane, Pock. pictured with wife Polly and brother to Fred.

Fred Easton's grave in Pocklington Cemetery

Fred was the son of a blacksmith who in 1871 lived on Scaife Lane. In 1881 the family had moved to Clarkson's Terrace. Fred's mother died in 1888 whilst his father passed on two years later in 1900. In the 1901 census Fred, now a blacksmith's apprentice, age 19, had moved in with his brother James, a blacksmith like his father, and his wife Polly onto Church Lane. His brother Harry, also a blacksmith, lived with them, he worked previously to joining up in the family business. Brother Arthur age 17 lived there as well as a saddlers apprentice. According to Kelly's Directory 1937 James is still a blacksmith on Church Lane. Fred died at Woolwich from pneumonia and his body was transported back to Pocklington by train.

It was sent to his brother James's home at 50 Chapmangate, (See his photograph with wife Polly). His funeral was military based with a band and a firing party of the 3rd Lancashire Fusiliers based at Ousethorpe camp. The family can be traced back to John Easton who, in 1841, lived on Church Lane and was a blacksmith. His son William, also a blacksmith, took over the home after John's death (date unknown) and married Charity from Fangfoss. Charity died in 1879 whilst William born 1794 died 1878. They had a son called James who is Fred Easton's father, four generations of blacksmith's living in Pocklington and working on Church Lane right up to 1937.

James Elliott - Driver Reg. No. 81157 (H10)

Born:	Pocklington in 1890
Date and age on death:	17th April 1917 aged 27. Died of wounds.
Enlisted:	Dewsbury, Yorks.
Regiment on Death:	"B" Battery. 51st Brigade Royal Field Artillery
Buried:	Aubigny Communal Cemetery Extension,
Pas	de Calais, France
Occupation:	Farm labourer
Father:	William Elliott (general labourer)
Mother:	Ann Elliott (charwoman)
Brothers:	Henry, Tom, Joseph
Sisters:	Ellen, Sarah, Ada, Fanny
Address pre-enlistment:	5 Southsea Terr., Bean Street, Hull Road, Anlaby, Hull

Photo: Chris Cosgrove

James' father William was born in Falsgrave, Scarborough in 1856. In 1881 he lived at 12 Hampton Road, with his wife Ann from Flixton. They moved to Pocklington between 1881 and 1891 and the family lived on Grape Lane. In the census Ann is still married but William but no longer resides at home. By 1901 Ann is recorded as being a widow, whilst Tom, the last son, is 7 years old giving William's death between 1894 and 1901. Ann died in 1908 aged 49. James known as 'Jim', worked on Coldwold as a Farm Labourer for a Mr Foxton. His sister Nellie Beckett is given as his closest living relative. On his death, she lived at No.2

South Parade. It is likely that Nellie was originally Ellen Elliott, the dates and place of birth agree. Nellie married George Beckett a brickmaker in 1895, and in 1901 they lived at the brickyard down Burnby Lane.

In 1911 he was 21 and living in Hull in his Brother Joseph's house who was married to Mary and had occupation of labourer. In the house was also his brother Tomas (age 17) with occupation of labourer and James had occupation of Farm Servant and was single. The 'in memoriam' is from his sisters with no mention of brothers. Fanny Elliott died in 1888 aged 9 years.

James is the Uncle of James Harrison also a 'Fallen Hero' from Pocklington, according to a newspaper cutting many of the men from this family group answered the call of the nation and went to war.

Robert Cecil English - Corporal Reg. No. 143807 (H11)

Born:	Pocklington in 1889
Date and age on death:	13th June 1919 aged 30
Enlisted:	Unknown
Regiment on Death:	Machine Gun Corps (Infantry)
Buried:	Pocklington Cemetery
Occupation:	Corn merchant's clerk and auctioneer
Father:	Richard Massey English J.P. (corn merchant, miller & auctioneer)
Mother:	Mary English
Brothers:	Thomas (corn merchant), George (farmer), Richard Loftus (corn merchant & auctioneer), Harry Turner (corn merchant & clerk)
Sisters:	Jane, Florence
Address pre-enlistment:	Lyndhurst, Kilnwick Road, Pocklington

Robert English joined up in the early days of the war and served throughout the conflict, seeing action in Italy and France. He survived being wounded in 1916, but became ill in late 1918 and was shipped home, dying in military hospital in June 1919. His brother Thomas was a Corn Merchant and according to the 1918 Electoral Role, lived at Mile Farm; brother Henry (Harry) Turner lived at 28 Regent Street and Richard Loftus lived at Lyndhurst, where Robert was raised in the family home. His father Richard Massey English died 7th November 1915 at age 66.

R.M. English

Robert was a noted sportsman who starred at Pocklington School at football, cricket and athletics before leaving school in 1902 to join his father's business, RM English & Son, millers, auctioneers & valuers and wool & corn merchants.

He was a popular citizen and sportsman in the town who started out as a clerk and became an auctioneer with English's. He joined up in 1914, initially with the Kings Royal Rifle Corps then switched to the Machine Gun Corps.

English's Mill in Pocklington

He was wounded on the Western Front in July 1916 and transferred to hospital in Glasgow, then returned to action after recovering from his wounds.

Robert contracted an illness while on active service in France in 1918. He battled on for seven months after the armistice was signed, but died from heart failure in Middlesex war hospital in St Albans on 13 June 1919 aged 30. He was brought back to Pocklington by train and his coffin carried by six Pocklington comrades to All Saints prior to being interred in the cemetery.

Thomas Wilfred Fisher - Lance Corporal Reg. No. 17851 (H12)

Born:	1894
Date and age on death:	21st Feb 1917 aged 23
Enlisted:	Unknown
Regiment on Death:	3rd Battalion 9th Border Regiment
Buried:	St Martin's Church Yard, Yapham
Father:	Rev. Arthur Thomas Fisher
	(All Saints vicar)
Mother:	Dora Jane Fisher
Brothers:	Arthur R, Godfrey Arthur, John Lionel, Cyril Martin
Sisters:	Dorothy M, Eva Margaret, Helen Auriol, Olive Winifred, Lilian Mabel
Address pre-enlistment:	The Vicarage, Pocklington

Thomas Wilfred was the son of Pocklington Vicar Arthur Thomas; the family lived at The Vicarage, Pocklington. Thomas's father Arthur was born in London on 16th February 1852, the son of John Fisher. He was educated at King's College London and Sidney Sussex College Cambridge, where he became a B.A (26th wrangler) in 1876. (a wrangler is someone with a 1st class maths degree.)

Arthur went on to become Assistant Master at Kings School, Ely before being ordained Deacon (Winchester) in 1877. He became priest at Rochester in 1878, curate of St Mathews, Brixton from 1877-1879. He was a church missionary for the Church Missionary Society at Amritsar in the Punjab, India 1879-1884 (where Dorothy was born). Curate of Nottingham 1885-6, Rector of Skelton Yorkshire 1886-1908 and vicar of Pocklington with Yapham-cum-Meltonby and Ousethorpe, 1908-21. The C.W.G.C has him living at 45 Esplanade Rd, Scarborough. Before his death in Dover on 17th April 1934, he resided c/o Netteswell Rectory, Harlow in Essex.

His father, the Rev. Arthur Thomas Fisher, vicar of Pocklington.

Thomas Wilfred was educated at Pocklington school, where he started in 1909 and left in 1912, his achievements at school were, 1st XV rugby 1910/11/12, and colours, 1st XI cricket 1910/11/12, 2nd XI football 09/10/11. Arthur R Fisher was also in service; he was Ships Surgeon aboard the Hospital Ship "Rewa" stationed off the Dardanelles. Thomas enlisted on the outbreak of war with the 9th Border Regiment with which he served in France before being sent with his regiment to Salonika. Unfortunately he contracted malaria and ended up in hospital in Malta. He was then shipped home to England. It was thought that he had fully recovered and was sent back after a brief visit home at Christmas 1916.

On his return to duty he studied for his commission but unfortunately he caught a chill which developed into pneumonia. He was once again shipped home and died in Barrow-in-Furness. Thomas was returned to Pocklington by train and was met by a band of the Border Regiment, who played the "Death March". The coffin was placed on a carriage with a Union Jack covering it. The coffin was then carried into the West entrance of the Parish Church accompanied by the Choir. After the service, conducted by Rev J Coates, the procession reformed and set off up George Street to Yapham under the strains once again of the "Death March" where his brother Rev John Fisher pronounced the committal service. "Abide with me" was sung, three volleys were fired and the last post sounded by bugles.

Charles Flint - Private Reg. No. 201226 (H13)

Born:	29th Nov 1881 at Pocklington, Christened 6th Dec.1881
Date and age on death:	16th September 1916, aged 34
Enlisted:	Pocklington
Regiment on Death:	1st/4th Battalion Northumberland Fusiliers (Territorials)
Buried:	Thiepval Memorial
Occupation:	Carter on farm, later brewery worker
Father:	Charles Flint (agricultural labourer)
Mother:	Elizabeth
Brothers:	James Henry
Sisters:	Alice Emma, Ada, Clara, Ann, Maud, Jessie
Address pre-enlistment:	19, Grape Lane, Pocklington

Charles, or Charlie as he was usually known, was born in Pocklington in November 1881 into a local family. We cannot find any reference to him being married or what date he enlisted.

In the 1891 census the Flint family lived on Grape Lane with Charles senior working as a bricklayer's carter, all ten of the family had been born in Pocklington.

The next census of 1901 has Charles junior still at home, aged 19, and was a carter on a farm, he later worked for a local brewery. Charles and his brothers James and Harry were also leading players for Pocklington's rugby team.

Artists impression of the advance of the Northumberland Infantry Brigade on April 26th 1915, during the second battle of Ypres.

The 1/4th Battalion Northumberland Fusiliers were posted to France in August 1915. From 15–22 September 1916 they were involved in heavy fighting in the battle of Flers-Courcelette, one of the engagements that made up the first battle of the Somme. The Regimental Diary reports on the 16th Sept. 1916, 22 Officers and 695 other ranks went into action. Total Casualties 17 Officers, 110 O.R's killed, 229 wounded, 143 missing. Only 213 of the 695 other ranks were unharmed.

Fred Foster - Private Reg. No. 70546 (H14)

Born:	1884 at Leeds
Date and age on death:	26th November 1917 Age 33
Enlisted:	Pocklington
Regiment on Death:	Durham Light Infantry
Buried:	Salonika (Lembet Road) Military Cemetery
Occupation:	Shoemaker
Father:	James Foster (storekeeper)
Mother:	Mary
Brothers:	John Jack, William
Address pre-enlistment:	Black Swan Inn, Market Place, Pocklington

Exhibit at the 2008 Exhibition

Fred was born in Leeds where his father was a storekeeper and one time brewer's labourer. He was the second grandson of J. W. Wells chemist and druggist Leeds and London, In 1898 he came to live in Pocklington with his Uncle, Mr John Allan Foster in Market Place, where he took up his uncle's trade and became a shoemaker. On his uncle's death he took over the shoemaking business with his brother John

Jack. In 1909 Fred married Emma Johnson proprietor of The Black Swan, a pub that the Johnson family had run from circa 1872. Fred and Emma had a daughter Grace Doreen Foster who was born 26th November 1910. Fred enlisted on the 7th December 1915 into the Kings Own Yorkshire Light Infantry Army Reserve, on the 4th April 1917 he was transferred to the Durham Light Infantry 2nd/9th Battalions. He embarked on board the Kingstonian with the 3rd Echelon at Marseilles on 13th April 1917. He disembarked at Salonika 23rd April 1917.

Fred was admitted to the 48th Field Hospital with pneumonia on the 26th October 1917 and died one month later on 26th November 1917, his personal effects were returned to Emma on 4th April 1918 and included photos, letters, big case, part of a mirror, tobacco pouch,

Fred Foster and his wife Emma (nee Johnson) who was landlady of the Black Swan Inn. They married in Leeds in September 1909. Fred died on November 25th 1917 in Salonika of Bronchial Pneumonia

disc, ring, knife, diary and a razor in a case. According to the 1921 Kelly's directory the Foster brothers shoemaking shop at 36 Market Place was still open for business. According to the 1937 Kelly's directory Emma was still running the pub. During the war Annie Johnson, Emma's sister still lived at the Black Swan, and in Fred's papers his mother Mary had also moved into the pub, his aunt, wife of the late John Allan Foster lived at Wells House on Burnby Lane, Pocklington.

Jim Giles - Private Reg. No. 21/855 (H15)

Born:	Pocklington in 1897
Date and age on death:	30th March 1918 aged 21
Enlisted:	Shipley
Regiment on Death:	D company 21st Wool Textile Pioneers (service) Battalion West Yorks. Reg.
Buried:	Duisans British Cemetery, Etrun
Occupation:	Apprentice butcher
Father:	Jim Giles (bricklayer)
Mother:	Hannah Giles
Brothers:	George
Sisters:	Elizabeth, Mellina, Hannah
Address pre-enlistment:	41 Union Street, Union Terrace, Pock.

In the 1901 census Jim and family were living in Union Street, but the story starts much earlier than that.

In 1871 William and Mary Giles lived on Chapmangate. William, born in Allerthorpe, was an agricultural labourer and Mary a bonnet maker from Pocklington. They must have emigrated to North America - where or why exactly is not known, as all their offspring John, Jim, and Elizabeth were born in North America.

Photo Source: Buttle Collection

In 1881 William and Mary's son Jim/James was living at 4 Deans Lane with his brother John Giles and his brother John's wife Martha from Millington. The census of 1881 also gives Jim/James' trade as an apprentice bricklayer and gives his place of birth as British North America (Canada). There is a William Giles who died in 1875 and a Mary Giles who died in 1878, this could account for the reason Jim/James is living with his brother.

In 1891 Jim/James has now moved to Union Street and has married Hannah they have a son called George aged 4 months. In 1901 Jim/James is still in Union Street and has several more children: George, Elizabeth, Mellina, Jim, and Hannah Mary, it is this Jim Giles that is on our memorial.

There is no record of our Jim Giles marrying but he did work at Thirsk's Flour Mill, Pocklington, before moving to Shipley to become an apprentice butcher in his uncle Mr George Brabiner's butcher shop. We do not know a great deal about Jim's service record other than he died in the 8th casualty clearing station from shell wounds to his left arm and thigh. Jim is commemorated on his parents' headstone in Pocklington cemetery, his mother Hannah Mary dying in 1954 aged 86 and his father aged 74 in 1936.

George Gilyead - Private Reg. No. 26066 (H16)

Born:	Pocklington in 1897	
Date and age on death:	28th March 1918 aged 24	
Enlisted:	Pocklington	
Regiment on Death:	10th Battalion East Yorkshire Regiment	
Buried:	Bienvillers Military Cemetery	
Occupation:	Corn merchants clerk	
Father:	James W Gilyead (auctioneers clerk)	
Mother:	Annie Gilyead	
Brothers:	Henry Read, Arthur	
Sisters:	Mary	
Address pre-enlistment:	Meltonby Villas, New Street, Pocklington	

George Gilyead's gravestone

In 1891 James Gilyead, George's father, had moved with his mother to Pocklington from Spaldington and was living on George Street next to the Royal Oak Inn. It is not certain what happened to James' father but in 1892 James married Annie. In 1901 the family were still at the same address where George was born in 1893.

George was never married and enlisted to the Army reserve on 23rd February 1916 aged 22 years and 256 days. He was mobilised on the 26 June 1916 to the 9th East Yorkshire Regiment, and was reposted on the 29th August to the 3rd East Yorkshire Regiment and embarked on the 21st October 1916. George's final posting came on the 4th November 1916 to the 10th East Yorkshire Regiment.

It is recorded that George had two weeks leave between 26th November 1917 and 11th December 1917. By this time the family had moved to Meltonby Villa, New Street, Pocklington.

George was killed on the 28th March 1918, his belongings were returned and contained a disc, pipe, 2 badges, knife, photos, 3 religious books, 2 diaries, Wesleyan Methodist book, wallet and an account paper.

George was employed by Messrs. English and Son in the role of clerk, he was a member of the Wesleyan Church becoming a teacher and secretary of the church Sunday school, and he was also secretary of the Wesley Guild. His two surviving brothers became leading Pocklington citizens, Henry was the town's cubmaster for decades, while Arthur was clerk to Pocklington council for 30 years.

George Henry Grainger - Private Reg. No. 28332 (H17)

Born:	Pocklington in 1896
Date and age on death:	24th April 1917 aged 21
Enlisted:	Pocklington
Regiment on Death:	7th Battalion East Yorkshire Regiment
Buried:	Arras Memorial

Occupation:	Rope worker
Father:	Jonathan Grainger (brickyard labourer)
Mother:	Hannah
Sisters:	Alice A, Fanny, Mary J
Address pre-enlistment:	23 Grape Lane, Pocklington

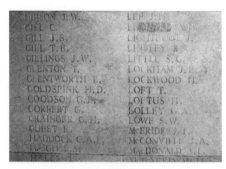

George Henry Grainger's name on the Arras memorial.

The Laister shop in Market Place (left)

In 1901 George lived at No 3 Alma Terrace. His mother was born in Leeds and they spent some time in Market Weighton as his sister Alice A was born there.

Before the war George was employed by Messrs Joseph Laister & Sons, rope makers, of 30-32 Market Place. He enlisted in November 1915 and had a years training before going to the front where he was wounded and spent two weeks in Base hospital. He went back to the front line and was killed in action 24th April 1917 at Arras. At 11.20am orders were issued to go over the top and make a strong and determined bombing attack. With the object to capture bayonet and rifle trenches. The bombing attack failed due to heavy artillery, rifle and machine gun fire. Some of the trenches were filled in so the men were in the open. In the operation their commanding officer Captain H.W. Brooke was mortally wounded. George Henry was also killed in this operation along with 26 others and 120 wounded

On the Pocklington memorial he has an "S" as his middle initial, but in the account of the dedication of that memorial, his family call him "Henry". He is correctly named on the Arras Memorial. There is a J Grainger on the picture of the 1899 – 1900 Pocklington Parish Church F C Rugby Club this could be George's father Jonathan (Right).

Stanley Hall - Private Reg. No. 1300 (H18)

Born:	Pocklington in 1895
Date and age on death:	17th September 1916 aged 21
Enlisted:	Pocklington
Regiment on Death:	5th Battalion P of W O Yorkshire Regiment
Buried:	Thiepval Memorial
Occupation:	Postal worker, ropers worker in 1911
Father:	Thomas Hall (brewers drayman)
Mother:	Lucy Hall
Brothers:	James
Address pre-enlistment:	George Street, Pocklington

Stanley Hall was killed in the battle of Flers-Courcelette on 17th September 1917 on the day of his 21st birthday.

He was born in Pocklington in September 1895, his father working as a drayman for a local brewery. The family lived on St. Helen's Gate and Stanley went to the National School in New Street. Unfortunately his father Thomas died early in 1916 when the family home was on George Street.

Stanley worked as a roper's worker before being employed by the Post Office. He was a member of the Pocklington Territorials and was in camp with the territorials when war was declared.

Troops follow a tank into battle at Flers-Courcelette

The 5th Yorks. went to France in April 1915 and was a front line unit throughout the war. They went straight into action at Ypres in 1915 and then moved on to the Somme offensive in 1916. Flers-Courcelette was the first battle of the war to see the use of tanks, Stanley was killed in action on the day of his 21st birthday as the 5th Yorks. suffered heavy casualties in the advance.

The Commonwealth War Graves Commission gives Rytham Gate, Seaton Ross, as the address of Stanley's mother, Lucy, when he was killed. It was a terrible year for Lucy as she lost a husband and a son within nine months of each other.

James Harrison - Private Reg. No. 38464 (H19)

Born:	1st October 1896
	Christened 18th October 1896 at Pocklington
Date and age on death:	24th March 1918 aged 21
Enlisted:	Pocklington
Regiment on Death:	2nd Battalion Highland Light Infantry
Buried:	Arras Memorial
Occupation:	Farm labourer
Father:	Thomas Harrison (farm labourer)
Mother:	Sarah
Brothers:	Thomas Redvers
Sisters:	Annie
Address pre-enlistment:	12 Chapmangate, Pocklington

This photograph is of Sarah Harrison and her son James he was in the 2nd Battalion Highland light infantry and died age 21 on 24th March 1918 and is commemorated on the Arras Memorial.

In 1901 the family lived on Waterloo Terrace, later moving to No 9 Church Lane. James enlisted with a special reserve unit named the "Wolds Wagoner's" Reg No Wg712. The Wolds Wagoner's were made up from farm workers who would deliver stores to the troops; he was later transferred to the 2nd Battalion Highland Light Infantry in August 1915 and was in full service one week later.

James was wounded three times and also gassed. He was, at some stage, recommended for the Military Medal, but it is unknown why he did not achieve this. His father Private Thomas William Harrison was serving in Salonika and the Balkans, his brother Thomas Redvers was in France with the Northumberland Fusiliers, having joined aged 16. After training at Ipswich and Doncaster he was shipped to France 6th of

February 1917. He fought at Cambrai, Champagne and Bullecourt before being wounded and held prisoner of war at Bullecourt.

James has no known grave but is remembered in the Roll of Honour book in Edinburgh castle, and also in the story of The Wolds Wagoner's, in which he is described as being 62 inches high, 105lb, with grey eyes and dark brown hair.

Clifford W Hayton - Bandsman Reg. No. 15553 (H20)

Born:	Pocklington, 24th April 1890
Date and age on death:	21st May 1915, Age 25
Enlisted:	Quebec, Canada, 28th September 1914
Regiment on Death:	10th Battalion Canadian Infantry
Buried:	Vimy Memorial, Pas de Calais
Occupation:	Cabinet maker
Father:	Thomas Hayton
Mother:	Lillian
Brothers:	Thomas Oswald
Sisters:	Laura Margaret
Address pre-enlistment:	Ross Avenue, Weston, Winnipeg, Canada

Clifford Hayton was born and grew up in Pocklington and is included on the Pocklington memorial, but he had lived in Canada for three years when he joined up at the outbreak of the war. The Hayton family was still living in Chapmangate in the 1911 census, with Clifford working in Pocklington as a cabinet maker and his father, Thomas, a foreman at a local flour mill. A few months later the family emigrated, getting a ship from Liverpool to Quebec then settling in Winnipeg.

The Canadian Expeditionary Force marching past Stonehenge in 1914 prior to going out to France.

When Britain declared war Canada was the Empire's biggest dominion and automatically joined the conflict, with more than half the volunteer Canadian forces of 600,000 men being ex-patriot Englishmen. Prior to emigrating Clifford had been in the Pocklington Volunteer Troop of the East Riding Territorials, and both he and his father enlisted in the Canadian Army when war was declared. Clifford signed up on 28th September 1914 and crossed the Atlantic again to England a few days later as a bandsman with the Canadian Expeditionary Force. They trained in Salisbury Plain in late 1914 before going to France in February 1915. Hayton's battalion was amongst the first Canadian troops into action. The 10th Battalion suffered heavy losses in April 1915 in the second battle of Ypres. Despite some 600 of the battalion's 800 troops being killed or wounded, the remaining soldiers were sent back into the front line a couple of weeks later. They took more heavy casualties in a first assault at Festubert on 20 May but were ordered to attack again at night on 21 May. A three and a half hour British artillery bombardment was ineffectual and the Canadians went over the top at 8.30 pm to meet heavy machine gun and artillery fire. Nevertheless they succeeded in driving back the Germans some 400 yards and took over their forward trenches. Hayton was killed during this action. Only a handful of the 10th Battalion had survived, and they were withdrawn 24 hours later, giving up the previous day's gains.

Henry Allison Holmes - Able Seaman Service No. J/4350 (H21)

Born:	Wilberfoss (1901 Census) 19 May 1893
Date and age on death:	31st May 1916, aged 23
Regiment on Death:	H M S Invincible, Royal Navy
Buried:	Portsmouth Naval Memorial
Mother:	Clara Holmes (pauper)
Brothers:	Arthur
Address pre-enlistment:	H M S Illustrious, Portland, age 17

Henry Holmes was born in Wilberfoss in 1896, and his brother Arthur in Pocklington. In the 1901 census the Holmes family lived in the Union Workhouse on Burnby Lane where Clara is listed as a pauper and her marital status given as single, not widowed. They were in the workhouse at the same time as the families of other 'Fallen Heroes', John Cross and William Cooper.

HMS Invincible (1907)

Henry joined the navy as teenager and was listed as a 17-year old seaman on HMS Illustrious in the 1911 census. Henry attended the National School Pocklington and on a return visit on leave visited his old school. Whilst at home he commented "without brag" that he felt very confident in the ability of the Navy to wipe out the Germans given the opportunity.

Clara is living in Marske by the Sea after her son's death, but she must have returned to Pocklington, as there is a record of her burial in Pocklington in 1925. Henry served on board the 'Invincible', the

Killed in Action aboard H.M.S. Invincible in the battle of Jutland Bank, 31st May 1916. This remarkable photograph records the moment Invincible exploded in the battle.

world's first battlecruiser, launched in 1907. The 'Invincible' had been involved in fighting off the Falkland Islands in December 1914 when the 'Scharnhorst' and 'Gneisenau' were sunk. It was in the battle of Jutland in May 1917 that the 'Invincible' met her fate after receiving three salvoes each from the German ships 'Lutzow' and 'Derflinger', the 'Invincible' taking only 90 seconds to sink. Of her full complement, 1026 Officers and men were killed, there were just six survivors.

Herbert Henry Holmes - Private Reg. No. 51347 (H22)

Born:	Holme on Spalding Moor, 1890
Date and age on death:	15th October 1918 aged 28
Enlisted:	Pocklington
Regiment on Death:	15th Battalion Cheshire regiment
Buried:	Lijssenthoek Military Cemetery
Occupation:	Butcher
Grandfather:	George Holmes
Grandmother:	Esther Holmes
Sisters:	Annie
Address pre-enlistment:	Pocklington

Herbert was born Herbert Henry Smith in Holme on Spalding Moor in 1890, but was brought up in Pocklington by his grandparents, George and Esther Holmes, and he later adopted their surname.

On 14 April 1908, Herbert joined the 5th Battalion Yorkshire Regiment Territorial Force Reg No 320 originally for one year aged 18 (his joining papers were countersigned by another Fallen Hero, Capt. George Scott), then re-signed for another five years with 3rd Battalion East Yorkshire Territorials.

Photo: Chris Cosgrove

He learned his trade as a butcher, apprenticed for four years to Robert Sherbourne in St Peters Square, Pocklington. His training with the Territorials included camps at Bridlington in 1908, Richmond 1909 and Haltwhistle 1911; in 1911 he also injured his thigh on the vaulting horse in the East Yorkshire's gymnasium at Beverley, a court of enquiry found him not to blame for his accident.

In 1912 he joined the Army as a regular soldier, becoming an Army butcher with the Royal Army Service Corps Reg No 31341 at Aldershot on the 4th of March. Herbert continued as a butcher with the Army Service Corps, and accompanied the British Expedit. Force to Flanders from August to November 1914. He returned to England and served as a butcher in home Army camps for the next three years.

The Cheshire Regiment's former title was '22nd Regiment of foot'

But the Army ran out of men for active service and Herbert was 'Compulsorily Transferred in the Interests of the Service' to the 16th Battalion Cheshire Regiment Reg No 51347 on 24th September 1917. The 16th was a 'Bantams' battalion – its soldiers had an average height of 5' 0" and so 5'3" Herbert fitted the bill. He was wounded in his back and spent time at Woodside Central Hospital Glasgow, then was sent to the Spa Hotel Aberdeen to convalesce.

Herbert was moved around the Cheshire Regiment probably because of amalgamations due to the losses incurred in battle. He was posted to France with 1/5th Battalion Cheshire Regiment on 11th April 1918, switched to the 11th Battalion on 14th April, then 6th Battalion on 17th June. He was finally posted to the 15th Battalion Cheshire Regiment another Bantams battalion. The 15th were heavily involved in the battles of Bapaume and Courtrai in August and September 1918, part of the allies 'Hundred Days Offensive' that was the turning point to winning the war. Herbert was reported as gassed on 26th August and he died from wounds at the 62nd casualty clearing station on 15th October 1918.

Alfred Hopper - Private Reg. No. 1731 (H23)

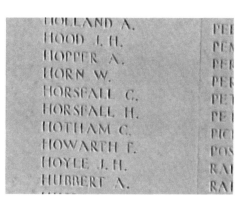

Born:	Driffield 1877
Date and age on death:	25th May 1915 aged 37
Enlisted:	Scarborough
Regiment on Death:	5th Battalion Alexandra Princess of Wales Own Yorkshire Regiment
Buried:	Ypres (Menin Gate) Memorial
Occupation:	Foundry worker
Father:	Thomas Hopper (licensed victualler "London Inn")
Mother:	Susannah Hopper
Brothers:	Percy
Address pre-enlistment:	12, Kirkland Street, Pocklington

Alfred's name is on the Menin Gate memorial

In 1891 Alfred resided with his parents at London Inn 24 Market Place, Driffield. He was employed at a local bookstall.

In 1901 he was married to Edith from Leven and lived at 32 Eastgate North, Driffield, his trade was now a tool moulder, and they had a daughter Marjorie 10 months old.

In 1911, he was 33 and a brass company iron moulder and living with his wife Edith in Kirkland Street, with his daughter Marjorie (age 10) and Harry (age 5). He worked in Mr Daniel Richardson's foundry at 3 Brunswick Place, making agricultural implements.

A newspaper cutting announcing his death said that Alfred was a keen rugby player. Alfred played for Driffield and Hull FC.

Sanctuary Wood. East of Ypres.

Before war was declared he was a territorial soldier with A Company (Pocklington) 5th Yorkshire Regiment, Green Howards, (dubbed 'The Pocklington Terriers' or 'The Pock Lads') and immediately volunteered for active service. The Terriers were sent to Hummersknott Camp, Durham, for basic training in September 1914 and were mobilised early in 1915, landing at Boulogne on April 17th 1915. They were straightaway ordered to the front to take part in the Ypres offensive, fighting in the battles of St Julien and Sanctuary Wood.

The battalion came under heavy artillery fire at Sanctuary Wood and Hopper was one of the men killed when a shell exploded in their trench. They were buried on the battlefield by their comrades. Commemorated on Menin Gate Memorial, Ypres.

Charles Hotham - Private Reg. No. 1451 (H24)

Born:	Pocklington 1894
Date and age on death:	11th June 1915, aged 22
Enlisted:	Pocklington
Regiment on Death:	5th Battalion Alexandra Princess of Wales Own Yorkshire Regiment
Buried:	Ypres (Menin gate) Memorial
Occupation:	Butcher
Father:	Charles Hotham (butcher)
Mother:	Mary Cecilia Hotham
Brothers:	Henry N, Frederick, Richard Albert
Sisters:	Kathleen
Address pre-enlistment:	11, The Pavement, Pocklington

The Hotham's can be traced back to Cottingham in 1841 where Thomas (shoemaker), his wife Sarah, son Frank and a lodger named William Otter lived on Buck Street.

In 1851 the Hotham's had moved to Pocklington living on New Street with siblings Frank, John, William Henry, Anthony, Ester and Albert. By 1861 Thomas (cordwainer) and Sarah had added to their brood with Alma, Charles and Sarah Jane being born. They now lived on Union Street. Unfortunately Thomas Hotham died in mid 1861 after the completion of the census, in the same census William Henry is described as being nearly blind.

The back of the above photograph records the death of Charles Hotham
Photo source: The Buttle Collection

William Henry embarked on his own life always employed as a bellman, first lodging on Chapmangate with 16 other people in Henry and Margaret's lodging house (1881 census). In 1891 he is living in the Black Swan yard with three children Thomas (4) Matilda (9) and Esther Leetham (7), not his offspring: why and how is not known. In 1901 he is living in Waterloo Terrace and died aged 64 in 1908.

In between 1851 and 1861 both John and Anthony had found positions in other households. John was a farm servant on William Bowman's 120-acre farm on The Green, Elvington, whilst Anthony was a carter on George Brigham's 358-acre farm at Millington.

In 1871 the Hotham's are still on Union Street with only William Henry (bellman), Charles Snr (scholar) and Sarah Jane living at home. By 1881 Esther has moved to Chapmangate and is living with Hannah P Monkman, whilst the rest of the family are living at No 6 Union Street. Sarah, now 66, is a shoe binder, Charles is a farm labourer and Sarah Jane a domestic servant. Also in the household is Arthur Hotham aged 1, parentage unknown, but is down as Sarah's grandson.

In 1891 Charles Snr is still at home and is now a butcher, Esther has now re-joined the household and is a charwoman, whilst Arthur is still there. Charles Hotham Snr father of our 'Fallen Hero' marries Mary Cecilia Wilson in 1891 and by 1897 has his own butchers shop at 11 New Pavement where the family also live.

Mary Cecilia Wilson was the daughter of Frederick Wilson who married Fanny Buttle a forebear of Francis Charles Buttle ('Fallen Hero'). Frederick is the son of Samuel Wilson Vicar of Warter

C. HOTHAM,

FAMILY BUTCHER,

The Pavement, - Pocklington.

Gimmer and Wether Mutton, Home-fed Hams and Bacon.

BRAWN and SAUSAGES in Season.

Esther Hotham is still at home (Union Street) with her mother Sarah, nephew Arthur, now a butcher presumably at Charles Hotham Snr's shop. Esther Ann Shaw (niece) is also living there, she is the daughter of John Robert Shaw (Pocklington) and Sarah Jane Hotham who married late 1881. Their mother Sarah died in 1904 aged 87.

Our 'Fallen hero' Charles, born in 1894, sang with the parish church choir for several years and was a popular local man working as a butcher. There are several comments as to how good he was with horses by comrades on the front reporting and giving consolation on his death.

On Friday June 11th 1915 at 5.45 pm Charles was shot in his side entering on the right side passing through both lungs and kidneys. He was semi conscious for ¾ of an hour, with his final words being "Remember me to mother" his Pocklington pals buried him under a shady tree in Sanctuary Wood 2 ½ miles east of Ypres

Tom Jennings who died one year later described how he could not go to see Charles buried and how he feared they did not know who would be next.

Charles Snr is still running the butcher's shop in New Pavement in 1921 but in 1937 Charles Jnr's brother Harry is running the shop and also has shoe repairers at 24 Market Place.

Private George William Javerley - Reg. No. 24325 (H25)

Born:	8th Feb 1884 at Pocklington, baptised 2nd Mar 1884
Date and age on death:	3rd May 1917, aged 33
Enlisted:	Pocklington
Regiment on Death:	2nd Battalion Duke of Wellingtons West Riding Regiment
Buried:	Arras Memorial
Occupation:	Tailor
Father:	Henry Javerley (agricultural labourer)
Mother:	Emma Javerley
Brothers:	Charles (painter), John (roper), Henry
Sisters:	Ellen
Address pre-enlistment:	Deans Lane, Pocklington

George Javerley was in the Pocklington Rugby team

George Javerley was born in Pocklington in 1884 and was married with a young family and working as a tailor at JT Everingham's factory in Railway Street on the corner with Station Road when he joined the West Yorkshire Regiment. He also played for the Pocklington Parish Church FC rugby team and he is pictured with the 1904 side after winning the York & District cup. His father was a farm labourer, originally from London, while his mother was from a Pocklington family, but born in Market Weighton. George grew up with his family in Chapmangate, became an apprentice tailor and married Clara King in Pocklington in March 1910. He lived in Deans Lane with his wife and four children.

He was killed by a sniper on 3 May 1917 and was with another Pocklington man, Walter Steel, who reported that they were both in no man's land, knocking in posts for barbed wire, when George was shot and died immediately.

Though the middle initial of his name was W for William, on the memorial it is incorrectly an M.

Corporal Thomas Jennings - Reg. No. 1452 (H26)

Born:	Storwood 1895
Date and age on death:	Died of Wounds 8th June 1916, aged 21.
Enlisted:	Pocklington
Regiment on Death:	5th Battalion Alexandra Princess of Wales Own Yorkshire Regiment
Buried:	Bailleul Communal cemetery Extension (Nord)
Occupation:	Ironmongers apprentice
Father:	Thomas Jennings (farmer)
Mother:	Jane H Jennings
Brothers:	Francis
Sisters:	Dorothy Beal, Bertha Mary, Jane Ann, Ethel
Address pre-enlistment:	In 1911 at 49, Chapmangate (Age 16 an ironmongers apprentice)

Thomas Jennings origins are in Manor Farm, Storwood, Melbourne. His father, also named Thomas, was a farmer who started with 105 acres in 1881 at an unknown location in Storwood, where he employed a hind (farm worker). In 1891 he was at Manor House where they were opulent enough to employ a school governess called Keturah Simpson aged 26.

Thomas Jnr. was born in 1895 at Storwood the same year his father dies. Some time between 1895 and 1901 the family move to Red House, Sherbuttgate, Pocklington, which, during the 2nd WW, had its top half taken off by plane crashing on its return to Pocklington Airfield.

Thomas Jennings Jnr. was educated at Pocklington School. He joined the Army at the outbreak of war and was in camp with the 5th Yorkshire Regiment (Green Howards) immediately volunteering for foreign service training at Newcastle.

On 5th April 1915 he left for France, in May of that year he was completely buried by earth from an exploding shell: only fourteen months later he met his death on 5th June 1916. Thomas was out wiring and was injured by shrapnel, dying later in the early hours of the morning of his wounds. He is commemorated at Bailleul Communal Cemetery Extension Nord.

Ethel Jennings married Lieutenant John Stanley Robson on the 16th July 1918 at St Michael All Angels Church Sutton-on-Derwent. John Stanley Robson was the fifth son of Thomas and Eva Robson. He was also brother to Captain Edward Moore Robson and Lieutenant Colonel Frederick William Robson, both Fallen Heroes of the Great War.

Private Arthur Jessop - Reg. No. 25982 (H27)

Born:	Pocklington 1884
Date and age on death:	22nd January 1918 aged 33
Enlisted:	Pocklington
Regiment on Death:	7th Battalion East Yorkshire Regiment
Buried:	Arras Memorial
Occupation:	Bricklayer and labourer
Father:	Walter Jessop (farm labourer)
Mother:	Mary Jane (Polly) Jessop
Brothers:	Walter, Herbert
Sisters:	Emily, Annie, Florrie, Lily
Address pre-enlistment:	3 Alma Terrace, Pocklington, Yorks.

Men of the 10th Battalion, East Yorkshire Regiment, returning from the trenches.
© Imperial War Museum

Arthur's father Walter came from Inglesom, Suffolk. He married a local girl Mary J, they first lived on Stather's Yard in 1881. In 1891 they had moved onto Smithy Hill. On the 1891 census it gives their 5 year old daughter Emily as being paralysed. In 1901 they had once again moved, this time they were at No 2 Alma Terrace. They were living next to Mr and Mrs Jonathon Grainger whose son George H is also a 'Fallen Hero'. Arthur by this time was working on James Coxon's, Skipgate Farm in Warter. The 1911 census gives the family address as moving next door to No. 3 Alma Terrace with Arthur a bricklayer and labourer.

In 1914 Arthur married Annie Heley. The marriage is registered in the Jul-Aug-Sept Quarter. In the same quarter Arthur Jessop is born, the mothers' maiden name is Annie Heley, obviously conceived out of wedlock. Arthur enlisted on the 24th June 1916 and was drafted to France in November 1916. He had been home on leave after fourteen months service abroad, and he arrived back in France 21st January where he was killed the following day.

In the newspaper accounts of his death it seems that Arthur was accidentally shot in the front line trenches with death being instantaneous. His commanding office found him a bright, cheerful, and efficient soldier, and would be greatly missed by his brother soldiers, and his platoon Officers

Arthur left a widow Annie Jessop of 2 Deans Lane, Pocklington and four young children, Kathleen, Arthur, Charles and Lily. He was also the brother of Fallen Hero Herbert Jessop who died 23rd July 1916.

Private Herbert Jessop - Reg. No. 21755 (H28)

Born:	Pocklington 1888
Date and age on death:	23rd July, 1916 aged 28
Enlisted:	Pocklington 10th December 1915
Regiment on Death:	1st Battalion East Yorks. Reg.
Buried:	Thiepval Memorial
Occupation:	Farm wagoner
Father:	Walter Jessop (farm labourer)
Mother:	Mary Jane (Polly) Jessop
Brothers:	Walter, Arthur
Sisters:	Emily, Annie, Florrie, Lily
Address pre-enlistment:	3 Alma Terrace, Pocklington, Yorks.

Herbert was the younger brother of Arthur Jessop, who enlisted the month before Herbert was killed. Arthur was killed by a bullet at the front in 1918.

Herbert's father, Walter, was a farm labourer who was born in Suffolk and married Mary Jane, known as Polly, from Pocklington. They had seven children and Herbert followed his father's footsteps into working on local farms. By 1911 he was aged 22 and had risen to being the wagoner at Wold House Farm near Driffield. It was a 700 acre farm and Herbert was one of 11 single young men who worked on the farm, all living 'on site' in the house of the farm foreman and his wife.

Herbert is down as back with his parents when he enlisted in December 1915 at Pocklington; and though he signed the forms himself it was noted that he was 'unable to read or write'.

He joined the 1st Battalion East Yorkshire Regiment and spent six months on home duties before being posted to France on 5th July 1916. His Army records indicate he was transferred 'in the field' to 2nd Battalion Yorkshire Regiment on 22nd July 1916, and he was listed as missing the following day – though it was several weeks before the Pocklington Weekly News reported that his family had been notified. On the 26th August 1916 the Pocklington Weekly News reported *"Mr. and Mrs. Jessop, of Kirkland Street, Pocklington, have received an intimation from the War Office that their son Private Herbert Jessop, of the East Yorks. Regt-, has been missing since the 23rd July. A box of eatables sent to him has been returned, and they are anxiously awaiting further news. "* On the 21st April 1917 *"From the Infantry Record Office, York, Mr. and Mrs. Jessop, Alma-terrace, Pocklington, have received notification that no further news has been received of their son, Private Herbert Jessop, East Yorks. Regiment, who left Withernsea for France, and has been missing since July 23rd last. The Army Council presume that his death took place on that date. He was 29 years of age, and was engaged in agricultural work in this neighbourhood up to his enlistment. One brother is now serving in France."*

Private Harold Johnson - Reg. No. 1281 (H29)

Born:	Pocklington 1897
Enlisted:	Pocklington 10th December 1915
Date and age on death:	26th September, 1916 aged 20.
Regiment on Death:	"A" Coy. 5th Battalion Alexandra Princess of Wales Own Yorkshire Regiment
Buried:	Thiepval Memorial
Occupation:	In 1911 a grocer's errand boy (age 14)
Father:	Thomas Johnson (shepherd)
Mother:	Edith Jane Johnson (Shown as a widow in 1911 census)
Brothers:	John Enzor, Robert
Sisters:	Dorothy
Address pre-enlistment:	46 Union Street, Pocklington, Yorks.

Harold (Harry) Johnson was born in Pocklington in 1897. He was from a local family, his grandfather was a Pocklington shoemaker and his father, Thomas, started out as a farm lad. Harold's two brothers and sister were also born in Pocklington but the family moved to Millington, living five doors away from the Gait Inn, when Thomas became a shepherd on a local farm.

Thomas Johnson died in 1910 at the age of 41 and the family moved back to Pocklington, living in 46 Union Street. In 1911 Harold is already working, aged 14, as a grocer's errand boy, and living with his widowed mother, Edith, brothers John Enzor (12) and Robert (2) and sister Dorothy (6). The Thiepval Memorial Index records he was brother of E. Johnson of 20, New St., Pocklington.

Private H. Johnson joined the Territorials at Pocklington before the war; and was one of 28 Officers, NCOs and men from the Pocklington Territorials who volunteered straightaway for overseas service in 1914. They were sent to a training camp at Hummersknot, Durham, before being posted to the front in 1915. Harold had a spell of home leave in February 1916; returning to France he was killed aged 20 on the 26th September 1916 by a bursting shell as his company attacked a German trench.

The Pocklington Weekly News subsequently carried an 'In Memoriam' which it is curiously signed 'Mother and Tom and brothers Enzor, Robert and Harry'. Tom had died in 1910. His younger brother Enzor survived the war and was in the 5th Yorks. See p.205 - C153.

Gunner Henry Johnson - Reg. No. 2599 (H30)

Born: 1897
Date and age on death: 26th December, 1915 aged 17
Regiment on Death: Royal Field Artillery
Buried: Pocklington Cemetery
Father: Mr Henry Johnson (horse man on
                               farm in 1901 and shepherd in 1911)
Mother: Mrs Elizabeth Johnson
Brothers: Albert, Percy, Ernest
Sisters: Emily, Lily, Ada Ann, Florence May
Address pre-enlistment: Burton Hall, Selby.

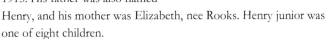

Henry Johnson was born in 1897 into a well known Pocklington family, and died in an accident on Boxing Day 1915. His father was also named Henry, and his mother was Elizabeth, nee Rooks. Henry junior was one of eight children.

He enlisted in 1915 at the age of 18 with the Royal Field Artillery, who provided horse drawn gun units to support infantry regiments. Henry was in an Army convoy in Doncaster on Boxing Day 1915 when some of the horses became restive. He jumped down from his wagon to help the driver calm them, but was kicked by a horse and crushed between the wagon and a wall. He was taken immediately to Doncaster Hospital but was dead on arrival.

Henry Johnson's grave in Pocklington Cemetery

The Pocklington Weekly News reported a rather sad description of his funeral. It was arranged quickly at the Army's request to accommodate a military funeral with a company of his unit in attendance. In the event only one soldier accompanied the body to Pocklington, a civil ceremony had to be conducted and he was interred at Pocklington cemetery.

Private George David Kemp - Reg. No. 2544 (H31)

Born:	Banham, Norfolk in 1888
Enlisted:	Pocklington
Date and age on death:	18th February, 1916 aged 28.
Regiment on Death:	5th Battalion Alexandra Princess of Wales Own Yorks. Regiment
Buried:	Railway Dugouts Burial Ground
Occupation:	Foreman on farm in 1911
Father:	David Kemp, farm labourer in Banham, Norfolk.
Mother:	Emma
Sisters:	Bessie, Gertrude and Freda
Address pre-enlistment:	Wold Farm, Burnby

George Kemp was born and brought up in Banham, Norfolk, where his father was a farm labourer. He left home as one of a group of young men who came to Yorkshire from East Anglia in search of farm work; and by 1911, aged 23, George was a farm foreman for James Scott at Burnby. He is believed to have been living at Pocklington when he enlisted.

In February 1916 the 5th Yorks were in front line action at Ypres and George was killed in action on 18th February; he is buried at the Railway Dugouts Burial Ground, Belgium, near where the Army had an advanced dressing station at a small farmstead in 1916 and 1917. George Kemp is also commemorated on the war memorial of his home village of Banham.

Bomber Edwin Kirby D.C.M. - Reg. No. 9998 (H32)

Born:	17 April 1885 - At Pocklington baptised 5th July 1885
Enlisted:	Market Rasen, Lincolnshire
Date and age on death:	20th Aug 1916 aged 31
Regiment on Death:	2nd Battalion Lincolnshire Regiment
Buried:	Vermelles British Cemetery
Occupation:	Ropers assistant (1901), labourer (in 1911)
Father:	Edwin Kirby (house painter)
Mother:	Elizabeth Kirby
Sisters:	Elizabeth
Address pre-enlistment:	3 Church Lane, Pocklington

Edwin Kirby was born and brought up in Pocklington and was a decorated war hero when he was shot and killed in August 1916.

Edwin's father, Edwin senior, was a house painter from Market Weighton, his mother, Elizabeth, was a Pocklington girl, thirteen years older than her husband. Edwin went to the National School in New Street, and in 1901 the Kirby's lived on Grape Lane with Edwin having started work locally as a roper's assistant. Ten years on the family had moved to Church Lane and both Edwin and his father are listed as labourers. It is believed that Elizabeth died in 1914, and both Edwin and his son went to live in Market Rasen, possibly with Edwin's married sister.

Edwin junior joined the 2nd Lincolnshire regiment. He won the Croix De Guerre (Cross of War) and the Distinguished Conduct Medal in 1915, and was presented with the D.C.M at a public parade in Grimsby on the 11th Dec by Brigadier General Hope Stobert, but was killed in action before receiving the French honours.

He was decorated when a lighted German bomb landed in a crater where 15 wounded men and 100 others were sheltering. Edwin picked up the bomb and threw it out of the crater saving serious loss of life.

Shortly after his gallant action Edwin was blown up by an explosion and shipped back to hospital in England. He recovered, visited Pocklington, and went back to his old school, then returned to the front.

According to a letter to Mrs Allgood of Prospect Place, Market Rasen from Lt H J Dickinson, Edwin died 20th August 1916 hit by a chance shot and is buried at Vermelles.

"Dear Mrs Allgood, it is with the utmost regret I have to inform you that your brother, No 9998, Pte E Kirby, DCM, has been killed by enemy sniper. He was out with me and a friend of his, Pte Pickering, on the night of the 20th inst, putting out wire entanglements in front of the fire trench. He was shot through the hip into the body. We immediately ran over to his aid, but on close examination we found he had passed away.

It was a very dark night and the moon had not yet risen, so you will see the German sniper was shooting blindly, and it was a chance shot that hit him. I must say I have been deeply moved by the occurrence, especially as I was with him at the time and exposed to the same danger.

I hope you accept my heartfelt sympathy in your sudden bereavement, which is shared not only by the Officers, N.C.O's and men of his company, but the whole battalion. He was, of course, very well known and respected among us, as a brave and cheerful soldier, who always did his duty faithfully and well. I am sure it will be of some consolation to you to know that he died a painless death whilst doing his duty.

I personally collected the articles he was carrying at the time, and am having them sent to you under separate cover. He was been buried with military honours behind the line. If there is anything more you would like to know concerning him you have only to drop me a line."

(This extract is taken from the book "Let Us Sleep Now", written and researched by the late Mr Douglas G Boyce)

Private John Lee - Reg. No. 16491 (H33)

Born:	Gardham, Cherry Burton - Dec 1877
Enlisted:	Peterborough
Date and age on death:	09/05/1915, Age 37. Reported missing, believed killed in action at Aubers Ridge.
Regiment on Death:	2nd Northamptonshire Regiment
Buried:	Commemorated on Ploegsteert Memorial, Panel 7.
Occupation:	Engineer and laundry worker
Father:	The late John Lee (farmer)
Mother:	Ann E. Lee
Sisters:	Mary, Frances and Hannah
Address pre-enlistment:	Peterborough or Percy Road, Pocklington

John Lee was born at Gardham in 1877. The Lee family farmed Gardham, near Bishop Burton, for most of the C19th. At over 1,000 acres it was one of the Wolds bigger and most productive farms. In 1881 his father, also John, employed 15 men on the farm and 11 servants in the house and they were renowned horse and sheep breeders and dealers. However, John Lee senior was declared bankrupt in

1884 and the family had to leave Gardham. Nevertheless they continued to live in some style, moving to Burnby House, the biggest dwelling in Burnby, where John Lee senior is listed as a 'retired farmer'. From there John Lee junior attended Pocklington School in the 1880s and 90s and in 1901 he was still living at home and working as a mechanical engineer.

The family moved again to Carlton House, Percy Road, Pocklington in the early 1900s, and it became the family home for some 25 years. John Lee junior's career appears to have taken a very different direction and in 1911 he was working in Peterborough as a laundry van driver. He joined the 2nd Northamptonshire Regiment in Peterborough early in the conflict and was killed in action at the start of the battle of Aubers Ridge. It was a disastrous allied offensive on 9th May that saw over 11,000 men killed but no ground won or tactical advantage gained. The Michaelmas 1915 'Pocklingtonian' magazine recorded the circumstances of his death. *'It is now certain that JOHN LEE of the Northants Regt was killed in action on May 9th. He died like a hero, being one of the first to volunteer on a dangerous wire-cutting expedition. He was 37 years of age.'* He appears on three war memorials at Pocklington, Peterborough and Pocklington School. In summer 1918 two of his sisters contributed to the school war memorial fund.

Private John Walter Plumb - Reg. No. 4574 (H34)

Born:	Fordham, Cambridgeshire, 1890
Enlisted:	Pocklington, April 1916
Date and age on death:	21st August 1916, aged 27.
Regiment on Death:	1st/7th Battalion Northumberland Fusiliers
Buried:	Lapugnoy Military Cemetery, Pas de Calais, Grave I.F.67
Occupation:	Dairyman
Father:	William Plumb
Address pre-enlistment:	West Green, Pocklington

Though he is named on the Pocklington war memorial as John W Plumb he was commonly known as Walter, and he appears as Walter Plumb on the memorial of his home village of Fordham in Cambridgeshire.

John Walter Plumb moved to East Yorkshire as a young man, likely in search of work – in the late 19th and early 20th century emigration to Yorkshire, where wages were higher, was commonplace from East Anglia and southern counties. In 1911 he was working as a cowman on a local farm, then became a dairyman for WH Spivey who had a butcher's shop in Market Street.

Photo: Chris Cosgrove

He got married in Pocklington in December 1914 to Annie Cooper, sister of John William Cooper who is also on the Pocklington memorial. Walter and Annie had a daughter, Dorothy, in June 1915. Though regarded as "not strong" Walter volunteered in April 1916 and was sent to France in July, just two weeks after his brother-in-law had been killed in action. He got a cold which developed into pneumonia and died a week later.

Private Robert Pratt - Reg. No. 240131 (H35)

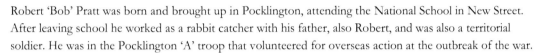

Born:	Pocklington
Enlisted:	Pocklington
Date and age on death:	27th May 1918, aged 27.
Regiment on Death:	5th Battalion Alexandra Princess of Wales Own Yorkshire Regiment
Buried:	Rosieres Communal Cemetery Extension
Occupation:	Rabbit catcher
Father:	Robert Pratt (rabbit catcher)
Mother:	Hannah
Brothers:	John
Sisters:	Martha, Annie, Lily
Address pre-enlistment:	3, Grape Lane, Pocklington

Robert 'Bob' Pratt was born and brought up in Pocklington, attending the National School in New Street. After leaving school he worked as a rabbit catcher with his father, also Robert, and was also a territorial soldier. He was in the Pocklington 'A' troop that volunteered for overseas action at the outbreak of the war.

In the 1901 census Robert, born Seaton Ross 1837, and Hannah Pratt, 24 years his junior, were living at Judson's Yard, Market Place, Pocklington with their children Annie, Robert, Lily and John. The 1911 census sees the family in Grape Lane.

The 'Pock Lads' – members of the Pocklington 'A' Troop Territorials – went to France in April 1915 and were immediately involved in some of the heaviest action. Bob's younger brother, John, was also in the 5th Yorkshire's; he was shot through the shoulder in May 1915 but survived the war.

The 5th Yorks. were a front line unit throughout the war and suffered heavy casualties. The battalion decimated in the first half of 1918 and Bob was reported missing during fierce fighting. CWGC gives the date of death as 27th May 1918, but more likely March as this cemetery is in the Somme region, in which case he may have been killed during the Battle of St Quentin, part of the final Somme battle. The Pocklington Weekly News newspaper's 'In Memoriam' section for May 1920 has a dedication by his sister from Martha and family, where they describe Robert (Bob) as being missing in action presumed dead after three years hard fighting.

Gunner Thomas Wilfred Rippon - Reg. No. 34339 (H36)

Born:	Pocklington in 1886
Enlisted:	Darlington
Date and age on death:	25th March 1917 aged 31
Regiment on Death:	133rd Company Machine gun Corps (Infantry)
Buried:	Baghdad (N. Gate) War Cemetery
Occupation:	Postman
Father:	John Cundy Rippon
Mother:	Mary Ann
Brothers:	John H, Frank, Arthur
Sisters:	Mary H, Eleanor
Address pre-enlistment:	John Cundy was in 9 Church Street Pocklington in 1911

A Machine Gun Corps (Infantry) gun team with their Vickers machine gun.

Thomas Wilfred Rippon was born late in 1886 at Pocklington. He was the son of a cordwainer from Beverley, John C. He married Amy E Barnes in 1913 they had a son, name unknown, and a daughter born 1914 called Annie. Amy was born 1888 the daughter of Mr George Barnes and Mrs Hannah Barnes. George was a farmer from Thornton, they farmed at Toft House, Bielby Lane, Pocklington. They then retired to Percy Road, Pocklington,

In 1891 the Rippon's lived on London Street moving to Church Lane and on Thomas's death they lived on Victoria Terrace. In 1901 Thomas's father, as well as being a shoemaker, was the caretaker of the Liberal Club in Pocklington and also a Lamp Lighter for the Urban Council.

Thomas was in the Volunteer Corps but resigned when he left to live in Darlington working as a postman. He re-enlisted in 1915, and went abroad September 1916. His brother John H (aka 'Jack' or 'Beesey') played rugby for Pocklington and Hull F.C.

We have an account of Thomas Rippon's death in the Pocklington Weekly News. It is a letter previously put into the Hull Times by a fellow named Corporal Herbert Jefferson from Beeford.

"I hear of rejoicings over our victories out here, but do people think of the lads marching daily in the boiling sun? We had a tight fight the other day. I was the senior N.C.O. left, and my worst job was to call the roll call at night. H Barker from Pocklington was with me at my gun, a fine brave fellow. He was cool as a cucumber, until he got two bullets, one in his right hand, and one in his left arm. Poor old Rippon, from Pocklington, got one in the stomach, so I pinched a stretcher, and got him away in a fast car, but he died the next day. It knocked the wind out of me for a bit to lose two of my special pals. You should have seen the four remaining Yorkshire boys that night, talking things over, and having a cup of tea and some broken biscuits for the first time that day."

"We have confirmation that Gunner Hawksworth Barker of the Machine Gun Corps, son of Mr & Mrs G. H Barker of Union Street was indeed wounded, suffering from gunshot wounds in both arms. His brother Lance Corporal Walter Barker was wounded in France at the same time, for the third occasion. John H Rippon is reputed to have died in Hull whilst refereeing a local rugby match. Eleanor married Wilfred Zilwood Swan from Saffron Walden, they lived at 96 Bridge Street and also Nailsea House, Chapmangate, they had six children, John, Paddy, Frank, Harry, Elsie and Hilda, they also had Cyril Rippon half brother to the six children living with them."

Paddy Swann became a local personality and sportsman who did so much good work for Pocklington Football Club, and in later life could be seen collecting waste paper from shops to help pay for their kits.

Captain Edward Moore Robson - M.C. (H37)

Born:	Pocklington in 1890
Enlisted:	Unknown
Date and age on death:	11th April 1918 aged 28
Regiment on Death:	"A" Company Alexandra Princess of Wales Own 5th Battalion East Yorkshire Regiment
Buried:	Ploegsteert Memorial
Occupation:	Solicitors articled clerk in 1911
Father:	Thomas Robson (solicitor)
Mother:	Eva Robson
Brothers:	Richard, Thomas, Edward Moore, John Stanley
Address pre-enlistment:	Pembroke Lodge, Pocklington

The Robson family was prominent in the town. The father Thomas Robson, Solicitor & Commissioner for Oaths; Perpetual Commissioner; clerk to the guardians assessment committee of the Pocklington union; clerk to the Pocklington Rural District Council, to the magistrates of Wilton Beacon & Holme Beacon divisions, & to the governors of the Pocklington Grammar School; steward of the manor of Pocklington, of Barmby-upon-the-Moor & Allerthorpe-with-Waplington; & agent for the Sun Fire & Life office, Waterloo buildings, and over the years much more to Pocklington.

He carried out these duties for 38 years retiring in April 1919. He was church warden for 12 years; President of the Yorkshire Law Society in 1905; treasurer to the church restoration fund; hon. sec to the Victoria Jubilee celebrations 1887 and chairman of the diamond jubilee celebrations in 1897.

Thomas Robson lost his wife Eva 4th July 1914, she died in a nursing home on Cavendish Square, London. He also lost two of his sons, Richard on 30th March of valvular disease at 20 Ladbroke Gardens, London and Frederick two days previous to Richard on 28th March 1918. When Edward died in April Thomas retired from public life and moved to Hatfield, Leeds where he lived with his second son Thomas Jnr. He eventually passed away in 1924.

Edward was the third son of four. They lived on Chapmangate at Pembroke Lodge. He was wounded several times, the second time in September 1916, when he suffered severe gunshot wounds whilst doing his duty. He was awarded the Military Cross for his bravery as a Lieutenant. According to reports, he took over the battalion front, establishing a connection with the brigade to his right, whilst carrying out his work with great courage and initiative on the Somme battlefield.

An extract from the Pocklington Weekly News dated 13th April 1918 (see Lieutenant Colonel Frederick William Robson D S O. for full account)

"Captain Edward Moore Robson (then Lieut') was wounded in four places in the same action. He received the Military Cross, and the two brothers were decorated by His Majesty at Buckingham Palace in December 1916."

Edward was reported missing in action on the 11th April 1918, he was later pronounced as being killed in action that same day.

Edwards passion, was to make sketches and draw cartoons that had a fun side to them concerning situations around him. One of his cartoons is above, the rest can be seen in the East Riding of Yorkshire Council Archives, quote catalogue number DDX1206.

Lieutenant Colonel Frederick William Robson - D.S.O. (H38)

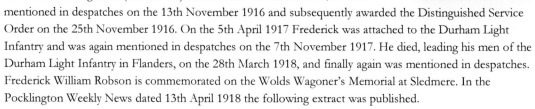

Born:	Pocklington in 1888
Enlisted:	Unknown
Date and age on death:	8th March 1918 aged 30
Regiment on Death:	Assigned to the Durham Light Infantry, from Alexandra Princess of Wales Own 5th Battalion Yorkshire Regiment
Buried:	Pozieres Memorial
Occupation:	Solicitor
Father:	Thomas Robson (solicitor)
Mother:	Eva Robson
Brothers:	Richard, Thomas, Edward Moore, John Stanley
Address pre-enlistment:	Pembroke Lodge, Pocklington

Frederick Robson was the elder brother of Edward Moore. Frederick joined the 5th Yorkshire Regiment (Territorials) on the 13th November 1909; he was mentioned in despatches on the 13th November 1916 and subsequently awarded the Distinguished Service Order on the 25th November 1916. On the 5th April 1917 Frederick was attached to the Durham Light Infantry and was again mentioned in despatches on the 7th November 1917. He died, leading his men of the Durham Light Infantry in Flanders, on the 28th March 1918, and finally again was mentioned in despatches. Frederick William Robson is commemorated on the Wolds Wagoner's Memorial at Sledmere. In the Pocklington Weekly News dated 13th April 1918 the following extract was published.

He was educated at Pocklington School where he attained many scholastic and athletic honours, including the sports championship two years in succession. He was a member of the Yorkshire Gentleman's Cricket Club, and the County Hockey team. He matriculated at the London University and served his articles with his father at Pocklington, where he afterwards practiced with him as a solicitor. He passed the Intermediate Law Examination in the first class, and at the final obtained honours, and was awarded the John Makerell prize for best practical candidate at the examination. He was awarded the prize of £5. 5s. 0d. by the Yorkshire Law Society for having obtained the highest position in the Honours list in 1908, he was a member of and took a keen interest in the Yorkshire Law Students Society, and frequently took part in debates. He was a churchman and for many years a sidesman at Pocklington parish church. At the outbreak of war he was a Captain in the local territorials (then under the command of Colonel Sir Mark Sykes. Bart M.P) and joining up immediately he went with his battalion to France in April 1915, and directly afterwards he was in action, being slightly wounded in the battle of St Julien, and in September 1916 during fighting at the front.

Captain Robson (as he was then) took command of the Battalion after Colonel Mortimer C.M.G was killed. He was promoted to Major and subsequently to Lieutenant Colonel, on being appointed Commandant of a Divisional School of Instruction overseas, for training Officers and non-commissioned Officers. On completion of his work in March 1917, he was appointed to the command of a battalion of the Durham Light Infantry and this position was held up to the time of his death.

He was twice mentioned in despatches for distinguished and gallant services and devotion to duty, and was awarded the D.S.O. Sir Douglas Haig's special mention stated that "Captain F. W. Robson assumed command of the battalion and carried out his duty with the greatest of courage and initiative. He set a splendid example to his men throughout the operations."

He was himself unwounded but his brother Captain Edward Moore Robson (then Lieut') was wounded in four places in the same action. He received the Military Cross, and the two brothers were decorated by His Majesty at Buckingham Palace in December 1916. Colonel Robson's two younger brothers Captain E. M. Robson and J. Stanley Robson (also wounded)

are serving in the Yorkshire Regiment and have been on active service overseas since July 1915. Mr Richard Robson a member of the firm Messrs Bell, Brodrick and Gray. Solicitors, Ormand House, London E.C. Colonel Robson's Eldest brother died on March 30th last."

Sergeant Arthur Rowntree - Reg. No. 52502 (H39)

Born:	Stamford Bridge in 1899
Enlisted:	Beverley
Date and age on death:	23rd October 1918 aged 19
Regiment on Death:	1st Battalion Prince of Wales Own West Yorkshire Regiment
Buried:	Vadencourt British Cemetery, Maissemy
Occupation:	School & newsboy in 1911 age 12
Father:	John Rowntree (labourer)
Mother:	Elizabeth Rowntree
Brothers:	Richard, Thomas, Alfred
Sisters:	Elsie/Eliza, Rose/Rosie
Address pre-enlistment:	20 New Street, Pocklington

Arthur Rowntree was born in Stamford Bridge in 1899 before the family moved to Pocklington. He was killed in October 1918, less than three weeks before the end of the war.

Arthur's father, John Rowntree, was originally from Cottingham and married Elizabeth from Stamford Bridge. They had five children, the eldest four being born in Stamford Bridge. In 1901 the family was living in Fangfoss, before they moved on to 20 New Street, Pocklington, John working as a general labourer.

Arthur and Alfred Rowntree

Arthur enlisted with the West Yorkshires in Beverley and died of wounds on the 23rd October 1918 aged just 19. In the Pocklington Weekly News he is classed as being Sergeant, but the Commonwealth War Graves Commission has his rank as Corporal.

Arthur's brother, Bombardier Alfred Rowntree MM, Royal Field Artillery, was awarded the Military Medal for gallantry in action in 1917 and survived the conflict.

Another brother (pictured right), Driver Thomas Rowntree, also served with the Royal Garrison Artillery.

Trooper Herbert Savage - Reg. No. 2447 (H40)

Born:	Anlaby in 1883
Enlisted:	Unknown
Date and age on death:	Died 2nd November 1914
	Age 31
Regiment on Death:	1st Life Guards
Buried:	Ypres (Menin Gate)
	Memorial (Panel 58)
Occupation:	Police constable
Father:	William Savage (police constable
	in Cottingham)
Mother:	Clara Savage
Brothers:	Arthur, Frederick
Sisters:	Emily, Maud
Address pre-enlistment:	Pocklington

Herbert Savage was Pocklington's first 'Fallen Hero' to die in World War One.

He was a Pocklington police constable when war was declared on 4th August 1914; and he was also a former soldier with the Life Guards who had remained an Army reservist so was immediately called up.

Herbert Savage was born in Anlaby in 1883 where his father, originally from a family of farm labourers from Speeton, near Filey, was an officer with the East Riding Constabulary. Herbert's four brothers and sisters were all born when William was a constable at nearby Cottingham. Herbert's first job was as a porter on the Hull & Barnsley Railway, but as soon as he reached 18, in 1901, he joined the Household Cavalry, being drafted into the Life Guards (Herbert was 6' ½ ", which fitted the Household Cavalry criteria of being between 5' 10" and 6' 1").

The usual term for signing on was seven years as a regular soldier then five years on the reserve list, so Herbert must have extended his time as a reservist for a further term.

When he came out of the Army in 1908 he immediately followed his father into the police. He was promoted to Constable 2nd Class in the East Riding Constabulary in 1911, and in 1912 married Annie Longfield and was posted to Pocklington.

In August 1914 he was straightaway sent to France with the British Expeditionary Force and the cavalry units were the first to see action in World War One, at Mons on 23 August.

Savage's unit was continued in the front line throughout September, and from 19 October to 22 November was in the forefront of the fighting at the 1st Battle of Ypres. It is regarded as an allied victory, but 56,000 British troops were killed or wounded, with the total allied casualties numbering 163,000.

Savage died on 2nd November 1914 and is listed on the Ypres (Menin Gate) Memorial which commemorates those men whose graves are not known.

Private Sidney Scaife - Reg. No. 32/426 (H41)

Born:	Pocklington in 1890
Enlisted:	February 1915
Date and age on death:	22nd November 1916 aged 26
Regiment on Death:	13th Battalion Northumberland Fusiliers
Buried:	Vermelles British Cemetery
Occupation:	Wagoner on farm in 1911, NE Railway in Pocklington Station
Father:	William Scaife (cab proprietor)
Mother:	Eliza Scaife
Brothers:	Christopher, Bertie, Sidney, Reginald, Percival
Sisters:	Ethel, Gladys, Mabel
Address pre-enlistment:	Chapmangate, Pocklington

Sidney Scaife was born and brought up in Pocklington and was working as a porter at Pocklington railway station when he joined the Northumberland Fusiliers in 1915.

His father, Thomas, was a groom who started up in business as a cab proprietor and livery stables at 52 Chapmangate, where he lived with his wife, Eliza, and their eight children. Eliza took on the business when Thomas died, aged 50, in 1914.

Sidney started out as an agricultural labourer and was a 20-year old wagoner on a farm in Burnby in 1911. He then got a job with the North Eastern Railway at Pocklington. He enlisted with the Northumberland Fusiliers in February 1915 and they were sent to France at the end of that year.

In the 9th November 1916 edition of the Pocklington Weekly News newspaper carried an obituary stating that he had been at the front for five months when he was killed on 22nd November. Right is a rare picture of his grave taken on the battlefield by his comrades who buried him.

A year later the paper's 'In Memorium' section had a memorial written from his brothers Chris, Bert and Reg, all of whom were in hospitals at the time.

Captain George Jefferson Scott (H42)

Born:	Market Weighton 1874
Enlisted:	Pocklington
Date and age on death:	25th December 1915 aged 42
Regiment on Death:	5th Battalion Alexandra Princess of Wales Own Yorkshire Regiment
Buried:	Poperinghe New Military Cemetery
Occupation:	Bank manager
Father:	George Scott
Mother:	Victoria Scott
Sisters:	Ida Mary
Address pre-enlistment:	44 Market Place, Pocklington (Barclays Bank)

George Jefferson Scott was born into a well-known Market Weighton family. He rose to become Bank Manager at Barclays Bank Pocklington. His military career started in the Old Volunteers, firstly as a cyclist; then in 1896 he took out a commission and rose to the rank of Captain. He later resigned but re-joined the Territorial Force in 1912. He was married in 1911 to a daughter of Mr Robert Bell of Market Weighton. They had two children. G. J Scott was a director of the Market Weighton Gas Light and Coke Company: a position he held for several years. He was educated at Pocklington School and took an active part in local cricket and football. He was the commanding officer of the Pocklington Troop of 5th Battalion Yorkshire Regiment Territorials that volunteered for overseas service as soon as war was declared.

G. J Scott was killed on Christmas day 1915 and a memorial service was held at Pocklington Parish Church on 27th December 1915, the

Capt. G. J. SCOTT, 5th Yorkshire Regt. (T.F.).

service being held by Rev. A. T Fisher, hymns sung were "O God our help in ages past": "On the resurrection morning" and "God of our life, to thee we call". The address was delivered by Rev. A. A. R Gill vicar of Market Weighton in which he read out a letter from Captain Scott's commanding officer Colonel Mortimer:

"Poor George was killed this morning, practically instantly, by a sniper. Piercy was with him at the time, and the only words he spoke were to the effect that he was shot through the back. The doctor tells me he was shot through the heart. The whole battalion, Officers and men, grieve for his widow.

I have lost a personal friend, and the battalion a very capable officer, who was always cheery and most resolute when any difficult work had to be done. He was loved by his company and very popular with us all, it is a sad Christmas day for us"

Another quote from a non commissioned officer prior to his death visiting the Scott family is as follows.

"His men all love him, and have perfect confidence in him, he always thinks of their comfort before his own, I believe we would all follow him wherever he might lead and no matter of the danger"

George Jefferson Scott with the Pocklington Territorials (see p.59)

George Jefferson Scott was mentioned in despatches and recommended for gallantry by Sir John French (Viscount French of Ypres).

Private George Henry Skelton - Reg. No. 241338 (H43)

Born:	Pocklington 1897
Enlisted:	Scarborough
Date and age on death:	15th July 1917 aged 21
Regiment on Death:	8th Battalion Alexandra Princess of Wales Own Yorks. Regiment
Buried:	Ypres (Menin Gate) Memorial
Father:	Richard Skelton (carter and labourer in 1911)
Mother:	Amy Skelton
Brothers:	Richard, Robert Samuel, John William
Sisters:	Hilda May
Address pre-enlistment:	1 Pem Lane, Pocklington.

Photo: Chris Cosgrove

George Skelton was the son of a Pocklington man Richard Skelton, carter, general labourer, and Amy from Leeds. They lived at Pocklington for several years before moving to North Bierley, Bradford around 1901. But by the 1911 census the family had returned to Pocklington and was living in Pem Lane.

They must have moved again before George signed up, as the Commonwealth War Graves Commission gives their address as "The Bungalow" Back Lane, Holme, York.

The 8th Battalion Yorkshire Regiment was posted to France in August 1915. It fought in most of the major battles of 1916 and 1917. George Skelton was killed in action on 15 July 1917 aged 21.

Alexandra Princess of Wales Own Yorkshire Regiment in Bridlington

Private Thomas Ross Skinner - Reg. No. 201120 (H44)

Born:	Pocklington 1888
Enlisted:	West Hartlepool
Date and age on death:	6th October 1918 age 30
Regiment on Death:	4th Battalion Yorkshire Regiment
Buried:	Glageon Communal Cemetery Extension
Occupation:	Newspaper employee
Father:	Atkinson Skinner (schoolmaster)
Mother:	Minnie Skinner (assistant teacher)
Brothers:	Frank (chemist apprentice in 1911), Arthur Baden, James Harold
Sisters:	Ethel May, Kate Eleanor
Address pre-enlistment:	32 Dovecot St., Stockton (journalist) visitor

Private Thomas Ross Skinner

His father Atkinson Skinner master at Pocklington National School from 1888-1923

Thomas Ross Skinner the son of Atkinson Skinner (born 1860) from Scotter, Lincolnshire who was the headmaster of National School on New Street, Pocklington and Minnie Ross from Stillington. In 1913, Atkinson had moved to Wold View, Yapham Road. Atkinson's parents were called Thomas (born 1827), and Ann (1834). They obviously commemorated the fathers name and Minnie's given surname. In an item on his death in the Pocklington Weekly News it was reported that the family had been told of Thomas's demise by a returning prisoner of war. It was not confirmed until April 1919. Thomas was taken prisoner on the 27th of May 1918 and died **on** or around 28th September 1918 (newspaper account) following a bout of dysentery.

Prior to his enlistment in May 1915 he was an employee of a Darlington newspaper: before that he was a member of the editorial staff on the Yorkshire Herald stationed at Malton and prior to that he was on the staff of the Pocklington Weekly News.

He was married in 1912 to Eleanor Bell Robinson. They had two children, but we do not know gender or names. They lived at No 11, Bickersteth Street, Stockton on Tees. He had a brother Frank Skinner, but in a newspaper article. *"Pte F Skinner, son of Mr & Mrs Skinner, Wold View, who was wounded early in the war, 26th April 1915, and after several operations recently had his leg amputated below the knee, arrived home this week."*
In a letter home Frank writes to a friend from his hospital bed in Ward 6a, 4th Northern General Hospital, Lincoln.

Dear Mrs Sergeant.

I must write to tell you how I am, and to thank you very much for the present you have so kindly sent me. My leg remnant is going on as well as can be expected, and I am pleased to say I am keeping in good spirits. I was pleased to see mother once more, I shall be glad when I get back to old Pock', and see everybody. I am afraid I must have great patience, I have already had more than a month in bed (ain't I lazy) I am afraid I have paid dearly for my little bit of experience but I am not going to worry about at all, it was for a good cause, and I would go through it again if sound, it is the duty of every single man to fight for his country. We get nicely cared for here, and I pass the time away by smoking, eating, reading and joking, and the pain does not seem so intense.

We have grand weather here, and to see chaps walking about makes me very envious, I have some very nice friends come to see me to brighten me up, so I think I shall keep alright. I must really close now, hoping you are in good health.
I remain, your sincere friend, F Skinner

Lance Corporal John William Smith - Reg. No. 243379 (H45)

Born:	Pocklington 1891
Enlisted:	Pocklington
Date and age on death:	Died of Wounds 29th April 1918, aged 27.
Regiment on Death:	5th Battalion Alexandra Princess of Wales Own Yorkshire Regiment
Buried:	Ham British Cemetery, Muille-Villette
Occupation:	Labourer and bricklayer
Father:	John William Smith
Mother:	Margaret A. Smith
Brothers:	Joseph, Ernest
Sisters:	Maggie
Address pre-enlistment:	5 Willow Lane North Featherstone (boarder) his widowed mother Margaret

was living in New Street, Pocklington with her son Ernest, adopted son Arthur and daughter Maggie.

John William Smith was born in Pocklington in 1891. His father, also John William Smith, was a Pocklington man who was born in the town in 1862 and died young in 1893. He married Margaret from Goodmanham. In census of the 1901 and 1911 Margaret and children lived in the School House, New Street, but in 1911 John William jnr. is working as a bricklayer and is a boarder at a house in Featherstone. By the time of the death of John William jnr., Margaret had moved to 11, Alma Terrace, Pocklington.

> **Died of Wounds.**
>
> News has been received that Corporal John William Smith, Yorkshire Regiment, youngest son of Mrs. Smith, School House, New Street, Pocklington, who was officially posted wounded and missing on the 30th March last, is now reported "died from the effects of wounds in the arms, whilst a prisoner of war in Germany." His death took place a fortnight after being captured. He was a well-built and popular young man, 27 years of age, and an athlete of considerable ability. Much sympathy is extended to Mrs. Smith and family in their sad loss.

In its edition of 13th April 1918 The Pocklington Weekly News newspaper carried a report that another Pocklington soldier had written home and stated: 'Cpl John Smith , third son of Mrs Smith of New Street, Pocklington, was wounded in the leg and afterwards taken prisoner by the Germans. Cpl Smith (who went to France on Christmas Day 1916) had previously been gassed.'

The newspaper carried another report on 10th August 1918: 'News has been received that Corporal John William Smith, youngest son of Mrs. Smith, School House, New Street, Pocklington, who was officially posted wounded and missing on 30th March last, is now reported "died from the effects of wounds in the arms, whilst a prisoner of war in Germany." His death took place a fortnight after being captured. He was a well-built and popular young man, 27 years of age, and an athlete of considerable ability.'

Captain Rev. Frederick Seaton Smith - Chaplain 4th Class (H46)

Born:	Pocklington in 1886
Enlisted:	Leeds 1916
Date and age on death:	15 November 1918 aged 31
Regiment on Death:	13th Battalion Yorks. and Lancs. Regiment
Buried:	Terlincthun British Cemetery, Wimille
Occupation:	Clergyman
Father:	Frank Smith of Regent St., Pocklington
Mother:	Jane
Address pre-enlistment:	18 Blenheim Square, Leeds.

According to the records of St Peter's School, York he was born 17th Aug. 1886 in Pocklington, however no birth record has been found. After leaving St Peter's School, in 1902 he went to work in the North Eastern Railway's estates office before following a calling to the church. He studied theology at Lampeter College in Wales from 1910 to 1913 where he captained the college tennis team, graduated with a B.A. then returned to Yorkshire to serve as a curate in parishes in St. John's Bradford and Leeds. Frederick married Martha Lilian Boyden daughter of Pocklington Chemist John AC Boyden at West Derby nr. Liverpool in 1911.

F S. SMITH

He enlisted with the Royal Army Chaplains office in 1916 and was initially posted to Egypt; then transferred to the Western Front and served in the trenches as a Chaplain 4th Class – the equivalent rank to an Army captain – attached to the 13th Battalion Yorkshire and Lancashire Regiment.

Spanish Influenza, which killed up to 100 million worldwide, more than the Black Death, is actually believed to have originated in a field hospital at Etaples, France. It peaked in autumn 1918 and Rev Smith died at nearby Boulogne after a few days illness on 15 November 1918, just four days after the war ended. He left a wife and two young children. The inscription on his gravestone reads "Death both hide but not divide thou art but on Christ's to other side".

A memorial message was posted in the Pocklington Weekly News dated November 18th 1920 by Mrs M Humble (nee) Sowerby.

Extract from Crockfords Clerical Directory:-

SMITH, Fred Seaton, 18, Blenheim-square, Leeds.—S.D.C. B.A. 1913, D 1913, p 1914 Rip. C. of All S. Leeds, Dio. Rip. 1916. T.C.F. 1918. F C. of St. John, Bradford, 1913-15.

E-mail from Lambeth Palace:-

'Crockford's Clerical Directory', maintained by the Church of England, provides the basic source of career information for most Anglican clergy. Please find the last and therefore the most complete entry relevant to Fred Seaton Smith from the 1918/19 edition of Crockford's attached to this email. As you will see, according to Crockford's he was ordained deacon in 1913 and then priest in 1914, he became a temporary chaplain of the forces in 1916 until his death in 1918 and he was formerly the curate at All Saints, Leeds in the diocese of Ripon.

Private Archie Spencer - Reg. No. 15542 (H47)

Born:	Thorganby 1896
Enlisted:	Pocklington
Date and age on death:	15th September 1916 aged 21
Regiment on Death:	3rd Battalion Coldstream Guards
Buried:	Thiepval Memorial
Occupation:	Farm worker
Father:	Frank Spencer (farmer)

Mother:	Emmaline Spencer
Brothers:	Henry H, Louis F, Harry R, Reginald
Address pre-enlistment:	Thorganby Gale, York

Archie Spencer was born and brought up with his four brothers at Thorganby, on the west bank of the River Derwent, where his father farmed at Thornganby Gale. He was a choirboy in the parish church at Thorganby; and in 1911 Archie was aged 15 and working on his father's farm.

As the boys grew up they left home to work as agricultural labourers on other farms, and Archie enlisted at Pocklington where he is believed to have moved to work. He joined the Coldstream Guards which had a longstanding connection with the Thorganby district.

Archie died on a fateful day of 15 September 1915 when three Coldstream Guard battalions fought side-by-side in line for the first time at Flers-Courcelette on the Somme. Their war diary reports: 'At 6.20 am the assault was launched. The battalion went over in half company waves at 50 paces intervals. The attack was met with great opposition…after this had been overcome the green line was taken…Here the battalion reorganised, then pushed forward to the evacuated brown line. About 6 pm the enemy made a counterattack which was easily repulsed…Total casualties, Officers 11, other ranks 414.'

Archibald Spencer, one time Thorganby Choir Boy

Photo source: http://www.thorganby.co.uk/the-first-world-war.html

Archie Spencer is also commemorated on a brass plate in St Helen's Church, Thorganby, with the nine other 1914-1918 war dead from the village; three of the ten were Coldstream Guardsmen.

Archie Spencer's elder brother, Louis Frank, fought in the King's Royal Rifles 1915-18. He was wounded in 1916 but survived the conflict.

Private Richard Mark Stubbs - Reg. No. 37251 (H48)

Born:	Malton 1897
Enlisted:	Bridlington
Date and age on death:	5th June 1917 aged 20
Regiment on Death:	21st Battalion (Tyneside Scottish) Northumberland Fusiliers
Buried:	Arras Memorial
Occupation:	Bank Cashier for Becketts Bank, Bridlington
Father:	Walter Stubbs (Poor Law Relieving Officer)
Mother:	Lucy Maria Stubbs
Brothers:	Reginald Mervyn, Louis Arthur Julian, Walter Carlton
Address pre-enlistment:	Aston Villa, Union Street, Pocklington.

The Stubbs family can be traced back to Malton, in 1881 on Old Maltongate. Richard M and Sarah J lived with seven children, one being Walter Stubbs.

Walter went on to marry Lucy Maria Lacey from Stoke Prior, Bromsgrove, Birmingham, whose father was Emanuel and mother Mary. Emanuel was employed as a blacksmith.

This extract was taken from Kelly's Directory of 1905:

'Stubbs Walter, registrar of births & deaths for Pocklington sub-district & relieving & vaccination officer for the union, Union Street.'

In 1901 Walter and Lucy show up living on Union Street in Kimberley House. They must have arrived after 1897 as they do not show up on the Kelly's Directory. They do however appear in the 1905, 1909, 1913, 1921 directories. Walter dies in 1922. In 1929, after the death of Walter, Reginald takes over his father's duties, but in 1937 only Lucy Maria is

Northumberland Fusiliers battalions in World War I

acting as an interim registrar of births & deaths for Pocklington sub-district, living and working at Aston Villa, Union Street.

Richard Mark Stubbs joined the Northumberland Fusiliers on his 19th birthday in March 1916, and went to France in July 1916.

He was a resident bank cashier for Messrs. Beckett and Co's, Bridlington, he was previously educated in Pocklington, Birmingham and York. He entered the service of the bank in York 1912, and was subsequently transferred to Bridlington six months later.

Richard was a good athlete, being 6 Feet 3 inches in height, he was selected to run in the seven mile race for his battalion, with around 1,800 other competitors, and in a letter to his parents his commanding officer wrote this.

"He was always a good soldier, and we are very sorry indeed to lose him. His name was sent forward from this company for a commission some months ago, and I am sure he would have made a good officer, if it had come through in time to save his life."

"For the last six months he had been in charge of a Lewis machine gun and since April had been waiting for a recall to England to undergo O.T.C training."

Private Arthur John Tayleure - Reg. No. 1692 (H49)

Born:	Pocklington March Qtr 1898
Enlisted:	Lincolnshire
Date and age on death:	20th May 1915 aged 17
Regiment on Death:	"D" Company 1st/5th Battalion Lincolnshire Regiment
Buried:	Packhorse Farm Shrine Cemetery
Occupation:	Unknown
Father:	William Tayleure (joiner in 1911)
Mother:	Emily Tayleure
Brothers:	William, Albert
Sisters:	Doris, Emily
Address pre-enlistment:	3 Sherbutt Cottage, Chapmangate, Pocklington

Photo: Amanda Nicholls

The Pocklington History website gives a background to the Tayleure family. Arthur John Tayleure (grandson of Pocklington's main Victorian photographer) was born in March 1898 two years after his father William Tayleure married Emily. William took his family to live in Lincolnshire, where is not known but at the time of Arthur John's death they lived at 127 Mary Street, Scunthorpe. (see p.241)

Private Arthur John Tayleure died aged 17

Arthur John was originally posted as missing, and his mother had known through one of Arthur's friends; Drummer Leaning, also of the "Fighting 5th", that he was dead. Arthur was declared dead on the 20th May 1915. His father William was also serving and had joined on the commencement of war.

Drummer Leaning wrote in a letter to his own mother:

"I will expect you have heard of my mate, Arthur Tayleure, getting killed, but it cannot be helped, you have to put up with these things. His time had come and everybody has to go when God thinks fit to take them to their everlasting home. At the time I am writing this letter there is an aeroplane over our lines and the Germans potting at it. About 3 to 5 o'clock every afternoon the Germans start to shell us with their big guns, then someone will say they're dishing iron rations out again, that is all we care, there are lots of "Jack Johnsons," "Little Willies," "Dirty Dicks," "Silent Creepers." God be with you till we meet again. Ralph"

Arthur John was in training at Stanstead when his regiment got the call to go the front; he was to be left behind for home duty, but on appeal to his commanding officer he was aloud to embark.

Footnote-

'Jack Johnson' – A large German/Austrian low velocity shell. 'Little Willie' was a nickname for early tanks. The others could not be found.

Private John Wilfred Thompson - Reg. No. 34691 (H50)

Born:	Stamford Bridge, 6th February 1897
Enlisted:	Pocklington
Date and age on death:	16th September 1916, aged 19
Regiment on Death:	10th Battalion Kings Own Yorkshire Light Infantry
Buried:	Dartmoor Cemetery, Becordel-Becourt
Occupation:	Unknown
Father:	John Thompson (farm/general labourer)
Mother:	Clara Thompson
Brothers:	Walter, Ernest
Sisters:	Edith Amy, Gladys Mary, Olive Maud
Address pre-enlistment:	Skins Lane, Chapmangate, Pocklington

Pte. WILFRED THOMPSON, K.O.Y.L.I., son of Mrs. Thompson, Chapmangate, died of wounds received in action, November 16th, 1916.

In 1901 the Thompson family was living in Grape Lane, Pocklington.
Father John Thompson, originally from Stamford Bridge, was a labourer aged 63 and married to Clara (nee

Tyrell) aged 36, twenty seven years his junior, from Full Sutton. They had five children between the ages of one and 13 (another daughter was born in 1902).

John Thompson senior died in February 1911, leaving his family in poor circumstances and in the census of April 1911, John Wilfred Thompson, usually known as Wilfred, is listed as a 14-year old schoolboy and an inmate in Pocklington workhouse with his widowed mother and two younger sisters. He attended Pocklington National School in New Street, where more than a dozen 'Fallen Heroes' went to school. Things improved for the Thompson family and they moved out of the workhouse in Burnby Lane to live in Skins Lane, Chapmangate.

He joined up in the first few months of the war and was posted to the 10th Battalion Kings Own Yorkshire Light Infantry. In 1916 the 10th Battalion KOYLI was involved in the battle of the Somme, which lasted for three and a half months with one million casualties. Wilfred Thompson died of his wounds on 16th September 1916 aged 19.

His two older brothers also served in WW1. Walter was a Lancashire Fusiliers and was shipped home to Warrington hospital after being wounded in the left side and arm in July 1918. His other brother Ernest returned safely after serving in France with the Royal Garrison Artillery for three years.

Private Thomas Richard Thorpe - Reg. No. 240569 (H51)

Born:	Pocklington 1894
Enlisted:	Scarborough
Date and age on death:	9th April 1918 aged 24
Regiment on Death:	4th Battalion Yorkshire Regiment (Green Howards)
Buried:	La Kreule Military Cemetery, Hazebrouck
Occupation:	Stonemason
Father:	James Thorpe (house painter)
Mother:	Ellen Thorpe
Brothers:	Fred (tailor), Frank (tin smith's apprentice)
Sisters:	Esther M
Address pre-enlistment:	5 Alma Terrace, Pocklington

Photo: Chris Cosgrove

Thomas R Thorpe was born in 1894 and lived with his family on Railway Street, Pocklington, attending Pocklington National School. He served a stonemasonry apprenticeship with Mr J Richardson of New Street (Richardsons produced the war memorial in Market Street, which was erected in 1921).

He joined the local Territorials and served from the outset of the war. He was with the regiment in France, where he was wounded twice, but he married Dorothy Steel, daughter of Mrs W Steel of Chapmangate, in Pocklington in 1916, only three weeks prior to his death when he had been home on leave. Though he served with the Green Howards, he is listed as attached to the East Yorkshire Regiment when he was fatally wounded in April 1918. At the time of his death the address of his wife, Mrs Dorothy Thorpe, is given as 83 Ainsworth Road, Radcliffe, Lancashire.

Private Thomas Thorpe, Yorkshire Regiment, is officially reported to have died on April 9th, in the Australian Casualty Clearing Station, from wounds received in action. He rejoined the local Territorials on the outbreak of war, and served with the Regiment in France, where he had been twice wounded. Only three weeks ago he was home on leave, and returning to France was attached to the East Yorks. Regiment, with which he was mortally wounded. In civil life he was a stonemason, serving his apprenticeship with Mr. J. Richardson, New Street, and his quiet and genial disposition gained him many friends, who deeply regret his early death at the age of 23 years. He leaves a widow, daughter of Mrs. W. Steels, Chapmangate.

Howdenshire Chronicle and Pocklington Weekly News for April 20th, 1918.

Private Richard Timbs - Reg. No. 3406 (H52)

Born:	Yapham 1897
Enlisted:	Pocklington
Date and age on death:	Died of wounds 15th April 1916, aged 19.
Regiment on Death:	5th Battalion Alexandra Princess of Wales Own Yorkshire Regiment
Buried:	Bailleul Communal Cemetery Extension (Nord)
Occupation:	Farm lad
Father:	William Timbs (cowman)
Mother:	Harriet Timbs
Brothers:	William, George, Alfred, Arthur, Daniel, Wilfred
Sisters:	Sarah, Amy, Mary Jane
Address pre-enlistment:	Pocklington

Richard Timbs and his brother Alfred from Yapham Mill.

Richard Timbs was born and brought up in Yapham, where his father, William, originally from Buckinghamshire, was a cowman on a local farm. William married Harriet, from York, in 1883 in Pocklington and had 17 children, 11 surviving to adulthood. In the 1911 census the family is still in Yapham, but Richard, aged 14, is a horse lad on Fordham Farm, on top of Garrowby Hill above Bishop Wilton. He is thought to have moved from there to a Pocklington farm before enlisting with 5th Battalion Yorkshire Regiment in Pocklington in 1915.

Richard was one of four brothers who enlisted in the armed forces, Alfred, William and Arthur; with Alfred and Arthur both serving in France. The 5th Battalion was involved in heavy fighting in early 1916, ending in front line trenches at Kemmel in April 1916. Richard was wounded in the head by a sniper. A letter from J E Jolly, Sister in Charge of No 2 Clearing Station, explains the situation to one of his sisters:

"Dear Miss Timbs

I hope this address will find you. I am sorry to say that Private R Timbs was brought here to No2 Clearing Station, severely wounded in the head and quite unconscious, and passed away at 1.30 today without regaining consciousness. He will be buried in part of the cemetery here reserved for our brave troops, and a little cross bearing the name and date marks each resting place. The name of the place and the number of his grave will be sent to you later from Headquarters. There is one consolation, from the nature of the wound you may be sure he did not suffer but would be unconscious at once.

With much sympathy.

Yours Sincerely,

J E Jolly Sister in Charge"

He is commemorated at Balleul Communal Cemetery Extension. According to the 1/5th War Diary, just before his death the 5th had relieved the 4th East Yorks. in the trenches at Lindehoek in the vicinity of Ypres (part of the second battle of Ypres).

Private William Walker - Reg. No. 203017 (H53)

Born:	Wilberfoss, January 1896
Enlisted:	Stockton on Tees
Date and age on death:	20th September 1917, aged 21
Regiment on Death:	13 Battalion Durham Light Infantry
Buried:	Ypres Reservoir Cemetery
Occupation:	Labourer
Father:	Robert Walker (agricultural/general labourer)
Mother:	Mary Jane Walker
Brothers:	Percy, James
Sisters:	Edith, Nellie, Fanny
Address pre-enlistment:	7 Church Lane, Pocklington

Photo: Chris Cosgrove

William Walker was from a Wilberfoss family that had a smallholding on
Bolton Lane. The family then moved to Pocklington, living in Church Lane, with his father, Robert,
becoming a general labourer and William attending the National School in New Street.

William enlisted with the 5th Battalion, Durham Light Infantry, and went to France in April 1915. The DLI

were in front line action at Ypres in 1915 and the
Somme in 1916, when William received a gunshot
wound and was shipped back to hospital in
England.

**The photographs (Imperial War Museum) are
of 13th Durham Light Infantry at the battle of
Menin Road ridge where William Walker was
killed.**

The 'Pocklington Weekly News' newspaper for
30th September 1916 gave a progress report:
'News has reached Pocklington that Pte William
Walker of 5th Battalion Durham Light Infantry,
who will attain his 21st birthday on January
next, has been wounded in the right thigh. He is
now in England and is going on as well as can
be expected and his many friends wish for his a
speedy and complete recovery.'

He did recover, went back to France to join 13th Battalion Durham Light Infantry and was killed on 20th
September 1917. The 13th Battalion was at the forefront of the Battle of Menin Road Ridge, 20-25
September 1917, part of the Passchendaele offensive, when it suffered almost 300 casualties.

Great War Exhibitions held in Pocklington Arts Centre

November 2008

Above: The Buttle bugle, later sold at a local auction. Contact PDLHG if you know of its current whereabouts.

This exhibition was researched and displayed in Pocklington Arts Centre thanks to the work of Martin Cooper, and other members of the Pocklington Town Council.

November 2014

Pocklington's Fallen Heroes exhibition took place in November 2014 to commemorate the town's World War One heritage and dedicated to those who gave their lives in the conflict. The display contained the updated research on each of the fallen on the war memorial and which is

Pocklington and District Local History Group

included in this publication. It got underway with a memorable opening ceremony on Friday 31st Oct. 2014, at Pocklington Arts Centre. An audience of over 150, which included several descendants of Pocklington's fallen heroes, were welcomed by the town mayor, Councillor Paul West, who then received a regimental plaque from Lieutenant Colonel Graham Whitmore in memory of all the Pocklington men from his regiment who died fighting in the war. Gareth Hughes, head of history at Pocklington School, set the context of the war, spoke about how his grandfather's experiences in 1914-18 first sparked his interest. An audio visual presentation included the reminiscences of local 'Tommy' Billy Harrison, who was interviewed for an aural history project in York circa 1980. Billy Harrison was born in Nunburnholme, started out as a gardener at Warter Priory, and became a well known local character and musician. He signed up at Pocklington in February 1917 and within weeks was in the front line in France. His interview was played to the captivated audience as he described going over the top with his platoon of 120 men, and how only ten survived unscathed. The fitting finale was provided the playing of a recording of the singing of veteran George Barker who died in Pocklington. A film was played of a memorial parade showing many of Pocklington's World War One veterans marching through the town in 1932, and Barker's moving renditions of the songs he sang in the trenches, such as 'Long Way to Tipperary' and 'Pack Up Your Troubles', were added as a soundtrack. The videos and sound tracks were running on a continuous loop in the exhibition. The exhibition closed on the 7th Nov. 2014.

November 2016

A further exhibition included photographs, memorabilia, extracted local newspaper articles and stories from across the district and was open 10-15th November 2016 in the Arts Centre studio.

Gareth Hughes was keynote speaker on the 100th anniversary of the Battle of the Somme.

Picture Gallery

The Pocklington "Terriers" (Territorials)

Back Row (Left to right): G. Sugden, C. Bennison, R. Pratt, Jim Eastwood, George Scott, Arthur Todd, Harry Hindwell
Middle Row (Left to right): Henry Johnson, Albert Hunter, G. Alderson, C. Hotham
Front Row (Left to right): R. Craggs, W. Hanley, Ben Allison, A. Hanley, J. Warters

Above:
A button of the Pocklington volunteers found at Pocklington

Left:
Pocklington School Cadets in 1916

Pocklington and District Local History Group

Alf Buttle who fought with
the Australian Forces

Fred Hotham
(p.204)

Bill Bentley
(p.192)

James Scott

Fred Barker

Hawksworth Barker
(p.191)

Walter Barker
(p.191)

Herbert Richardson who was the
chauffeur at Warter Priory

Henry Silburn & his wife
Alexandrina (p.215)

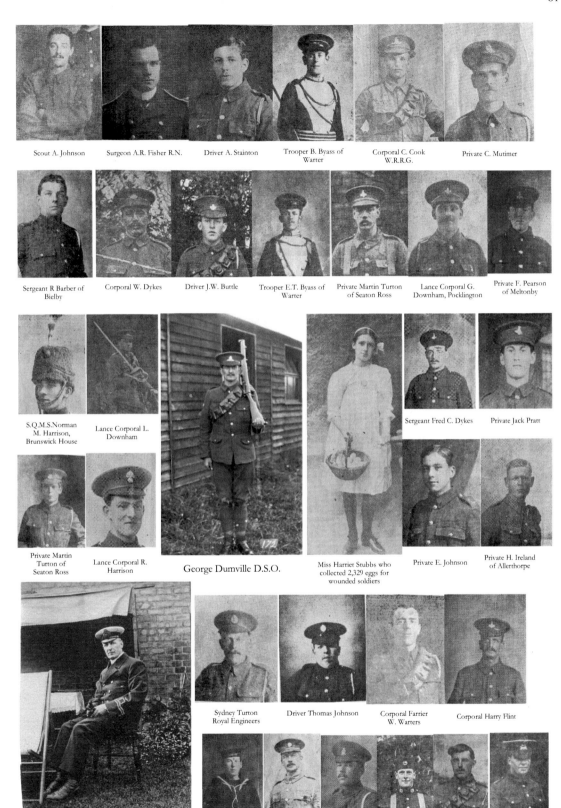

Scout A. Johnson

Surgeon A.R. Fisher R.N.

Driver A. Stainton

Trooper B. Byass of Warter

Corporal C. Cook W.R.R.G.

Private C. Mutimer

Sergeant R Barber of Bielby

Corporal W. Dykes

Driver J.W. Buttle

Trooper E.T. Byass of Warter

Private Martin Turton of Seaton Ross

Lance Corporal G. Downham, Pocklington

Private F. Pearson of Meltonby

S.Q.M.S.Norman M. Harrison, Brunswick House

Lance Corporal L. Downham

George Dumville D.S.O.

Miss Harriet Stubbs who collected 2,329 eggs for wounded soldiers

Sergeant Fred C. Dykes

Private Jack Pratt

Private Martin Turton of Seaton Ross

Lance Corporal R. Harrison

Private E. Johnson

Private H. Ireland of Allerthorpe

Wycliffe Galland Everingham

Sydney Turton Royal Engineers

Driver Thomas Johnson

Corporal Farrier W. Warters

Corporal Harry Flint

Son of Mr and Mrs Webster of Bolton Hall

Sgt W. Walker of Melbourne

Private H. Preston of Seaton Ross

Harry Webster of Bolton Hall

Driver G. Mouncey of Pocklington

Harry Holmes 3rd-5th West Yks. A nephew of Mr. Whitehead

Pocklington and District Local History Group

Market Place musters

We can date this picture by the film being shown at Fred Lee's Central Hall Cinema "The Sign of the Cross" which was touring the local Cinema's in October 1914

Pocklington and District Local History Group

From Eric Buttle's collection
—the back reads
"For Aunt Hannah Bielby"

From a set of photos from Warter

From a set of photos from
Warter

Trooper E.T. Byass of Warter

Corporal Alf Rowntree RFA

**All
Unknowns
from Eric
Buttle's
collection**

Pocklington and District Local History Group

George Gray is on the top row 2nd right, Herbert Ezard kneeling at the front right & brother Charles is behind him far right.

The Kings Royal Rifles—Top left Harold Buttle, 3rd from left at the back Walter Barker, front row left Sidney Gray, 2nd from left Veiney Waite, front row 2nd from right Harry Morris, Front row far right Herbert Ezzard.

From the Buttle Collection. The back reads "To Eric, Best of Luck, hoping you are well. Yours Bill. 21/7/17."

Herbert Theodore Cliff Killed in Action on 13th Oct. 1914 and whose monument is in Barmby Moor Church

Pocklington Military Band

Pocklington and District Local History Group

Left: Percy Robinson of the 10th Royal Hussars

Harold Harrison from Bishop Wilton

Lyth Downham is in the centre

Wilberfoss soldiers

Mounted troops at Wilberfoss

John Snow

Charles
Vernon
Waite

Chris & Reg Scaife

Pocklington and District Local History Group

Arthur Henry Todd | Harry Gospel Killed in Action 23 Oct 1917 | Corporal Richard Wright Webster (left) & Mr. Steel ? | David Claude Balmford Legion of Frontiersmen

Mr Alfred Edward Boulton paralysed by a bullet in 1915 in his electric wheelchair and later joined the Board of Guardians and became a town councillor in 1929.

Kath Hotham dated 20 Dec 1916, 11 New Pavement.

A young cadet from the Buttle Archive

An Officers gathering (inc. Mark Sykes) thought to be at Pocklington School from the late W Brown

Billy Hardy with the ASC (Seated 2nd from Right)

Pocklington Military Recruiting Band c.1915 (thought to be practising in a garden in George Street)

Pocklington and District Local History Group

From the
Pocklington
Post
Newspaper

Our Memory Lane picture this week shows the East Yorkshire Volunteer
Brigade on parade at Pocklington railway station. The photograph was loaned to
us by Mr M J Wood of Foggathorpe. Can anyone help us identify the brigade
members and perhaps pin-point the date on which it was taken?

From the Buttle
Collection. The
back reads:

"*Baggy Topham, Charlie
Spivey, Percy Knaggs, L
Downham, Chap who
worked at one of Pock
banks.*"

Postmark is for
Darlington and
dated 2 Sep 14

Billy Harrison
from
Nunburnholme

Reproduced
with permission
from Peter
Halkon, author
of "Bills Book"
published by
Hutton Press.

William Ernest
Walker of
Hayton and
Ousethorpe.
Killed in action
on 14th July of
1915.

Pocklington and District Local History Group

5th September 1914 — Pocklington rally to raise
money for the Prince of Wales Relief Fund from a
glass slide (from the PDLHG Everingham collection)

Billy 1915 - Private William Hardy #39053
Wolds Wagoners (standing in middle)

A Call to Arms

GREAT RALLY AT POCKLINGTON.

THE PRINCE OF WALES IS OFFERING HIS LIFE FOR THE NATION—
COME AND LET US KNOW WHAT YOU ARE GOING TO DO.

— ON —

Saturday, the 5th Sept.,
1914, THERE WILL BE A
MONSTER RALLY

In the MARKET PLACE at POCKLINGTON, for the purpose of
raising money for the National Relief Fund.

At 6-15 p.m., the following Bodies are requested to line up in
consecutive order in the Market Place :—

The Coronation Band.
The National Reservists.
Magistrates.
Clergy and Ministers of all Denominations.
Members and Officers of the Urban District Council.
Members and Officers of the Pocklington Guardians.
Members of the Red Cross Society.
Members of the Manchester Unity of Oddfellows.
The Cycling Club.
Pocklington Merry Makers.
All the School Children with Flags.
The Fire Brigade.
The General Public.

At 6-30 p.m. the Procession will pass through Union Street, Bridge Street,
Chapmangate, Pavement, and back to the Market Place, where short Patriotic
Speeches will be made. Everybody will then be asked to pass in double file in
front of Collecting Bags into which they will drop their copper, silver, and gold according
to their means.

Our Gallant Prince as Treasurer of the National Relief Fund says—" My first duty is
to ask for generous and ready support ; and I know I shall not ask in vain."

By helping this Fund you are doing your best to make sure that the wives and children
of our brave soldiers shall be cared for whilst they are nobly fighting our Battles, and guarding
our beloved Shores. Give, and give generously.

GOD SAVE THE KING.

Ousethorpe Camp from 1907/8

Pocklington and District Local History Group

Pocklington Peace Celebrations in 1920 with Mr Boulton in his wheelchair (see p.67) and it is thought to be Margaret Warters with the pram and her twin grandsons (Ref. Ken Durkin).

The gentleman with the moustache in the centre ring is Alfred Summerson, Clerk of the Council and organiser of many war activities including air-raid precautions, war savings, help for Belgian refugees.

Pocklington and District Local History Group

The diary of John Brook

(Transcribed with the kind permission of Caroline Hanna)

John Brook fought throughout the Great War conflict. Brook was a
Pocklington plumber when he joined the 5th Yorkshire (Green
Howards) Territorials in August 1914. He was sent to France in
April 1915 and was plunged straight into the battle of Ypres.
Keeping a diary at the front was prohibited in case it fell into enemy
hands, but Brook had a remarkable memory for detail and wrote a
retrospective log of his wartime experiences, including life in the
trenches and in no-mans land at the Somme and meeting up with
friends from back home. He was still at the front when the war
ended in November 1918, being repatriated and returning to
Pocklington to start up in business again in The Pavement in early
1919.

1914 - 18 WAR

I joined the 5th Yorkshire Regiment (Green Howards) in Aug 31st
1914 and was sent to Scarborough for training. Captain Scott was
our officer. We were stationed at Falsgrave Barracks and got our meals at a Café near the station opposite a
cinema. One day after our lunch we went outside to wait for our sergeant
(Windy Taylor we called him). Some of our lads sat down on the cinema steps
and the Sergeant was furious when he saw them, and said "Fall In" and he
marched us all back to barracks, and said "you street corner boys, I'll teach you
to lounge about". He made us run round that yard, he was a regular soldier and
he put us thorough it all right. After a while we were billeted out, I was sent
with a few more to Bell View Hotel near the station. We had beds to sleep on
and good food. Some mornings we went for a bathe in the sea before breakfast.
Other mornings we had to run round the Marine Drive, stop half way for a rest
and if anyone said they were tired he would say "lie down and die you are not
tired until blood runs out of your boots". Some lads used to run up a passage
when they could and wait until we came back, he soon found out and then he
got a bicycle and rode behind us. We used to go to the cricket field for drills.

John Brook in later life

After our training we were sent to Newcastle to join the battalion. My brother
Maurice had just come over to England with the first Canadian contingent, and I got one day leave to see
him, and had to meet the other boys on the train at York station as they came through. We were billeted at
the Old Infirmary for a time and then at Mitford St.
School. We used to go to the swimming baths but I used
to pay for a hot bath. Of course we had to parade with
the company, we did not get any time off only a few
passes were allowed each night as we had a lot of guard
duty to do, we always had to sleep on the floor. The tea
was made in the same dixie as the stew had been boiled
in and we all had to wash them out in turn very often in
cold water and rub some sand on to get the grease off.
We had to sit on the floor to have our meals, one
morning while we were sat having breakfast one of our

J. E. BROOK,

PAVEMENT, POCKLINGTON

PRACTICAL PLUMBER, GLAZIER, PAINTER,
PAPERHANGER and HOUSE DECORATOR.

HOT and COLD WATER and
GAS FITTER

PAPERHANGINGS in large variety.

BATHS, LAVATORIES,
WATER CLOSETS.

CYLINDERS, TIGHT BOILERS and CISTERNS always in Stock

Estimates Given.

lads shot himself in the shoulder. We used to parade every morning and then march several miles with the battalion through Newcastle up Scotswood Road, and then we went in fields to drill. We had two Scotch sergeants to drill us, one wore kilts, the other plaid trousers, he was a Scottish Borderer. Colonel Mark Sykes used to come with us sometimes, he was real tough and used to make us push through hedges and lay down anywhere in the mud and rub mud on your face so as planes could not see you. If it was pouring with rain he would not let you put your overcoat on, we had to get hardened to it.

One night at Newcastle I was on guard at the High Level Bridge, two hours on and four hours off. After my first two hours one of the workmen on the bridge gave me a drink of Cocoa and something to eat and then I laid down to sleep. After four hours I should have gone on guard again but someone made a mistake, forgot I should have gone on guard and put W. Moor on again, he had done his guard twice that night. When the Germans shelled Hartlepool and Scarborough we were out all night up Scotswood Road and we were rushed back to barracks on trams and issued with extra ammunition, and sent by train to Hartlepool. Breakfast was waiting for us on the platform, then we were posted to places in the streets, when all had quietened down at night we were put on a railway siding and slept in the carriages. Next morning our band arrived and we marched around the town to cheer the people up as a lot of houses were damaged, after that we returned to Newcastle. We were first line of the defence up there and always carried rifles when on church parade and piled arms in the street with a sentry over them. We always had early morning service on our own. Captain Robson was our A. Company Officer. One night when Captain Robson had gone home on leave, a machine gun officer walked into our room and looked around. Then he said to me I want some more men for machine gun section would I like to transfer to them and I said yes, when I told Alf Hopper he also joined. Next morning we were sent by train to Hurworth, near Darlington. We had lectures and practice putting the gun together and repairing parts. Then we were sent on the range two or three times a day, sometimes at night we had lights on the target, then I got my M.G. badge. After that we were posted to Redcar on coast defence, we were billeted at the convalescent home close to the sands. We had two Maxim guns and two lots of trenches and dugouts on the sands, one lot at Marske and one at Tod Point. Some of us were on duty day and night a week at a time and as soon as day break the other gunners used to come and stay and work making positions and trenches., no civilians were allowed near to us as sentries were on patrol on the sands. I bought Marie a ring and a necklace in Redcar. After several weeks I got leave, but after two days at home I got a telegram to return at once to Newcastle. My brother Maurice an officer was at home on leave, and I was thinking of staying another day but he told me I had better go back. Well he went up to York on the same train with some other Officers. I was a private so I could not travel with my brother. After we got to Newcastle they were busy getting ready to go to France, it was April 1915. Two days after at night time we were marched to the goods station to load up wagons and horses and food and ammunition, then we were off to Southampton. On the train Clemmy Hill had a revolver, he started messing about with it and it went off and a lad called Wackie got shot in the wrist so they had to stop at Southampton for a court marshall and they never got back to us. At Southampton we had to unload and carry everything to the side of the boat. It was amusing to see horses being lifted up with a belt under their body on to the boat, they did kick.

We got to Le Havre harbour 11am next day then we marched to a camp several miles away, and arrived about 10-30 pm next day. We went by train to Cassel and met our Battalion as we had set off night before them. Now we were 22 Kilometres from the front and a shell burst near our train on the line just behind, that was a good start. After a few days we were put on some old London buses, the windows were well boarded up and we were rushed to Ouderdom near Vlamertinge and went into some huts, we had orders not to take our boots off but some did, during the night we had orders to get out, there was a scramble as we only had a few matches. The Germans had broken through at St. Julien and Langemarch and Pilham [Pilkem] by using poison cloud gas. At 5 o'clock in the morning, the Germans came forward in a kind of divers costume, then behind them came bomb throwers they came past the corner of the Canadian line but masses were caught in offloading fire and suffered heavy losses. Then the bomb throwers got into range of the French lines and a breakthrough occurred. Two Battalions of Canadians were hurled against the Germans and they retired into a wood between Pilham and St. Julien and rapidly made a fortress with machine guns, this halted our advance. Early on Friday morning the Canadians attacked the wood led by bomb throwers. This lasted all day and the Germans were driven out of the wood. Then orders came to retire to keep intact with the French. Now reinforcements were brought up from behind Ypres, our 50 Division Territorials. Some Buffs were already there, the others included 4th & 5th Yorkshire Regiments, West Kents and Gloucesters. Indian Gurkhas were there up the road and along the banks of the river Hannebeck, they paused, mown down by machine gun fire from the ruined houses, then with a final push they captured a lot of machine guns, then the line had to be abandoned again. During this time the German heaviest artillery were firing from Houthulet Wood and Poelcappelle near Wieltze. A 17" shell nearly wiped out Headquarters. The officer had a very bad time exposed to shrapnel from two sides, a lot of villages in the district were destroyed; St. Julien, Wieltje, St Jean, the suburbs of Ypres, Brielen and in Vlamertinghe a lot of transport horses were shot down. The shooting was so deadly, supplies could not get up and ammunition and rations had to be carried 1½ miles. As we came up through Ypres all the houses on both sides of the streets were on fire, and when we got on the open road we were in view of the Germans so our transport men had to throw all the ammunition and rations by the roadside and gallop back, it was Saturday night and raining. We stayed until morning in gutters and then moved further up the road and got into a farmhouse the people had gone and left everything. We let the horse and cows and poultry loose and then cut a hole through the room wall for our machine gun and then one man went to the attic to see where the Germans were. We got some chocolate and sweets out of the house. Gurkhas and French Algerians were running about with knives. One Gurkha said to me 'drink' so I gave him my water bottle and he held it up but did not touch his lips just poured it down his throat. Bob Boyes started to pray that upset us a bit. Soon we got shelled out and moved further up and dug trenches. Then an Officer I thought he was a spy came along and asked me about where the stores was, and I said what for? And he would not answer. So Alf Hopper and me stood guard over him and a soldier he had with him. Captain Purvis searched him and his papers seemed alright, but they were tapping our wires and they got caught later on. A lot of wounded were coming down the road and the Gurkhas was making awful noises, a lot had been gassed. Some Gurkhas were working by the roadside mending wires they had mules and rolls of wire, all was confusion. After we got relieved, we marched to a place near Vlamertinghe for a rest, it was just a field, we laid on a ground sheet and threw another over us. It was raining and we slept out in the open. Then we got shelled out and moved further back for five days. We had a lot of horses killed in the field we went near Poperinge. We were tired marching back so during the night we came to a farmhouse and our officer knocked at the door. The farmer popped his head out of the bedroom window and said he had no room, however, we went into a barn and slept there. Next day we moved further back, Lord French came to see us and congratulated us. He said we had been rushed into action soon after coming from England but we were the nearest troops available and the gap had to be filled. This was the 2nd Battle of Ypres April 1915. General Sir Henry Plumer conveyed personal thanks to Colonel Maurice Bell of 4th Yorks. for bravery by the North Riding troops. The losses were heavy with 200 missing, the 5th Yorks. losses were not known but the Battalion exhibited great gallantry.

We had no gas masks only black muslin dipped in solution to tie round our mouths and the bombers had to make bombs out of old jam tins filled with metal and powder and a wick to light with matches and throw into the trenches. Captain Scott was in the Battalion, Frank Skinner was wounded and lost one leg, Sergeant John Eastwood got to England he was gassed. Early in May we went near to Hill 60 and helped engineers to build trenches for a week, we had to march several miles there every night and march back before daylight. It was hard work carrying boxes of ammunition and rolls or wire a long way down a railway line and then fill sand bags. After this we went to Sanctuary Wood to make machine gun positions, this lasted about a week we went every night and came back in the morning. At midnight on Whit Sunday we were called out as the Germans were attacking again at Ypres we waited on the roadside until Monday night then marched up through Ypres to the Menin Road past *Hell Fire*

Hell Fire Corner at Ypres in Belgium, one of the most dangerous places in the war

Corner. It was a crossroads and was shelled continuously day and night. Horses and wagons were blocking the road, dead all over the place we had a job to get past all the confusion. Then we got in the open, and had to dig a trench for cover. After a while I got out of the trench and washed my feet in a shell hole and then I fell asleep. Soon I got woke up as the Germans were shelling and one shell fell and killed Alf Hopper and three others, one was a painter from Scarborough. We could only see Alf Hopper, all his side was blown in, the others were buried under him. Captain Purvis got a few belongings of his and sent to his wife. There was a sunken railway near us and seven of our men got killed, dead were laid all over on the lines, we had to move it was so bad, and we made our way to Sanctuary Wood. Then 'Cuddy' Layburn got shot in the shoulder we waited on the roadside then an ambulance took him away, he was never heard of after that, we think the ambulance got blown up. Charles Hotham got killed before we got to the wood, Captain Purvis and Bob Boyes later put a wooden cross where Alf Hopper was killed, later his name and Chas Hotham's was put on the Menin Gate Memorial. Some time after we moved into Hoodge [Hooge] Village all the water was poisoned we were lost. We fixed our gun up at a corner of the street facing a chateau then our artillery started shelling the village and we went into a house. There was a lot of our soldiers laid on the floor wounded. The Germans were in houses on the opposite side of the street and we kept firing at one another. When it was dark we carried all the wounded out and then returned into Zouave Wood trenches, we had nothing to eat that day.

We saw a Zeppelin going over to England. We had not been in the wood long before we were spotted by an observation balloon. Then shells rained at us in the wood. We had to run and leave one gun and we found shelter in a deep 11ft Trench at the edge of the wood. Corporal Dove got wounded when we were shelled for 16½ hours, about 15 shells a minute. Sergeant Warriner got killed soon after. Bill Barrot and Kelly Creacer got wounded. When things had quietened down two of us crept on our stomachs to a pump to get some water but as soon as we got to the pump we were fired on by machine guns. When we got back into the wood our Maxim gun had been hit and broken. Nearly every tree was knocked down and over 90 soldiers killed. Captain Purvis brought us some bully beef and biscuits and said I did not expect to see you alive. Our Company were at a camp when we got relieved, we had to march six miles to them and they wanted to know where we had been. They gave us some tea and bread, soon we were moved further back, then slept two nights in the open fields. We dug a trench and threw some tree branches over the top and then laid our waterproof sheet on top. After that we marched to Dranoute for a week. Our officer got billeted in a house and we got into dugouts, they were on a bank side. After that we went to trenches, we never went back to the same trench as our front was over 100 miles. Then there was at least 200 miles the French and Belgians held. We went to Cammel [Kemmel] near Messines only 45 yards from the German trenches. They blew three mines up near our trench and a lot of rifle grenades, you cannot hear them until they explode. An officer came up one day and looked over the top but he was soon down. I saw one of our lads get shot right through the chest with looking over and Sergeant Flankish from Sledmere got killed the same way. We used to use a periscope to look over. Every night thousands of flares or vary lights were fired up in the air all night long, you could see if anyone was creeping across. When we wanted artillery to help us we used to fire S.O.S. with red rockets or flares. One cold and wet night Joe Cromack and me were on duty, and we just went into a dugout for shelter about midnight, and Captain Fred Robson came round on visiting patrol. He popped his head in and said "who's on guard here?". We told him we were. He said "on guard in the dugout?". However, he did not report us or it would have been a court marshall for us. The Germans used to blow a bugle to us and shout to us and tell us what regiment we belonged to. One said he used to work in England as a butcher. After we got relieved we went to Dranoutre for a short rest. Then we went to Armentiers 67 Trench there was a babies grave on the side of the trench with a wood cross and a pair of shoes tied on. A house had been there, there was still a water pump left. We used to climb out of the trench at night and dig a few potatoes up between our trench and the Germans. We also found a lot of bottles of red and white wine under brick rubbish, it had been a cellar. We used to bluff the Germans make them believe we had a lot of machine guns we used to fire several rounds and keep moving to another part and fire again. We used to have two guns to the battalion and we used to let one another know if we were alright by firing like this 'Tom-tiddly-om-pom-pom'. We lost Private Warde, Jude and Codgy Warton killed. Soon after this a few were allowed leave to England. Someone had to draw and I was drawn first, but I let a married man called Pobby Clarke go before me and I went a few days after. I walked from the trenches and down a railway line there was a big hedge across the railway line to screen us from the Germans. Our company then went to a rest camp at Outersteen near Bailleul. First time we went into Armentieres it was for a bath at a disused brewery. We lined up in a street and undressed, left our clothes and ran about 100 yards up a yard and then climbed up and got into some very large tubs, six of us at a time. Well I came to England on leave Nov. 1915. We got to London late at night. A few of us got a horse drawn taxi to go from Victoria Station to Kings Cross, when I got to York someone took me to the Guildhall until I could get a train home. I got married on Nov. 15th 1915. Next day we went to London and stayed one day with Elsie, then I returned to France.

I went up to Ypres 48 Trench near Hill 60. We had to wade knee deep in parts of the trench, our overcoats touched the water so we had some to cut off our coats. We were there about 10 days then got relieved for a few days then we

German Soldiers in trenches at Hill 60

went to the trenches again. We had not much shelter, they gave us thigh boots as there was so much water. The RAMC [Royal Army Medical Corps] used to come round and rub our feet with whale oil to get circulation going. Our feet were white and swollen. We were in trenches Christmas Day 1915, Captain Scott got killed, shot through the head. The Germans had underground shelters, and they had a band playing on Xmas day. We had to get our drinking water from a stream that ran between our trench and the Germans at night, we had to be careful not to get captured. There was so much mud we had to climb out of the trench and walk on the top to fetch rations from near a wood. The transport wagons used to wait there up to their axles in mud, if you fell down you had not much chance, there was a lot drowned in shell holes. One night we lost a bag of rations so we were without food next day. We used to get a large dog biscuit or a piece of bread, a piece of cooked meat or bully beef, tea and sugar, some jam or raisins instead and boiled bacon all in one bag and we had to share it out for five or six of us. We used to cut pieces of wood to make a coke fire to boil water to make tea, we got charcoal sometimes. If we made a lot of smoke we got shelled with trench mortars, the shells dropped down on your trench like a football.

Jan. 1916 we were at Dickiebush [Dickebusch] and got a heavy shelling, after a rest of two weeks we went to Kemmel Trenches for about 10 days, then to St. Jans Cappel. From there for several nights we used to go and make a raid on German trenches, then came back to St. Jans Cappel. After that we went back up the line, but stayed one night in a house in a village as the people had run away to hide by the roadside. We occupied the house and laid down to sleep, it was a shop and house. At daybreak we were getting some breakfast ready when in walked a woman and her daughter she had a shock just folded her arms and wept. We gave her some money as we had helped ourselves to some food and then we went further up to trenches, after that we came back so far and stayed at a camp but there was nowhere for us to sleep and it was raining, so we pinched a tent from a Chinese camp nearby while they were away working on the roads, then we moved again and slept in tents. One night Tommy Tailor went out and pinched a case of whiskey from a wagon, we heard him come back as there was a thump when he fell over our tent ropes. He brought me a drink and said he had it sent from England as it was his birthday. That night someone set my trousers on fire, it must have been with a cigarette someone had thrown on them not knowing, they smouldered to bits. Then next morning someone got me an old pair of breeches until I could get some trousers. Some time after we had a kit inspection, some lads had eaten their emergency rations, bully beef and biscuits without orders, and I think it was eight of them were tied to trees, hands behind them, at Armentiers.

Now we have moved on to the Somme at Bazentin-Le-Grand and Le-Petit, the villages are among trees. Then we went to Mametz Wood, it is September and tanks are lined up on the roadside ready for action for first time. We advanced and helped to capture High Wood near Martinpuich, a lot of tanks got stuck in shell holes and mud, and the trenches were too wide to get across and it was too late in year to do much good, then the Germans had tanks soon after. In Nov 1916 we went over the top at Butt-De-Warling Court [Butte -de-Warlencourt] near a hill called the Mound. There was dead all over, I was sent back to the headquarters with a new kind of egg bomb the Germans had used on us and machine gun parts. I had to crawl over dead bodies, not safe to stand up, too many bullets were whizzing around. Then we got relieved, after a while I was transferred to the 19th Division, I did not want to go as I should have got another stripe and my leave was delayed. We travelled most of the day by road, at night we rested at camp, Captain Pocklington was there he knew me. Next day we arrived at 19th Division HQ at 3 o'clock in the afternoon, had some tea and was sent to trenches at Beaumont Hamel, there was heavy fighting at the time. Next day we found a deep dugout, perhaps 20 steps down, that the Germans had occupied and we found some coffee and other food in tins, but the black bread we did not eat. Some of our lads had German overcoats on what had been left, it was very cold, we were near Theipvall. After several days we moved to Beanaville and to Domesmount until after Xmas.

Then we went to Herbeaton on the Somme it was very cold we got some eggs and they were frozen in the shells. We used get a rum ration, when we first went into the trenches we had two gallon of rum to share between two machine gun teams, that was alright. After some time we only got a small quantity, perhaps two spoonfuls, it was real stuff. I got my second leave early in 1917. I stayed at the Salvation Army Hostel near Victoria Station, had something to eat and drink and a hot bath and then went to bed, that was lovely and cost very little, and someone woke me up early to catch my train to Pocklington. We only stayed a day in Pock then went back to London, there was a Zeppelin raid on John Bull Place while I was there. But we went to a theatre and I met one of our Officers there as we came out to go to Elsie's, the guns were firing on Hyde Park. Fred came to see me when I was at Elsie's. After I had returned to France, we moved to

Zillebeke Canal Bank, a German aeroplane was shot down and dropped near to us. Also a German fighter chased one of ours nearly down to the ground a few yards off us, but we were not allowed to fire on it. Some time after we moved again to Kemmel Railway Shelters then on to Steework, then every night we used to go up to the line near Whychette making gun positions ready for the attack on Hill 60 and St.Eloy. I think it is June now, we found a gallon stone bottle of rum and hid it in a wagon and Captain Flood, transport officer, saw it and threw it against a bridge wall, we saw it all run down into the water, we were mad as it had been left on a dump. After that we were moved up to trenches near Whychette for the attack on Hill 60, Captain Flood sent up pack mules and ammunition right up behind our front line ready to move forward, two of us thought we had time to make a drink of tea we were in an iron dugout and lit a primus stove, then gas shells started to come over and we could not get our gas masks on in time. We both got a dose and I paced up and down trying to get my breath, the other lad laid down. The officer called me a 'B.Fool' and made a report of the other lad, he thought he was trying to dodge going over the top. Well about 2-50 am one big gun fired, then hundreds of shells were fired, it was hell let loose, all the ground shook. We saw Hill 60 blown sky high and St. Eloy, the hill had taken years to mine, the shock was felt 200 miles away in London. After the bombardment had ceased we climbed out of trench and moved forward, we met a lot of Germans with their hands above their heads, their hair was stood straight up with fright. We came across a big dugout, it had an engine for making electric light for their underground shelters, they had beds underground made of wood and wire and stoves for heat, one German was laid dead in the doorway. As we got to a roadway, Captain Purvis said to us you stay here while I go to look for a suitable position to fix our guns, he was in his short sleeves as it was June but he did not come back to us, he got killed. When it was dark someone went out and carried him back and he was buried at Vierstratt, a wooden cross was put up for him. I picked up a saw bayonet, but lost it when we moved. Next night I was sent down with other wounded lads to Bailleul Hospital, we called at a few dressing stations on the way to get some of the wounded first aid. When we got to hospital, the yard was full of stretcher cases, 250 laid all over, one of our Officers was among them Captain Black. There was at least two marquees in the yard and a lot of lads were put in there when there was no chance for them. The operating shed was in the yard and we could see them. A doctor asked one of us to hold an arm while he sawed it off, then they carried the limbs in a bucket and burnt them in a garden with bloodstained clothes.

After a day or two I was sent back to Kemmel then to Locre Huts. While I was in Locre a lot of artillery was moving through the village, and a supposed Belgian officer was watching them pass. He was on horseback, he was a spy because he went into a shop and was asking two girls questions, because I went into the shop and they said he was not a Belgian. So I went across the road and reported him but he galloped off and they missed him. One man did get hold of the horses bridle but had to let go. We were at Dickebusch a few weeks and used to go up to trenches near Ypres. When we came out, our Captain took us a near [short] cut across the fields. He had a long stick like a pole and he walked in front of us prodding on the ground in case we fell in shell holes as it was dark. When we got back he washed our feet in Condy's fluid and saw to our blistered feet. Well after he got killed, we got a fresh officer from England, Captain Hartley. We were taken up to a wood in front of Warneton where we were going to make an attack. He said we will chase the Bosch back to Berlin. He slept in a dugout, the night before the attack he wrote a few addresses out of his relations and gave them to me and said if I get killed and you got back alright would I write and let them know. I went forward with the Sergeant Major Cummings and got back and brought some prisoners back. Captain Hartley got captured, he let a German walk in front of the gun team and he led them straight into the German lines and six or seven of ours got captured. A lad called Turton managed run back firing a revolver and he got awarded a medal. We were sheltered a short time in a trench and one German showed me some family photographs and gave me a dagger. After that two of us escorted the prisoners out of the trenches and on to the road and then handed them over, and some Cavalry men marched them away. Then we went back to the trenches at night, we went back to camp and I gave an officer the addresses Captain Hartley had given me. I was reported missing and some of my letters were returned to England. Now we have got another officer Captain Champion, he was alright. I had made a small model aeroplane out of a bullet and a piece of brass for wings and he bought it from me for his little girl. He gave me 5 Francs and then he said how long have you been out here. It was about 3 years and he said you ought to be back in England. He said he was going to Camiers on a refresher Machine Gun course and taking some more lads and I could go with them. When we got there we slept in tents. It was a stormy night, poured with rain and blew our tent down. Next morning we were marched to a big building near the sea front occupied by Americans and we were given different duties. I got a good job, nothing to do but wait on the Officers at meal times. We got good food porridge and eggs for breakfast and I slept in a tent on the sands with two Americans. For four weeks there was no one else on the sands only French patrols, we could see ships out at sea. After this we moved to Bellicourt and Metz and Havrincourt Wood then into the Hindenburg line and had orders no more retirement, we had to make a stand at all costs. There was miles of barbed wire yards and yards thick, if you got through one lot you had to go through a lot more. It was impossible without tanks then when you reached the trenches, they were very wide for tanks to get over. Then they had very deep dugouts with wire beds and electric light. We occupied one for a short time, I think the Guards had captured them before we took over. After we got relieved we went to Le-Transloy near a sugar factory. You had to be careful where you walked as there was a lot of wells, they just had a covering of branches, they were traps. We were doing a course of map reading and range finding. We had to go forward and bring a report back of what we had seen, also positions we had to take when the attack came.

It is March 1918, one day we were in camp near Le Transloy below a hill, then the Germans opened up a heavy bombardment. About midday orders came for ours to go to help the 51st Scottish as they were being attacked and were due to be relieved, they had a rough time. The Germans were now coming over the hill, a few of us had been left behind to clear things up and pack blankets and kits, but we had to clear out. We set fire to what we could first then we walked up the road. We had an officer with us and we came to a store and they gave us some machine gun parts and we fixed them together and then we had a new machine gun. We fired a few shots to see if it was in order, we also got several boxes of belts and ammunition and some rations of food. I was put in charge of the gun and Spencer was my second, he had to put belts into the gun. We had a few chaps that had never been up the line before, they were transport men, but we had lost heavily and everybody had to go into the line even orderly room clerks. It was some Americans that fixed us up and then they arranged for a lorry to take us to another part of the line, I think it was a village called Grievilles near Pozières. While we were waiting Harry Spears fell down in a faint. We went to the other side of the village and there were stores but everybody had cleared out so some of our lads got some rum and were dazed, so I said go and lay down in that hole and we fixed our gun up on the bank near a sunken road and fired through a gap in the hedge. Before dawn I said we had better have something to eat, it was a good job we did as we did not get any more for a day or two because the Germans came forward. We could scarcely see them, our officer came to us and looked through his field glasses and said all those are Germans, fire and stay as long as you can but don't get your gun pinched. One lad beside me got shot in the shoulder, I fired several belts of ammunition and the gun was hot. The Germans were now getting round the village, Willie Love, orderly room clerk, got killed. The infantry made a counter attack at the right hand side of us, and drove the Germans back a bit. They lost the Captain, a regular soldier, and then had to retire back. We had not time to wake the other lads that were asleep in a shell hole, I suppose they got captured. As we retired through the village, a drunken corporal said to me "stick that gun up there". It was right in the middle of the road, I took no notice of him, he would get captured, he was waving his arms about and saying "where are the B's". We had to leave a lot of things behind as there was only two of us now. We walked through the village, then we were in the open, the Germans were sending flares up in the air to show where we were. Then an Officer came up on his horseback and said we must now turn our face to the Boche, then some shells burst near us and he galloped off, and never saw him again, and one Scottish soldier was shouting come back the 51st. A bit further back we met a few soldiers, they were waiting and one Officer said to me "is your gun in order?". I said yes, so he took it and fired a few shots. Then we kept going back like a flock of lost sheep no one to give orders, then a Scotch Officer came up to us and said "now lads shall we make a stand, I want 14 volunteers". Nobody spoke so I stepped forward for one and he said "well if that's it, you, you and you" and he made about 14 stay with him. We stayed in a valley all night, he did manage to get us some biscuits and ammunition, he found a transport man and he went on horseback for them. The other men we had gathered up kept going back as we did not need them when we only had one gun. Next morning we wandered round and saw a deserted camp, we found some cold tea in a dixie and some cold potato what the transport men had left and we all shared it, the Officer drank out of an old jam tin same as us. We were near to Herberton village the same day, and we went into any empty house for a sleep but soon somebody shouted "everybody out they are all round the village". There was now about 35 of us and the Germans had surrounded the village, we helped to keep the road clear as there was a lot of transport to get away, after that we had orders to return to a camp several miles away. When we reached the camp they were preparing to move, they wanted to know where we had been and what had happened, then we had something to eat and drink. Then we moved further back with them to a camp, we stayed with them for a short time, then we went by train to Belgium, near to Neuve Eglize near to Kemmel. One morning I went into a village and went into a shop to buy something and the shopkeeper said "we sell you nothing, the Germans are advancing on the village". A train had just come into the station near by with food and stores so the Germans would capture all that as they had broken through the Portuguese in the Neuve Eglize sector. I hurried back to camp and met some of our lot going up to help to check the Germans and some of us retired further back in reserve near Mont De Cats monastery on a hill. This was the third battle for Ypres April 1918.

The French came up and soon their 75 guns, as they were called, went into action, I slept under a wagon that night. As we came through Lockre the nuns were coming out of a convent moving further back to safety, they carried a cross in front of them. Some of our men were putting tins of fruit and other things into a limber as the shopkeeper and everybody had cleared out and the Germans would have got it, cattle were turned loose and some of our lads milked some cows. The Germans were trying to get to the coast, all these years had been trench warfare, first the Germans would bomb you out of your trench, then you had to go and take it back. We could never advance very far, the Germans captured Kemmel, Locre, Dranoute, Bailleul and Outersteene. After that we were sent by train to help the Americans at Chateau Therry, we got off the train at Eperney in Picardy, they were trying to capture Paris and Rheimes. We had pulled up at St. Dennis Station on the way and some French people brought us some wine to drink, one of our lads jumped off the train when we stopped and deserted, we were close to the Marne. My name was down to go up to the line but somehow I was put down to fetch rations, and when the transport came for reinforcements I was not there, so I was on reserve. We could see the battle going on from a hill near to us and grapes were growing in the open. After our lads came out of the line we had a pay day and the officer wanted to know where I had been as I was supposed to have been up the line. After about 12 days we went by train to Belgium, we always went on trucks and were fastened in like cattle, we pinched some coal and made a fire inside the truck and burnt a hole in the truck bottom. A lot of the railway line had been captured so we had to go a long way round, when we got off the train we went to Bethune and Locon near La Basse Canal. The bridges were blown up and we had to cross the canal by planks fastened on top of boats with ropes for handrails. All the houses were deserted. We used to make raids on German positions, we came across a few snipers. We used to fetch our rations in small trucks on a light railway, we only went at night. Now the Germans showed signs of returning. After a week or two we were put on a miniature railway with a small engine and trucks, then we went to another part of the line, first in buses, and then on train to the outskirts of Cambrai. Thousands of German prisoners are coming in, they are first put in a very big pit with sentries posted on the top, they are quite happy and singing away. We slept in bivouacs near to them, paper money was no good to them now and they were throwing marks away. In the morning we came in Cambrai, there was dead bodies laid in the streets some were kneeling where they had been firing. We went into a house and saw one dead German strapped up in bed and others dead on the room floor. Horses were dead in a school, and pictures were still hung on the walls. We had orders not to touch any ornaments or pianos or anything in case there was any explosives, as there was a lot of delayed action bombs going off and there was fire coming up on the roads on the sides of cobbles. One of our lads found a gold sovereign and a good German helmet had been left behind, I did once send a German helmet home. We kept advancing as the Germans were retiring and we kept getting news that the war was going to end soon. It was a change for us to be advancing after being in trenches for years firing at one another and creeping out in the open. When we had to creep up to the German trenches on listening patrol, getting news re what they were doing. We had trip wire laid out in front of our trench and tins fastened on to them, and if anyone knocked them they used to rattle and we knew if the Germans were coming to our trench. But all through the night and every night the sky was lit up with thousands of Verry Lights fired from both us and the Germans. I remember Lieut. Stanley Robson coming back to our trench, he had been out on listening patrol, we shouted "who goes there", we put the wind up him as he crept through a hole near our machine gun. If we wanted artillery to fire we sent up a red light S.O.S. We kept moving forward every day, not much opposition, when we were on the road we met a lot of civilians pushing barrows and carts with some of their belongings and they shouted "Aya La Englal", long live England. We were on the Mons Valencinnes Road near to Mons, we were told to halt then we went through an opening near a farm into the yard and rested in some buildings and had some food, then waited. After some hours a dispatch rider on motor bike came up with orders the war's over. There was no cheers as we could not believe it, however at night we started to move back, we met a lot of our own soldiers coming up the road and they shouted "is the war finished?". They had been getting cleaned up and rested to move into Germany. But we had been advancing and needed rest. We were attached to the 5th Army and I think the 2nd and 4th went to Germany, we should have liked to go to see what it was like.

This was Nov. 11 1918. We marched most of the night and stayed in Candas village two days. We went into a house where two old ladies were, they had been there during the German occupation, they seemed dazed they had only dark coloured bread, they gave us some coffee and did not ask for any money but we threw some on the table. The Germans had all these years to prepare and had got fortified with cement strong points and gun positions and deep underground shelters and electric light and wire beds, and miles of wire 20 ft. in front of trenches. Our lads had to have it rough. Well we moved back again through Arras, Cambrai, Houdain, Haussay, St. Amand, Douai, Malplazuet to Candas. I joined the band and Jimmy Warters came to us as bugler, we stayed there over Christmas 1918, we had a bucket full of beer in the hut, it was poor stuff, nobody had much of it. After Xmas they started letting miners and other lads go to England if they had a job to go to. I got my leave Jan 3 1919, I remember getting to London and going on the top of the tram to Elsie's. It was snowing heavy, I got to Elsies about 10pm. While I was at home, the last day of my leave, I got notice to report to Nr. Ripon for my discharge. I got discharged Feb 18 1919, it was the greatest and most terrible war the world had ever known, nearly 1 million Britons were killed in it and some more than 2 million wounded. In just one battle of the 1914-18 war, the Somme, the British suffered more casualties than died in the whole of the second world war 1939-45.

We were not allowed to keep a diary in case we got captured, so I made this up from memory after I got home.

John Brook

ODE TO THE 5th YORKS—THE GALLANT

By John Brook

Its Saturday morning at Newcastle
April15th is the date
There's a hustle around the station
The 5th Yorks going to meet fate

They are a true Yorkshire lot going to action
Against Kaiser and Germanys Huns
Their off to battle for Britain
In front of Von Krupps famous guns

They are not afraid of the steel lads
And powder is food for the grit
Soon they will be showing the world lads
That the Yorkshires still know how to hit

They are off—what a cheer in the station
And the bands playing glorious airs
They are off—and what an ovation
Is gen to those doing their share

Now its Sunday and 2 in the morning
No longer in England they stand
But on France's fair soil they are standing
As brave as ought to be found in the land

Just a week since they left Dear Old England
And the battle is raging around
The Yorkshires are holding the centre
Whilst shells are rending the ground

They are whizzing and cracking like thunder
And deafening is the sound
But not one of those brave lads does waver
They lose not an inch of the ground

We are not going back either
But we'll bear the battles hard brunt

Eagerly they move their positions
And take up a line on the left
The Royal Irish are fighting on one side
Whilst Canadians draw blood on the left

These 3 fine Regiments fighting
Had stemmed a great German advance
And the Yorkshires first time in action
Had wrought their great fame in France

Many poor chaps there went under
But the glory they won will not fade
They had saved a grave situation
And thus opened a glorious page

They were once called the fireside soldiers
But when England their service did need
They were know as the Yorkshire Ghurkas

And for their dear country did bleed

Thrice since they have been in action
And wrought some glorious deeds
But the one that was fought at St. Julian
Was where they proved more than weeds

England has known all about them
And heard too of all their fame
Which the Green Howards as they call them
Made on the blood splattered plains

Then off with hats to the Yorkshires
The great service they rendered the land
They fought and bled for their country
And proved they are real British brand

They are only lads at the most now
But their hearts are in the right spot
They are full of grit as can be
And for fighting can do quite a lot

So when the fighting is over
To England they'll come with the rest
And be classed at last as the bravest
The loyalist truest and best

In history they will be mentioned
As adding to Englands great name
And for ever their name will be written
As a glorious symbol of fame.

Pocklington and District Local History Group

Extracts from the Howdenshire Chronicle and Pocklington Weekly News for the years 1914—1918 by kind permission of the British Library Board.

(The newspaper diligently reported in great detail the events pertaining to the district throughout the war. Below is a very small selection from its columns. The complete volumes can be viewed at the British Newspaper Library)

22nd August, 1914

A Service of Intercession will be held in the Parish Church this (Friday) evening at 7-30, when a collection will be taken in aid of the Prince of Wales' Fund. Despite the inconvenience caused by the war the harvest operations in the district around Pocklington proceeds briskly, and there has been much good corn stacked this week, thanks to the favourable weather conditions which have prevailed. The many friends in this neighbourhood of Mr. C. E. Ringstead, the light-weight jockey, who has been fulfilling a riding engagement in Austria this season, are getting anxious about him, for there has been no news from him for some time. His brother Mr. 'Neily' Ringstead volunteered for service and left Pocklington on Saturday last to join the 5th Yorkshire Battalion.

There has been much military activity displayed in the Pocklington district lately and last week-end was no exception, for the high-road through Canal head presented quite a busy appearance. On Friday evening a Battery of Artillery passed through each gun drawn by eight horses. On Saturday afternoon another lot of Horses (55) which had been obtained locally, were sent from the Feathers Hotel, to York, travelling by road; and at intervals on Sunday there was another battery of big guns, each drawn by a powerful Simplex car, a large number of Cavalry, and the commissariat and supply convoys, which camped overnight near Shipton Thorpe, whilst a large detachment of the Red Cross men passed through Pocklington and spent the night at Kilnwick Percy.

OUR LOCAL WARRIORS—Pocklington has supplied its quota of Territorials, many of whom have volunteered for active service if required. On Saturday last our representative interviewed several of the Pocklington contingent in Scarborough, including Private B. Allison, Private C. Ringstead, Private W. Irons, Private A.H. Todd, Corporal Rooks, Private Smith, and others. All were in the best of health and spirits, and in the pink of condition. Their superior Officers are also on duty at various posts in the town, which presents quite a military appearance with representatives of the Yeomanry and Territorial forces. The remainder of the Corps have been moved northwards, in order to carry out flanking movement, if necessary.

Old Hay

Yorkshire farmers who have any old hay are requested to send particulars to the War Office stating quantity, place, whether cut or in rick, nearest railway station, and price per ton of 2,240lb on rail.

The Horse Supply

AMPLY SUFFICIENT FOR AGRICULTURAL PURPOSES

The Board of Agriculture in an official statement regarding the effect of mobilisation the number or horses available for agricultural purposes, says the returns in June show that the estimated number of horses used for agriculture, including mares kept for breeding, but excluding saddle horses, carriage or trap horses, and vanners, is 793,436. The number of heavy draught horses obtained recently from agricultural holdings is estimated at 9,000, only slightly over 1 per cent of the whole. It is clear, therefore, that the number of heavy draught horses on agricultural holdings is amply sufficient to meet the requirements of the Army without interfering seriously with the cultivation of the land.

Pocklington Board of Guardians - Relief of distress during the war.

At the meeting of the Pocklington Board of Guardians, held at the workhouse on Monday, Mr. G.W. Appleton presided. Mr G.W. Appleton said that since their last meeting the King had been compelled to declare war on Germany. He was sure they would all agree with him that England had not been seeking war. It was the duty of all the inhabitants of this country, including the Board of Guardians, loyally to support the Government in its present tremendous responsibilities. There was another matter which they would have to face, and that was in reference to the maintenance of the wives and families of those who were away on active service. It was desirable that they should give all the relief they could, taking each case on its merits. The Rev. A.W. Welch said he was sure they would, as Guardians, with all due regard to the rates, do all they could to help the sick and wounded, and to help the wives and families of the soldiers abroad.

29th August, 1914

Arrival of Military

Pocklington just now presents quite a military appearance, for on Thursday there arrived the Royal Army Medical Corps, under the command of Colonel Clayton; a troop of East Riding Yeomanry, an Army Service Corps, the Dragoons and Regimental Staff; and expect to remain about a fortnight. They are stationed at Kilnwick Hall and the Grammar School, whilst the other regiments are in the vicinity of Londesborough. We anticipate a nice sprinkling of military will be in attendance at the Grand Whist Drive and Dance to be held in the Victoria Hall, Pocklington on Wednesday next, in aid of the Prince of Wales' Relief Fund.

CENTRAL HALL, POCKLINGTON, the all British Picture Palace. Fred Lee is showing a Magnificent Programme of Animated Pictures, including a splendid Detective Story and pleant of Comics. Next week we are showing a splendid Military Programme; this is one of the best programmes we have had the pleasure of submitting to the public during the two years we have been showing. The Star Picture, entitled "The Curse of the War," is magnificent and thrilling and should be seen by everybody.

A Call to Arms

GREAT RALLY AT POCKLINGTON.

THE PRINCE OF WALES IS OFFERING HIS LIFE FOR THE NATION— COME AND LET US KNOW WHAT YOU ARE GOING TO DO.

— ON —

Saturday, the 5th Sept.,

1914, THERE WILL BE A

MONSTER RALLY

In the MARKET PLACE at POCKLINGTON, for the purpose of raising money for the National Relief Fund.

At 6-15 p.m., the following Bodies are requested to line up in consecutive order in the Market Place :—

The Coronation Band.
The National Reservists.
Magistrates.
Clergy and Ministers of all Denominations.
Members and Officers of the Urban District Council.
Members and Officers of the Pocklington Guardians.
Members of the Red Cross Society.
Members of the Manchester Unity of Oddfellows.
The Cycling Club.
Pocklington Merry Makers.
All the School Children with Flags.
The Fire Brigade.
The General Public.

At 6-30 p.m. the Procession will pass through Union Street, Bridge Street, Chapmangate, Pavement, and back to the Market Place, where short Patriotic Speeches will be made. Everybody will then be asked to pass in double file in front of Collecting Bags into which they will drop their copper, silver, and gold according to their means.

Our Gallant Prince as Treasurer of the National Relief Fund says :—" My first duty is to ask for generous and ready support ; and I know I shall not ask in vain."

By helping this Fund you are doing your best to make sure that the wives and children of our brave soldiers shall be cared for whilst they are nobly fighting our Battles, and guarding our beloved Shores. Give, and give generously.

GOD SAVE THE KING.

It is a Military Drama, reproducing some of the most sensational aviation scenes as applied to modern warfare. This film was produced under the supervision and with the assistance of the Belgian Imperial Army and the Belgian Imperial Flying Corps. Over 300 feet in length. The rest of the programme is all star pictures, depicting realistic war scenes and including some screamingly funny comics one of which is entitled "When Papa came Home from drill." Your patronage on this occasion is earnestly requested. Admission 6d. and 3d. Seats booked, no extra charge.

12th September, 1914

BRISK RECRUITING AT POCKLINGTON.

Pocklington and district have been well to the fore in the matter of recruiting this week. Mr. Harry English (son of Mr. R. M. English, J. P., of Lyndhurst, Pocklington) has joined the East Riding Yeomanry, and along with several others has offered for foreign service during the war, This is a splendid lead to the young men of the town, because it means that Mr. English is, like many others, leaving his business to respond to the call of his country. Surely this will act as a spur to others ! We have young men in the town whose paramount duty it is to offer their services to the King. Some of them have no business or other ties, and if they fail to respond to the Call they must not be surprised if in the future they are looked upon as laggards and cowards.

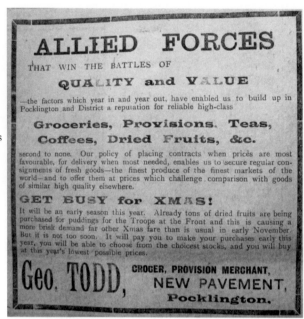

Pocklington Weekly News - Nov. 14th, 1914

In addition to Mr. English no less than 25 other recruits have been sent to the different depots namely for 5th Battalion Yorkshire Regiment:

H. Suggitt, H. Brigham, W. Shepherd, C. Oliver; J. Thody, T. Thorpe, Frank Skinner;
and for Lord Kitchener's Army : Frederick L. F. Rees, Campbell L. John Rees, Robert Briskham, Wilfrid Young, Robert Craven, James Craven, John Bennett, George Drury, William Plumb, James Smith, Ernest Jenkins, Robert Yellop, George Noble, Roy Thomas, Arthur Moyser, Richard Squires, John H. Harrison, James Loft.

8th May, 1915

GALLANT STAND BY POCKLINGTON TERRITORIALS.

INTERESTING LETTERS FROM THE FRONT.

Sergt. JAS. EASTWOOD, of the 5th Yorkshire Brigade, writing from France, to his wife at Pocklington, Says:—

"I write to tell you that I am safe at present after going through what I hope win never happen again. No doubt the news will have reached Pocklington about the awful time we have had. Never in all the South African War was there such a time. Shot and shell simply raining down upon us, but we stuck to our posts until the enemy ran.

"I was too near a 'Jack Johnson,' with the result that I was thrown into the air about eight yards and landed on a lucky heap of sand many yards away. It happened on Sunday morning at six o'clock and for some time after I have not known much of anything, but I am in an hospital train now, and will soon be in the line again. Take care of Les and Ron, and remember me to all my friends.

"Trusting you are well, I close with love to you and my two little pets.
Your loving husband, Jim." P.S. - Keep smiling.

On a Postcard, which arrived on Monday morning, from Sergt. Eastwood, bearing the Birmingham postmark. He says:—

Birmingham, May 2nd, 1916.,

"I am now in England, and on my way to Scotland to a Hospital there. I will write as soon as I land, and tell you where I am."

Sergt. Eastwood is now in Glasgow, and progressing favourably.

———

Private FRANK SKINNER, son of Mr. A. Skinner, schoolmaster, of Pocklington, is wounded in the left leg and right arm from shrapnel fire. He is now in hospital in Lincoln.

Sergt. C. BENNISON, of Pocklington, is wounded in the shoulder and is now in the Base Hospital.

We regret to hear that Private PRATT, of Pocklington, was shot through the shoulder, and that Private Buttle (late of Pocklington), a member of the Regular Army, has been wounded in action.

Lance-Corporal T. Jennings was completely buried in earth thrown up by a shell, and was none the worse for his unique experience.
Private Sydney Lawson, of Driffield, of the gallant 5th Yorkshires, has died of wounds in the recent battle. His father, Mr. John Lawson, received the news from the base hospital. The doctor said the wound was mortal and left no hope of recovery. Private S. Lawson was married to a Middlesbrough girl, and he also leaves a young baby. He had been with John Smith's Brewery Company at Driffield since boyhood. He was 22 years of age.

12th June, 1915

A POCKLINGTON HERO.

YOUNG SOLDIER KILLED IN THE TRENCHES.

On Wednesday morning official news was received by Mrs. W. Tayleure, of 12, Mary street, Scunthorpe (and late of Pocklington), that her son Arthur (a grandson of Mrs. Walsh, of the Black Bull Hotel, Pocklington), who was a private in the 15th Lincolnshire Regiment, was posted as missing, and believed to be killed on the 20th May. This notification was signed by Captain Simpson, and although it came as a great shock to the gallant soldier's mother, and her husband (the deceased's father also being on active service, having joined since the commencement of the war), she had had previous news of his death from his mate, Drummer R. Leaning, another Scunthorpe lad, who is with the "Fighting 5th."

Drummer Leaning, in his letter to his mother says he has just come out of the trenches. Continuing, he says, "I expect you will have heard of my mate, Arthur Tayleure, getting killed, but it cannot be helped. You have to put up with these things. His time had come, and everybody has to go when God thinks fit to take them to their everlasting home. At the time I am writing this letter there is an aeroplane over our lines and the Germans potting at it. About 3 to 5 o'clock every afternoon the Germans start to shell us with their big guns. Then someone will say 'They are dishing, iron rations out again.'

That is all we care. There are lots of shells—"Jack Johnsons," "Little Willies," "Dirty Dicks," "Silent Creepers." God be with you till we meet again.—Ralph."

Although only 17 years of age, our gallant hero always displayed a keen desire to go to the front, and when his regiment left Stanstead, where they were in training, he was being left for home service, but his appeal to the officer commanding removed the difficulty, and he was allowed to proceed. He was always of a cheerful disposition, and has been described by one of his sergeants as "the life of the company."— He will be greatly missed by his comrades in arms.

12th June, 1915

PTE. CHARLES HOTHAM, KILLED IN ACTION.

Quite a gloom was cast over Pocklington and neighbourhood on Monday last, when it became known that one of the brave lads who so nobly volunteered for the Front had fallen in battle. We refer to Private Charles Hotham, second son of Mr. and Mrs. Chas. Hotham, butcher, Pavement, Pocklington, who got sniped at the top of a trench on Friday last. He was of a bright and happy disposition, very daring, and had rendered valuable service in the able handling of young and spirited horses. A few years ago he was respected member of the Parish Church Choir, and was extremely popular throughout the town and neighbourhood, and much sympathy is expressed for his bereaved parents and their family in their great loss.

Letter From:

Corpl. B. Allison, 1792, "A" Coy., 5th Yorks. Regt. Northumb. Divn., British Expeditionary Force, France.

Dear Mrs. C. Hotham,

Just a line to express my deepest sympathy with you in your sad bereavement.
I saw Charlie just after he was shot and stayed with him until he died. His last words were "Remember me to Mother." All the Pocklington boys were present at his burial. He is laid to rest in Sanctuary Wood, about 2½ miles east of Ypres, where a cross marks his grave. With best wishes to you and all inquiring friends allow me to remain, Yours sincerely, BERNARD ALLISON, B.E.F., G.P.O. 11-6-15

MORE LETTERS FROM OUR POCKLINGTON LADS.

The following letters provide additional proof, if any were needed, that our Pocklington Territorials are possessed of the real grit, and have the right spirit, and the recipients on that account appreciate them very highly, as we are sure will all our readers. The first letter, printed below, has been received by Mrs. Sargeant from Private Frank Skinner, and the second by Mr. A. Skinner from Private John Pratt.

6a Ward, 4th Northern General Hospital, Lincoln.

Dear. Mrs. Sargeant,—

I must write to tell you how I am, and to thank you very much for the present you have so kindly sent me. My leg remnant is going on as fast as can be expected, and I am pleased to say I am keeping in good spirits. I was pleased to see Mother once more, but I shall be glad when I get back to old Pock, and see everybody. I'm afraid I must have great patience. I have already had more than a month in bed (ain't I lazy?).

I am afraid I have paid dearly for my little bit of experience but I am not going to worry at all. It was for a good cause, and I would go through it again if sound. It is the duty of every single man to "fight for his country." We get nicely cared for here, and I pass the time away by smoking, eating, reading, and joking, and the pain does not seem so intense. We have had grand weather here, and to see chaps walking about makes me very envious, I have very nice friends come to see me to brighten me up; so I think I shall keep all right. I must really close now. Hoping you are in good health.

I remain,

Your sincere friend,

F. SKINNER.

———

Pte. J. Pratt, 5th Batt. Yorks. Regt., Ampthill House, Ampthill, Bedfordshire, June 8th, 1915.

Dear Sir,—Just a few lines hoping they will find you in the very best of health. I was very pleased to see the Roll of Honour in the Pocklington Paper. I think you will have got to know that I have been wounded by a bullet in the chest, but it has healed up, and I am ready to go back when I have had my furlough. I was against your son when he got wounded. I got wounded the following morning. I hope he is getting better. It was the 25th of April when I got hit by the bullet. I walked five miles right through Ypres. The big fight was at St. Julien. It was awful all the morning. I think my brother Bob is all right yet. I isn't afraid to go back, no, not I, but I wish it was over so that we all could get home again. It will soon be a year since we were called up. I think we shall win the war because there are the nuts from Pocklington. I am not as good a writer now as when I went to your school. Please write a few lines back.

J. PRATT

———

INTERESTING LETTER FROM SERGT. J. W. EASTWOOD.

To the Editor of the "Pocklington News.", Ward 12 B, No.3 Scottish G. Hospital, Stobhill, Glasgow.

Dear Sir,—In last week's issue of your popular paper I read with interest a letter from the Pocklington "Terriers" at the Front in which they made enquiries after your humble servant.

Well, seeing your paper gets well read in the trenches by others besides the Pock, lads, and as my letters to my Platoon have not seemed to have reached them, I venture, for their benefit, to add a little more to their letter as effecting me and other Pock. "Terriers" with me.

My experiences were the same as recorded by last week's correspondent up to where we made our memorable advance. We had orders to go up to support another Unit who were severely pressed, and right well the Boys behaved for the rain of shells was awful, but through it all they kept their heads. Whatever I saw or went through in the South African War does not want mentioning after that.

Well, it was during a rush forward, headed by our Adjutant, who was a brick, that I ran up against a "Jack Johnson" which burst near me and flung me yards away on a heap of sand, the result being two broken ribs and a broken bone in my foot. When I came round I was laid in a hole , and what with the ribs and the fumes from the shell could hardly breath. I don't know how long I had laid when Sergt. Bennison and Pte. Leo Hunter (a Scarboro' lad) crawled into the hole to get out of the hurricane of shells—both of whom were wounded. There we laid until an Officer out of the Canadians, with another chap, fetched us to a shelter that happened to be near. There we were joined later by A. Johnson, N Kendall (Pock, lads), J. T. Elliott (Market

Weighton), Cundall (Bishop Wilton), and Talentyre, H (of Brid.) all of my Platoon. We stayed there all next day, attended to by a Scout of the Hull "Terriers" and Lieut. Clark of our Batt. without whose assistance several would have bled to death, and seeing neither had ought to eat or drink while with us, as we only had very little water, I consider they were bricks. During this time the shells were bursting all round our place, and as the entrance faced the enemy we expected every moment to be our last.

During the night that followed, Cundall, Elliott, and Talentyre died. In the early hours of the morning after that a couple of stretchers took two of the worst cases, and those who could walk at all went with them. I was left with a lot more as it was too light for stretcher work so near the German lines. We had to stay there next day, when we got a few more in, and next night. Somewhere about 4 a.m. next day the shelling of the Germans increased and it fairly rained shells, and one dropped near our place and killed three and further wounded several more who were near the door; we expected every moment to be our last, and it nearly came when shortly after a shell charged with gas-burst right in front of the entrance and filled the place with its deadly fumes. Those who were not killed outright tried to creep out, but I was overpowered and I know nothing what went on after that until three days after, when I came round I was in a French Hospital where I had been kept alive by the use of oxygen, which I lived on nearly a week. They told me only three had survived, and the other two poor fellows died when we got to Rouen Hospital, from where I was sent to Le Harve, and then to this Hospital, where I am well looked after. I was the colour of Marco when I came here, but I am getting on well now.

Soldiers would gladly risk a wound rather than a mouthful of the infernal gas, for the devil himself could not invent a worse torture.

I have heard from Sergt. Bennison and he tells me he is getting on fine, and when he left France, A. Johnson was getting on all right. I am able to get up a bit now, and with the aid of a stick, get about; so we shall soon all be fit again and back among the boys. Hoping this will relieve the minds of the boys in my Platoon who kindly asked after me, and wishing your Paper, which is looked forward to by us Pock, lads, every success,

I remain, Yours sincerely, 309, SERGT. EASTWOOD, J.W.

19th June, 1915

Letter to the paper:

1293, Sergt. F.C. Dykes, Wm "A" Coy., 5th Yorks., Northumbrian Division, British Expeditionary Force, June 9th.

Dear Sir,—

Having read with much interest your Church School Roll of Honour, I am very pleased to inform you that all the boys, with the exception of one, that are serving out here were educated at your School, and they wish me to write and let you know of the fact as they feel proud that their old Teacher should take so much interest in them although they are far away in a land ruined by the barbarism of an enemy. I only wish they would let us describe it the best way we could to you, but the Censor won't, so we have to be content as we are, plodding along sometimes in the thick of it; but, thank God, we have been spared so far. When they get a start it is complete Hell, as Tommy

OUR PORTRAIT GALLERY.

We herewith produce a recent photo of the late Corporal Thomas Jennings, whose death (in action) it was our painful duty to record in our last week's issue. He was the second son of the late Mr. Thomas Jennings, of Storwood Manor, York, was born at Storwood, on January 5th, 1895, and educated at the Pocklington Grammar School. At the outbreak of the War he was in Camp with the 5th Yorkshire Regiment (Green Howards), and immediately volunteered for Foreign Service, proceeding later to Newcastle-on-Tyne for training.

Corporal Thomas Jennings.
F. Slights, photo., Pocklington.

On April 17th, 1915, he left England with his Regiment for France, where after fourteen months' faithful service he died, on June 8th, 1916, for his King and Country, succumbing to serious wounds received by shrapnel at one o'clock on the morning of the 7th June, whilst out wiring.

Pocklington Weekly News, 24th Jun 1916

calls it. You can see your friends "go down" but still we keep going, praying to be spared to be able to return home again. We are all very sorry about poor Frank as to was a nice lad, and a good soldier; may he soon be well again is the wish of the boys out here. I hope you will not think us forward in letting you know we are your old Scholars.

Yours very sincerely, F. C. DYKES

P.S.—We are in the trenches so have not much time for anything at present. But should you wish it I will forward you a letter from the boys every week.

3rd July, 1915

POCKLINGTON HERO.

SERGT. H. ROWLEY MENTIONED IN DESPATCHES.

General satisfaction is expressed in Pocklington that the name of Sergeant H. Rowley, 2nd Est. Yorks., who has been mentioned in despatches, appears in the Distinguished Service List just published, for he is a son of the late Mr. W. Rowley and Mrs. Rowley, Chapmangate, Pocklington. He enlisted nearly nine years ago, rising to pioneer sergeant, and after serving seven years in India, he arrived in Pocklington New Year's Eve for a short furlough before proceeding to the front.

It is not known in what manner Sergt. Rowley has distinguished himself, but those acquainted with him are not surprised at the special honour gained, for he is one of a family of soldiers, having three brothers at present serving the country, viz., Colour Sergeant W. Rowley, 5th Yorks.; Driver F. Rowley, R.A.M.C., who both served in the Boer War and Private Alf. Rowley, Motor Transport. In addition, his nephew, Private W. Rowley (son of Col.-Sergt. Rowley) is serving with the 5th Yorks. (Home Defence), and his brother-in-law, Driver J. Musgrave, R.F.A., was drowned in the Dardenelles, whilst Private W. Prole, another brother-in-law, is serving in France.

Since he gained distinction Sergt. Rowley has been wounded, and is at present in the base hospital.

17th July, 1915

Pte. H. Flint, "A" Company, 6th Yorks. Regt, 1st Northumbrian Division, B.E.F., G.P.O.

My dear Niece,—

Just a few lines to you, hoping they will find you well, as it leaves me at present.. I am sorry I have not written you a letter before, but you will know we have plenty to do whilst we are in the trenches. I had a parcel from your Grandmother last Saturday morning, it was eatables, and I can tell you me and Bob Pratt had a good feed from it, and I am keeping the sponge cake for Sunday tea. It is more like being at home when we get a bit of old Yorkshire cake, I am writing these lines to you whilst I am in the trenches. We have to sit and then stand to watch for the Germans to see if they will come forward, but they not alarm us. It is rather a tiring job, but we have to get used to it. They keep knocking one or two of our lads out. Well, you will have heard, I dare say, about Charlie Hotham getting killed. Poor, lad, me and Pratt and Hotham had been having a sleep, and Hotham got up and made us some tea ready, and then we got up, and had our teas, and then we wanted him to go for a wash, but he would not, so me and Bob Pratt and Arthur Johnson went. We had not been away more than ten minutes before we got told he was shot. He did not live much longer than 16 minutes. He asked for his Mother, said a prayer, and then said good-bye. The Pock. Lads dug him a grave, and we buried him after it got dark, so as we should not be seen by the enemy. Lieut. Thompson read the burial service. He is our Officer, and a very good one, too. It would be a great shock to his Mother when she got to know about it, but he was a credit to his country.

Soldier portraits from the Howdenshire Chronicle and Pocklington Weekly News

Driver J. W. BUTTLE, 5th Yorks. Transport Division, just arrived from France, on a visit to his relatives at Pocklington. He is in the pink of health and has seen much fighting.

Pocklington Weekly News - Nov 6th, 1915

Sergt. W. WALKER, R.R.A.S.C, of Melbourne, now in Wiltshire, is shortly expecting to go out on foreign service.

Pocklington Weekly News - Nov 6th, 1915

Private J. PRATT, of Pocklington, 5th Yorkshires, who was shot clean through the shoulder at St. Julien, came over to Pocklington a short time ago to recuperate, and has since returned to France.

Pocklington Weekly News - Nov 6th, 1915

SURGEON A. R. FISHER, R.N., son of the Rev. A. T. Fisher (vicar of Pocklington) who is on H.M. Hospital Ship, "Rewa," at the Dardanelles.

Pocklington Weekly News - Nov 20th, 1915

Private H. IRELAND, 10th Batt. King's Own Y.L.I., the dearly-beloved son of Mrs. and Mr. Roberts of Allerthorpe, who was killed in action, in France, on the 26th September.

Pocklington Weekly News - Nov 20th, 1915

Private F. PEARSON, 1-5th Yorkshire Regiment, of Meltonby, now on active service.

Pocklington Weekly News - Nov 20th, 1915

Private H. A. HOLMES, Royal Marines, who was errand boy in this office three years ago. He is a nephew of Mrs. Whitehead, of Pocklington.

Pocklington Weekly News - Dec 4th, 1915

Trooper B. BYASS (No. 1114), of Warter, 1st Troop, "A" Squadron, 1st East Riding Yeomanry, now at the Dardanelles.

Pocklington Weekly News - Dec 4th, 1915

Trooper E. T. BYASS (No. 1115), of Warter, 3rd Troop, "A" Squadron, 1st East Riding Yeomanry, now at the Dardanelles.

Pocklington Weekly News - Dec 4th, 1915

Driver R. B. DAVISON, 9th Cavalry Fld Ambulance, 1st Cav. Div., British Expeditionary Force. He has been in France 15 months. He is 18 years of age, not been wounded, is quite well, and says they are very comfortable in winter billets.

Pocklington Weekly News - Dec 11th, 1915

Sergt. FRED C. DYKES, of Pocklington, is one of the 5th Yorkshires, and has done good service in France. He is one of the "boys" of whom Pocklington people are very proud, springing from a good fighting family, who have done good service for their country.

Pocklington Weekly News - Dec 11th, 1915

Corporal W. DYKES, of the Waggoners Reserve (brother of Sergt. F. C. Dykes whose photo we also give in this column) is a son of Mr. and Mrs. Dykes, of Market Street, Pocklington, has distinguished himself in his profession and soon been promoted to the rank of Corporal.

Pocklington Weekly News - Dec 11th, 1915

Private JOHN P. DAY 10th (Service) E.Y., Hull Commercials. Trained in Hull, Hornsea, Ripon, and on Salisbury Plain. Now left with his regiment for that vague somewhere.

Pocklington Weekly News - Dec 18th, 1915

Private HARRY WEBSTER, R.M.L.I., the second son of Mr. and Mrs. Webster, of Bolton Hall, who was killed in action near the Dardanelles.

Pocklington Weekly News - Dec 18th, 1915

WILLIAM WEBSTER, signalman, youngest son of Mr. and Mrs. Webster, of Bolton Hall, who is on H.M.S. Prince Edward. Place unknown.

Pocklington Weekly News - Dec 18th, 1915

Corporal C. COOK, W.R.R.G. Artillery, now in France, sends us a very interesting letter, to be found on page 1.

Pocklington Weekly News - Dec 25th, 1915

Pocklington and District Local History Group

Farrier-Sergeant R. BARBER, R.F.A., of Bielby, who is now stationed at Edinborough, Scotland, was wounded at La Basse in November, 1914. He is well-known in Pocklington, having worked at the Albion Foundry, prior to joining the Army five years ago.

Pocklington Weekly News, 15th Jan 1916

Driver Arthur STAINTON, 1st Yorks. Transport, 5th West Yorks. He has been on active service in France since April last, and has seen much fighting. He is well, and has had good luck so far.

Pocklington Weekly News, 15th Jan 1916

Private THOS. ROWNTREE, son of the late Mr. John Rowntree, of Pocklington, a member of the Royal Garrison Artillery, now in training in London, and shortly expected to proceed to the Front.

Pocklington Weekly News, 15th Jan 1916

Private ALFRED ROWNTREE, a brother of the above, now serving in the Royal Field Artillery, leaves England this week for active service at the front.

Pocklington Weekly News, 15th Jan 1916

Private F. SKINNER, wounded by shrapnel on the 26th April, 1915. He is now convalescent in Hospital (Red Cross), at Skegness.

Pocklington Weekly News, 5th Feb 1916

S.Q.M.S. Norman M. HARRISON, 1416, son of Mr. Mansfield Harrison, Brunswick House, Pocklington, now serving with the "A" Squadron, Sherwood Ranger Yeomanry, who was in the English Gunners thrilling march from Lala Baba, in the afternoon of August 21st.

Pocklington Weekly News, 5th Feb 1916

Lance-Corporal R. HARRISON, P.S. 450, second son of Mr. Mansfield Harrison, now serving with the Royal Fusiliers, B.E.F.

Pocklington Weekly News, 5th Feb 1916

Lance-Corporal T. W. FISHER, who is serving with the 9th Border Regiment, in France.

Pocklington Weekly News, 5th Feb 1916

Private J. W. WHITEHEAD, 3rd-5th West Yorks., in training at Clipstone Camp, Mansfield, Notts. He is a nephew of Mr. Whitehead, of Pocklington.

Pocklington Weekly News, 5th Feb 1916

Private HARRY HOLMES, 3rd-5th West Yorkshires, is in training as a bomb-thrower. He is also a nephew of Mr. Whitehead, of Pocklington.

Pocklington Weekly News, 5th Feb 1916

Private H. PRESTON, 60182, R.A.M.C., No. 27 General Hospital, Mudros West, Isle of Lemnos, Dardanelles Army, B.M.E.F.

Pocklington Weekly News, 12th Feb 1916

King and Queen's Condolence. Mr. and Mrs. Johnson, of George Street, Pocklington, have received the following message from Lord Kitchener, on the death of their son, Henry Johnson, who was accidentally killed at Doncaster on the 29th of December last:—

"The King commands me to assure you of the true sympathy of His Majesty and the Queen in your sorrow.
KITCHENER."

Pocklington Weekly News, 19th Feb 1916

Private H. JOHNSON, 1281, "A" Company, 5th Yorks. Regiment, Northumbrian Division, B.E.F., now serving in France. He was over at Pocklington the other week (on leave), looking exceedingly well.

Pocklington Weekly News, 4th Mar 1916

Private E. JOHNSON, 3433, "C" Company, 5th Yorks. Regiment, B.E.F. (brother to the above) also serving his country in France.

Pocklington Weekly News, 4th Mar 1916

Private GEORGE KEMP, 5th East Yorks, killed in action on 18th February, 1916. The deceased was well-known in this district, having been in the employ of Mr. Jas. Scott, Burnby Wold, and also at Millington Grange.

Pocklington Weekly News, 4th Mar 1916

Lance-Corporal G. DOWNHAM, 1443, "A" Company, 5th Batt. Yorkshire Regiment, B.E.F. He is now enjoying the best of health, and has been on active service over twelve months.

Lce.-Corpl. L. DOWNHAM transferred from the 5th Yorks, into the Yeomanry, and is stationed at 6th Squadron, E.R.Y.Y., Room 19, 5th Cavalry Barracks, Pulford Barracks, York.

Pocklington Weekly News, 4th Mar 1916

Private R. HARRISON, "A" Squadron, 18th Hussars, B.E.F.

Pocklington Weekly News, 11th Mar 1916

Private H. HARRISON, "A" Company, 5th Yorks. Regiment, B.E.F.
Both the above are sons of ex-Police Constable Harrison, of Bishop Wilton. They have been serving in France for many months, and neither has yet been home on leave.

Pocklington Weekly News, 11th Mar 1916

Driver THOMAS JOHNSON, of Lockington, has just been over on short leave, having been out in France one year.

Pocklington Weekly News, 25th Mar 1916

Corpl. Geo. Ernest DUMVILLE (shoeing Instructor), now serving in the Royal Field Artillery, and shortly expected to go to the Front.

Pocklington Weekly News, 1st Apr 1916

Scout A. JOHNSON, 1621, 1st Line 5th Yorks., 1st York and Durham Brigade, 1st Northumbrian Division, B.E.F., went out to France in April, 1915, wounded in the leg with shrapnel, and now fully recovered.

Pocklington Weekly News, 1st Apr 1916

Private R. W. BUTTLE, of Pocklington, 2nd East Yorks., served in India for six years, now in France, and looks in the pink of condition after being reported killed.

Pocklington Weekly News - Dec 25th, 1915

Private C. MUTIMER, of Pocklington, serving in the Royal Field Artillery, now in France.

Pocklington Weekly News - Dec 25th, 1915

Private BOB PRATT, of Pocklington, Local Territorial, been having a good time in France since April last.

Pocklington Weekly News - Dec 25th, 1915

Private MARTIN TURTON, 3rd East Yorks., enlisted in April, 1915, now in training at Hedon.

Pocklington Weekly News
4th Mar 1916

Gunner H. Johnson of Pocklington
Pocklington Weekly News, 1st Jan 1916

Lieutenant-Colonel Frederick William ROBSON, D.S.O.

Pocklington Weekly News
16th Dec 1916

TROOPER B. BYASS,
East Yorks. Yeomanry. Killed in action in Palestine, 1917. Son of Mr and Mrs. T. Byass, Middlebridges Farm, Warter.

Pocklington Weekly News
Christmas Supplement 1917

Sapper G. HUNTER (Royal Engineers), of Pocklington, joined the army a year ago and likely to go to the Front shortly.

Pocklington Weekly News
22nd Sep 1917

Lieutenant Edward Moore ROBSON, M.C.

Pocklington Weekly News
16th Dec 1916

Pte. WILFRED THOMPSON, K.O.Y.L.I., son of Mrs. Thompson, Chapmangate, died of wounds received in action, November 16th, 1916.

Pocklington Weekly News
20th Oct 1917

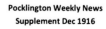

Private JOHN P. DAY,
of Pocklington, of the 10th (Service) E.Y., Hull Commercials, who has been wounded whilst serving at the Front.

Pocklington Weekly News
Supplement Dec 1916

Pocklington and District Local History Group

He was not a White Mouse. We are having it very hot out here in the day time and it comes in very cold at night, and we cannot walk about to keep ourselves warm. Remember me to Arthur when you write him again; tell him I am on the go yet, Remember me to all at home. I think this is all this time, from

Your loving Uncle, HARRY.

P.S. I think there is a few more Pock, lads joining. It is time they did; they ought to be out here helping us, and then they would know what War is. It is not a Cake Walk for as, we have something to do yet. The Germans are hot stuff yet, and don't forget it. I am just going to have dinner—Bully Beef and Biscuits.

17th July, 1915

INTERESTING LETTERS FROM THE FRONT.

1285, Pte. E. Pratt, "A" Coy., 5th Yorks., Northumbrian Division, British Expeditionary Force, G.P.O. July 6th, 1915.

Dear Mother,—

I received your parcel and letter on Friday, and have enjoyed the contents very much, so write to thank you for same. I am very pleased to hear you are all keeping, in good health and hope you will continue to do so. Myself, I am in the best of health, and as long as I have the same luck all through I can't grumble. We are again in the trenches and are having a nice time. The weather still keeps fine for us, but during the day the heat from the sun is terrible. We are in another part of the line now, and within eighty yards of the German trenches, but up to now nothing startling has happened. If you send another parcel next week as you said, please let me have some more Woodbines as I am about run out again. How are things in Pocklington. I hear the chaps from the Camp have left you, but that some more have come. I hope they are a decent set of chaps, and that it will liven the Old Place up a bit for you. Do you hear from Jack often? I have not had a line from him for a long time, and hope he is getting all right again. We have had two good parcels from Pocklington—one from Mrs. Hotham and the other from Mrs. Thomas (Grammar School), and I can tell you that there was a lot of good things in both and were much enjoyed by us all. It is nice to think we are not forgotten by the people, and if we are spared to get through this none of us will ever forget the kindness the people from dear old Pock have shown towards us while we have been out here. I could do with a little cash, if you can manage to send some! We can get it changed out here all right, so please oblige if possible, as we shall soon be going for a rest, and shall be able to have a good time, if we have any money to spend. Hope all the others are keeping well; give them all my very best love, and accept the same for yourself. News is very scarce out here, so please excuse more this time. I will write again soon, so will ring off now.— Wishing to be remembered to all friends in Pocklington.

Best love to all, Your loving Son, BOB.

P.S.—The letter got delayed, and we have been relieved since and are at a very good billet.

14th August, 1915

THREATENED AIR RAID OVER POCKLINGTON.

To the Editor of the "Pocklington News."

Dear Sir,—Kindly allow me a little space to ventilate a grievance which gas consumers of Pocklington suffered by being deprived of the use of gas on Tuesday, until ten, o'clock in the forenoon on that particular day.

Whilst admitting that it is a proper course to turn the gas off during a threatened air-raid, I am quite at a loss to see why we should be deprived of the use of gas until ten o'clock in the forenoon.

What was there to prevent the Bellman being sent out at seven o'clock, instead of nearly ten, to notify the public that the gas would be turned on at 7-30 or 8 a.m.?

Of late, stick and coal fires have not been in use, in many homes, and much inconvenience and annoyance was occasioned by cutting off the gas supply to such a late hour. My old man played steam with me because his breakfast was not ready for him at the usual hour—8 a.m.,—but I put all the blame on the Gas Manager.

Yours truly,

A GAS CONSUMER.

14th August, 1915

INTERESTING LETTERS FROM THE FRONT.

1st Line 5th Yorks. Trans., York and Durham Inf. Brigade., 50th. Division, British Expeditionary Force France, 8-8-1915.

Dear Mr. Whitehead,—

Many thanks for the parcel which was sent to us from the people of Pocklington. The articles enclosed were very acceptable, seeing that we don't get such luxuries out here. By the way, what we can buy is as dear as possible, and with not getting much pay we have to do without unless the people in the dear old place think of us and send a few such things. I think it is very kind indeed of them to think of us. But I dare say that still in Pocklington there are a few that could be doing there bit as well as us instead of staying at home. Sir, I must now close my letter, thanking all very much for their kind gifts.

Believe me,
To remain,
Yours obediently, Driver J.W. Buttle

To the Editor of the 'Pocklington News."

Driver J. Harrison, 712, A.S.C., No. 8 Squadron, No. 1 Batt., Remount Dept., Rouen.

Dear Sir,—Happening to meet another lad from Pocklington in Camp here, we fell to discussing the Town from a recruiting point of view. As a result we find Pocklington very much wanting; scores of Pocklington lads of my acquaintance, I find, have never given a thought to enlisting. I wonder if they can guess what the men who are camping outside the town are saying about them. I have a good idea what they say! It is nice, I daresay, to turn out in full force when troops are leaving these camps for the front, and send them off with a ringing cheer. It is far more patriotic, however, to be leaving for the front with them and to receive the ringing cheers of womenfolk; to have your sweethearts and sisters, wives, and mothers shaking your hand and bidding you God speed. It is a fair-sized place, and boasts at least two recruiting Officers. I should very much like to hear that they were having their work cut out to cope with eager applicants for khaki suits. All can't be "Edwin Kirby's" we know, but all can do their share and put their shoulders to the wheel. Apropos of my own share, I have been actually in France since August 24th last; and still going strong. It is rumoured about Pocklington lads, when the war started, and troops began to leave England, that they said "We'll be amongst the first to go and see the boys off at the Station." Try and make them buck up. We want them out here. Do they think they will be away from Mother too long, or what? Can you guess how I feel when other Yorkshire Lads boast of the hundreds that have gone from their own respective districts? Sir, please wake them up to the fact that England is involved in War, and oblige.

Yours sincerely,

Driver J. Harrison.

Pocklington and District Local History Group

Sunday, August 8th, 1915.

Dear Brother,—

I am sending you another short address, and hope you will get it published in the Local Paper. Remember me to all in Pocklington. I hope all the boys of Pock have rallied round the flag. Don't let it be said we had any shirkers hanging round our place. I have met a good few lads from our place out of the 5th Yorks. and they seem very jolly. I hope you will send some of the boys who have been trained round Pock, We will all wish them the best of luck, hoping to be with you soon for a short leave.

from your loving Brother, WILLIAM.

14th August, 1915

Precis of Speeches delivered by Sir John French, Commander in Chief of the British in the Field to Brigades 27th and 28th Divisions, on the 21st and 22nd May, 1915.

"I came over to say a few words to you to tell you how much I, as Commander-in-Chief of this Army, appreciate the splendid work that you have all done during the recent fighting. You have fought the Second Battle of Ypres, which will rank amongst the most desperate and hardest fights of the war. You may have thoughts because you were attacking the enemy that you were not helping to shorten the war. On the contrary, by your splendid endurance and bravery you have done a great deal to shorten it. In this, the Second Battle of Ypres, the Germans tried by every means in their power to get possession of that unfortunate town. They concentrated large forces of troops and artillery, and further than that they had recourse to that mean and dastardly practice hitherto unheard of in civilised warfare, namely, the use of asphyxiating gases. You have performed the most difficult, arduous and terrific task of withstanding a stupendous bombardment by heavy artillery, probably the fiercest artillery fire ever directed against troops, and warded off the enemy's attacks with magnificent bravery. By your steadiness and devotion both the German plans were frustrated. He was unable to get possession of Ypres. If he had done this he would probably have succeeded in preventing Neutral Powers from intervening, and he was also unable to distract us from delivering our attack. In conjunction with the French in Arras-Armentiers district had you failed to repulse his attacks and made it necessary for more troops to be sent to your assistance, our operations in the south might not have been able to take place, and would certainly not have been as successful as they have been. Your colours have many famous name emblazoned on them, but none will be more famous or more well deserved than that of the Second Battle of Ypres. I want you one and all to understand how thoroughly I realise and appreciate what you have done. I wish to thank each Officer, Non-Commissioned Officer, and man for the services you have done by doing your duty so magnificently, and I am sure that your country will thank you, too." Best wishes to the Editor.

11th September, 1915

TERRIBLE TRAGEDY AT POCKLINGTON

A SOLDIER MURDERS HIS WIFE.

About 10 o'clock on Thursday night a terrible tragedy occurred at Pocklington in which the parties concerned are from Hull. It appears that Henry Macdonald (40), a Hull soldier, in camp at Ousethorpe, and his wife Bertha Macdonald (32), who came to Pocklington in June, assisted the proprietor of a fish and chip saloon in his business in order to be near her husband.

Macdonald brought his wife from the shop to the private house of Mr. Rodgers, and they were sitting in the kitchen talking, which led to a quarrel, Mrs. Rodgers being present. Macdonald, who appeared to be sober, wanted his wife to go out with him, but she refused and said she would go in the morning. She had previously told Mrs. Rodgers not to leave them as she was afraid of his threats, and not to let him stay the night. He pressed her to go to the front of the house and bid him good-night, but she said she was going to stay where she was that night. Macdonald then got hold of his wife's head and pulled it back and cut her throat with a razor and then drew the razor across his own throat three times. Mrs. Macdonald fell across Mrs. Rodgers's knee, and Mrs. Rodgers got out of the back of the house down the garden screaming for help. Macdonald appears to have dragged his wife from the kitchen to the front door step where her body was found with the head nearly severed from the body. He then went across the road to Mr. Dale's and asked for a drink, but then went back to a grass plot in the front of the houses, and a drink was taken to him, there being no thought of any tragedy until the neighbours saw that his throat was bleeding

Dr. Fairweather was sent for but nothing could be done for Mrs. MacDonald, whose body was removed to the premises of the Feathers Hotel, Pocklington. The doctor stitched Macdonald's throat and he was re-moved to the Military Hospital in Union Street. In an interview Mrs. Rodgers says the whole affair happened so quickly that she was helpless to prevent it, and when Mrs. Macdonald fell across her knee all she said was "Oh! Mrs. Rodgers."

The cause of the crime appears to have been jealousy on Macdonald's part for which there was no reason, and Mrs. Macdonald said that he had threatened to "do her in" on several occasions, and Mrs. Rodgers had advised her to go and live with her mother in Wednesbury, if the man was so jealous of her.   The unfortunate woman was in Mrs. Rodgers opinion, "As nice a woman as you could wish for," and hardly dare speak to a man owing to her husband's jealousy, Macdonald lies in a precarious condition this (Friday) morning. In his Possession was a late pass for the camp for that particular night. Macdonald was removed from Pocklington by Military Motor Ambulance to York at 4-15 yesterday (Friday) afternoon. Macdonald still lies in a precarious condition

An inquest will be held this (Saturday) morning, a report of which will appear in our special edition issued about noon the same day.

11th September, 1915

A LETTER FROM POCKLINGTON "GHURKAS."

To the Editor of the "Pocklington News,"

Sir,—With the arrival of the last mail we read in your paper that you had been having a chat with Private Topham with regard to his experiences while in France. We should be pleased if you would insert in your Paper a slight contradiction to the very elaborate tale he told you.   He was sent to Hospital suffering from weak eyes and was fortunate enough to reach England from same cause.   First he says we had a few hours rest in Boulogne, then we marched to a station where we entrained for the Front. Topham must have mistaken kilometres for miles, as the distance to the station was not much over three miles.   On reaching the Railhead we had a stiff march, again kilometres,—he stated 16 miles. We should also like to state that from our baptism of fire at St. Julien up to the time Topham was "wounded" with a glass marble (which is a myth), we had some vivid experiences.   We wonder if he can show the scar of his wound. As for having had the misfortune to lose his right eye, we think it was caused with looking for somewhere to sleep, as every time he was wanted for duty it took us all our time to wake him up.   He also refers to a Crucifixion; the same did happen, but long before we arrived in France.

(Signed), POCKLINGTON GHURKAS.

25th September, 1915

POCKLINGTON.

A Strange Find.

A soldier's uniform (without anyone in them) was found in a field near South Moor House, Pocklington, on Saturday last. Information was given to the police, who took possession of the outfit. They did not belong to anyone from the Ousethorpe Camp but belonging another regiment stationed elsewhere.

Closing of N.E.R. Stations.

Owing to the enlistment of Railwaymen and the consequent shortage of staff, the undermentioned stations will be temporarily closed on and after Monday, 20th September, 1915:—Bernton Square, Cayton, Fyling Hall, Hessay, Newby Wiske, Smardale: also Newport (closed from 8th August, 1915).

2nd October, 1915

PHOTOGRAPHS OF WARSHIPS.

Admiralty warning to picture postcard dealers.

The following instruction has been received from the Admiralty for communication to the Press and for publication:—

The attention of all concerned in the publication or sale of picture postcards or photographs is drawn to the fact that photographs, profile outlines, drawings, or silhouettes of any of H.M. ships, or picture postcards of the same character that might in any way assist enemy agents in the identification of H.M. ships, must be regarded as coming under Regulation 1 of the Defence of the Realm Regulations, which forbids the collecting, recording, publishing, or communicating of any information with respect to the description or condition of any of H.M. ships of such a nature as is calculated to be, or might be, directly or indirectly, useful to the enemy, or the possession without lawful authority or excuse of any document containing such information.

Photographs, profile outlines, drawings, or silhouettes, and picture postcards of this nature, therefore should no longer be exposed for sale, and no dealings in such articles, whether by sale or otherwise, should take place during the continuance of the war.

1st January, 1916

A POCKLINGTON GUNNER

CRUSHED TO DEATH.

It is with feelings of sincere regret that we have to record the death of Mr. Henry Johnson. 18 years of age, of George Street. Pocklington, who lost his life at Doncaster on Sunday last, under most tragic circumstances. He belongs to a Pocklington family who are held in high esteem, and for whom much sympathy has been expressed.

The soldier, Gunner H. Johnson, No. 2599, attached to R.F.A.. was proceeding with other soldiers, horses, and wagons along West Laithe Gate, Doncaster, about 10-30 a.m., to draw stores.

The horses suddenly became restive through a congestion of traffic, and Johnson jumped down, and attempted to assist the driver in quietening them. In doing so he was crushed between the wall and the wagon, and was kicked by one of the horses.

Before he could be rescued he was caught by the front part of the wagon and terribly crushed.

The unfortunate man was convoyed with all speed to the Doncaster Infirmary, but on arrival there was found to be dead.

THE FUNERAL was to have taken place at Pocklington Cemetery on Tuesday afternoon. The bereaved family received a wire to that effect and stating that a Company of Military would accompany the corpse and give to it a military funeral. They therefore fully expected their arrival but were much put out on finding that only Bombardier Conroy was instructed to journey to Pocklington, the Doncaster contingent only journeying as far as Doncaster Station. Moreover the military changed the hour to 10-45 a.m. and thus the hurried interment (arranged for the convenience of the military, who failed to turn up) prevented the attendance of relatives from a distance, or the arranging of a firing-party from Ousethorpe. Had all gone as was expected, a very imposing funeral would have taken place in honour, of one who had laid down his life in the service of his King and Country. The chief mourners were:—Mr. and Mrs. H. Johnson (father and mother), Pocklington; Misses Emily, Lily, Ada, and Florence Johnson (sisters); Albert, Percy, and Ernest Johnson (brothers); Mr. and Mrs. Rooks (grandfather and grandmother); Corporal L. Rooks (uncle), Pocklington; Mrs. Downham (aunt), Pocklington; Mr. L. Downham (cousin); Miss L. Downham (cousin); Mrs. Walsh (aunt); Mr. and Mrs. Todd (cousins); Mrs. Gilyead; Mr. T. H.Headley. and Mr. H. Jackson, Barmby Moor. Mr. John Johnson, Driffield (uncle). Mr. George Johnson, Driffield, (cousin), Miss L. Dounham. York (cousin), Mrs. Wilson, Bishop Wilton (aunt).

There were also present:—Bombardier Conroy (Doncaster), Spnt. J. W. Robson, Sergt. Spriggs, Mr. Harold Scaife, Mr. Syd. Everingham, Mr. Whitehead, Mrs. J. Wilson, junr., Mr. W. Warters, Miss Eastwood, Mr. Bateson, Mrs. W. Coupland, Mr. Vincent, Mrs. F. Thorpe, Mrs. Witty, Miss N. Scaife, Miss Giles, Mrs. Hunter, Mr. Holderness, Mrs. B. Tinson, Miss Richardson, Mrs. Rowley, Mrs. Douthwaite, Mrs. Atkinson, Mrs. H. Skelton. Mrs. Lockwood, Miss Dorsey, Miss Turner, Miss Toyne, and other sympathetic friends.

Letters of sympathy were received from the following:—Miss Richardson, of Field Farm, Barmby Moor; Miss Richardson, Kimberley House, Barmby Moor; Mr. and Mrs. Potter, West Field Farm, Barmby Moor; Mr. and Mrs. Javerley. York; W. Barber, Bielby; from Relatives at. Leeds; from Mrs. Bontoft, Hessle: Mr. and Mrs. Richardson, Greenland, Barmby Moor. **The Wreaths**.: The floral tributes were very choice, and as follows:—
"With deepest sympathy from his follow comrades, the cooks, stewards, and orderlies of the Officers' Mess, 3, Regent's Square, Northumbrian Brigade R.F.A. (T).-R.I.P.
"In loving memory from Grandfather and Grandmother—Lythe and Connie."
"A token of regret from the N.C.O. and Men of the Ammunition Column, 2nd Northumbrian Brigade, R.F.A."
"In deepest sympathy from Mr. and Mrs. C. Hotham."
"To dear Harry, from Albert, Percy, and Ernest."
"With sincere sympathy from the Officers of the Ammunition Column. 2-2nd Northumbrian Brigade, R.F.A."
"In loving memory from his sorrowing Father and Mother."
"To our dear brother, from Emily, Lillie, Ada, Florrie, and Doris."
"Mr. H Johnson, Cosy Cottage, George Street, Pocklington.

15th January, 1916

MILITARY FUNERAL AT POCKLINGTON.

THE LATE MR. FRED EASTON.

As briefly reported in in these columns, Mr. Fred Easton, shoeing-smith, passed away at Woolwich from pneumonia on January 6th. His remains arrived in Pocklington on Saturday by the 3-25 p.m. train and were conveyed by hearse to his brother's residence in Chapmangate, to await interment which took place in Pocklington Cemetery on Monday afternoon.'.

A very large number of tradesmen and friends assembled to pay a last tribute to one who was highly esteemed. The funeral was of a military character. The band and firing party of the 3rd Lancashire Fusiliers (from Ousethorpe camp) were present and under Bandmaster Miles the band played Chopin's Funeral March as the procession passed through the streets. At the cemetery the Rev. A. E. Clarke (Wesleyan) officiated in the presence of a large crowd.

The firing party, in charge of Sergeant Robinson, fired the customary three volleys over the grave, and Sergeant Green sounded the "Last Post" at the conclusion of an impressive ceremony. Some lovely floral tributes were received., including two from the Officers and non-commissioned Officers of deceased's battery, and one from the Pocklington Conservative Club., the following being the full list of floral tributes.:—

The Wreaths:

"From his sorrowing Brothers and Sisters."
"From the Officers, P.R.H.A., Woolwich, with deepest sympathy."
"From the non-commissioned Officers and Men of the P. Battery, R.H.A., Woolwich, with deepest sympathy."
"With deepest sympathy from the Committee and Members of the Pocklington Conservative Club."
"In affectionate memory of a good friend, from Mrs. Scaife and Family, cab proprietors. Chapmangate, Pocklington."
"With deepest sympathy from Bill, Alf, Jim, and Jack."
"With deepest sympathy from Mr. and Mrs. C. Hotham."
"To dear Fred, with, deepest sympathy, from Lance-Corporal and Mrs. Hindwell"
"With deepest sympathy From Mr. and Mrs. T. Hunter, Gate House."
"In loving memory of a dear friend, from Mr. and Mrs. A. Wilson."
"To dear Fred, with deepest sympathy, from Miss S. Hindwell."
"With, deepest sympathy, from Millicent.", "To dear Fred, from M.A.H."

The family mourners were Mr. and Mrs. J. Easton, Mr. and Mrs. H. Easton (of Market Weighton), Mr. and Mrs. Clark (Escrick), Mr. and Mrs. G. Bell (brothers and sisters), Mr. B. Shepherdson (uncle, Driffield), Mrs.

This photograph was from the Buttle collection and has the above writing on the back. The cap badge looks like the Army Service Corps.

Watson (Riccall). Miss Shepherdson, Mr. T. Playforth (Londesborough), Miss A. Appleton (Cliffe), Mr. and Mrs. Wilson. Mr. and Mrs. Gordon, Mrs. Noble, and Miss M. Bell (niece).

Amongst others, present we noticed:— Councillor C. Stather. Councillor Scaife, Mr. A. Moor, Mr. and Mrs. G. Buttle, Mr. H. Kendall,. Mr. J. Rippon. Mr. W. F. Hill, Mr. Tinson Stubbs, Mr. and Mrs. E. J. Lamb, Mr. R. Manners, Mr. J. Manners, Mr. Walter Askham, Mr. T. Grant, Mr. J. Whitehead, Mr. Henry Thomas, Mr. T. Smithson, Mr. Sellers, Mr. and Mrs. J. Glaisby, Miss Glaisby, Superintendent Robson, Sergt. Spriggs, Mr. G. Harrison, Mr. Fred Thorpe, Mr. Pearson. Mr. J. White, Mrs. and Miss Watson. Mrs. Thomas (of Canal Head), Mr. Mennell, Mrs. Baxter, Mr. G. Thorpe, Mr. I. Everingham, Mrs. Boyden, Mrs. Cooper, Mr. W. Spivey, Lance-Corpl. Horace Laister and Private W. Bean (representing 5th Yorks.), and Private Syd. Gray. (representing the 21st K.R.R.), Mr. L. A. J. Stubbs, Mrs Snow, Mrs. Wright, Mr. T. Smith, Mrs. Thomas, Mr. and Mrs. Guppy, Mr. H. Scaife; Mr. Harold Procter. Mr. and Mrs. Jas. Scott (Burnby Wold), Mrs. Hunter, Mrs. Spray, Mr. J. Brown, Mrs. Lister, Mrs. Hodgson, Mr. W. Wilson, Mons. Mamet, Mr. Chris. Scaife, Mrs. Fisher, Mr. H. Meynell, Mrs. Sellers, Mr. C. Rowley, Mr. T. Towle, Mr. J. Johnson, Mr. G. Gray, Mr. Fred Lee, Mr. J. Nicholson. Mr. R. D. Gray, Mr. and Mrs, J. Johnson (Burnbv). Mr. H. W. Curtis (Allerthorpe), Mr. N. Cattle. Mr. C. Turner, Mr. J. Cook, Mr. F. E. N. Todd, Mr. Holderness, Mr. Drake, Miss Precious, Mr. R. Hotham, Mr. H. Hotham, Mr. Linfoot, Mrs. Richard Todd, Mrs. J. Wilson, junr., Mr. Ralph Scaife, Mr. J. Douthwaite, Mr. T. Fairweather, Mrs. Dales (Callis Wold). Miss Brewer, Miss B. Brown, Mrs. J. H. Buttle, Mrs. T. Warters, Mrs. Rowley, Mrs. H. Topham, Mrs. Scaife;. Mrs. G. H. Barker, and other friends.

The coffin was of oak, with brass fittings, and bore the inscription:—

FRED EASTON, Died January 6th, 1916. Aged 33 Years.

Mrs. Scaife and Son, cab proprietors, had charge of the funeral arrangements. which were efficiently discharged, whilst Mr. Watson Wright superintended the duties of undertaker.

29th January, 1916

A Local D.C.M. Winner

Private Edwin Kirby, a native of Pocklington, and winner of the D.C.M., who is spending a short leave with his brother at Pocklington, paid a visit to his old School (the National School) this week. He was wearing his medal, and was warmly congratulated by his old Master, Mr. Skinner, on his achievement. Taking advantage of the opportunity the School was assembled and told how an old scholar had distinguished himself in the War waged for honour, freedom, and right, and brought not only honour to himself, but also credit to his School and has given them an example of unflinching courage and devotion to duty. The Master then called for three cheers which were given with the utmost heartiness. The medal (of silver) with bar and clasp, bearing the words "For distinguished conduct in the field" was viewed by the children and teachers and greatly admired. The presentation of the medal was made to Private Kirby by the General Officer Commanding the 3rd Battalion of the Lincolnshire Regiment, and was accompanied by the following words describing the circumstances under which the distinction was won :-

"Presentation of the Distinguished Conduct Medal to N. R2-9998, Private E. Kirby, 2nd Battalion, the Lincolnshire Regiment for gallant conduct on the 9th May, 1915, at Rouge Banns in throwing a lighted German bomb out of a mine crater where about 15 wounded and 100 other men were taking cover, therby saving serious loss of life."

Like other British soldiers who have received recognition for heroic deeds, Pte. Edwin Kirby wears his decoration with becoming modesty, and does not claim to have done more than his duty.

1st April, 1916

POCKLINGTON.

PLEASANT MEMORIES OF POCKLINGTON

We have received the following interesting letter

Sergeant H.E. Lambert, 28th Reserve Park, A.S.C. France, 19th March, 1916.

Sir, -

I wish to place on record my appreciation of the kindness and generosity of the inhabitants of Pocklington.

It was in January, 1915, that I bid adieu to dear old Pocklington, where, as a recruit in the Yorkshire Mounted Brigade. T. and S. Column, A.S.C. I had been stationed for close on five months. It was home away from home. The suppers provided for us in the Wesleyan Schoolroom were a veritable God-send, and after my first introduction to the "nocturnal beanfeasts" I need hardly say that I was seldom an absentee.

Nearly twelve months "somewhere in France" has not obliterated the memories of happy days spent amongst the good people of Pocklington, and if I'm spared to see the finish of this "business" you can rest assured that one of the visitors to good old Pock, will be

Yours truly, H. E. LAMBERT.

8th April, 1916

POCKLINGTON.

Air Raid.

On account of Wednesday night's air-raid the 8-42 p.m. train from York was stopped in Pocklington Station, where it remained until 2 a.m., when all danger was passed.

Whist Drive and Dance.

On Wednesday evening a whist drive and dance was being held in the Victoria Hall, Pocklington and when the drive was half completed, the gas was turned off on account of the threatened air raid; and the party quietly dispersed. Those in attendance were each presented with a Complimentary Ticket, admitting them to the Fancy Dress Ball to be held at Easter, when it is hoped Zeppelins will be conspicuous by their absence. This was rough luck, not I only on those present, but also upon Mrs. H. Kendall, who had provided an excellent supply of choice refreshments.

29th April, 1916

A YAPHAM SOLDIER KILLED.

News has just been received at Yapham that Private Richard Timbs. 5th Yorks. son of Mr. and Mrs. W. Timbs. of that village, has been killed by a sniper in France and was buried last Sunday. The unfortunate young man was 20 years of age, and enlisted a year ago, being one of four brothers who are serving their country and who are much respected in the district.

15-4-16

Dear Miss Timbs,—

I hope this address will find you. I am very sorry to tell you that Private R. Timbs was brought in here to No. 2 Casualty Clearing Station very severely wounded in the head and quite unconscious and passed peacefully away at 1-30 to-day without regaining consciousness. He will be buried in a part of the cemetery here reserved for our brave troops, and a little wooden cross bearing the name and date marks each resting place. The name of place and number of his grave will be sent to you later from Headquarters. There is one consolation, from the nature of the wound you may be sure he did not suffer, but would be unconscious at once. With much sympathy.

Yours sincerely,

L. E. JOLLEY. Sister-in-Charge.

2nd Lieut. Bredrick writes as follows:—
"I very much regret to write to tell you that Private R. Timbs was shot with a rifle bullet whilst out with a working party. The short time I have known your son, who was in my platoon, I had got to like him, for he was most popular with Officers and men. His companion was killed the same night, and both are greatly missed by their companions."

6th May, 1916

Wounded in Action

News was received in Pocklington on Monday that Private T. B. Thorpe, of Pocklington, of the 5th Yorkshire Regiment, has been wounded in action. Along with some of his comrades in the same regiment, he was taking shelter from shell-fire in a dug-out, when a shell fell right on the top of their shelter, and Private Thorpe was badly wounded, receiving a broken arm, a broken rib and several severe bruises, and his comrades were fortunate in escaping with nothing but a severe shaking. This is the second time Pte. Thorpe has been wounded since going out to the front in April of last year. He is now in Hospital at Birmingham, and we are pleased to hear that he is making satisfactory progress.

6th May, 1916

A Gigantic Retail Turnover.

The Officials of the Pocklington Co-operative Society have watched with pleasure the steadily increasing weekly sales of the Society, but the total recorded for the week —April 29th, 1916, was so highly satisfactory that we feel that we ought not to let the matter pass without drawing our members attention to it. Although the premises of the Society were closed one day (Easter Monday) the Cash receipts for goods sold during this week amounted to £1,141 5s. 9d., which constitutes a week's sales record for the Society. We take this opportunity of thanking all our Members who by their "more than average" purchases enabled us to reach such splendid figure, and trust that with their increased loyalty to their own Society we shall in due coarse register this total every week.— Shop at your own Stores.

War! War!

Now is the time to economise. It is imperative at the present time, that every penny should be spent to the greatest advantage. "A penny saved is a penny earned." We can help you to save many pennies by buying one of our Patent Vacuum Swift Washers. The only good Washer on the market. It saves time, labour, soap, coals, and clothes, besides putting the housewife in a good temper. Hard work made easy. A tub full of clothes can be washed perfectly clean in four minutes, no steeping, rubbing, or boiling required. You simply put the clothes into a tub of boiling water, use the Vacuum Washer for four minutes, rinse the clothes as usual, hang on the line, work completed. To verify the above statement we are willing to demonstrate the Washer at your own homes upon application, or at our Depot. Market Place. Furthermore, to convince you, we are willing to lend out one of these Washers for a week, free of charge, and you are under no obligation to buy unless perfectly satisfied. This is what we call a real and fair test. The nett Cash Plans of this wonderful invention is only 15s. 6d. The Washer pays for itself in the course of a few weeks. Owing to the scarcity of the Washers it is essential that you should place your order with us at once, otherwise you be disappointed. Please see our Windows for display of Washers during the next few days. All enquires promptly attended to. Sole Agent for Pocklington and Market Weighton District: FRED LEE. Cycle and Motor Engineer, Pocklington.

20th May, 1916

POCKLINGTON.

A Prisoner of War

News has been received this week that Private W. A. Aston, of the 20th Canadian Battalion, 2nd son of the late Rev. Edward Aston, Presbyterian Minister, and Mrs. Aston, of Ebenezer House, Pocklington, who has been missing for some time, may be now a prisoner of war in Germany, having been captured whilst gallantly assisting in the defence of a crater.

Somewhere in Belgium,

April 26th, 1916.

Dear Mrs. Aston,—

I have to write you that your gallant son, H.H., has been missing since the 20th inst., when he and his comrades, holding one of the craters, were subjected to an intense shelling by the enemy. The story of how they held that position in the face of an awful fire is one that will add fresh honour and glory to deeds of our Army. Your son I do hope will be found to be among those who were forced to surrender, but it will be some weeks before any definite news will be received. I can only say that out of my Company of some hundred and forty odd men and Officers but two Officers remain and some sixty men. Your boy has been in my Co. since November 8th, 1914, and he was a fine man, a good soldier, cheerful, and very highly thought of by his Officers and comrades. We seemed to be more like some large family.

Yours very truly, P. H. SROUTT, Captain, "D" Company, 29th Battalion.

10th June, 1916

A Local Man in the Naval Engagement.

We regret to hear that Henry Holmes, at one time a scholar at the National School, Pocklington, went down in the Invincible in the Naval engagement of the 31st of May.

He was very recently on a short leave from his ship and paid a visit to his old school on the 16th of May. He was in the sea fights off the Falkland Islands and saw the Scharnhorst and the Gueisenau sunk. He had the

---

Pocklington Co-Operative Society, Ltd.

SALE OF SUGAR

RESTRICTIONS.

In consequence of the restriction of supplies of Sugar to Traders by the Government, we are compelled to limit the supply to our Members. We have given this matter careful consideration, and have decided to allot supplies as follows:—

One Pound of Granulated and One Pound of Lump Sugar with each order for Groceries to the value of 2s. 6d., and One Pound of each kind for every additional order to the value of 2s. 6d., such amount to be exclusive of the value of Sugar and Offals.

This course has been adopted in the interests of the Members generally, and will prevent any undue proportion of Sugar being purchased by some Members, resulting in short supplies for others. The proportion of Sugar allocated pro rata to purchases is about the usual quantity bought by consumers in normal times, and we anticipate no hardship will be caused. We have a reserve stock of a few tons on hand, which, together with our direct weekly supplies from the Refiners will enable us to provide regular supplies to our Members if above conditions are observed.

On behalf of the Committee,
GEO. W. HAW,
General Manager.

P.S.—In genuine cases of temporary shortage 1 lb. of Sugar will be supplied at the counter to Members only without restrictions.

To-day's Prices.

Tate's Standard Gran.		$5\frac{1}{4}$d. per lb.
Fairries' Med. Castor		
McFie's Fine Gran.	Two lbs	$10\frac{1}{2}$d
LOAF SUGAR, Tate's, Fairies', & American.		6d p e lb.
Demerara and Raw, 6d. per lb.		
Tate's "Fourths" - 5d. per lb.		

Pocklington Weekly News, 17th Jun 1916

---

utmost confidence in our ability to wipe out the German Navy, given the opportunity, and was looking forward to the day of the mighty conflict. There was no "brag" in Henry's composition, and his feeling of confidence was expressed, only as the result of interrogation. His Schoolmaster, who had an extremely favourable opinion of the lad, says he is sure that Henry Holmes would die at the post of duty, and would fight to the last. To his mother we offer our sympathy and this consolation.

1st July, 1916

THE SHORTAGE OF PAPER

NEED FOR COLLECTION OF WASTE MATERIAL.

REMEMBER THE BOYS
Fighting on all Fronts and at Sea
THEY WANT THEIR FAVOURITE BRANDS OF CIGARETTES
Direct from Factory to Soldier by Post

Order			
280	"WILD WOODBINE"	Cigarettes	3/-
280	"GOLD FLAKE"	Cigarettes	5/-
1000	"WILD WOODBINE"	Cigarettes	8/-
500	"NAVY CUT"	Cigarettes	8/6
500	"THREE CASTLES"	Cigarettes	10/6
1000	"GOLD FLAKE"	Cigarettes	15/-
1000	"NAVY CUT"	Cigarettes	16/-

Pocklington Weekly News, 24th June 1916

Sir Thomas P. Whittaker, M.P., chairman of the Royal Commission on paper, in a letter to the Press points out that while shortage of supplies of paper making material is causing great inconvenience and seriously increasing the price a large quantity of waste paper, now quite valuable, and which paper makers would be glad to buy is being thrown away or destroyed. He has already suggested that local municipal authorities should organise the collection of waste paper, and while something has already been done in some localities there is still a large quantity of useful and valuable material lying waste or being destroyed. All that is required, is that some person or persons in each locality should organise the collecting, sorting, and forwarding of this badly wanted material. Considerable sums may thus be obtained for deserving local war funds, and he suggests that local authorities and local societies should make an effort to do what is necessary.

OUR PORTRAIT GALLERY.

Farrier W. WARTERS, 9323, of Pocklington, 486 Co., A.S.C., 27th Divisional Train, Salonika Forces, is enjoying the best of health, and has had a most interesting experience. We wish him the best of luck, and a safe return.

Pocklington Weekly News, 1st Jul 1916

22nd July, 1916

A Pocklington Soldier Wounded.

Lc.-Corpl. R. C. English, King's Royal Rifles, who was recently wounded, in France, is at present in the Scottish National Military Hospital, Bellahouston, Glasgow, where be is making satisfactory progress towards recovery. He was one of a party of six who were proceeding for rations when a shrapnel shell burst, killing two of the men instantly, a third dying shortly after. Lc. Corpl. English was wounded in the head, hip, and thigh, one of the others was slightly wounded, and the remaining one luckily escaped injury.

Another Local Hero Wounded.

The news was received on Thursday that Pte. Harold Seller, East Yorks., had been admitted to Hospital suffering from shell shock. He is one of three sons of Mr. and Mrs. D. Seller, of Rose Cottage. Millington. who are serving their country, and his many friends hope he may make a speedy recovery.

Public and Air-Raid Relics.

With reference to the Order in Council of the 10th May. amending the Defence of the Realm Regulations, the War Office request that the public will render assistant by notifying at once to the military authorities, or to a Police Constable in the neighbourhood, the finding of any bomb of projectile or fragments thereof, or any other article discharged, dropped, or lost from any enemy aircraft or vessel.

22nd July, 1916

Wounded In Action.

News has just come to hand that one of Dunnington's heroes. Private Steven Stabler, has been wounded in action, previous to joining the King's Royal Rifles, Steven was employed as a gardener by Capt. P. M. Stewart, at Ivy Hall, Pocklington, but, along with several of his pals, in Pocklington, he heard, and answered his country's call. He was wounded in the thigh, whilst taking part in an attack on a German trench. Private Stabler is at present in hospital at Gravesend, and his many friends wish for him a speedy recovery.

5th August, 1916

CORPORAL JACK MOOR WOUNDED.

DESIROUS OF HAVING ANOTHER GO AT THE HUNS.

Corporal Jack Moor, of the R.G.A., son of Mr. J. J. Moor, Avondale House, Carnaby, nr. Bridlington, and formerly of Barmby Grange, near Pocklington, has been wounded in action and has returned to Hospital in England, where he is making good progress towards recovery.

Corporal Jack Moor writes as follows: — Military Hospital. Paddock House. Osbaldtwistle, near Accrington.

Dear Brother and Sister,—

Many thanks for your card and welcome letter, and glad to tell you that I am improving wonderfully now. I was out yesterday with the wife, she came to see me. I get up now at dinner-time, so you can judge how I am going on, and expect to be fit again in a fortnight. I don't mind having another do, but don't like wintering out there as it is awful getting about., being up to the knees in mud.

I was not out there long, but I know I have done enough for our family. I had some clever gunners under me. One of them wrote me during the week. He says they are having some fine fun in the advance, and that our artillery are doing some terrible slaughter, now that they have plenty of shells. I greatly relished the change of food when I arrived in hospital. It is a fine place and we got the best - of everything—living like lords, and have an ounce of tobacco allowed daily.

Kind love and best wishes to all. Your loving Brother, JACK.

12th August, 1916

INTERESTING LETTER FROM CORPORAL FARRIER W. WARTERS

Farrier W. WARTERS, 9328, of Pocklington, 486 Co., A. S.C, 27th Divisional Train, Salonika, writes as follows:—

Dear Sir,—It is my privilege to receive one of your "Weekly News" out here every week, for which I always look forward to, and I was greatly surprised on receiving the last one a few days ago, to find in your paper my photo, and I must congratulate you on the excellent photo produced in your columns of me,—it was such a surprise to me, I never had any idea of seeing it there. I hear of several Pocklingtonians being out in this country but it has never been my luck to meet with a single one up to the present, and I have travelled some scores of miles round about on the different tracks. We have some very heavy thunderstorms occasionally, and the heat is most awful during the day. It is all mountains for miles and miles. It is a noted place for snakes of many different kinds, and tortoises by the hundred are crawling about. What little plots of land they till are all worked by teams of oxen, and no grain is grown round here, but rye. No carts are used; all the loads are carried about on donkeys and ponies on pack saddles, whilst the dress of men is most amusing, and hundreds of both men and women never have a boot on their feet. I may say I have received promotion, on the 10th July, to full Corporal Farrier. I am sorry I am not able to give any details on military matters of what is going on out here. I may say how sorry I am when I see in your paper the names of our Pocklingtonians that have 'gone under' recently. I am amused at the different excuses that are made at the meetings of the Tribunals. I think there can't be many loafers left in Pocklington, and won't be after a time. Now I must thank you once again, and I am sorry I am not able to give you any details as regards military matters. So with my kind regards to all Pocklington friends, I remain,

LANCE-CORPORAL G. DOWNHAM WOUNDED.

Lance-Corporal G. Downham, 1-5th Yorkshire Regiment, of Pocklington, has been wounded in the calf of the leg, in France. He is now in hospital in Leeds, and is going on as well as can be expected.

Pocklington Weekly News, 12th Aug. 1916

Yours sincerely, Corpl. W. Warters. July 27th.

19th August, 1916

Another Distinction for Pocklington.

Sergt. John McNeil Francis, of the 5th Yorkshire Regiment, who left Pocklington shortly after the outbreak of the War, and has been serving in France some months, has been awarded the Military Medal for gallant action one dark night among the Boches, and we congratulate him very heartily on attaining this honour.

No Longer a Novelty.

Not so long since, the whirr of an aeroplane over Pocklington was sufficient to bring out an eager throng of sky-gazers, but the visits of those mechanical birds have become so frequent of late that they no longer excite surprise. By the way, the name of Mr. John Nicholson was inadvertently omitted from our report last week of the aeroplane landing at Meltonby. The visitor dropped in a field adjoining Mr. Nicholson's farm, and he rendered assistance and guidance to the lost aviator.

The Local Ambulance Corps.

Some little time ago, a splendid ambulance equipment was provided at Pocklington to deal with any cases of emergency, and at first members turned up in pretty good numbers for free instruction in this important work. Latterly, however, the numbers have dwindled down to very small proportions, which in very discouraging to Mr. J. Nicholson (the hon. instructor), and to others who have the welfare of the Corps at heart. We trust members will take a gentle hint, and attend practices more regularly in future.

POCKLINGTON GUARDIANS AND RURAL COUNCIL.

INTERNMENT OF ALL ALIENS DEMANDED.

The monthly meetings of the Pocklington Board of Guardians and Rural District Council were held at the Workhouse, Pocklington, on Monday. In the unavoidable absence of both the Chairman (Mr. G. W. Appleton) and the Vice-Chairman (Mr. E. Johnson) of the Guardians, Mr. G. Cobb, J.P., presided, and there were also present the Rev. A. W. Welch the Rev. E. Peters, Messrs. G. Johnson, W. Sampson, John Johnson. J. T. Laverack, B. H. B. White. T. A. Stephenson, J. Sawyer, 8. Stephenson, J. Green, A. G. Fraser, J. E. Dalgliesh, W. H. Johnson, R. H. Stocks. T. B. Fisher. R. T. Richardson, J. Byass J. E. Pearson, and R. Wilson, with the Clerk (Mr. A. J. Oliver). The Master reported that for the week ending July 29th there were 42 inmates in the House, against 46 in the corresponding week of last year. Of the 42, 12 were casuals.

A letter from the Coventry Union asking the Board to support a resolution as to the alleged inadequacy of the pensions at present being paid to soldiers and sailors and to the widows and children, of these men was laid on the table, but it was unanimously decided to support the following resolution, also forwarded by the Coventry Union: "That it is the opinion of this Board that the recent statement by the Home Secretary in the House of Commons on the subject of enemy aliens was unsatisfactory, and that the internment of aliens has been carried but in a very lax manner. We strongly urge the Government to act more vigorously and intern all enemy aliens without exception."

26th August, 1916

INTERESTING LETTER FROM THE FRONT

Mr. F. Scaife, of Neswick Villa, Pocklington, has received the following letter from the Front:-

France, 17th August, 1916.

Dear Mr. Scaife,—

I was so pleased to receive yours of the 23rd July and to hear you had got my letter, but you do not mention having had a Field Post Card dated somewhere about 28th June, and another about the 30th. I sent one home on those dates, but they don't seem to have received them. I wonder if they have got lost or have they since turned up? It was very strange the letters should have crossed in the post. You would learn from the papers that things were busy round here at the time I sent the Field Post Cards, and you will know we had no time for letter-writing. It took us all our time to look after ourselves, and get through the work we had to do, which was by no means light. It was not very pleasant clearing and building up trenches which had been blown in by shell fire, and the work had to be done with all speed on account of the continual bombardment. We lived for days under such conditions as these, but through all the crashing of guns, &c, you could have seen the men going about for the better part with smiles on their faces, apparently oblivious to the din. I believe it would have made Conscientious Objectors join a fighting unit when they saw those men. This will give you an idea of the spirit of the men, it is only one of many I saw myself:— One poor chap had his leg broken just below the knee, and his foot was hanging only by torn flesh, A couple of stretcher bearers came along and would have carried 'him off, but he said: "Nay, lad, ahm all-reet, theers worse behind me than ah am," and he struggled off, dragging his maimed leg. I was told that a little further on he had fastened his knife lanyard to his leg and kept the latter off the ground by holding the loose end of the cord in his teeth. This brave chap died a few hours later. Did you hear of young Carlyon's death.? He was killed in action somewhere about July 14th. I could, tell you more fully where it was if I was permitted to do so. At the same time I lost a dozen or more of my pals who were with me in the Depot at Pocklington. I like to hear how my old friends are getting on. Many thanks for sending me Stockdale's address. have dropped him a line and hope to hear from him shortly. The Zepps. have again been busy.

This time they passed over my home, and you can imagine what state they would be in. My sister tells me they took refuge in a deep ditch in one of the lanes which runs off the street in which they reside. I am glad to say they are none the worse for their first attempt at "trench life." I have exhausted my, stock of news, so will conclude hoping Mrs. Scaife and you an keeping well. I am,

Yours affectionately,

CHARLIE.

An Appointment

Nurse Sheard, of Pocklington, has accepted an appointment as nurse on a hospital ship, and her many Pocklington friends wish her the best of luck in her new sphere of labour.

A Pocklington Soldier Missing.

Mr. and Mrs. Jessop, of Kirkland Street, Pocklington, have received an intimation from the War Office that their son Private Herbert Jessop, of the East Yorks. Regt., has been missing since the 23rd July. A box of eatables sent to him has been returned, and they are anxiously awaiting further news.

Aviation Thrills

Last Monday evening a most obliging Aviator gave a very fine display of looping-the-loop over Pocklington. He approached from the South-East riding in a biplane at a great height, and after passing over the East-end of the town he took a wide sweep and then returned. When he reached a point about over the railway near the Barmby-road Crossing he looped-the-loop about three times, rode in a horizontal position whilst completely upside down, and also whilst his plane was in a vertical position. It was a lovely evening, with a brilliant sun shining, and scores of people witnessed the performance. We do not know the Aviator's name, but on behalf of a most grateful public we tender him very sincere thanks for giving little Pocklington such a fine opportunity of seeing to what perfection flying has attained in the hands of a skilful pilot. We have heard of various heart-displacements as a consequence. Some say their hearts were in their throats, others in their mouths, whilst many aver that theirs were in their boots. All the patients, however, are now quite convalescent, and are willing to run further risks if granted the opportunity.

Death of Private Walter Plumb.

Many of our readers will learn with feelings of the deepest regret of the somewhat sudden death of Private Walter Plumb, of Pocklington. He was 26 yrs. of age on the 9th June last, and is a native of Cambridgeshire. Prior to joining the Army he was in the employ of Mr. W. H. Spivey, dairyman, for over twelve months. Although he was not strong he joined the Army in April last, and was attached to the 22nd Northumberland Fusiliers (3rd Tyneside Scottish), and went out to France exactly a month ago. Last week he got cold and was taken seriously ill with an affection of the lungs and passed away on Monday last. He leaves a widow and one little girl 1 year and 5 months old, for whom much sympathy is expressed. The deceased young man was of a quiet and pleasant disposition, and was highly respected by a wide circle of friends in the Pocklington district.

9th September, 1916

SEATON ROSS MAN KILLED IN ACTION.

Private Albert E. Chapman, son of Mr. and Mrs. Joseph, Chapman, is the first Seaton Ross patriot to lay down his life for his King and country. The

Private A. E. Chapman is standing, and his friend Private Gell is seated

following letter conveying the sad intelligence was received by Mrs. Chapman on the 25th of August:—

45, Machine-Gun Coy., B.E.F., France, 21.8-16.

To Mrs. J. Chapman, Seaton Ross, Everingham, Yorks.

Dear Madam,— I sincerely regret to announce to you the death of your son, No. 44628, Pte. A. E. Chapman, who was killed in action on the 20th inst, by shell fire, and was buried where this unfortunate incident took place. During the short time he was under my command he made a number of friends in the Company, who with me beg to tender their deepest sympathy to you in your great loss.

I am, Madam, Yours truly, H. W. WILKINSON, Capt.

The deepest sympathy is felt for the sorrowing family by all the people of the village and neighbourhood. Deceased enlisted voluntarily in the early part of 1915, and had bean in training in England until a brief fortnight before he made the supreme sacrifice. He was 22 years of age, of a bright and cheery disposition, and left home in the best of spirits. While deeply grieving the loss of a young and valuable fife, all who knew him are proud to link with his memory all that is noble and manly. His brother, Private George Chapman, who went to France in May last, is now recovering from wounds in a Sheffield hospital.

16th September, 1916

BARMBY MOOR.

Lieut. Rees awarded the Military Cross.

Second-Lieuteuant F. L. F. Rees, third son of the Vicar of Barmby Moor, has been 'awarded the "Military Cross." The following will explain the circumstances:—

"On 4-8-16, in trenches near ———, of ———2nd-Lieut. Rees led two bombing parties up ——— Ally, capturing the enemy forward, block, driving the enemy back to their second block, at point ——— protected by barbed wire and defended by two machine-guns which resisted all 2nd-Lieut. Rees efforts to capture it, so he established only 18 yards away from it and held on to it the whole night in spite of fierce and sustained efforts by the enemy to drive him out."

Frederick Llwelyn Forsaith Rees 3rd son of Rev. Rees Vicar of Barmby Moor

H. WILKINSON, Lieut.—Col. A.A. 2M., G-23 Division, 31-8-1916

23rd September, 1916

Lieutenant Edward Robson Wounded

Mr. Thomas Robson solicitor, Pocklington, has been informed that his fourth son, Lieut. Edward M Robson of the 5th Yorks. Regiment has been wounded in action, and Is in hospital suffering from a severe gunshot wound. This is the second time Lieut. Robson has been wounded whilst serving with the colours. We sincerely hope that he will have a speedy and complete recovery. Much sympathy is felt for Mr. Robson in the town and district.

Wounded In Action

On Tuesday morning, Mr. and Mrs. G. H. Barker, of Union Street, Pocklington, received intimation the one of their four soldier sons, Rifleman Walter Barker, of the Kings Royal Rifles, had been wounded in the right arm, and is at present in the Base Hospital in France, but he expects being sent to "Blighty." We hope his wound is not serious, and he will have a speedy recovery. Prior to enlisting Rifleman Barker was employed as a tailor by Messrs. J.T. Everingham and Sons, Pocklington.

Another Pocklington Soldier Wounded

News has reached Pocklington that Private Sydney Gray, of the King's Royal Rifles, has been wounded in action. The nature of his wounds has not yet come to hand, but it is hoped they are not serious and that he will be soon convalescent. Pte. Gray is the only son of Mr. and Mrs. Wm. Gray, of Market Square, Pock.

Killed In Action.

News has been received in Pocklington this week that Corporal Jack Thompson has been killed in action. Soon after the outbreak of war he joined a Highland Regiment, and was soon drafted to the Front. Before joining the Colours he was employed on the N.E.R. and for some time was stationed at Pocklington, where he made many friends.

Concert at Ousethorpe Camp

A very enjoyable concert was given in the Y.M.C.A. Hut. Pocklington, by the "Royal York Pierrot Troupe," under the direction of Miss R. Morten and Lieut. Storey. There was a large attendance of troops. Amongst those present were the Commanding Officer (Captain Hill) and Lieut. Bean. The programme was contributed to by the following artistes, each of whom were encored:- Miss R. Morten, Miss McLaurie, Miss R. Storey, Lieut. Storey, and Mr. R. Wilde. The proceedings terminated with the singing of the National Anthem. The men showed their appreciation of the entertainment by giving the party a hearty send off.

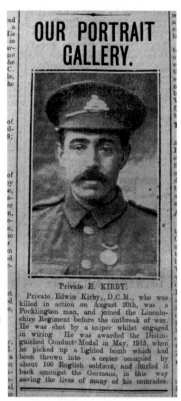

OUR PORTRAIT GALLERY.

Private E. KIRBY.

Private Edwin Kirby, D.C.M., who was killed in action on August 20th, was a Pocklington man, and joined the Lincolnshire Regiment before the outbreak of war. He was shot by a sniper whilst engaged in wiring. He was awarded the Distinguished Conduct Medal in May, 1915, when he picked up a lighted bomb which had been thrown into a crater occupied by about 100 English soldiers, and hurled it back amongst the Germans, in this way saving the lives of many of his comrades.

Pocklington Weekly News, 16th Sep. 1916

Important Announcement.

Fred Lee begs to announce that at an enormous cost he has booked the Celebrated Government Film. "The Battle of the Somme," 5,000 feet in length, and will positively show this famous picture in the Central Hall, Pocklington, on October 26, 27 and 28. Owing to the great cost of this picture Mr. Lee is obliged to advance his prices as follows: Back Seats, 1s 2d.; Front Seats, 6d., both including Tax. Owing to the immense success of this famous film of the Battle of the Somme it behoves you to book seats at once - only 100 per night booked. No extra charge for booking. Several seats already booked, Note the date: October 26th, 27th and 28th.

A Big Output

Mr J. E, Law, 16, Market Street, Pocklington, is just executing 1000 pairs of Army Repairs for the Camp (apart from Town and Country work). Mr Law's one study is to oblige all who so generally entrust their repairs to him. Through his gift of mechanism he has fitted his workshops with modern machinery which enables him to turn work out in up-to-date style and finish, on the shortest notice.

30th September, 1916

A CHEERFUL LETTER FROM A WOUNDED SOLDIER—AN HEROIC CHARACTER.

September 21st, 1919.

Dear Dad and Mother,—

Just a few lines to let you know I'm going on as well as can be expected, considering the nature of my wounds. Fritz has planted me right this time. I was hit in the back and it went through into my body, but they have operated and the result is I have a big hole back and front, but don't worry, I shall soon be alright, and I am coming to dear old "Blighty" to-morrow, and have been marked for the boat.

I am quite happy in spite of the pain, and, of course, I can't walk, and don't think I shall be able to for a long while yet. But I shall pull through in the long run. You would not know me if you saw me now, all my hair cut off and not had a shave for a fortnight, I look like Mr. Fairburn. Well, remember me to all at the Swan and Mr. Moran, and tell him I shall soon be seeing him again, and will go rabbiting. So no more this time. If the Pocklington Paper has anything in about me, keep one for me.

Kind regards, from.

Your loving son,

ARTHUR.

WARNING.

To the Editor of the "Pocklington News." - Pocklington, 30th September, 1916.

Sir,-

Owing to a considerable number of complaints having been received from Special Constables, and private persons, that the following offences are committed on Air Raid nights, viz.:—

1. Striking matches, using flash-lights, cigarette lighters, etc.;

2. Entering rooms, passages, and going upstairs with lights without previously taking precautions to obscure the windows and fanlights;

3. Congregating in the streets;—

In future, all persons so offending will be proceeded against without further notice

All persons are requested not to stand in the streets, but to go into their houses, or out into the country, and to make as little noise as possible.

C. PROCTER, Group Loader, No. 6 Area, Wilton Beacon Division.

POCKLINGTON MEN WOUNDED

News has been received at Pocklington that the following soldiers have been wounded in recent fighting:—'

Sergeant F. C. Dykes, Yorkshire Regiment, son of Mr. and Mrs. Dykes, Market Street, Pocklington, Wounded in the arm and thigh. He is in Firvale Hospital, Sheffield. Sergeant Dykes, who has been mentioned in despatches for gallant conduct, has five brothers in the war.

Rifleman Sydney Gray, K.R.R.O., the son of Mr. W. and Mrs. Gray, Market place, Pocklington, is at present in Cardiff Hospital, wounded in the thigh.

Rifleman Walter Barker, K.R.R.C., son of Mr. G. H. Barker and Mrs. Barker, of Union-street, Pocklington, is also in hospital, suffering from wounds in the arm and leg.

Scout A. Johnson, Yorkshire Regiment, son of Mr. and Mrs. F. Johnson, New-street Pocklington, has been wounded for the second time, and is in hospital.

Private E. Fox, nephew of Mr. J. Magee, Bridge Street, Pocklington, serving with the Northumberland Fusiliers, has been wounded in the chest; and

Private A. Wreghitt, Northumberland Fusiliers, son of Mr. W. Wreghitt, Pocklington, has been wounded in the right shoulder.

30th September, 1916

News has reached Pocklington that Pte William Walker of 5th Battalion Durham Light Infantry, who will attain his 21st birthday on January next, has been wounded in the right thigh. He is now in England and is going on as well as can be expected and his many friends wish for his a speedy and complete recovery.

14th October, 1916

Central Hall, Pocklington.

Mr. Lee begs to remind you that the famous Government picture. "The Battle of the Somme," will be shown on October 26th. 27th, and 28th. Please note the dates. If you intend seeing this wonderful Picture, I strongly advise you to book your seats to-day, as there ' are already 300 seats booked. Application, for seats are coming in from far and near. By booking to-day you will ensure it and not be disappointed when the night arrives. In every town where it has been shown hundreds have been turned away. This is not an ordinary film but a picture of national interest. We have arranged for a Matinee on Friday and Saturday afternoons, owing to the large booking of seats. Prices, 6d. and 1s. 2d., including tax.

Wounded.

Ex-police Constable Harrison has received notice that his son Harold Harrison has been wounded at the Front. Private Harrison went out to France with the 5th Yorks. In the early stages of the War, and has never been fortunate enough to get home on leave. A few days since he received shrapnel wounds in the left arm, and is at present in hospital at Leith, where he is progressing favourably. At the out-break of the War he was apprenticed with Messrs. J.T. Stubbs and Sons, Joiners and Wheelwrights, Pocklington.

21st October, 1916

Wounded.

News has been received that Rifleman Herbert Ezard, King's Royal Rifles, second son of Mr. and Mrs. H. Ezard of London Street, Pocklington., has been wounded in the back. His comrade, Rifleman Harold Buttle, son of Mr. and Mrs. Geo. Buttle. Union. Street, was with him at the time, and assisted in his removal to the Field Dressing Station, where he was attended to, and he in now at the General Hospital, Manchester.

Wounded In Action.

Private George Scaife, 67th Western Scots. Batt. (Vancouver Contingent), Canada, son of Mrs. Scaife, Waterloo Square, Pocklington, was wounded last Saturday, and is at present in a Base Hospital. His injuries are in the leg and ankle.

Wedding.

At the Parish Church, Pocklington, on Wednesday the marriage took place, in the presence of many relatives and friends, of Mr. George Hunter, eldest son of Mr. and Mrs. T. Hunter, Burnby Gates, and Miss Elizabeth. eldest daughter of Mr. and Mrs. T. W. Johnson, of Lockington, near Beverley, the Rev. A. T. Fisher officiated. The bride, who was given away by Mr. T. Warters, was attired in a brown costume with hat to match. Miss Hilda Hunter, sister of the bridegroom and Miss E. Warters (cousin) acted as bridesmaid. They wore brown dresses and brown felt hats, trimmed with blue silk ribbon.

28th October, 1916

LCE.-CORPL. C. B. FLOWER KILLED IN ACTION.

We deeply regret to record the death of Lance-Corporal Henry Bernard Flower, who was attached to the Northumberland Fusiliers. He was of Warter, where he was much beloved by all who knew him. Official intimation has just come to hand that he was killed in action on the 28th September, 1916, aged 22 years.

A Chum writes as follows:— 22424, Lce.-Corpl. H. Martin, "A" Co., 2 Platoon, 13th N.F., B.B.F., France. September 30th.

Dear Mrs. Flower,—

It is with deepest sympathy, and regret, that I write to inform you that your dear son, Bernard, was killed in action on the 28th inst., while assisting to carry out some wounded. He had only been away from me about twenty minutes, and it was a great shock to me on hearing of his death, because, as you know, we have been the best of chums these last fifteen months. His death was instantaneous, therefore it is some consolation to us to know that he suffered no pain. He was a general favourite in our platoon and well-liked in the whole company both by Officers and men. Other platoon friends and myself buried him on September 28th, and on the 29th a friend and myself erected a cross to his memory. He was buried on the Somme battlefield, facing Geudecourt (I don't think the Censor will object to this). I offered a few words of prayer at his grave-side, and, believe me, it is a heavy blow for me, because I have lost the best chum I had, and I shall miss him more as the days go by. His belongings will be forwarded to you in due time.—Yours, in your great bereavement.

HARRY MARTIN.

George Hunter

Pocklington Weekly News, 11th Nov. 1916

"A" Co., 13th N.F., B.E.F., France, 2nd October, 1916.

Dear Mrs. Flower,—

It is with the deepest feelings of regret that I write now to inform you of the death of Lance-Corporal H. B. Flower in action. He was killed in the execution of his duties by a fragment of a shell which burst in the trench. Flower was one of the best men I have had the fortune to know and was universally popular. I believe his great friend, Lance-Corporal Martin has already written you, and I assure you he can feel the loss no more keenly than I do. He has been buried near where he fell, and a cross has been erected by the many friends. It was fortunate that he was killed instantaneously instead of having any pain—those who were near said he did not suffer at all. All the Officers and men of the company join with me in expressing the deepest sympathy with you in your great loss.

Yours very sincerely, ARTHUR PATON Lieut.

Killed In Action

Official intimation has been received by Mrs. Haywood, Snr. of Yapham Mill, that her son, Private Bernard Haywood, of the 10th York and Lancaster Regiment, who was reported missing for so long, was killed in action on or about 25th September, 1915.

4th November, 1916

POCKLINGTON.

Flash Lamps.

Why endanger your own limbs and those of other people, when Flash Lamps CAN be used. The only regulation being, that a piece of tissue paper must be placed between the bulb and the lens, in order to stop the blinding rays. Observance of this will keep you within the Lighting Restrictions Act. Everingham Brothers have a large and varied assortment in stock at prices from 1s. 6d. Or we can Repair and Recharge the old one you have carefully put away until after the War. We also hold a large stock of new and Second-hand Gramophones, and Records. Come and hear the Latest.—Everingham Bros., Railway Street, (Next door to Post Office), Pocklington.— N.B. Flash Lamps must NOT be used out-of-doors on Raid nights.

Light Clothes for Dark Streets.

The advisability of wearing light clothes during our period of enforced darkness in the streets is suggested by a witness at an inquest. A woman was knocked down by a motor-car, and the driver said he was unable to see her in the darkness because she was dressed in black.

11th November, 1916

DRIFFIELD LOCAL TRIBUNAL.

A SUGGESTION THAT COLOURED TROOPS SHOULD BE USED.

At a sitting of the Driffield Urban Tribunal. A member suggested that they should ask the Government to make use of coloured troops rather than draw men from civil occupations from which they can ill be spared. After some discussion it was decided to draw up a formal motion and

Pocklington Weekly News, 11th Nov. 1916

submit it at the next sitting. The clerk was instructed to write to men granted, exemption conditionally, on their joining the Volunteers, requesting them to conform with the conditions. It was stated that a number of men had not complied with the request of Tribunal.

Lighting Prosecution at Pocklington.

Joseph, Layfield, fruiterer, of Market Place, Pocklington, was summoned for exhibiting a naked light from his sitting room in Market Place, Pocklington.

Extra Constable Tinker said that he was on duty in Market Place, Pocklington, at 9-30 p.m. on the 28th September, 1916, in company with Supt. Robson, when he saw a naked light in the defendant's house, which cast a reflection across Market Place on to Mills' shop front owing to the window blind not being properly drawn. He went into the shop and there saw the defendant, and asked him if he would go into the street and have a look at his light. He did so, and then shaded the inside of the glass in the door.

Defendant: How could it be a naked light when there was, a curtain in, front of it?

Witness; The blind was not properly drawn,

Supt. Robson said, the curtain was pulled to the side, and there was a light from the inner room through the shop into the street. A fine of 5s. was imposed.

25th November, 1916

Killed in Action.

We regret to have to announce that Private Stanley Hall, 5th Yorkshires, son of the late Mr. T. and Mrs. Hall, of George Street, Pocklington, is officially reported killed in action on September 17th, his 21st , birthday. Deceased, who was formerly employed at the Post Office, was a member of the local Territorials in camp when war commenced, and has been on active service some time. Much sympathy is expressed with Mrs. Hall in her bereavement.

The Xmas Pudding Effort.

The Military Concert was a big delight, as we anticipated. The Silver Bond and every artiste, from the most experienced to little Miss Nancy Parminter, added honours to their previous successes. Wretched weather prevailed both on the flag Day and for the Concert; but notwithstanding this the result was so satisfactory that enough money has been raised to provide a plum pudding for every man in the Battalion to which our Pocklington men are attached, and there will be a balance sufficient also to provide many more puddings for their comrades. We knew the Pocklington people would not forget the brave boys at the Front.

The Light that Failed.

Accidents will certainly happen, but it was somewhat unfortunate on Monday night that those in authority did not take the precaution to have sufficient gas in the holders at the Gas Works to tide them over any leakage that might be expected during the installation of the new retorts. The result was that before the Concert had proceeded an hour the light failed; and had it not been that the Committee were able to secure lamps and candles at once, the proceedings would have had to be abandoned before half the programme was completed. A few minutes before the gas failed news reached the room that the supply of gas was running short, whereupon an announcement was made to that effect, which prevented any panic. Both the audience and the performers took the matter very good-naturedly, and the room presented more the appearance of a theatre than a concert hall.

The public are also entitled to the exercise of more care at the Gas Works than has been shown lately. Quite early last Sunday night the gas was lowered to such an extent that several lights in the houses were entirely extinguished. Now many people leave their gas lights burning when they go out, and many more have gas stoves burning from which, if the gas is out off, serious explosions might occur.

A Boon for the Soldiers.

We understand that a recreation room is shortly to be opened in Pocklington for the benefit of the soldiers from the Camp, where they will be able to buy light refreshment end have an opportunity of writing letters, reading, and indulging in music every evening. A Committee of ladies has been formed to carry out the details of the scheme. The idea is to give the men an opportunity of getting away for a time from the routine of camp life, and to surround thorn to a certain extent with the amenities of home.

Victims of the Darkness.

We continue to hear frequently of people who come to grief owing to the entire absence of light in the streets. Last Monday night was notorious in this respect. If Phlebotomy was still in repute, there would be no need to call in the Doctor; all the patient need do would be to step out-side his house and attempt to walk the length of the street without a light, and the darkness would complete the operation.

Two Interesting Shop Windows.

There are two windows in Pocklington attractive at the present time. Messrs. J. T. Everingham and Sons have on view several souvenirs of the war, ranging from a German helmet to a pair of spurs, and including a shell and a hand grenade; whilst there is on view in Mr. Whitehead's window the vellum Testimonial from the Royal Humane Society presented to Mr. Herbert Fisher last Monday night for gallantry in saving life.

Gone at Last

We are glad to observe that the advertisement of German goods so conspicuously displayed in Railway Street, to which we drew attention in this column some weeks since, has been removed during the lest few days.

Stampeding the Tribunals?

We are informed that at a recent meeting of a County Appeal Tribunal the Military were represented in quite strong force. What does this mean? Many people think it was for the purpose of putting pressure on the Tribunal: but, if so. we hardly think this is a method which will commend itself to the public. Tribunals, both Local and Appeal, were constituted to act impartially as between the public and the Army, they should not be subjected to any influence from one side or the other, but should decide every case brought before them strictly on the evidence presented.

Reports of Petrol Consumption.

Those of our readers who possess or are interested in motor cars ought to secure a copy of "The Autocar" of the 16th November, which contains a very useful summarised and tabulated report of returns as to the number of miles per gallon obtained by readers of that Paper concerning 290 different types of cars. Particulars are given of the H.P. and name of each car, bore and stroke, number of seats, type of body, average petrol consumption M.P.G., and also the best petrol consumption M.P.G., together with the make of carburettor and general remarks. The collection and tabulation of the information has taken three months.

2nd December, 1916

BISHOP WILTON.

Wounded In Action.

Sergeant Francis Norman Wilson, third son of Mr. W. H. Wilson, of Garrowby Lodge, Bishop Wilton, was wounded in the early stages of the fighting on the Somme. He is 21 years of up. enlisted in the Royal Field Artillery on November 27th, 1914, and had been on active service for twelve months before receiving wounds in the leg; he has now recovered and is engaged in training recruits. Sergeant Wilson's father is a well-known farmer. He founded the Thirsk Agricultural Society, of which he was secretary until he left the district eight years ago, and was also a member of the Thirsk District Council; later he removed to Poppleton, and now occupies a farm on the estate of Sir Mark Sykes, Bart., MP. Two cousins of Sergt. Wilson are serving in the Army.

More Honours for Pocklington

We informed that Capt, F. W. Robson, the son of Mr. T. Robson of Pembroke Lodge who was quite recently awarded the Distinguished Service Order, has now been offered and has accepted the post of Commandant of the 50th Divisional School of Instruction with the temporary rank of Lieutenant Colonel. We offer him our heartiest congratulations.

WAR HONOURS

A Special Supplement of the London Gazette dated Saturday contained the following awards :-

Captain Frederick William Robson, Yorkshire Regiment, was awarded the D.S.O. for conspicuous gallantry in action. He assumed command of his battalion, and carried out his duty with the greatest courage and initiative. He set a splendid example to his men throughout operations.

Second Lieut. (temp. Lieut.) Edward Moore Robson, Yorkshire Regiment, received the Military Cross for conspicuous gallantry in action. He took over the battalion front, established connection with the Brigade on his right and carrying out his work with great courage and initiative. Both the above Officers are sons of Mr. Thomas Robson, solicitor, Pembroke Lodge, Pocklington.

Home for a Holiday

The hearts of some parents in Pocklington were cheered by the unexpected arrival this week of their sons from the Front. We are glad to hear that leave has been granted to those who have been taking part in the great push on the Somme. The boys richly deserve it.

SHOOTING AT CARRIER PIGEONS
MILITARY WARNING

Admiral Nicholson, commanding the East Coast of England, has issued a notice warning people who kill, wound, or molest any carrier or homing pigeon, or take such pigeon and neglect to inform the military or authorities, that they will be summarily dealt with.

The notice states that carrier pigeons have failed to return or have returned to their lofts wounded.

9th December, 1916

Killed in Action.

Official news has been received that Pte. Sydney Scaife, Northumberland Fusiliers, third son of Mrs. T. Scaife, Cab proprietor, Chapmangate, Pocklington, was killed in action on November 27th. He was 26 years of age, enlisted last February, and had been as the front five months. Previous to enlistment he was employed as porter on the N.E. Railway at Pocklington. Much sympathy is expressed with his mother and family in their bereavement.

Pocklington Co-operative Society Ltd.

We are advised that the Royal Commission on the Sugar Supply are contemplating reducing the supplies of Sugar to the Trade by another 10 per cent, on January 1st 1917. This is in addition to the 10 percent reduction announced in advertisement appearing on this page, making a 20 percent, reduction on the already inadequate supplies now available. Our scheme of Sugar Tickets has had a very favourable reception, and whilst we hope that our supplies will be sufficient to meet requirements, in view of the further curtailment of supplies foreshadowed we must use every care and we appeal to our Members to restrict their consumption to the lowest possible limits. The reduction announced above apply equally to the trade.

23rd December, 1916

IN MEMORIAM.

JOHNSON—In loving memory of our dear son, Gunner Henry Johnson, R.F.A. killed on December 26th 1915.

In the Pocklington graveyard.
Where the tree their branches were.
Lies a loving son and brother
In his cold and silent grave

We think of him in silence,
And his name we often call,
Though there's nothing left to answer
But his photo on the wail.

A faithful son, so true and kind.
No one on earth like him we find;
One year has passed, but none can tell
The loss of the one we loved so well.

Silent love is always truest;
At his post he met his fate.
As he answered his country's call.

Sweet be thy rest, thy memory dear,
Tis sweet to breathe thy name.
In life we loved you very dear,
In death we do the same.

We have to mourn the loss of one.

We did our best to save;

Beloved on earth, regretted gone

Remembered in the grave.

From his loving Mother, Father, Sisters and Brothers.

23rd December, 1916

FOOD CONTROL.

REGULATION OF MEALS

MEATLESS DAYS TO BE ENFORCED.

The Board of Trade on Tuesday made an Order under the Defence of the Realm Regulations regulating meals in hotels, restaurants, and' other places of public eating. The operative provisions: of the Order are as follows:—

(a) Except -with the express authority of the Board of Trade, no articles of food be served by or consumed in any inn, or hotel, restaurant, refreshment house, boarding house, club, mess, canteen, hall, or any other place of public eating, in the form of or as part of a meal, consisting of more than three courses if the meal begins between the hours of 6 p.m. and 9-30 p.m., or of more than two courses if the meal begins at any other time. For the purpose of this provision plain cheese shall not be regarded as a course; and hors d'oeuvre (not containing any preserved or freshly cooked fish, meat, poultry, or game) dessert (consisting only of raw and dried fruit), and soup prepared in the ordinary way, which does not contain any meat, poultry, or game in a solid form, shall each be computed as half a course.

(b) Any person acting in contravention of the above recited provision as applied by this Order is guilty of a summary offence against the Defence of the Realm (Regulations. The Order' applies to the ' United Kingdom of. Great Britain and Ireland, and comes into force on December 18th, 1916.

30th December, 1916

A LETTER OF THANKS.

France,

Thursday, December 14th, 1916.

Sir,—We hope you will give us a little space in your valuable paper to thank the people of Pocklington for the nice parcels we have received. We think it is very good of them to think of us out here; we know they will have had a great deal of trouble gathering subscriptions and packing the parcels up and sending them off. So we thank the kind and generous people who gave towards such nice parcels, and the kind friends who sent them off to us. From three of the Boys.

F. ALLISON, A. DYKES (Minnie), G SCAIFE.

F.A. also thanks the kind and good-hearted people of Everingham for the Xmas parcel he received with the money they gave towards it. - It shows someone has a kind thought for the boys doing their bit. He also thanks the kind ladies who collected for them and sent them off, for it would not be done without a lot of trouble, but he hopes they will be rewarded in the long run for their good deeds.

And we are thanking you, Mr. Whitehead, for letting us put it in your paper, but we are thanking before we get it in, but still we know what kind of a business gentleman you are for we have lived in the good old town long enough to know that, and hope to come back to it. So we again thank you for going to the trouble of printing this letter. We get a copy of your paper every week out here, and it is read with the keenest interest.

December 17th.

Dear Sir,—Will you kindly allow me a small space in your paper to express my thanks to the people of Pocklington for the nice Parcel of Xmas Cheer which I have received. I am confident the other Boys along with me will appreciate the kindness of all who have so generously subscribed and taken such on interest towards our comforts. Again thanking you and wishing you all a bright and prosperous New Year.

I remain, Yours sincerely, Lce.-Corpl. BROOK, 56, M.G. Coy.

———

6th January, 1917

LETTERS OF THANKS.

France, 24-12-16.

Dear Mr. Editor,—

Will your allow me through the medium of your valuable paper, to thank the people of Pocklington for the parcel which they so kindly sent to me. I received it early this morning, in good condition, and the contents be very useful and highly appreciated. By yours sincerely. Private C. EZARD, 56670, R.A.M.C., att. 1st. Mons, B.E.F.

———

December 26th, 1916,

Dear Sir,— '

I have the pleasure in writing to thank the Pocklington people, one and all, for their kindness in sending all the boys of that town a parcel this Christmas time, and I can assure you that we are all very pleased to have lived to accept them, and that, such things as these are looked forward to by the boys out hero, because there is nothing that puts more life into us than a parcel or any news from our own town. Well, I thought I could do no more than write to you, seeing that everyone has had a hand in this, to thank them one and all and I can say that every one of the Pocklington Boys are highly satisfied with what they have received. We all join in wishing good luck for all in the New Year, and we all hope to be back in the dear old town next Christmas. Again thanking you, one and all, for the kindness you have all shown to us out here.

Yours sincerely. Corpl. BECKETT. 5th Yorkshire Regt., France.

———

Somewhere in France December 21-16.

Dear Sir,—

Just a few lines to you, hoping that you will convey thanks to the inhabitants of Pocklington through the columns of your popular paper, which I am pleased to receive every week and quite a cheering paper, too, to all boys from Pocklington, who like to know all they can about the old town. Well, I hope you will give my best thanks to all the people who subscribed and sent out to us a nice Xmas parcel, which was much appreciated. This is my second Christmas here, and I have been serving in the 1st West Riding R.G.A. I joined the Regiment shortly after the outbreak of war, and after about three months training left England on the 16th of April, 1915. I have been through all the fighting on the Somme Front, and pleased to say I am still going well, and I soon hope to be back amongst old friends. Again, I wish to thank all for their kindness.

Yours truly, Driver E. W. THOMPSON.

To the Editor of the "Weekly News."

December 26th. Dear Sir,—I shall be very pleased If you will, through your paper, kindly thank the good friends in Pocklington for so kindly sending the nice and useful parcel to cheer us up, which I received with many thanks.

Yours –truly, E. BLISSETT, 280. Army Troop Coy., Royal Engineers. B.E.F., France.

13th January, 1917

INTERESTING PRESENTATION OF THE D.C.M., AT POCKLINGTON.

On Thursday evening, an interesting presentation took place in the Central Hall, Pocklington. when Sergt. F. C. Dykes, of Pocklington, had the D.C.M. pinned on his breast.

The presentation was organised by the members of the Pocklington Urban District Council, who took their place on the platform, immediately followed by Sergt. F. Dykes, D.C.M., to the strains of "For he's a jolly good fellow."

Mr. A. Summerson said it only came to his knowledge the previous day that Sergt. F Dykes was in the town, and that he had not been officially presented with the medal that he had so gallantly won (Applause). He also learned that as a loyal townsman he preferred to have the presentation made by a fellow-townsman. The difficulty that dawned upon him (Mr. Summerson) was the question of a room, and then he remembered from previous experience that Mr Fred Lee would assist them in every possible way. Mr. Lee's answer was that he would only be too pleased to grant them the use of his room during the interval in the Cinema performance, for such a useful and gallant purpose. He thought there was hardly a town of the size of Pocklington in the whole of the British Isles that had gained such distinction as Pocklington during the present war. The King has been pleased to decorate Captain, now Lieut. Col. F. W. Robson: he has conferred the military Cross upon Lieut. Ed M Robson; Private E. Kirby had been awarded the D.C.M.: he believed Sergt. Francis had won a medal, and the other was that won by Sergt. F. C. Dykes, to whom it was their privilege to present the medal that evening. Sergt. Dykes comes of a military family - his father served a good, many years in the Army, went through the Zulu War, and has no less than six sons fighting for his King and country at the present time. That was a record that any man might be justly proud of. The 5th Yorkshires, of which Sergt. Dykes is a member, were attached to the Northumbrian Brigade, and at one time that Brigade was the only one that stood between the German Army and Calais. (Applause.) When the history of the war comes to be written they will find that the 5th Yorkshires have won unheard of distinction by their gallantry. On one side of the medal there is the King's initials and the inscription "For bravery in the field, and on the other side you have a very good portrait of file King, and round the edge this inscription: "12093, Sergt. F. C. Dykes, 5th Yorkshire Territorial Forces." He therefore, in the unavoidable absence of Mr. Procter, the chairman of the Council, had much pleasure in asking Councillor,. J. W. Laister, the vice-chairman, 'to make the presentation. (Loud 'Applause.) Councillor J. W. Laister said it was with mingled feelings of pleasure and regret that he occupied the position that night. Mr. Procter would have had the greatest possible pleasure in making the presentation, but his enforced absence over the local Alps, in such inclement weather, made the time, of his return uncertain, and he was therefore unable to be present. Personally, he thought Pocklington had done nobly throughout the war. There was its gifts to the Belgians, to the Red Cross, and Plum Pudding Fund, and other deserving objects. Mr. Dykes had six sons serving in the Army, and he thought he came next with four. (Applause.) He would not like that moment to pass without saying how deeply we all sympathize with those families who' have lost sons in the great battle. They also extended their sympathy to those who have been wounded, and sincerely trust that they will soon recover from their wounds. It gave him the greatest possible pleasure to pin that Distinguished Conduct Medal to the breast of Sergt. Dykes, hoping that he would live long to wear it, and still attain greater acts of gallantry and noble deeds.

"God Save the King" was next sung, Sergt. Dykes standing at the salute, which was most impressive.

Sergeant Dykes, in a few words, suitably responded.

———

It was Sydney Smith who was responsible for the remark that "His whole life has been passed like a razor - in hot water or a scrape."

———

Thanks for Christmas Parcel.

Private Joe Eagan, of the Northumberland Fusiliers, writes to thank the Pocklington friends for the splendid parcel he received from them at Christmas. He is in hospital in France, through illness, and the parcel he received was most acceptable. We trust this popular young soldier will have a speedy recovery.

Central Hall, Pocklington.

The Celebrated Picture House. Mr. Fred Lee begs to announce that at a greatly increased cost he has booked the Famous Government Picture, "The King Visits his Armies in France," which will be shown On January 18th, 19th, and 20th. Mr. Lee has not been able to show the Picture earlier, owing to its great demand and popularity, although it has been booked three months. It is a Film 2,500 feet in length, and should be seen by everybody. The rest of the miscellaneous programme will be of the highest quality. Prices of Admission, 7d. and 4d. Reserved Seats booked, which will be necessary on this occasion. 1s. including Tax. Plan at Mr-Lee's Tobacco Shop only. The Public who have seen this Government Picture say it is far superior to the Picture, "The Battle of the Somme." Remember the bookings then, and book early.

20th January, 1917

LETTERS OF THANKS.

Mrs. Suddaby, The Bank, Pocklington, has received the following letters of thanks from Pocklington men now serving in France:—

B.E.F., France,
December 22, 1916.

Dear Mrs.

Will you please convey my best thanks to the people of Pocklington for the lovely Xmas parcel they so kindly sent me. The contents were very much enjoyed, and I would mention that I especially appreciate the kindness of the people who worked and raised funds in order to distribute such parcels.

Yours sincerely,

JOHN P. DAY.

Private JOHN P. DAY, of Pocklington, of the 10th (Service) E.Y., Hull Commercials, who has been wounded whilst serving at the Front.

———

Saturday, 6th Jan., 1917.

Dear Madam,—

Just a few lines, thanking you and all the kind ladies of Pocklington for the Xmas parcel which I received on the 4th; also for the kind wishes. I am sure it gives me great pleasure to think that although so far away from the old town we are not forgotten.

Wishing you all a Happy New Year.
Yours sincerely, Rfm. C. V. WAITE.

———

Gunner G. W. Javerley writes as follows:—"I received a welcome parcel on December 24th, all safe and sound, for which please accept my grateful thanks. Wishing you a Happy Now Year. I remain, Yours truly, G. W. JAVERLEY.

A LETTER OF THANKS.

10,884, D Company, 6th Batt., E. York Regiment, B.E.F., France.

January 4th, 1917.

Dear Sir —

Will you kindly allow me a small space in your valuable paper to thank the many friends in Pocklington for the splendid parcel, which I received when I arrived back. I am sure it is very good to know that we are thought of so much. I happened to be one of the lucky ones and was at home for Xmas, and I am sure the many friends I have nearly killed me with kindness, and I shall never forget the Xmas of 1916. I often have your Paper sent out and enjoy reading it very much. Thanking you all once again, and the Compliments of the Season to All, I remain,

Yours truly,

Pte. J. SELLERS.

LETTER FROM A POCKLINGTON MAN AT THE FRONT.

Corpl. Scaife, R., 35065, B Coy., 5th Platoon, 10th Batt., K.O.Y.L.I., British Expeditionary Force.

January 3rd, 1917,

Dear Mr. Editor —

If you will allow me a small space in your weekly paper, which I was always glad to receive weekly when in Blighty, but I only get it now and then, and it is always very acceptable in the trenches to see the little goings on in the town, and also to see if there are any letters from any of the boys out here, as we do not meet often. During my length of time out here I have only met one Pocklington lad since leaving the Base and that was Harry Skelton, who is in the same Battalion as I—and then we do not often meet. Of course when we do we tell each other the news we receive from the old town.

No doubt you kind people will have heard the sad news concerning the death of my brother, and I am sorry to say we never saw each other the whole time out here, and at times we were only two to three miles from each other. Our Battalion was out for a short rest and I got to know where he was in the line and wanted to see him. I asked permission to go and see him, which was granted, and I went, only to find the sad news, but

I got news as to where he was buried and went the next day. I am glad to say he was put away with all the care a British Tommy could wish, and is in one of the prettiest Cemeteries I have yet seen in France, which is called the British Cemetery, where thousands of British heroes are from the battle fields.

I have up to the present been in several battles and hot fighting and have come out without a scratch. All the boys in my company are all happy and cheerful and when in the line work like Turks, and at this time there is work to be done for their own benefit, and we have had a fearful lot of rain which makes the trenches above the knee in mud and water, and it is not very comfortable, and the boys all say we have Johnny on his last legs, and do their work singing and always in a merry mood.

Hoping you won't be troubled with the Zepps. any more in England. Fritz is No Bon with his wings out here, we beat him upside down.

I will now close, wishing all the inhabitants the best of luck, and love to all home.

I am, Yours sincerely, REG SCAIFE, Cpl.

27th January, 1917

LETTERS OF THANKS

Jan 3rd, 1917. My dear Miss Robson,—

Just a line to thank you and the kind friends of Pocklington for the parcel I received on the 28th December. You may think me a long time before I write to thank you for it, but I have not had much time to spare, but I have done so at the first opportunity. I hope you and all the kind friends of the town have had a happy Christmas and will have a prosperous New Year, for we have had a very lovely time of it out here, which, can only be expected, for it does not matter where you go, you are up to the knees in mud, but we are looking forward for being at home before another one comes round; if not we shall have to keep smiling same as we have to do now. I shall have to close now, as I am going to a fatigue, but before doing so, I will thank you once again for the parcel which you were so good to send me.

I remain, Your sincere Friend, Gnr. ALFRED ROWNTREE.

———

H.M.S. Royal Arthur, c-o. G.P.O., London. 11-1-17.

Dear Mr. and Mrs. Perry,

No doubt you will think it very unkind of me not writing to you before this to thank you for the Parcel you sent to me for Xmas, but I was at a loss to know who sent it, as there was no note to say who it came from. It is with pleasure I thank all the ladies for their kindness to think of those who are away from their homes fighting for their King and country. It is for a just cause, and we will do our best to save the Flag that has floated over every wave—the Union Jack of Old England. I must now conclude, thanking you all once more for your kindness.   I remain, Yours sincerely, W. ANDREWS.

———

A1 Ward, Billinge Military Hospital, nr. Wigan, 27-12-16.

Dear Madam —

Just a few lines to express my sincerest thanks for the splendid Xmas Parcel from the people of Pocklington, which I was pleased to receive. Its nice to know that we are thought of by those at home, and I personally appreciate their endeavour to make our Xmas a happy one. We have had a decent time here this Xmas, as every effort has been made to make our lot a happy one. Again thanking you, and wishing you all a Happy New Year, I beg to remain, Yours sincerely, J. W. EASTWOOD.

———

Hut 12, F Company, 7th Training Res., Rugeley, Staffs. December 20th, 1916.

Dear Mrs. Perry,—

Please excuse my taking the liberty of writing to you, but I just want to thank, through you, all the kind people of Pocklington who have sent all of us boys your best wishes and a present this Xmas time.

Although I am at present better situated than the boys in the trenches, yet my thanks are just as hearty as those and when Fate decrees that I am to go back out yonder, my only wish, is that I may go with the same spirit and determination that has characterised all the Pocklington Boys departure.

Thanking you all again, I remain, A Pocklingtonian, C. CYRIL STATHER.

10th February, 1917

LETTERS OF THANKS.

France,

15-1-17.

Dear Madam,—

I wish to thank you and the inhabitants of Pocklington for the Christmas Parcel which you so kindly sent., I received it in good condition, and I most heartily enjoyed the contents. You will be pleased to know that on the part of the line I am in we beat the enemy in all his scientific appliances for modern warfare.

I am serving with the 2nd Tyneside Scottish, and this is the first Christmas I have had in France, and I think I can safely say that if all goes well it will be my last. I am convinced that the Germans are playing a losing game, and those in authority know it but they keep on struggling in the hope of getting such peace conditions as will satisfy their people. What a difference from their attitude and expectations at the beginning.

I may say I have had some very exciting times out here, and I am pleased to say that so far. I have come through safe and that I am able to pride myself in taking part in the most colossal adventure the world has ever seen.

As you will be aware, we are allowed to say very little, so I must now close. Again thanking you one and all.

Yours very sincerely,

R. M. STUBBS.

Mrs. Perry.

In the Field, 14-1-17.

To the Editor of the "Pocklington News."

Sir,—I am writing in the hope that you will allow me to use your paper as a medium in which to thank the People of Pocklington for so kindly remembering those serving in this part of the world.

The parcel did not arrive in time for Xmas Day but it was very welcome nevertheless. We are at present in a rather isolated part of Macedonia, and anything in, the way of a luxury is much appreciated. We hope that the good people will not be required to provide Xmas fare for the troops for Xmas, 1917. We trust that we shall have Peace, with Victory, some time before 26-12-17. Best wishes for the New Year.

Believe me to be, Yours sincerely, HARRY ROWLEY.

17th February, 1917

A Letter of Thanks.

Dear Madam.—I take this my first opportunity of sending my sincere thanks for parcel I received on Christmas Day). We are in the trenches at present and I must say it was most acceptable and appreciated very much indeed. We don't get the good things out here like we do at home, but wish your kindness things were more like home. Well, I will close my short letter, once more thanking you and all the lady workers of Pocklington for the good work. Wishing you all the compliments of the season.

Yours truly, Rfm. G. H. BUTTLE.

24th February, 1917

DEATH OF CORPL. TOM FISHER.

With deep regret the news was received in Pocklington of the death, of Corpl. T. Fisher: son of the Vicar, Rev. A. T. Fisher, and Mrs. Fisher, The Vicarage, Pocklington, which occurred on Wednesday morning at Barrow-in-Furness. Educated at Pocklington Grammar School, he shortly after war commenced enlisted in the 9th Border Regiment, with which he served in Salonika where he suffered from an attack of malarial fever which necessitated his removal to a military hospital at Malta, and from thence to England. It was thought he had completely, recovered and visited home last Christmas. On returning to duty and when studying for a Commission, he caught a chill. which developed into pneumonia and ended in death, Just entering manhood his early demise cuts off a distinctly promising life. The interment takes place at Yapham this (Friday) afternoon. Owing to early postal arrangements we are compelled to hold over a report of the Military Funeral which takes place at Yapham, as we go to press.

A comrade in the regiment-; named F. W. Read, writing to Mr. F. Scaife, of Neswick Villa, Pocklington, says:— "I am very glad to hear that Tom has quite recovered, and I hope they don't send him out again, because he has done his bit if he never does any more."

The above letter arrived on the day of the death of Mr. Fisher.

3rd March, 1917

A LETTER OF THANKS

Gunner Geo. Giles, Nv. 113541, R.G A.

Feb. 18th, 1917.
To the Editor of the "Pocklington News."

Dear Sir,—I am just writing to ask your kind permission for a little space in your weekly paper (which I receive every week, and pass an hour or so good reading) to thank the inhabitants of Pocklington for the parcel which I received on the 17th. It is very thoughtful of them, seeing that I have not been amongst you for a matter of 12 years, and I am not forgotten, but still I am one of the Pocklington lads

Again thanking you all, and with the best good wishes, I remain, Yours truly, GEO. GILES.

FUNERAL OF L-CORPL. THOMAS W. FISHER.

Amidst many manifestations of sympathy the funeral took place last Friday, with full military honours, of L-Corpl. Thomas Wilfred Fisher, son of the vicar and Mrs. Fisher, the Vicarage, Pocklington, whose death occurred on Wednesday morning at Barrow-in-Furness. Educated at Pocklington Grammar School, he shortly after war commenced enlisted in the 9th Border Regiment, with which he served in France before proceeding to Salonika where he suffered from, an attack of malarial fever which necessitated his removal to a military hospital at Malta, and from thence to England. It was thought he had completely recovered and visited home last Christmas. On returning to duty and when studying for a Commission, he caught a chill which developed into pneumonia and ended in death. Just entering manhood his early demise cuts off a distinctly promising life.

The remains arrived in Pocklington by train in the afternoon, where they were met at the station by a detachment of the Durham T.R.'s, under Col. F. C. Cheverton, Major Longden, Captain Giles, and Regt. Sergt.-Major Toes, the firing party being in charge of Sergt. McKenzie. Headed by the fine band of the Regiment playing the "Dead March" in "Saul," the coffin, placed on a carriage and covered with the Union Jack, was conveyed to the West entrance of the Parish Church, and preceded by the choir, the coffin was carried into the Church by soldiers, where a solemn service was conducted by the Rev. J. Coates, in the presence of a large and sympathetic gathering The 90th Psalm was chanted and the hymns "For all the Saints" and "On the Resurrection morning'" were sung, Miss Ottley presiding at the organ. After the service the procession re-formed and the cortege passed through George-street, the band again playing the "Dead March," and also at Yapham, where in the Churchyard the Rev. John Fisher, brother of the deceased, pronounced the Committal portion of the service, and the hymn "Abide with me" was sung. Three Volleys were fired over the grave, and with fine effect the bugles sounded the "Last Post." The chief mourners were:—The Vicar and Mrs. Fisher, the Rev. John Fisher (brother), Cyril Fisher (brother), Misses Eva, Ellen, Olive, and Lilian Fisher, Mrs. and Miss Tonge Smith, Miss N. Hodgson, Dr. Tonge Smith. Staff-Surgeon A.R. Fisher R.N., and Vice Consul G. A. Fisher, brothers, were prevented by official duties from being present.

Among others present in the church or at Yapham were Mr. T. Robson, Mr. H. S. Powell, Mr. F. Scaife, Mr. and Mrs. Mansfield Harrison, Mr. and Mrs. Suddaby, Mrs. Thomas, Mrs. Lewis, Mrs. Grant, Miss Grant, Mrs. Brigham, Miss McConkey, Mr. and Miss Wilkinson, Mrs. and Miss Skinner, Mrs. Sargeant, Mr. and Mrs. Boyden, Mr. McCartney, Mr. Linfoot, Mrs. Robinson, Mr. Sands. Mr. Thomas, Mr. Perry, and the Boys from the Pocklington' School, Mr. and Mrs. Flint, Mr. and Miss Petch, Mrs. Stewart, Mr. and Mrs. Toder, Mr. and Mrs. J. Matthews, Mr. Askwith, Mr. R. R. Young, Mr. Bower, Mrs. Duggleby, Miss Precious, Miss Skinn, Mr. and Mrs. W. W, Cattle, Mrs. A. G. Nelson, Miss H. Theakston, Miss Stewart, Mr. J. H. Brown, Mr. Stenton, Mr., and Mrs. G. Harrison, Mrs. C. Procter, Mrs. Barnes, Mrs. E. Skinner, Mrs. T. Scaife, Mrs. Meynell, Mrs. Lockerbie, Miss Shepherdson, Mr. T. Towle, Mr. Connell (Sancton), Miss Beal (Rosewalden), Mrs, Dunn, Misses Braithwaite, Mrs. R. Tinson, Mrs. Southcoat, Miss Lister, Miss Flowers, Mr. Mamet, Mr. Jas. Johnson, Miss Laister, Mrs. Hatfield, Mrs. Wilson, Mrs, Stather, Miss Ottley, Misses Silburn, Mrs. J. T. Stubbs, Miss Clark, Miss Bell, and many others, including the choirmen, Messrs, H. E. Currell, W. Coupland, R. Gray, E, J. Lamb, A.G. Nelson, P. Scaife, A. Skinner, and W. E. Todd.

There were several beautiful floral tributes. The coffin bore the inscription:--"Corporal T. W. Fisher, died February 21st, aged 23 years."

A comrade in the regiment, named F. W. Read, writing to Mr. P. Scaife, of Neswick Villa, Pocklington, says:-

I am very glad to hear that Tom has quite recovered, and I hope they don't send him out again, because he has done his bit if he never does any more." The above letter arrived on the day of death of Mr. Fisher.

10th March, 1917

BISHOP WILTON.

Lieut. Gerard Peters Dies at the Front

Sec.-Lieut, Gerard Peters, who is reported to have died on Active Service in France, on February 24th, was the youngest son of the Rev. and Mr. E. Peters. Bishop Wilton Vicarage. Born in 1891, he was educated at St. Peter's School, York. Choosing the Law as his profession, he served his Articles with Mr. H. S. Powell, solicitor, of Pocklington, and in June, 1914, was placed among the thirteen successful candidates who obtained Honours at the final Examination held by the Law Society, and was admitted a solicitor the same year. He was also awarded a prize by the Yorkshire Law Society. He accepted a post in the office of Messrs. Collyer, Bristow, and Co., 4, Bedford Bow, London, which he relinquished in October, 1916, in order to join the Inns of Court O.T.C. After undergoing the usual training at a Cadet School Berk Lansted, he headed the list of successful candidates at the Final Examination required by the War Office, and received his Commission in the 4th Gloucester Regiment in the following September. Lieut. Peters went out to the Front only in January last. His Commanding Officer writes: "It is a great loss to the whole Company. Officers and men. He was a splendid soldier, always willing to do his utmost to help, and I shall miss him more than I can say." There will be a Memorial Service in Bishop Wilton Church on Sunday evening next, at 6.30, conducted by the Rev. Lieut. Col. Cheverton.

17th March, 1917

Local Hero gains Military Medal

News has been received that Bombardier Ernest William Brown, a native of Bishop Wilton, has been awarded the Military Medal for meritorious conduct in putting out a fire in an ammunition dump in France on November 18th last, thereby saving a serious explosion. The Bombardier is well known in Pocklington and district, having served an apprenticeship with Mr. Chas. Stather, draper, before taking an engagement at Hull. He afterwards enlisted in the Royal Field Artillery with which he was called up off reserve on 1st August 1914, being wounded in October the same year. After recovering from his wound he served in Egypt and France, winning his medal on the Somme front. He has been twice previously recommended for distinction, once for assisting a wounded officer out of danger, and later for working a gun. He was over on leave in January last. His brother-in-law, Driver Frank Walker, whom many will remember as driver of Mr. G. Todd's, grocer, motor-van, is at present acting as despatch rider in France.

PRIVATE C W. MOORE, OF SHIPTONTHORPE, REPORTED KILLED,

IS NOW A PRISONER OF WAR IN GERMANY.

Our readers will rejoice to learn that Mrs. C. Moore, of Shiptonthorpe, has received a letter from her son (reported to be killed by a sniper last November), who is now a prisoner of war in Germany. The following are copies of letters forwarded to for publications :—

B.E.F. December 4th, 1916.

Dear Mrs. Moore, - It grieves me very much to inform you that your son, 21548 Pte. C. W. Moore, was killed on November 13th, shot by a sniper, and it is little consolation to know his death was instantaneous. His effects will be forwarded to you in due course through the necessary military channels. Offering you my deepest sympathy in your sad bereavement, and the loss of a gallant soldier who always did his duty.

H. HANN, 2nd—Lieut. O.C., A Coy.

Shiptonthorpe, Market Weighton.

Dear Sir, - Will you please publish in your paper this week the following :-

My son Private C. W. Moore, E. Yorks., was reported missing on the 13th November last by War Office. I also had a letter from his Commanding Officer, which I enclose. Great was our surprise on Monday morning to have a letter from my son saying he was alive and well, but a prisoner of war in Germany, and asked for food, shirt, socks, etc. to be sent. I feel so thankful it has not turned out as his Officer wrote last November.

Yours truly, (Mrs.) C. MOORE.

7th April, 1917

Home on Leave.

Private Wm. Harrison, of the East Yorks. Regiment, who is now over on leave from Salonica, joined His Majesty's forces in January, 1907, and shortly afterwards went to India, where he remained eight years, and came home with his regiment in 1915. He then went out to France, where he remained twelve months, and afterwards was drafted to Salonica, where he has been fifteen months up to coming home on fifteen days' leave. Private Harrison is a successful knock-about comedian and has spent his spare time entertaining troops behind the firing line and is extremely popular with both the Officers and men of his regiment. He went through the first and second battle of Ypres and Loos without injury. Our local hero also entertains wounded soldiers at the front. He is having a fine old time at Pocklington (amongst his numerous friends, after his tedious and exciting journey from Salonica. On Wednesday evening, Private Harrison gave a couple of turns at the Central Hall, Pocklington, singing with great success "The Tanks that broke the ranks out in Picardy," and that fine patriotic song "We are under the same old flag." His success was such as to merit a re-engagement for the following night, and he is also expected to give a turn at the Victoria Hall social on Saturday night.

Lt.-Col. F. W. Robson and Private Ensor Johnson, of the Yorkshire Regiment, are also over on leave from France, and their many friends are delighted to see them looking so well.

7th April, 1917

POCKLINGTON LADS IN MESOPOTAMIA.

Machine Gun Coy., Mesopotamia Ex. Force. D. February 12th, 1917

Dear Sir, - We shall be very grateful if you will allow us through your weekly paper to tender our thanks to the people of Pocklington for so kindly remembering us at Christmas. The parcels arrived here on February 10th, and were in excellent condition considering the distance they had travelled. Since we came out here we have had an exciting time. It is very queer climate—very hot during the day and as the sun sets it is time for overcoats. There are no trees or hedges to see, just bare desert land. Things are going on very favourable out here, although we cannot say what we would like to, but the Turks are getting some stick now. We are looking forward to the time when it is all over and we shall be coming back again to good old "Blighty." We shall have to draw to a close as time is precious. Thanking you again, one and all, we remain

Yours faithfully,

Gunner H BARKER, 34330.
Gunner T. W. RIPPON, 34339.

21st April, 1917

A Local Soldier Missing.

From the Infantry Record Office, York, Mr. and Mrs. Jessop, Alma-terrace, Pocklington, have received notification that no further news has been received of their son, Private Herbert Jessop, East Yorks. Regiment, who left Withernsea for France, and has been missing since July 23rd last. The Army Council presume that his death took place on that date. He was 29 years of age, and was engaged in agricultural work in this neighbourhood up to his enlistment. One brother is now serving in France.

Wounded in Action.

News was received on Wednesday morning that Corpl. Percy Moor, son of Mr. and Mrs. W. Moor, Throstle Nest, Pocklington, has been wounded in action. He is now in hospital in France, but the nature of his wound is not yet known. We wish for him a speedy recovery.

Killed in Action

Official news has been received that Gunner Wilfred Rippon, youngest son of Mr. and Mrs. J. Rippon, Victoria-terrace, Pocklington, was killed in action in Mesopotamia on March 26th. He was a popular postman, and a member of the local Volunteer Corps, from which he resigned on taking up duties as a sorter at Darlington. He re-enlisted two years ago, and went abroad last September. Thirty-one years of age, he leaves a widow (a daughter of Mr. and Mrs. Barnes, of Percy-road, Pocklington), and two children. He is brother to J. H. Rippon, the old Hull N.U. Rugby player, and two brothers (Frank and Arthur) are recuperating in England from illness contracted whilst serving in France.

28th April, 1917

POCKLINGTON.

All the latest Military Cap Badges, Brooches, and Canes are now on sale at Whitehead's, in Market Square. Pocklington.

The Victoria Hall

is again at liberty for hire for concerts, dances, or any public meeting. For terms apply to J. Whitehead, lessee. Market Sq. Pocklington.

Wounded In Action.

Official news was received from the War Office on Sunday morning last, by Mr. and Mrs. G. H. Barker, Union Street. Pocklington that one of their four soldier sons, Gunner Hawksworth Barker, who was serving with the Machine Gunners in Mesopotamia, had been wounded in action. He joined the Yorkshire Regiment about two years ago, and after serving several months with that Regiment, he transferred to the M.G.C. and was sent out to Mesopotamia. Two of his brothers—Shoeing-smith Fred Barker and Lce.-Corpl. Walter Barker, K.R.B. are also serving abroad, the latter having been twice wounded some months ago, and is now back again in the firing line. Another brother, Sergt. H. Barker, is serving in a Home Defence Battalion, and a brother-in-law, Pte. R. Brewer, is serving in France. We sincerely hope Gunner Barker's wounds are not serious, and wish for him a speedy recovery.

28th April, 1917

CORRESPONDENCE.

To the Editor of the 'Pocklington News."

April 23rd, 1917.

Dear Sir.—Should you find any merit in these crude verses of mine, and appreciate the feelings I had for your dear old town as I write them, I should be pleased if you I saw fit to publish them in your paper.

Yours sincerely,

Private J. R. CAMPBELL.

ADIEU TO DEAR OLD POCK

Adieu, you dear old Yorkshire town,
We've no good-bye for you;
We leave in hopes of coming back,
And coming early, too.

There's not a lad in the Battalion
But shares this joyous hope,
And many a lad now over seas
Will remember dear old Pock.

Your many acts of homely love
Are Cherished by our men;
But Providence is kind, and will
To you rich blessings send.

Once more. Old Pock, Adieu;
We men, with grateful hearts,
Will, aye remember you,
As we do our little part

To bring you back the joys of old,
And peace that should be thine;
We'll stroll with you your Yorkshire Wolds,
When we have crossed the Rhine.

Howdenshire Chronicle and Pocklington Weekly News for April 28th 1917

n.b. Thought to be John George Campbell b. Bolton 1891, who married Sarah Annie Claybourn in Goole in 1909. He was son of James and Martha Campbell a farmer at Bolton in 1901 and then at Fir Tree Farm, Fangfoss, and later at Clayfield Farm, Pocklington (Martha died at Clayfield Farm in 1916 and is buried at Bolton Chapel). In the 1920's & 30's John George farmed at The Grange in Bielby Lane, Pocklington. Or, it may be James Colin Campbell b. Bolton 1893, John George's brother who later farmed at Cliff Farm, Bishop Wilton.

12th May, 1917

Wounded in Action

Now was rewired on Tuesday morning that Lce.-Corpl. Walter Barker, of the King's Royal Rifles, son of Mr. and Mrs. G.H. Barker, of Union Street, Pocklington, had again been wounded in action and had been admitted to Hospital in France. This is the third wound Lce.-Corpl. Barker has received at the hands of the Boche, having this time sustained a bullet wound in the head. He went "over the top" with his regiment at 3 a.m. and was wounded at 11. He was in action a few weeks ago with the K.R.R.'s when that battalion was complimented by Sir Douglas Haig for smart work in the field.—A brother, Gunner Hawksworth Barker, of the M.G.C., is also in hospital, suffering from gunshot wounds in both arms.

News has been received that Private R. E. Young, of Oak Hill Lodge, Moortown, Leeds (late in the employ of Mr. R. M. English, of Pocklington), has been wounded in action, and is now in hospital in Newcastle. Prior to enlistment, he was employed as Head Gardener to Mr. L. Clayton, of Moortown.

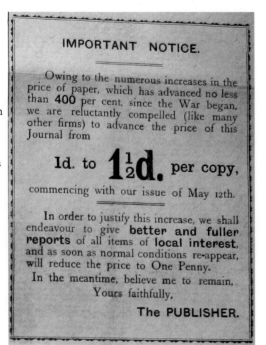

Pocklington Weekly News, 5th May 1917

Killed in Action

Official news has been received that Pte. George Henry Grainger, East Yorks., eldest son of Mr. and Mrs. J. Grainger, of Grape Lane, Pocklington, was killed in action in France on the 24th April. Formerly employed in the rope works of Messrs. Laister and Sons, he enlisted in November, 1915, and after a years' training proceeded to the Front, where he was wounded, but after being attended to at the base hospital for a fortnight, went back to the trenches. The deceased young fellow was of happy disposition, and his many friends will learn of his death with feelings of sincere regret. He had never spent a night away from home up to the time of enlistment. He was 21 years of age. His brother-in-law Private Mutimer, is at present in Preston hospital wounded.

SAFETY OF MARKET WEIGHTON SOLDIER

It was feared that Trooper W.H. Johnson (Yeomanry) had been drowned at sea but Councillor and Mrs Johnson, Rectory Farm, Goodmanham, have received information that their son is safe.

19th May, 1917

TRAGIC FATE OF TWO LOVERS.

DROWNED TOGETHER. Another love tragedy was brought to light at Beverley on Tuesday, the victim being a youth of 18 and a girl of 16 years Of age. They were found drowned in the Beck at Beverley, and it would appear that the tragedy was due to the fact that the young man had received his calling-up notice.

The unhappy couple were David George McDonald (18), a joiner's apprentice, of 4, Mason-street, and Doris Hudson (16), of 14, Rose-terrace, Alfred-street, Hull, the latter of whom, was employed as a brush-maker. They had been missing since Monday, the 7th instant.

Hands Tied Together.

About one o'clock on Tuesday the lock-keeper at Beverley, Mr. John Hoggard, was walking along the Beckside, when he saw the two bodies floating in the water. He got assistance, and the bodies were drawn to the bank. It was found that a boot lace was tied round one of the girl's hands and one of the boy's, hands.

The Beverley police had been notified that the couple were missing, and inquiries were afterwards, made at Hull, with the result that the bodies were identified. The girl left home about 6-15 on the morning of the 7th inst., saying she was going to the station to see-her sweetheart off by train. An hour and a half later, however, her mother found a note in the sitting-room stating she would never see her again, and asking for forgiveness.

Call to the Army.

The following day McDonald's parents received a letter in the lad s handwriting, bearing the Beverley postmark, to the effect that he and the girl were going away, and making reference to the calling up notice he had received. He said he did not want to join the Army. From that day until the recovery of the bodies nothing was heard of them.

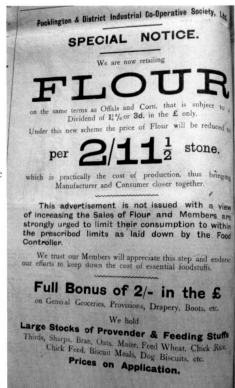

Pocklington Weekly News, 12th May 1917

The youthful couple had kept company for some time, and it is stated that their impending separation had caused them great depression..

The sad occurrence was made still more pathetic when it became known that on the very day the bodies were found, the boy's employers had been successful in their appeal for his exemption from military service, as a joiner's apprentice engaged on important national work.

An Old Pocklingtonian Killed.

News was received on Thursday last that Pte. F. S. Beckworth, stepson of the Rev. W. E. Daw, late curate of the Parish Church, Pocklington, and now of Shrewsbury, was killed in action on May 3rd. Pte. Beckworth, who will be remembered by many of our readers, was educated at the Pocklington Grammar School, afterwards taking a position in the office of Messrs. Wright and Vine clothiers accountants, Shrewsbury. He enlisted two years ago in the King's Shropshire Light Infantry, when 18 years of age. Much local sympathy will be extended to the Rev. and Mrs Daw in their bereavement.

A Pocklington Soldier Loses his right eye.

We regret to learn that Private Thomas William Herrington, of the East Yorks. got wounded in the right eye on the 3rd May, whilst on active service in France. He has since been removed to Edinburgh, and has had the injured eye removed. It is a year this month since he first joined up, and he went out to France last December. He was the rullyman at the Cooperative Stores, Pocklington, before joining the Army. Private Herrington was very popular throughout the district, and much sympathy is expressed for him and his wife on the injury he has sustained.

26th May, 1917

Corpl. Richard Beckett Gains the Military Medal.

Pocklington has received a big share of honours during the War, and it is now our privilege and pleasure to record the fact that Corporal Richard Beckett, son of Mr, George Beckett, lately in the employ of the N.E.R.. Company, has been awarded the Military Medal for conspicuous bravery in the field. He joined the Army on the 1st of March, 1915, and went out to France on April 16th, 1915, being invalided home exactly a year later. He returned to the front in August, 1916, and on April 23rd of the present year he gained the honour previously referred to. He expects being presented with his ribbon in billets at a rest camp. Our readers at home and abroad will join us in hearty congratulations to Corporal Beckett on his well-deserved honour.

Private Herbert Frear Killed in Action.

We regret to learn that Private Herbert Frear, of the Royal Field Artillery, and late of Hayton, has been killed in action. He is brother to Mr. Frear, who resides at Clock Mill farm, Pocklington, and much sympathy is felt for the bereaved relatives.

ELVINGTON

Private Harold Cooper Killed in Action

We regret to learn that Private Harold Cooper, second son of Mr. and Mrs. Alfred Cooper, has been killed in France. The deceased, who was 32 years of age, and single, joined the Northumberland Fusiliers in October last, was drafted to the front in January, and fell in action on April 29th. Previous to entering the Army, he was in farm service with Mr. Galtry, of Stockton-On-Forest. Private Ernest Cooper, a younger brother, is at the front with the Machine Gun Corps, while brother-in-law of the deceased, Private Widderstone, has been invalided home.

IN MEMORIUM

HOPPER—In loving memory of Alfred Hopper of Pocklington, who was killed in action on May 25th, 1915. "Greater love hath no man than this, that he lay down his life for others." - From his Wife and Children.

2nd-Lieut. Cyril Stather

We notice that Mr. C. Cyril Stather has been gazetted a 2nd Lieutenant in his Northamptonshire Regiment. He will be reporting for duty, at Chatham, on Monday next.

2nd June, 1917

Pocklington Soldier in Mesopotamia.

The following appeared in "Bumble's" Letter from Beeford in the "Hull Times" of Saturday last:- "Five of our Beeford boys have given their lives for their country. Another of our boys who is in Mesopotamia, Corporal Herbert Jefferson, has had a warm time lately. He says in a letter to his parents: 'I hear of the rejoicings over our victories out here, but do people think of the lads marching daily in the boiling sun? We had a tight fight the other day. I was the senior N.C.O. left, and my worst job was to call the roll at night. H. Barker, from Pocklington, was with me at my gun, a fine brave fellow. He was as cool as a cucumber, until he got two bullets, one in his right hand, and the other in his left arm. Poor old Rippon, from Pocklington, got one in the stomach, so I pinched a stretcher, and got him away in a fast car, but be died the next day.

It knocked the wind out of me for a bit to lose two of my special pals. You should have seen the four remaining Yorkshire's boys that night, talking things over, and having a cup of tea and some broken biscuits for the first time that day. As long as the British Army is composed of men like Corporal Jefferson there is no wonder at the Turks being on the move."

A Local Soldier Missing.

Mr. A. Jackson who was formerly cashier at the Pocklington Branch of Barclay's Bank, has been reported missing since the 29th April, and it is feared he has made the great sacrifice. He was son of the late Dr. Jackson, of Market Weighton, and much respected in the district.

Private Joe Eagan Killed.

Mrs. Eagan, of Church Lane, Pocklington, has received information that her fourth son. Private Joe Eagan, Northumberland Fusiliers, has been killed in France. Though not yet official, the news which was received in a letter from his Company Sergt. Major appears to be only too true. The unfortunate young man was 36 years of age, and leaves a widow and two children. For some time he worked at the Pocklington Cooperative Stores, before removing to Hull, where he was employed at Needler's Sweet Factory. He enlisted in the East Yorks. and afterwards transferred to the Northumberland Fusiliers. His three older brothers have served in this war, viz.: Farrier-Sergt. H. Eagan, who was at Salonika; Pte. Luke Eagan, who has been two years in France; and Pte. D. Eagan, who was discharged medically unfit after nine months' service. Much sympathy is extended to Mrs. Eagan and family in their bereavement.

Wounded

Lance-Corporal Walter Barker, of the King's Royal Rifles, who was badly wounded in the head some weeks ago, is at present in hospital at Aberdeen, and, after a successful operation, is going on as well as can be expected.

Awarded the Military Cross.

Captain R. F. Hayward, of the London Regiment, attached to the Machine Gun Corps, has been awarded the Military Cross. Mr. Hayward is one of a well-known Lincoln family, and brother of Mr. C. T. Hayward, Implement Works, Pocklington. Prior to the war he practised as a barrister on the Midland circuit, and has appeared in several cases at Lincoln Assizes and Quarter Sessions.

Private Arthur Jessop Wounded

We regret to learn that official news has reached Pocklington that Private Arthur Jessop, of the East Yorks., is suffering from a bullet wound. We hope the wound is not severe, and that he will have a speedy recovery. His younger brother has been reported missing over twelve months..

9th June, 1917

BOLTON.

Local Soldier Drowned at Sea.

We deeply regret to record the death of Private David William Walker, the beloved son of Mr. and Mrs. Charles Walker, of Bolton Grange Farm, which occurred through the sinking of a hospital ship on April 11th last. The deceased young fellow was attached to the East Yorkshire Regiment, and was held in high esteem by a wide circle of friends in the Bolton and Wilberfoss districts. He was only 20 years of age, and much sympathy is expressed for his bereaved parents.

The American Expeditionary Force.

News that an American Expeditionary Force will before long be fighting in France has been received with the greatest enthusiasm here.   General Pershing is well known to many Americans in London, and he has evidently the faculty of inspiring unbounded confidence among all who meet him.   He has seen hard service in Mexico, and was attached to the Russian General Kuroki's staff as an observer in the Russo-Japanese War.   The American Medical Unit which reached London had a great reception. They had, I believe, an uneventful voyage. Everybody is full of admiration for the remarkable speed and thoroughness with which the unit has been equipped and sent across.   They were greeted here, on their arrival, by a company of the R.A.M.C. The blue cloak and Red Cross of the nurses has, of course, already been seen in London.

INTERESTING LETTERS FROM THE FRONT.

188, M.G. Corp, Mesopotamia, 12-4-17.

Dear Mrs. Rjppon,—I am sending just a line to offer to you my heartfelt sympathy in the death of your husband, he was one of the best men in my section, and a splendid soldier, and died in action doing his duty. He was hit in the stomach and died next day. I must apologise for not writing before, but we have been so busy lately. Again assuring you of my sympathy in your great loss.

Yours truly, E. A. HILL, Lieut., 3rd Sec, 133 Coy.

———

34336, Cpl. H. Jefferson. 133 Coy. M.G. Corps., Mesopotamia Ex. Force, G.P.O., London. 8-4-17.

Dear Mrs. Rippon,—I am writing to send you my heartfelt sympathy in the loss of your dear husband. Wilf and I have been great pals since we first went to Newcastle. We had a fearful fight with the Turks on the 25th of March. I'm not allowed to tell you what part of the country, but it was far above Bagdad. Wilf got hit with shrapnel in the body. The men on his gun got him out of the range of guns. I came up with the few men I had left, pinched a stretcher, got Wilf down to a dressing station in a fast car. I never thought he would die; he even said "I don't think its real serious." The last words he said to me were: "I'll write home in a few days. Jeff." He died the next day. Oh! I could have dropped; I had such good hopes for him. Our other pal Hawksworth Barker also got wounded, so I'm feeling like a fish out of water with both of them away. You know, dear Mrs. Rippon, we had been together so long we always confided in each other, the three of us. I know what he thought of you and his dear little children, and how he longed to be back with you. If there is anything you would like to know don't be afraid to write me, I will only be too pleased to do anything for you for a dear pal's sake. Trusting God will help you over this great trouble, I remain,

Yours very sincerely, H. JEFFERSON.

16th June, 1917

BIRTHS, MARRIAGES AND DEATHS

IN MEMORIUM

BUTTLE.– In loving memory of Pte. R. W. Buttle. East Yorks., killed in action on the 18th June 1916, eldest son of Mrs. Huck, of Pocklington.
Not dead to those who love him.
Not lost but gone before;
He lives with us in memory still,
And will for evermore,

From his sorrowing Mother and Father, Brothers and Sisters.

The German Air-Raid.

Mr. Q. W. Jameson, an old Pocklingtonian, who is now in a flourishing way of business in London, has very kindly sent us a small piece of shrapnel dropped in London by the Germans on Wednesday forenoon, as a memento of the inhuman conduct of the Germans in taking the lives of in innocent people. Seven people were killed within fifty yards of where he stood, and he had the satisfaction of seeing one of the machines brought down.

The Price of Clothing in the near future

One has only to get in touch with representatives of the leading firms of clothing manufacturers to be convinced of the fact that there will, in the near future, be great difficulty in obtaining many kinds of cloth, and at considerable enhanced prices. Some shrewd men, who are in the know, are, as it were, preparing for a rainy day by placing orders for two or more suits, whilst they have choice and opportunity. As previously stated in these columns. Mr. Chas. Rowley, of Market Street, Pocklington, has secured a good stock of reliable cloth, and can offer extraordinary value to early customers—a fact well worth bearing in mind.

GUNNER HERBERT FREAR.

Above we reproduce a photo of Gunner Herbert Frear, the fifth, and much-beloved son of Mr. and Mrs. Jas. Frear, of the Post Office, Hayton, who was killed in action, in France, on May 19th, 1917. Prior to enlistment in the Royal Field Artillery the deceased young man was in the employ of Messrs. R. M. English & Sons, for a period of three-and-a-half years, by whom he was held in high esteem as a faithful and conscientious workman. After donning His Majesty's uniform two years ago last May, he was stationed at several important Yorkshire Camps before being drafted off to France a year later, and was at the Front exactly twelve months when he met his death in action. He was 29 years of age, and was highly respected by everyone who had the pleasure of his acquaintance and much sympathy is expressed for the bereaved family in their great trouble. A Memorial Service will be held at Hayton Church to-morrow (Sunday) evening.

Pocklington Weekly News, 16th June 1917

Patriotic Family

A local patriotic family is that of the late Mr. Seth Fieldhouse, of Pocklington, for his three sons, two sons-in-law, and a grandson have all served in the war. The eldest son, Walter, enlisted in the Royal Engineers two years ago; Seth Whittam, the second son has been enrolled in the R.F.A., for three years; and the youngest, John Thomas, enlisted in the A.S.C., nearly two years ago. Louis Swaby, son-in-law, has been nearly two years service in France, and Walter Tate, R.A.M.C. son-in-law, has served 8 years in the Army, and been on active service a considerable time. Seth Ablett (Hull), grandson, has served six years in the Navy. Though having served so long in the field, we are pleased to state that up to the present none of them have been injured, though John Thomas has been discharged owing to ill-health.— Mrs. Fieldhouse now lives in Hull.

23rd June, 1917

HAYTON.

Memorial Service.

A Memorial Service was held at the Parish Church, Hayton, in memory of Herbert Frear, the second soldier who has given his life for his King and country from this village. A special form of service was used, with suitable hymns and lessons. The Vicar officiated and preached an appropriate sermon, making reference of the sad loss, and expressing sympathy of the village people with the family in their bereavement.

SHIPTONTHORPE

Mr. and Mrs. J. W. Oxtoby, of York Road, Shiptonthorpe, have sustained a great bereavement in the loss of their eldest son, Private George William Oxtoby, of the East Yorkshire Regiment, who was killed in action on April 9th, 1917, at the age of 20 years. He was a particularly fine young man, and was well-known and highly respected throughout the district. An impressive memorial service was recently held in Shiptonthorpe Parish Church by the Rev. —. Chester (vicar), and was well attended by sympathetic friends. The deceased's brother—Gunner John Clark Oxtoby, aged 19 years, is now serving in France, and we sincerely hope he will be spared to see the war finished, with success to the cause of the Allies.

30th June, 1917

MARKET WEIGHTON

Volunteer Orders.

2-3rd Batt. East Yorkshire. Regt. (Volunteers). "A" Company, Market Weighton Platoon.

Monday, July 2nd-—The platoon will parade at the Drill Hall at 7-10 p.m. for bayonet fighting half-hour and drill half-hour. Dress, belt and side arms.

Tuesday. July 3rd—The platoon will parade at the Drill Hall at 7-10 p.m. for musketry half-hour, bombing half hour, whilst the machine gun section will parade for one hour's machine gun drill. Dress, as above.

Thursday, July 5th.—The platoon will parade at the Drill Hall at 7 p.m. for one hour's musketry, whilst the machine gun section will parade at the same time for one hour's machine gun drill. Dress, as above,

Sunday, July 8th.-—The platoon will parade at the Drill Hall at 9-30 a.m. for bombing half-hour, extended order drill half-hour, drill one and a half hours, and half-hour's physical training. Dress, drill order.

WILLIAM THOMPSON, Sec.-Lieut.

Soldiers on Leave.

Amongst the Market Weighton soldiers who have been home on leave during the week have been the following:—Pte. S. B. W. Brown (Canadian Contingent), son of Mr- and Mrs. George Brown, of Northgate; Pte. Harry Arnot (Lancers), one of the three soldier sons of Mr. and Mrs. Henry Arnott, of Hungate, who has been overseas for some considerable time, and has been wounded two or three times. Pte. Wm, Dorsey (East Yorks. Regt.) of South Parade, one of the soldier sons of Mr. Amos Dorsey, of Shipton Thorpe; Pte. Albert Lusher (Machine, Gun Corps.), of Market Place; Pte. Alfred Bell (Northumberland Fusiliers), one of the two soldier sons of Mrs. James Bell, of Northgate, who is home for a few days recuperating after again being wounded; Gunner Thomas Cook (Canadian Artillery), son of Mr. and Mrs. James Cook, of Southgate, who is spending a short leave at home after being in Canada for over four years; Lce.-Corpl. Alfred Jackson (A.S.C.), of South Parade, one of the two soldier sons of Mr. and Mrs. W. Jackson, of Northgate, who has already served one and a-half years with the East Yorks. Wagoners Reserve; Pte. Sydney Smith (East Yorks. Regt.). one of the three soldier sons of Councillor and Mrs. W. J. Smith, of the Railway Cottages; Driver Albert Marshall (A.S.C.). who previous to enlistment was employed at the Market Weighton Railway Station; Corpl. George Bramley (King's Royal Rifle Corps), son of Mr. and Mrs. G. Bramley, of York-road, who has been wounded but is making good progress; Pte. Atkinson (East Yorks.), one of the two soldier sons of Mrs. Atkinson, of Londesborough Park; Lce.-Corpl. Arthur Gordon (Northumberland Fusiliers), one of the three soldier sons of Mr. and Mrs. Henry Arnott. of Hungate; Private Harold Mitchell (Northumberland Fusilliers) one of the three soldier sons of Mr. and Mrs. William Mitchell, of Railway View Cottages; Gunner Fred Saltmer (R.F.A.), one of the two soldier sons of Mr. and Mrs. Richard Saltmer, of Garden Place, who has been on the Western front for some considerable time; Boy Telegraphist Alfred Richardson (H.M. Navy), one of the three soldier and sailor sons of Mr. and Mrs. J. T. Richardson, of Westfield-terrace; and Pte William Maynard (East Yorks.), High St., one of the two soldier sons of Mr. and Mrs. William Maynard, of Southgate.

MARKET WEIGHTON M.C.

FORMER POCKLINGTON CONSTABLES GALLANTRY IN WAR.

Official information has reached Market Weighton that the Military Cross, for meritorious service in the field, has been awarded Temp. Sec-Lieut. (Act. Captain) Thomas William Baron.

The official report of Capt. Baron's recommendation for the Military Cross intimates that when in command of a support company, he engaged three strong positions held by snipers in strength, and, in the face of heavy rifle and shell fire, he generally succeeded in capturing the coveted positions.

The report also states that Captain Baron set a splendid example to his men throughout a most difficult and dangerous operation.

Captain Baron was a police-constable, stationed at Melbourne, Pocklington, and Stamford Bridge, near York, prior to coming to Market Weighton, where his great success and honour will be well received.

When a constable in the force, P.C. Baron was of a refined disposition, kind, courteous, alert, a conscientious officer, and above all—a thorough gentleman. No one is more delighted at his success than the editor of the local newspaper, who has watched his career with keen interest for some years past.

Another officer in the force with a splendid record is Sergt. Long, of Stamford Bridge, which will bear investigation. He has several very smart cases to his credit, and if he is anything like lucky he will still gain further promotion.

7th July, 1917

KILLED IN ACTION

STUBBS—Killed in Action, June 5th 1917, Richard Mark Stubbs (Dick), Tyneside Scottish. N.F., the dearly beloved eldest son of Walter and Lucy M. Stubbs, Aston Villa, Pocklington, aged 20 years and 3 months. "A brief bright life, a glorious death"

A Local Soldier Wounded

Official intimation has been received that Sapper T. Flint, R.E., son of Mr. and Mrs. T. Flint, Kirkland Street, Pocklington, has been wounded whilst serving in France. The wound is not a serious one, and we hope for a speedy recovery.

Bank Cashier Killed in Action

We regret to record that Pte. Richard Stubbs, eldest son of Mr. Walter Mark Stubbs, Relieving Officer, Pocklington, fell in action in France on the 5th June. He joined the Northumberland Fusiliers on attaining the age of 19 in March, 1916, and went abroad at the beginning of July last year being afterwards transferred to the Tyneside Scottish. In private life he was resident Bank Cashier at Messrs. Beckett & Co., Bridlington. He was a very popular young man of bright and cheerful disposition, and pleasant and unassuming manner, and his loss is keenly felt by his relatives and friends. Educated at Pocklington, Birmingham and York, he entered the service of the Bank over five years ago in York, being removed to Bridlington six months later. A good athlete (over 6ft 1in in height) he was selected to represent the Battalion in the Great Northern Command Seven Miles Race held in June last year, when about 1800 competitors started.

In a letter conveying the sad news, his Commanding Officer states :— "He was always a good soldier and we were very sorry indeed to lose him. His name was sent forward from his Company for a Commission some months ago, and I am sure he would have made a good officer if it had come through in time to save his death." For the last few months he had charge of a Lewis Machine Gun, and since April was daily awaiting his recall to England to undergo his needed O.T.C. training. His brother Reginald was recently appointed to the Life Guards, and a third brother, Louis joined the West Yorks. V.T.C. last Summer at the age of 15½ years.

STAMFORD BRIDGE.

Local Soldier Killed in Action

We much, regret to learn that Private "Dick" Ward, of Stamford Bridge, has been instantaneously killed in France. He was well-known and highly respected throughout the district, and much sympathy is expressed for the bereaved family.

YAPHAM.

Military Medal Awarded.

Private Fred Leeson, Border Regiment, been awarded the Military Medal for keeping up communication on the wires under heavy fighting. He is the youngest son of Mr. and Mrs. Leeson, Yapham. He enlisted September, 1914, was drafted out to France in September, 1915. Before enlisting he was a gardener at Levens Hall, Westmoreland. They have also two sons-in-law serving in France.

FRANCE THANKS BRITISH SOLDIERS AND FARMERS

Grateful recognition of the part played by British soldiers and by British farmers in re-establishing the agriculture in the reconquered French Territory has been conveyed by French farmers, through the medium of the Agricultural Academy of France to Sir Douglas Haig and also to the President of the Royal Agricultural Society (Mr. C. Adeane). British troops have laboured hard and successfully in the preparation of the soil, and the practical help given by the Agricultural Relief of Allies Fund (which was initiated by the Royal Agricultural Society) has proved of the greatest utility in the invaded regions. The French Agricultural Academy has been deeply impressed by the splendid work of our soldiers and by the help of English Farmers through the instrumentality of the Agricultural Relief Allies fund.
It is the object of the fund to offer assistance to the farmers in the invaded districts of our Allies as those districts are recovered from the enemy.

14th July, 1917

BIRTHS. MARRIAGES AND DEATHS

IN MEMORIAM,

WALKER-- In loving memory of our dear son, Private W. E. Walker, late of Hayton, killed in action on July 14th, 1915.
From Father, Mother, and Brother

WALKER— In loving memory- of our dear brother, Private W. E. Walker (late of Hayton) killed in action on July 14th, 1915.
Sleep on, dear Brother, thy troubles o'er. Thy willing hands will toil no more; On earth they strove, in heaven they rest; We miss thee most who loved thee best.

From Jack and Ben (Salonica and France.)

Mrs Atkinson, wife of Mr. J. Atkinson, Pocklington, on receiving an urgent telegram from the Military Hospital Authorities, journeyed to France to see her son, Gunner J.E. Atkinson, Machine Gun Corps, who was seriously wounded by gunshot wounds in the neck whilst serving in a tank. On arrival Mrs Atkinson found her son was a deal better than the doctors anticipated he would be. She stayed from Friday until Monday night, and speaks highly of the care and attention bestowed upon the wounded in the Australian Hospital where her son is a patient. She arrived home again on Tuesday evening, and on Wednesday received a telegram stating he was out of danger. She has another son serving in Mesopotamia.

A Pocklingtonian in London

Mr G.W. Jameson, formerly of Pocklington, witnessed the air-raid on London last Saturday. He had only one square of glass broken in his office, although the adjoining building was wrecked. In his opinion, the enemy aeroplanes were flying very low, and he is much surprised that more were not fetched down. He counted 29 German planes.

THE GREAT AIR RAID OF LONDON.

To the Editor of the "Pocklington News."

Saturday, July 7th, 1917.

Dear Sir.—I thought perhaps it would interest your readers to know that I was an eye-witness to the Air Raid carried out this morning. I may say that we are getting used to air-raids as we get the alarm regularly, but this morning put everything that has occurred before into the shade completely. We got the alarm "Air-Raid Action," and we got a very good view of 26 German aeroplanes (we counted them several times to make sure), flying fairly low and very slowly, making for London, and they were in full view nearly all the time. I can safely say that we did not lose sight of them for ten minutes the whole of the time until they went back over the coast about 11 a.m. When they got nearer London our airmen seemed to swarm on top of them from all sides, and there must have been 60 or 70 in the air altogether; fighting for all they were worth and shrapnel was bursting all round them. I never saw such a sight in all my life, it was simply great— if they had not been doing damage to civilian people. But what gets over me was that all the buzzers round here never gave the warning to the townspeople until were right over the centre of the town.

Why cannot our airmen meet them before they get so far inland? We have scores flying round here daily when there is nothing doing, but when there is a raid you hardly ever see one.

I am, Yours respectfully, G.H. BARKER.

POCKLINGTON GRAMMAR SCHOOL

To the Editor,. "Howdenshire Chronicle"

7th July, 1917. Dear Sir,- I have been reading your weekly paper as usual and have noticed a list of old boys now serving in this most serious World's War. If I am not mistaken, there is one name omitted Appleton, Corporal, J. K., East Riding ,Yeomanry. Perhaps you can explain.

A WEEKLY READER.

[We regret to find the names of Corpl., J. K. Appleton, Trooper W. Dunning, and others have been inadvertently omitted from the official list published by the School, which is the cause of their omission from our list, given last week] - Editor P.W.N.

21st July, 1917

Men Available for Harvest.

The East Riding of Yorkshire War Agricultural Executive Committee have been informed that a further number of Soldiers have been sent to assist in harvest work. The men are available at once, and application for them should be made at an early date as the number is limited. Applications must be made on forms, which can be obtained from Mr. John Bickersteth, Clerk of the Committee.

Local Soldier Missing

Official intimation has been received by Mr. I. Eastwood, of London Street, Pocklington, that his adopted son, Pte. William Lorne, Northumberland Fusiliers, has been missing since the engagement of June 16th last, and as no letter hits been received from him since that date grave fears are entertained as to his being alive. A quiet, well disposed young man of 23 years of age, he was well known to a large circle of acquaintances by the name of his adoption, Eastwood, and will be remembered by our readers as being in employment at Hill's and Lee's motor garages, and afterwards with Dr. Fairweather. About two years ago, when working in the N.E.R. warehouses at Hull, he enlisted in the Railway Battalion, with which he went to France.

28th July, 1917

Killed in Action.

We deeply regret to record the death of Private James Elliott, R.F.A., who has died of wounds received in action. He was a particularly nice young man, and was for six years in the employ of Mr. Foxton, at Coldwold, before joining the Army.

Aeroplane Damaged.

On Saturday afternoon on aeroplane passed over Pocklington, and the pilot for some reason came down. He thought he was alighting in a seeds field. It proved, however, to be a field of wheat, among the stalks of which the propeller became entangled, and caused such damage that the pilot could not resume his journey. The growing corn choked the wheels and propeller, and caused it to turn completely over. Three of the blades of the propeller were broken off, but the young pilot and observer jumped clear, and thereby escaped injury.

4th August, 1917

Gassed

Official news has been received by Mrs. T. Tinson, London Street, Pocklington, that her husband, Sapper Travis Tinson, R.E. has been badly "gassed" during the fighting in Belgium last week. Pte. James Ferisy, East Yorks., son of Mr. and Mrs. Ferisy, London Street, is also officially reported "gassed" during last week's operations.

Wounded

Intimation has been received that Lance-Corpl. Charles Spivey, Yorkshire Regiment, son of the late Mr. Ralph and Mrs. Spivey, has been shot in the stomach, and that he is making satisfactory progress.—Sapper Thomas Flint, son of Mr. and Mrs. T. Flint, Kirkland Street, is also reported seriously wounded. Both these local heroes have been previously wounded.

11th August, 1917

Wounded

Driver E. Thompson, R.F.A., son of Mrs. Thompson, Chapmangate, Pocklington, has, after two years service in France, been admitted to a Base Hospital, wounded in the right knee. He is progressing favourably.

A Prisoner of War.

Mr. I. Eastwood, London Street, Pocklington, on Thursday received official intimation that his adopted son, Pte. Wm. Lorne. Northumberland Fusiliers, who has been reported missing since June 23rd, is a prisoner of war at Dulmen Camp, Westphalia..

A Pocklington D.C.M.

Sergt. Harry Rowley, East Yorks., son of Mrs. Rowley, Chapmangate, Pocklington, who has been awarded the Distinguished Conduct Medal for conspicuous gallantry, in action, has been previously honoured; being one of the four non-commissioned Officers mentioned in General French's first Despatch from the Front. —His brother, Rev. Frank Rowley, who was an acceptable local preacher in this Circuit before proceeding to College, and who has served three years in different circuits, was ordained minister at the recent Wesleyan Conference in London.

Another Pocklington Soldier Wounded

Rifleman Harold Buttle, K.R.R., son of Mr. and Mrs. Geo. Buttle, of Union Street, Pocklington, is officially reported wounded by a bullet entering the body under the left shoulder, during recent fighting. His younger brother, Frank, died a short time ago from wounds received in action.

18th August, 1917

Local Soldier Honoured.

Corpl. Arthur Dykes, Yorkshire Regt., son of Mr. and Mrs. Dykes, of Market Street, Pocklington, has been awarded the Military Medal for distinguished services in the field. The Official Card, which his wife, Mrs. Dykes, junr., of Market Street, has received bears this notification: "— Division. B.E.F., Cpl. A. Dykes, Batt. Yorkshire Regiment,——Your Commanding Officer and Brigade Commander have informed me that you distinguished yourself in the field on the 30th and 31st July, 1917. I congratulate you on your fine work," Corpl. Dykes is one of six brothers who are serving their country, and the second of the family to receive distinction, his brother, Sergt. F. C. Dykes, having received the Military Medal some months ago. Another brother, Corpl. T. Dykes, has been wounded but has recovered and returned to his Regirnent.

25th August, 1917

KILLED IN ACTION.

CATTLE, —August 13th, 1917, killed: in action, Henry, Irving Cattle, dearly-loved eldest son of Henry and Annie Cattle, Panel House, Pocklington.

IN MEMORIAM.

THORPE,——In loving memory of our dear Mother, the late Mrs. J. Thorpe, of Pocklington, who died, 27th August, 1913.

"To memory ever dear."

THANKS FOR SYMPATHY.

MR. and MRS. H. W. CATTLE and Family are deeply grateful for the many expressions of sympathy shown to them in their great sorrow.

Panel House, Pocklington. August, 1917.

Killed in Action

On Sunday morning news was received by Mr. and Mrs. H. W. Cattle, of Pannal House, Pocklington, that their eldest son Sapper Irving Cattle R.E., had been instantly killed by enemy shellfire whilst in action on the 13th August, and was buried in the British Cemetery in Flanders next day. When the sad news was known in the town much sympathy was expressed with the family in their bereavement, for the deceased was a popular young man, who had gained a large circle of friends in the district. Only 25 years of age, he had been at the front over twelve months, during which period he had been in much of the heavy fighting without injury, until recently, when he was "gassed." he arrived home on sick leave. His brothers, Norman, who is in the Royal Flying Corps, and Ronnie, who is a Wireless Operator in the Marconi Company, also obtained home leave, and there was a family reunion until the 8th August, when Irving returned to the Front, being killed five days later. Before enlistment he was acting manager, for his father, at the Old Brewery, Chapmangate, Pocklington.

A SPLENDID ACHIEVEMENT

The inhabitants of Pocklington can feel justly proud of the brave soldiers who have gone from our midst to take part in the greatest war for right and freedom that England has ever been called upon to wage, for that they are worthily upholding the country's traditions and prestige is manifested by the fact that no less than eight Military Decorations have been bestowed upon them for distinguished bravery in the field. Whether this is a record for a small town of less than 3,000 people we are not able to state, but of this we are certain, that it is a record which will take some beating, and is a highly creditable tribute to the courage and example shown by our local boys. The Honours bestowed are:—

The Distinguished Service Order—Lieut. Colonel F. W. Robson, D.S.O., Durhams.
Military Cross—Lieut., now acting Captain, E. M. Robson, M.C., Yorkshire Regt. (Twice wounded).
Distinguished Conduct Medal and French Croix-de-Guerre—Bomber E. Kirby, Lincolns, since killed in action.
Military Medal—Sergt. F. C. Dykes, Yorks. Regt. (wounded).
Military Medal— Corpl. A. Dykes, Yorks. Regt.
Military Medal—Corpl. R. Beckett, Yks. Regt.
Military Medal—Sergt. J. Francis, Yorks. Regt. (wounded).
Military Medal—Sergt. H. Rowley, East Yorks. (wounded).

In addition another local soldier, who is at present seriously wounded and in hospital, is recommended for the Military Medal.
Whilst congratulating these heroes on their achievements which has brought so much honour to themselves and the town, we must remember that the Regiment to which our Territorials are attached have been especially complimented on the fine work which it has accomplished in the field, whilst other Regiments which contain several of our townsmen have been similarly congratulated. When we consider the fact that these men, with few exceptions, were following civil occupations, living ordinary lives in our midst, with no thought of being called upon to train for warfare, it speaks well for the nation's system of military training, which in so short a period enables men to turn from these duties and become such proficient soldiers. But as we read with satisfaction of these successes we should not forget that they have not been achieved

without sacrifice, for many of our local soldiers have been wounded, and, alas! several killed, whilst others have died on service, and we feel sure the sympathies of our readers are extended to the families of those who have been thus bereaved, who whilst feeling a natural grief at the loss of their loved ones, must also feel a thrill of pride in the knowledge that their loved ones nobly died in the defence of our homes. Having been asked the question how many of our parishioners have laid down their lives in the War, we publish, as far as we know, a complete list; if any name is omitted it is unintentional, and we will publish the name in future issues upon reliable information.

They are as follows:

Buttle, R. W.

Buttle, F. C.

Cattle, H. I.

Cooper, J.

Crisp, W.

Eagan, J.

Easton F.

Flint C.

Fisher, T. W.

Flower, C.

Flower, H.

Grainger, G.

Hall S.

Haywood B.

Holmes H.

Hopper A.

Hotham, C.

Jennings, T.

Jessop, H.

Johnson Henry

Johnson, Harold

Kirby, E. (D.C.M)

Lee, J.

Plumb, W.

Rippon, T. W.

Savage, H.

Scaife, S.

Scott, Capt., G.

Skelton, G.

Stairs, F.

Stubbs, R. M.

1st September, 1917

Private J. Allison Wounded

Mr. and Mrs. J. Allison, of 22, Regent Street, Pocklington, have received news that their son (Pte. J. Allison, Machine Gun Corps) has been wounded in the leg and is now in hospital at Liverpool and progressing favourably. We trust be will have a speedy and complete recovery.

8th September, 1917

ELVINGTON.

Memorial Service.

A memorial service was held in the Parish Church. Elvington, for the late Private Ernest Cooper, who died on June 15th at Ingoestadt, in Bavaria, where he was a prisoner of war, The deceased was wounded in the knee and his leg was amputated, but he never rallied. An impressive service was conducted by the rector, the Rev. W. W. Phillips, who preached an appropriate sermon from the words. "He loved me and gave Himself-for me." The rector paid a tribute to the deceased soldier. He said he was a Sunday School scholar, a member of the choir, and a regular attendant at church when in private service in the village. He went; willingly to defend his country, and died a glorious death. He left a widow to mourn his loss.

LONDESBOROUGH.

Killed in Action.

Much sympathy has been extended to Mr. George Martin, Easthorpe Farm, Londesborough, who has been notified that his son, Private Tom Martin, of the Duke of Wellington's (West Riding) Regiment, has been killed in action. Private Martin, who would have celebrated his 21st birthday in January next was, previous to enlisting in the Army, in the employment of Mr. Henry Beachill, Wallis Grange, near Market Weighton. He had been in the Army about 15 months, and served abroad for some months. From the information to hand it appears that he was killed, along with other three of his comrades, by a shell bursting in the billet. Mr. Martin has received the following letter from Sec.-Lieut. C. Everitt: "I am sorry that I have to write this letter to inform you of the death of your son. Private T. Martin. He died last night, August 21th, about 11-30 p.m. He and four others were in a small billet some little way behind the line, and a high explosive shell came and killed four and wounded one. They died instantly and suffered no pain. We buried them yesterday in the British Cemetery; the chaplain taking the service. A cross will be put over his grave. Although your son has not been with our platoon very long, he will be missed by all."

POCKLINGTON.

Ice Cream

Is now on sale at 10 a.m. daily at Whitehead's, Market Square, Pocklington.

Wounded in Action.

Rfl. C. Mills-Trout (Mills and Co.), Market Place. Pocklington, has been wounded in action, in the right shoulder, and is now in hospital. He enlisted in the London Rifle Brigade. We are pleased to hear that he is going on nicely.

A Belgian's Thanks.

Mademoiselle Rossel (Belgian Refugee), who has been staying in Pocklington for some considerable time, wishes to express her sincere thanks to the many kind friends she has made in the town here, she leaves for the South of England, on account of her somewhat indifferent health.

A Local Soldier Injured.

Pte. J.H. Hatfield, R.G.A. who has only been in France a few weeks, is at present in hospital suffering from a dislocated shoulder. The many friends of Mr. Hatfield, who, prior to enlistment, was in business as hairdresser in Market Place, Pocklington, will wish him a speedy recovery from his injury.

Charlie Chaplin has arrived

After months of waiting, we have pleasure in announcing the fact that Charlie Chaplin has actually arrived in Pocklington, and will appear at the Central Hall Cinema to-night (Friday) and to-morrow (Saturday) in all his new turns. Charlie is funnier than ever, and if you have not had a good laugh for a long time, Charlie will draw it. There will be no extra charge of admission, so we anticipate large and enthusiastic houses to witness the funniest of all comedians.

15th September, 1917

BIRTHS, MARRIAGES AND DEATHS.

IN MEMORIAM.

FLINT.—With ever-loving remembrance of Charlie Flint, of Pocklington, who was killed in action in France, September 15th, 1916.

Dear Brother, the memory of thy sacrifice; We cherish now with pride; Sweetest thoughts shall ever linger, Around the grave where you are laid.

From his Sister Ada (Sheffield), and Brother Harry (France).

FLINT.—In ever-loving memory of a dear Brother, Charlie Flint, of Pocklington, who was killed in action September 15. 1916.

We little thought when he left home
That he'd no more return,
But God has willed it otherwise,
And left us here to mourn.

Gone from us, but not forgotten,
Never will his memory fade,
And loving thoughts will ever linger
Around the spot where he is laid.

His loving Sister, M. E. Harper.

ROWLEY.—In loving memory of Margaret Ann Rowley, the beloved daughter of Private and Mrs. J. Rowley of Pocklington, who died September 15th, 1916.

Days of sadness still come over us,
Hidden tears ofttimes flow,
For memory keeps our dear one near us,
Though she died one year ago.

THOMPSON.—In loving memory of Pte. Wilfrid Thompson who died of wounds, September 16th, 1916.

Dear is the grave where our loved one is laid,
Sweet is the memory that never will fade;
Roses may whither, leaves fade and die,
But you, dear one, from our memories will never die.

From his loving Mother, Sisters, Brothers (in France), and Maggie.

Pocklington Weekly News, 6th Oct. 1917

EFFECT OF AMERICA'S ENTRY INTO THE WAR.

SIR MARK SYKES'S VIEWS. Sir Mark Sykes, Bart., M.P.. speaking at a
War Aims meeting, told the hearers that politics and war had nothing in
common. In politics every word counted and blows did not, but in war the
contrary was the case. It was wrong of anybody to try and think of politics
during the war. After the war. we should go into a new world. We were like
Columbus beating across to an unknown shore, which he (the speaker) believed would be the promised land. But don't let us make the mistake that
the Spaniards made in carrying with us any of the frivolities and follies, the
wraths and contentions of the world we had left behind. (Applause.)
Continuing, Sir Mark said he thought that November, 1916, was one of the
turning-points of the war, because it was in that month that the enemy
made the first sign that he wanted to get out of the war somehow or
another. He attributed that to the fact that those who directed the war in
Germany could perceive the time when the country would be exhausted.
His own deduction at that time was that the end of the war and the defeat

OUR PORTRAIT GALLERY.

Bombardier ALFRED ROWNTREE, M.M., of Pocklington, who has been awarded the Military Medal for gallantry in action.

Pocklington Weekly News, 20th Oct. 1917

of the enemy would happen within nine months. But since that time the disorganisation of the Russian
armies had taken place. That was a serious matter—a disaster; but it was at once counter-balanced by the
equally great disaster for the enemy and enormous advantage to ourselves of the entry on our side of the
United States. (Applause.) He would ask them to regard what had happened in Russia as negative. It had
given the enemy respite in that quarter, but so severely tried had the German military machine been that the
enemy had not been able to take military advantage of his opportunity. The Russian trouble was also purely
negative because Russia continued in the war and would remain in the war; whereas America's entry was
positive in the highest degree. There was the positive advantage of having on our side eighty millions of the
best educated people in the world, the immediate material advantage of the help of American finance, and,
when the day of greatest strain arrived,   there were the great potential reserves of the man power of the
United States on our side. (Applause.)

Homing Pigeons Missing.

We are sorry to learn from an advertisement in another column that Mr. Arthur Todd has lost several
homing pigeons. Mr. Todd's birds are being usefully employed by the Government Pigeon Service, and it is
a very serious offence under the Defence of the Realm Act, by not reporting homing pigeons to the police,
as they may be doing great service to the country.

22nd September, 1917

MARKET WEIGHTON.

Death of Discharged Soldier.

Information has been received at Market Weighton of the death of Mr. Joseph Lambert, who formerly
served in the Royal Field Artillery. The deceased, who was 22 years of age, was a member of a family of
eight sons and six daughters. and five respectively of whom survive. He was one of the three soldier and
sailor sons of the late Mr. William and Mrs. Lambert, of Southgate, and previous to joining the colours was
engaged in agriculture, being in the employment of Mr. Howard, Fisher-street, Kiplingcoates, as beastman.
Deceased two years ago last May decided to join the Royal Field Artillery, and his brother Walter the Royal
Navy. Walter was in the employment of the famous hackney breeder, Mr. John Wreghitt, Easthorpe,
Londesborough, for seven years, and at the time of joining the Navy was working for Mr. William Galtry,

Middlethorpe, Londesborough as farm foreman. Deceased, after seven months service was drafted overseas. He had the misfortune to be gassed in July, 1916, and was admitted to a base hospital, where after treatment for some time he was sent to England. In January last, shortly after the death of his father, he was discharged, and arrived home in poor health. He was taken ill about a month later, and had relapses from time to time, until death occurred this week.

SHIPTON

Local Soldier Wounded.

Mr. and Mrs. Pickering, Council Cottage, Shiptonthorpe, have received information that their son, Private Albert Pickering, East Yorks. Regt., has been wounded in action, in France, in his right- hand and leg, and is in the General Hospital.

Local Soldiers

We regret to learn that Lance Corporal John William Smith, of the Yorkshire Regiment; is suffering from shell-gas wound (mild), and is now in hospital. Rifleman Mills-Trout still lies in a critical condition injuries to his arm, and his wife was summoned to France the other day to see her husband. Gunner Jas. Marjerrison, Pocklington, has been admitted to hospital, suffering from the effects of gas.   We are sure our readers hope for them a speedy recovery.

Pte. WILFRED THOMPSON, K.O.Y.L.I., son of Mrs. Thompson, Chapmangate, died of wounds received in action, November 16th, 1916.

Pocklington Weekly News, 20th Oct. 1917

13th October, 1917

Sergt. Reg. Scaife Wounded.

Official intimation has been received that Sergt. Reg. Scaife, fourth son of Mrs. T. Scaife, Chapmangate, Pocklington, was wounded in the advance of Thursday, October 4th, by a bullet passing through his left arm, and is now in Birkenhead Hospital. Of his three brothers who have served, Sydney was killed nearly 12 months ago; Chris, is at present in a Newcastle hospital suffering from trench fever; and Bert, is now in the trenches.

27th October, 1917

Private William Walker Missing.

We regret to learn that Private William Walter (Durham Light Infantry), son of Mr. and Mrs. Robert Walker, of Pocklington, aged 22 years, is reported missing on the 24th September.   He joined the Army voluntarily on the 1st September, 1914. Official news has been received that he is missing after serving two years in France. He has seen much hard fighting in the two battles at Ypres, and on the Somme. His brother Percy, lately in the employ of Mr. Fred Steel, butcher, Pocklington, is now on military duties in Staffordshire.

EVERINGHAM.

Pte. J. W. Withell recommended for the D.C.M.

Many of our readers will be pleased to learn that Private J. W. Withell, Royal Marine Light Infantry, son of Mr. and Mrs. T. Withell, Everingham, has been recommended for the D.C.M., for bravery on the battlefield on the 29th April last, and for defeating the Germans when they counter-attacked seven times. Pte. Withell went out into a shell-hole with a Lewis gun, and remained there alone for 48 hours without either food or water. It was a severe fight in which many of his comrades fell. We congratulate Private Withell on this distinction as a mark of his bravery in action.

10th November, 1917

BISHOP WILTON.

Sapper Harry Gospel dies of Wounds.

We are sure our readers will learn with feelings of sincere regret of the death of Sapper Harry Gospel, of Bishop Wilton, who died on October 24th, from wounds received in action. The deceased young fellow was well-known and highly respected by a wide circle of friends throughout the district, and much sympathy is extended to the widow and a large family.

Another Local Military Medallist.

We are pleased to state that another of our local soldiers has been awarded the Military Medal for bravery in the field, Corpl. Frank Allison having gained the distinction a fortnight ago for an exceptionally smart piece of work, in taking rations up to an outpost party who had been isolated for several hours by enemy shell-fire. Corpl. Allison ventured through the barrage, and on his return was warmly congratulated by both Officers and men. He is one of the three sons of Mr. and Mrs. Allison, of Kirkland Street, Pocklington, serving, who have also three sons-in-law with the Colours.

17th November, 1917

Pocklington Soldier Wounded

News has been received that Corpl. Harry Flint, Yorks. Regt.. son of Mr. and Mrs. C. Flint, Grape Lane, Pocklington, has been admitted to Springburn Hospital, at Glasgow, suffering from a severe shrapnel wound in the thigh, which be received on the morning of October 31st, whilst distributing rations. He is progressing favourably. His brother, Charles, was killed in action a year ago.

We also regret to learn that Private Herbert Holmes (who was employed in this office about four years ago) has been injured in the arm by shell fire, and is now in hospital in France. He is progressing favourably.

Military Medal

Our readers will be pleased to know that another of our local soldiers has gained the Military Medal for distinguished conduct in the field. Riflemen C. V. Waite, of the K.R.R.O., son of Mr. and Mrs. J.H. Waite, Baden House, Pocklington, having been awarded the medal for fine work on 20th September. He is attached to the Divisional Signalling Company and the official notice of the award is as follows: - "Your Gallantry and devotion to duty 20th September, when you repeatedly carried urgent messages and acted as guide under heavy shell and machine-gun fire. Your coolness under heavy fire enabled communications to be kept up during a very anxious period. — Major-General." This is the second occasion on which Rfl. Waite has been recommended.

Soldiers on Leave

Corporal Mutimer, Private Bob Pratt, Private P. Hotham, Private H. Buttle, Trooper Harry Hotham and Private W. Rowley have recently been home on leave and some of them have already returned to the front. We wish them all the best of luck and a speedy return to their native town.

Wounded.

Official intimation has been received that Pte. John Henry Skelton. K O.Y.L.I., son of Mr. and Mrs. H. Skelton, Dean's Lane, Pocklington, has been admitted to the Canadian Hospital, Boulogne, suffering from a wounded contused back, caused by being buried by a shell explosion on October 25th. whilst acting as a stretcher-bearer. He is making satisfactory progress.

8th December, 1917

Death of Private Fred Foster

The sad news has been received that Pte. Fred Foster, Durham Light Infantry, died in hospital in Salonica on November 26th. from bronchial pneumonia, following fever. Deceased, who was 33 years of ago, came to reside at Pocklington 19 years ago, and at the death of his uncle (the late Mr Allan Foster), he, in partnership with his brother, carried on the shoe-making business in the Market Place. He enlisted on December 6th last year, and after training went abroad on April 4th of this year. A quiet genial dispositioned man of good physique, he was well-known and much respected in the district. He leaves a widow (licensee of the Black Swan) and one child, and to them and his mother and brother much sympathy is extended in their bereavement.

POCKLINGTON.

Whitehead's Local Almanack for 1918 is now ready. It is meeting with a quick sale, and you should secure your copy today.

A Local Soldier in Hospital.

The many friends of Private Chris. Scaife of Pocklington will be pleased to learn that he is progressing favourably. He is in hospital in Newcastle-on-Tyne, and is just about convalescent. His two brothers are also in hospital, and are reported to be going on satisfactorily, whilst another brother has made the supreme sacrifice.

Military Service.

A Military service will be held in the Wesleyan Methodist Church, Pocklington, to-morrow (Sunday) evening at 6 o'clock. Preacher. Lieut. Sawyer; soloists, Staff - Sergt. Marlborough and Private Hollingsworth.

On Leave.

Quite recently a number of Pocklington soldiers have been over on leave, and their many friends are delighted to see them looking so well. Sergt. Reg. Scaife, Corpl. C. Spivey, and Private Hutchinson are here this week, whilst quite a nice batch visited their native town a week ago, and have returned to the front.

A Soldier's Thanks.

Private Hutchinson, of Canal Head, Pocklington, is over on leave from France, and begs to acknowledge with grateful thanks, the receipt of a postal order which some kind friends in Pocklington sent to him whilst he was in France.

Another Local Military Medallist.

Corpl. A. Dykes, Military Medallist, one of the six sons of Mr. and Mrs. Dykes, of Market Street, Pocklington, who are serving with the Colours, paid a visit to the National School the other week, where he received a hearty welcome from the Master, Teaching Staff, and children. Mr. Skinner congratulated his old scholar on his achievement and pointed out to the school children how honour was reflected on the school by the distinction gained. The medal was won on the night of July 3lst. Taking over charge, from an officer, of a raiding party of 48 men, Corpl. Dykes and his men came into contact with 150 of the enemy, armed with bombs, bayonets, and daggers. Superior in numbers the enemy attacked, but this was met with exceptional skill and daring by the small British Force, who used bombs and bayonets to such good effect that the enemy were completely defeated, a number being left dead in "No Man a Land."

Their Officer in charge was captured and important documents seized. Corpl. Dykes is the second member of his family to receive distinction, his brother, Sergt. F. C. Dykes, having gained the medal a year ago.

BIRTHS, MARRIAGES AND DEATHS

FOSTER.—On November 26th, at Salonica, Pte. Fred Foster, D.L.I., the beloved husband of Emma Foster, Black Swan Inn, Pocklington.

"Those who have lost will understand."

FOSTER.– On November 26th, at Salonica, Pte. Fred Foster, D.L.I., second son on M.E. Foster and the late James Foster, and second grandson of the late J.W. Wells, chemist and druggist, Leeds and London.

From Mother and Brothers (Jack and William.)

IN MEMORIAM.

LOFT.---In loving memory of my dear son, Pte. Albert James Loft (East Yorkshire Regiment), of Bishop Wilton, who died from wounds received in action, on the 5th day of December. 1915, aged 27 years.

Though buried in a distant land,
Amid the shot and shell,
No one knows the parting
When we couldn't say "farewell."
But his memory will never fade.

15th December, 1917

WARTER.

Death of Trooper Bernard Byass.

We deeply regret to record the death of Trooper Bernard Byass, the beloved son of Mr. and Mrs. T. Byass, of Warter, who was killed in action in Palestine recently. Much sympathy is expressed for Mr. and Mrs. Byass in their great bereavement. We also regret to learn that the deceased's brother (Trooper E.T. Byass) was severely wounded.

Wounded.

Pte. George Warrior, D.L.I., son of Mr. and Mrs Warrior, The Balk, Pocklington, was wounded in the foot during last week's operations in France. He is now in Harehills Road Hospital, Leeds where he is progressing favourably.

22nd December, 1917

CORRESPONDENCE.

To the Editor of the "Pocklington News"
Dear Sir,—
Will you kindly allow me a small piece in your paper to thank the ladies of the Pocklington Parcels Fund for their kindness in forwarding to me such a delightful Christmas gift. It was somewhat a surprise to me to receive such an amount, as I thought with there being such a lot of lads to send to, it would not run out so much as it did. I am sure it will be a most handsome gift for the lads out at the front now. Although I am not there myself I know what it is to be there, and I also know how even a very little is appreciated from the

dear old home town. I am sure you most have had a very successful social and everybody must have had their shoulders to the wheel to bring forth such splendid results as shown. Therefore once more thanking the ladies of the Committee, also all who have in any way helped to try and make Tommy's Christmas a little brighter.

I remain,

Yours faithfully, Lce.-Corpl. BARKER, W.

———

London Street,
Pocklington
December 20th, 1917

To the Editor of the "Pocklington News."

Dear Sir, - Will you allow me through your paper to thank the people of Pocklington for the Christmas gift I received from Mrs. Thomas, on behalf of the residents of Pocklington. Wishing you all a happy Xmas and a brighter New Year.

Yours respectfully, Private J. Ferisy

———

Portsmouth,

December 17th, 1917,
Dear Sir,—Permit me to thank the good people of Pocklington for a much-appreciated Xmas Gift, which I received recently. I assure you the P.O. just came in nick of time.
Again thanking you all.
Believe me to remain.
Yours truly, Rifleman H.E. EZARD, K.R.R.

———

Dublin,
December 15-17,
Dear Mr. Editor,—
I cannot find words to sufficiently express my gratitude to the Pocklingtonians who have been the means of providing local soldiers with a welcome Postal Order with which to provide a few luxuries at this Season of the Year;   I sincerely wish you all a Merry Xmas and a Bright New Year.
Yours faithfully.
Bugler J. WARTERS, H.L.I.

———

George Street, Pocklington
December 21st, 1917

Dear Mr. Editor,- Will you kindly all me to express through your columns, my sincere thanks to the many kind friends in Pocklington who have been the means of sending each local soldier a welcome P.O., I am sure their kindness is much appreciated by us all.

Yours truly, J. MARJERRISON, R.G.A..

———

Pocklington Officer Mentioned In Despatches

Amongst the names mentioned in the Dispatch (dated 7th November, 1917) of Field Marshal Sir Doulas Haig, Commander in Chief of the British Armies in France, for distinguished and gallant services, and devotion to duty, is that of Major (Acting Lieut. Colonel) F.W. Robson, D.S.O. (Yorkshire Regiment), who new commands a Battalion of Durham Light Infantry.—This the second time that Lieut.-Col. Robson has been mentioned in despatches.

Soldiers on Leave.

We are pleased to see several of our local soldiers at home on leave from the front for a few days, looking fit and well. Amongst them are: Lce.-Corpl. Richard Brewer, who has seen some hard fighting, and taken part in all the big battles since April last. He is serving with the machine gunners, and has been fortunate in come through without a scratch. He tells an interesting story of a pal out yonder, whom he considers to be the luckiest man he has ever met. One day they were in a warm corner and very tired, and although shells and bullets were flying in all directions Lce. Corpl. Brewer's pal was dead-beat, and he threw himself on the ground and was soon fast asleep; He had been asleep but a few minutes when a shell dropped between his legs, but it didn't explode and the lucky chap is still alive and doing his bit. Private W. Bean, son of Mr. Thomas Bean, George Street, Pocklington, is also at home for a few days, after serving eighteen months on the Western front. Leading Stoker Harry Windebank, is spending a month's leave at home, after being away for five years, serving in the Navy, somewhere in the Tropics.

SPLENDID RECORD OF A POCKLINGTON FAMILY.

SIX SONS WITH THE FORCES: TWO WIN THE MILITARY MEDAL.

"The Yorkshire Herald" of Tuesday last contains splendid photos of the six sons of Mr. and Mrs, W. Dykes, of Market Street, Pocklington. All now serving in His Majesty's Forces, and says:—An interesting record of service is held by the family of Mr. and Mrs. W. Dykes, Pocklington. Their six sons are enrolled with his Majesty's Forces, and two of them have been made recipients of the Military Medal for splendid gallantry in action.

William Dykes, aged 33, the eldest son, was employed in a maltkiln at Market Weighton when he was called up as an old Volunteer on the outbreak of war. He took part in the Retreat from Mons, and altogether was in France for sixteen months. A year ago last January he completed a long period of service as a Territorial; then he joined the Navy, and is now serving on a submarine chaser. He is married, and has four children. Private Tom Dykes, aged 30, was in the Territorial Force when war was declared, was called to the Colour on

mobilisation, and was drafted overseas in July, 1916. He has been once wounded, receiving a machine-gun bullet through one of his legs. Before the war he was a bricklayer's labourer.

Sergeant Fred Chapman Dykes, the third son, was also in the Territorial Force, and called up when hostilities were begun, being sent to the front in April 1915. He was awarded the Military Medal for bravery in the field, going out under heavy shell fire and carrying a wounded officer to a place of safety. He is married, has two children, and before the war was employed in the wagon works at Horbury.

Corporal Arthur Dykes, aged 26, joined the Territorial Force soon after the outbreak of war and went to the front with his brother Tom. He was awarded the Military Medal for his courageous work during the night of July 31st—August 1st last. Corporal Dykes, acting on instructions, took charge of a raiding party of 48 men, and came in contact with 160 of the enemy, armed with bombs, bayonets, and daggers. The enemy made an attack, which was met with great skill and daring. Cpl. Dykes led the men, and they used their bombs and bayonets to such good effect that the enemy were completely repulsed, a number of the party being left dead in No-Man's-Land. Their officer in charge was captured, and important documents seized. Corpl. Dykes is an old scholar of the Pocklington National School, of which Mr. A. Skinner is the head teacher.

George Dykes, aged 24, has been accepted for the Royal Flying Corps, but has not yet received his call to the Colours, He is a member of the Metropolitan Police Force, and wears a medal received as one of the guard of honour at the coronation of King George V.

"Private Albert Dykes, the sixth son, joined the Army Service Corps early in the war, was sent to a Mediterranean base, but is now serving in another theatre of war. He is 22 years of age and married, and previous to entering the Army was employed in the Post Office Telegraph Department."

29th December, 1917

POCKLINGTON.
War Time

Owing to the orders of the Food Controller there was no distribution of bread at the Parish Church as in former years.

Wedding.

A marriage of local interest was solemnized in the Wesleyan Methodist Church. Pocklington, on Boxing Day, December 26. the contracting: parties being Private Wm. Lister to Miss Lottie May Shillito Longthorn, both of Pocklington.

Flag Day

A Flag Day in aid of the Church Army Huts was held at Pocklington on Saturday week and realised £8 16s. Mrs. Fisher is the hon. secretary, and the collectors were; Mrs. T. Harrison (South View), Mrs. Seaton Smith, Miss M. Harrison, Miss Thirsk, Miss O. Fisher, Miss Aston, Miss Skinn, Miss C. Skinn, Miss G. Silburn. and Miss Ablitt.

TROOPER B. BYASS, East Yorks. Yeomanry, Killed in action in Palestine, 1917. Son of Mr and Mrs. T. Byass, Middlebridges Farm, Warter.

Pocklington Weekly News, 22nd Dec. 1917

Christmas Day in Pocklington.

The weather proved most seasonable, snow falling freely soon after noon on Christmas Day giving the fine old town a truly winterly appearance, whilst the church bells added enchantment to the scene by ringing out merry peals throughout the day. Juvenile "boxing" fraternity were again in strong force, and appeared to have a fairly successful time.

Dance on Boxing Day.

The long-night dance, held in the Central Hall, Pocklington, on Boxing Day, was a great success, there being a large company of town and country people, who thoroughly enjoyed themselves, dancing being kept up until 1-30 a.m. Miss "Kathie" Hotham played excellent dance music, and the duties of M.C.'s were ably discharged by Mr. Fred Lee and Mr. M. Washington.

Local Soldiers Home on Leave.

Private Percy Walker, Sherwood Foresters, has been over on leave, visiting his parents in Church Lane, Pocklington. He looked exceedingly well, and is the making of a very smart soldier. We are pleased to learn that he received the first prize for the cleanest equipment in his company numbering about 400 men, before leaving Staffordshire for the north, where he is now training.

12th January, 1918

POCKLINGTON RURAL DISTRICT FOOD CONTROL COMMITTEE.

NOTICE IS HEREBY GIVEN that the above Committee have fixed the following maximum retail prices for BUTTER and MILK in their area:—

FARMER'S BUTTER, 2s. 6d. per lb., 1s. 3d. per half-pound.
MILK, for January and February, 2s. 4d. per gall, delivered; 2s. per gall, not delivered.

ARTHUR J. OLIVER, Executive Officer., 17, Market Street, Pocklington. January, 1918.

N.B.—The Butter (Maximum Prices) Order, 1917, provides that the expression "retail sale" shall include any sale of a quantity not exceeding 4lb. of butter by the maker of such butter, where the total quantity of butter so sold by the maker by the buyer in any one calendar week does not exceed 8lb.

EAST RIDING OF YORKSHIRE.

WAR AGRICULTURAL EXECUTIVE COMMITTEE.

SALE OF HORSES ORDER, 1917.

NOTICE TO FARMERS.

The Food Production Department of the Board of Agriculture have appointed Mr. T. P. Foster, of Sewerby Fields, Bridlington, to be their Horse Purchasing Officer for the East Riding.

Mr. Foster has received instructions from the Government to purchase a large number of horses. The War Agricultural Executive Committee in consequence of this, have decided that until further notice no unconditional licences will be issued.

Conditional licences may be issued on receipt of the application form, which may be obtained from me, duly completed.

These licences are subject to the condition that the horses specified in the licences, are not to be sold or transferred except to an occupier of an agricultural holding or to a person duly authorised by the Board of Agriculture and Fisheries, or the Army Council to purchase the same.

JOHN BICKERSTETH, Clerk of the Committee. County Hall, Beverley. 8th January, 1918.

D.C.M.

We are please to record that another Pocklington soldier has distinguished himself. Corporal Charles Spivey, Yorkshire Regiment, son of the late Mr. Ralph Spivey, for many years manager of the Pocklington Gas Works, and of Mrs. Spivey, now residing at Bradford, having been awarded the Distinguished Conduct

Medal for bravery in the Field. Corpl. Spivey was a member of the local Territorials Force in camp when war broke out, and which was at once placed on active training. He went out with the Battalion and was severely wounded but made satisfactory recovery and returned to France, where he is now serving.

Military Medal.

Gunner T. Armitage, second son of Mr. and Mrs. G. Armitage, Haxby Road, York, late of Pocklington, has been awarded the Military Medal for bravery on the 10th and 11th June, 1917, in assisting to save a quantity of cartridges. He is 34 years of ago and previous to enlistment in a Siege Battery, R.G.A., was employed at Messrs. Rowntree's Works. York.

Home on Leave.

Private Charlie Ezard and Private Chas. Bean are both home, on leave from the front, looking in the pink of condition.

Millington Camp.

A very enjoyable evening was spent on Wednesday at the Y.M.C.A. Hut when Mrs. C. T. Hayward and Miss Patty Robson arranged a concert. Capt. Robinson presided, and the following kindly took part:—Capt. Robinson. Lieut. Smith, Lieut. Willis, Miss Queenie Dunn, Miss Aston, Master Claude Brook, Corpl. Gaddass, Cpl. Blacklesley, Lce.-Corpl. Gathercoli, Pte. Smythson and Pte. Vobias. At the close, Lieut. Power thanked Capt. Robinson for presiding, and the artistes for their splendid efforts. A word of thanks to Mr. Parker for having the hut so beautifully warm and comfortable, was heartily accorded.

ELVINGTON.

Killed in Action.

Pte. Alfred Atkin, West Yorks. Regiment, who was killed in action on December 21st, was the son of Mr. and Mrs. E. Atkin, Kirby lane, Elvington, York. The deceased was 42 years of age, and only returned to the front on December 4th last, after his second leave; before joining the Army he was engaged at Elvington as a farm labourer.

SHIPTONTHORPE.

A Local Soldier's Distinguished Service.

The many friends of Driver G. Pickering. A.S.C., will be pleased to learn that he has received a certificate from his Commanding Officer for distinguished service in the field from 20th March. to 20th September, 1917, and says "that although promotion and decorations cannot be given in every case, your good services are recognised and greatly appreciated."

19th January, 1918

The Late Private E. H. Porrill

It will be remembered that Private Ernest Hartland Porrill of the East Yorkshire Regiment, died at Millington Camp, a few weeks ago, following depression. The Coroner (Mr. J. R. Wood) in summing, up at the inquest which followed said that it was quite probable that an open-air life had cured Porrill of his old-standing mental trouble to a large extent, but that the effect of him being ordered overseas the second time had caused him to break down again. To him it was incredible that a man with a medical record like that of the deceased man could, under any circumstances whatever, be placed on draft to go out overseas a second time. From the evidence it appeared that when the deceased went overseas the first time he had in his possession a doctor's letter which would probably have prevented him being sent out had he produced it.

He seemed to have been a gallant fellow, however, who was determined to "do his bit," and he went out and did it. There could be no doubt that he took his own life, but it was not an act of cowardice; he was a brave man, and it was undoubtedly because his mind gave way that he took his own life. The Jury recommended that the widow of deceased should receive full pension as though he had died on the battlefield. The Coroner approved of the suggestion and a petition has been drawn up and Mr. T. Towle, who is ever ready to help any deserving cause, has received many signatures to the petition for a full pension for the widow and family. The petition is now in the care of Mr. Whitehead, stationer in Market Square, Pocklington, from Saturday. December 19th, to Saturday, December 26th, where it can be signed by anyone who is in sympathy with the movement, after which it will be despatched to the proper authority.

KILNWICK PERCY

On Leave.

Sapper B. B. Sellers, of the Royal Engineers, one of the four sons of Mr. D. Sellers, Kilnwick Percy, who are serving; with the Colours is at home on 14 days holiday, after spending two years in France.

26th January, 1918

The Injuries to Private W Preston

Private W Preston, of the Scottish Rifles, son of Mr. and Mrs. Charles Preston, of Seaton Ross, who was badly wounded in France last September, resulting in amputation of the left foot, has recently had a serious relapse, necessitating further amputation above the knee. His condition has been critical, but latest reports state that he is now making good progress towards what it is hoped may prove, a permanent recovery. We are sure our readers in all parts of the Riding, will sympathise with Mr. and Mrs. Preston to their soldier son.

9th February, 1918

A Local Officer Shipwrecked.

Staff-Surgeon Arthur Ronald Fisher, R.N., son of the Rev. A. T. and Mrs. Fisher, Vicarage, Pocklington, was on board H.M.S. Lizard, which was sunk in collision on Sunday night, January 22nd. Though losing his belongings, Surgeon Fisher was uninjured and has since been appointed to H.M. hospital ship.

16th February, 1918

A LETTER FROM PALESTINE By Pte. H. PRESTON (late of Seaton Ross) (Passed by Censor.)

After a period of silence quite a batch of most interesting letters have been received from Pte. H. Preston, R.A.M.C., by his parents. He joined up in June, 1915, spent four months at Nottingham as Hospital Orderly and in October of the same year was sent out in connection with the Dardanelles Expedition. After four months duty on a rather desolate island Pte. H. Preston was transferred to a Hospital in Egypt, where he had much strenuous work and formed many friendships. Last Summer he was drafted into the Field Ambulance in connection with General Allenby's successful operations in Palestine. During the whole of his time in the Army he has only had one brief week-end leave home, in August, 1915; and, as may be gathered from his letters home, looks anxiously and hopefully forward to the dawn of victory and peace.

The following extracts from one of his letters dated December 31st, 1917, will doubtless prove interesting to his many old friends and comrades in the district. After, dealing with letters from home and family matters he says:-

"Now that I have answered your letter it might interest you to know how I am getting on. Well, under the circumstances very well indeed. Having got thoroughly rid of an attack of Irinsy, I have been back to duty four days and feel quite fit. In spite of tempestuous winds and torrential rains I spent a very quiet but happy Christmas. My parcel arrived on Christmas morning in the best of condition, and improved things very much. I reckon I did very well—made it last four days. It was a lovely change from the hard biscuits, but I hope you did not rob yourselves in order to send it. Yesterday (Sunday) we re-joined our Headquarters, after three weeks at an Advance Dressing Station. The A.D.S.'s are good jobs. Sometimes they are a bit rough, and sometimes very new to the front, but we generally manage to get a sheltered place behind some hill, and when a small party is out it is always better than a lot. We are not troubled with a lot of red tape, the Officers are free and easy, and everybody seems happy. I think we enjoyed our Christmas better than we would have done at Headquarters. Our Camp was in a wood, nothing but olive trees, and it was a fine camp. When old "Johnny" was driven far enough back, we made little camp fires and sat round them like Gipsies. Oh! it was nice after dark to sit round a fire

POTATOES in 1918

LAST YEAR the COUNTY of YORK

Produced 297,000 Tons of Potatoes.

Consumed 387,700 Tons of Potatoes.

Deficit 90,700 Tons.

LORD RHONDDA and Mr. PROTHERO appeal to every man who has a Farm, a Garden, or an Allotment, to **PLANT MORE POTATOES** and make the County SELF-SUPPORTING.

Pocklington Weekly News, 23rd March, 1918

and spin yarns and discuss various things, such as our training days, past experiences, and especially the war and how long it is going to last (we are giving it until next Christmas). These olive trees are supposed to be sacred and we are told not to chop at them, so very carefully we managed to gather enough for a fire each night we were up there. It is surprising how it burns. A branch newly cut off burns like dried oak soaked in oil, no matter how green. We are now camping in a village (a Jewish settlement), a very nice place. The houses are built of brick with tiled roofs and floors. Some of the natives have cleared off and our Hospital Staff are using one house for patients. Those who remain are very clean industrious people, and a few can speak English very well. One very fine house, still inhabited, has a nice garden and beautiful shrubs. They have also bee-hives; fancy hen huts and runs. I saw a couple of hay stacks here, the first I have seen since I left the dear home-land. There are about eight acres of corn quite near, which looks very healthy, also a plot of cabbages and cauliflower. I have seen one or two large farms, but very little stock yet. They have fine stables and fold yards, and their implements seem very up-to-date. I had a glance through the village to-day, but to-morrow I hope to go again and find out what make these implements are (German, I should think.) A few of the people are carrying on with their farming, &c. All to-day two girls and a boy have been planting spring onions. The military are warned by notices all over to keep to the tracks, thus avoiding damage to crops. The old Turks shelled the place a few days ago and killed the prettiest little girl in the village. I often wonder what the natives think when they see the Turks being driven out, and our men occupying the places. I know I would not like our places in England to be over-run like this. It is of necessity bad enough with a friendly Army, but what it would be with a fiendish enemy like the German has proved himself to be, is too awful to contemplate. The natives here are very quiet, and rather sad. I saw one of them to-day grinding grain such as we used to grind, but just cracking it, his motive power being an oil-engine, it reminded me of happy bygone days. The people here sell bread; it looks very nice, and I dare say I shall have a taste before I leave the place. Life here is certainly interesting and enjoyable when the weather is fine, and I am pleased to say it is passable at present, resembling the English climate, rather on the cold side.

Well, we are just at the close of another year, and God grant that the New Year may see peace proclaimed and us safely back to our dear old homes. Under these conditions I cannot sit up to see the Old Year out and the New Year in, but I dare say some of you will. News being about exhausted I must conclude and turn in for the night. I sincerely hope and pray that when I awake we have started out on the happiest year we have ever known. I thought it well to close the year with a little chat home, so Good Night all. With dearest love and best wishes for the New Year. From your affectionate Son and Brother, HARRY.

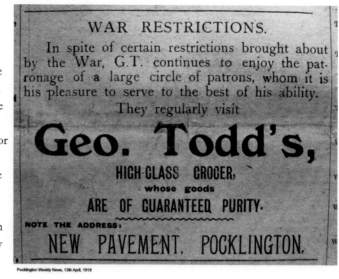

P.8.—Please excuse the scribble as my only illumination is a candle blowing in the wind. I am writing laid on my bed under a bivouac."

23rd February, 1918

Letter from a Pocklington man

Meedham Red Cross Hospital, Harlow, Essex.

To the Editor of the "Pocklington News."

Dear Sir, -Just a line to say that I am progressing very well with my wound in the left leg, which I received in action on the 15th December, 1917. It was at Ypres, about two or three miles from St. Julian. I am in a very good hospital in Essex, and hope to be well again soon., Well, I will close, hoping to be in Pocklington soon at Mr. F. Lee's Pictures.

I am, your obedient servant, Lce.-Corpl. J. PRATT.

2nd March, 1918

Killed in Action.

Private Arthur Jessop, formerly of Pocklington, whose death is recorded in another column, enlisted in the East Yorks. Regiment on June 24th. 1916, and was drafted to France in November 1916. He had been home on fourteen days leave and arrived back to France on January 21st., and was killed the following day. In a letter received by his widow from deceased's Commanding Officer, he states he was killed by a bullet in the front line of trenches, death being instantaneous and that during the time he was out he found him a bright, cheerful, and efficient soldier, and would be greatly missed by his brother soldiers, and his platoon Officers. He leaves a widow and four young children to mourn his loss.

30th March, 1918

SEATON ROSS.

Military Funeral

The funeral of the late Rifleman J. H. Henley of a reserve battalion, West Yorkshire Regiment, and eldest son of Mr. and the late Mrs. Jesse Henley, took place in St. Edith's Churchyard. Seaton Ross, on Friday last. The remains were conveyed by rail from Cannock Chase, where death took place, to Foggathorpe Station. A detachment of 50 cadets from the Pocklington Grammar School in command of Captain Ross, headed the cortege, while the coffin, covered by the Union Jack, on which were placed the deceased's cap and belt, was borne into the church by four of the cadets, and preceded by the Rev. George Deane (rector of Harswell and curate in charge of St. Edmund's). Miss Preston, organist, played "O rest in the Lord." During the service the hymns "Peace, perfect peace" and "Fight the good fight" were sung, and on the procession re-forming the organist played the "Dead March" in "Saul." The chief mourners were Mr. Jesse Henley (father). Miss Jessie and Miss Mary Henley (sisters), Masters Charles and Robert Henley (brothers), Mr. Charles Henley (Seaton Ross) and Mr. George Henley (York) uncles, Mr. and Mrs. Charles Ogle (Yapham) uncle and aunt, Mr. and Mrs. Herbert Tinson (Pocklington), Mr. George Linfoot (Pocklington), Mrs. Wm. Walker (Melbourne) aunt, Mr. and Mrs. Wm. Featherby (Harswell), Mr. Maxwell Stewart (Everingham Park), Mr. Burden (headmaster of Beverley Grammar School), Mrs. Burden, Mr. and Mrs. Michael Nichols (Melbourne), Mrs. Geo. Todd, Mr. Charles Preston, Private Preston, Private Middleton (Seaton Ross), Mrs. Macgarr, Mrs. H. Hammond. and Mrs. G. Gardam (teachers at the Council School), Mr. Richmond, Mrs. T. Gardam, Mrs. T. Drakes, and Sergt. Farrar (representing the Reserve Battalion West Yorkshire Regiment).

Memorial Services for Two Bishop Wilton Heroes.

On Sunday, 7th March, Memorial Services were held in St. Edith's Church, Bishop Wilton, to commemorate two men belonging to the Parish who have given their lives for King and Country. Pte. Hartley Slater (West Yorks. Regt.), who was commemorated at the morning service, was the third son of Mr. and Mrs. Wm. Slater, of Bishop Wilton. He had been in France for some months, and had been missing since October. 1917, and a few weeks ago, was officially reported to have been killed in action.

In the evening the Memorial Service was for Pte. John Cooper Walkington (Durham Light Infantry), who was killed in France, 20th February last. He was the youngest son of Mr. Wm. Walkington, and had spent nearly all his life in the Parish, and was a general favourite and greatly respected by all. He had been married only a few months and very much sympathy is felt with the widow, in her early bereavement.

The Vicar (Rev. E. Peters) officiated at both services, which were attended by a large number of parishioners and friends of the two fallen soldiers. The Vicar took as his text St. John. xii. 25, the subject being "Self-saving is death; Self-giving is life"; and in the course of his address paid, a fitting tribute to the memory of the two heroes, and expressed deep sympathy with their families.

13th April, 1918
PRIVATE JIM GILES, West Yorks. Regt.

Mr. and Mrs. J. Giles, of Union Street, Pocklington, have received the sad official news that their second son, Pte. Jim Giles, aged 21 years, died in a casualty clearing station in France on March 30th, from the effects of shell wounds to left arm and thigh, received in action. After leaving school he was for some time employed at Messrs. Thirsk and Sons Flour Mill, Pocklington, before proceeding to Shipley, where he was apprenticed to the butchering trade with his uncle, Mr. George Brabiner, a native of Pocklington. He enlisted in the West Yorks. Regt., with which he served over two years in France. Being of tall physique, good appearance, and happy disposition, he was generally respected, and much sympathy is expressed with the parents and members of the family in their heavy bereavement. His elder brother is at present in a military hospital suffering from illness contracted on active service.

France, 4th April, 1918.

Dear Mr. Giles,—It is with great regret that I have to inform you of the death of your son, No. 855, Pte. J. Giles. He died in hospital from wounds received in action on March 28th. He was a good and hard working lad, and I can assure you he will be greatly missed by the fellows of the platoon with which he has been so long.

I know his death will be a great loss to you. May I offer my deepest sympathy in your sorrow. He died a soldiers death, in a great and just cause, a cause which, please God, will triumph.

Again offering my sympathy,
Yours very truly, G. W. MAYO.
P.S.—If there is any further information you would like I shall be only too pleased to give it you.—G.W.M

ROLL OF HONOUR.

LIEUTENANT-COLONEL FREDERICK WILLIAM ROBSON, D.S.O.

BATTALION COMMANDER FALLS IN ACTION.

Official news was received on Monday last by Mr. Thomas Robson. solicitor, Pocklington, that his third son, Lieutenant Colonel Frederick William Robson. D.S.O., Yorkshire Regiment (Green Howards), attached Durham Light Infantry, had been killed in action. It has since been ascertained that this took place on the 28th March. He was educated at Pocklington Grammar School, where he gained many scholastic and athletic honours, including the sports championship for two years in succession. He was a member of the Yorkshire Gentlemen's Cricket Club, and the Yorkshire County Hockey team. He matriculated at the London University, and served his articles with his father at Pocklington, where he afterwards practised with him as a solicitor. He passed the Intermediate Law Examination in the first class, and at the final, obtained honours, and was awarded the John Mackerell prize for the best practical candidate at the examination. He was also awarded a prize of £5 6s. 0d. by the Yorkshire Law Society, for having obtained the highest position in the Honours List during the year 1908. He was a member of, and took a very keen interest in, the Yorkshire Law Students Society, and

Food Control Notes

There is a hint of a **General Rationing Scheme** to come into operation about the middle of July.

Domestic Sugar Ration.

The Director of Sugar Distribution desires it to be clearly understood:
(a) That there is no intention in the early future to reduce the amount of weekly domestic ration of Sugar.
(b) That in making special allotments of Sugar through the Local Food Committees, under the scheme for providing fruit growers with Sugar for domestic preserving, no account will be taken of any Sugar saved out of the weekly ration.
(c) That the saving of Sugar out of the domestic ration for Jam making not only DOES NOT constitute hoarding, but is a course which is eminently desirable in the public interest under existing circumstances.

Paper.

The gradual shrinkage in supplies of Paper-making materials is now causing a famine in all classes of paper, and prices are soaring upward, and the scarcity has now become so serious that unless we are able to supply the various Mills with Waste Paper we cannot get New Paper. We therefore appeal to you to collect all the waste you possibly can and bring it to us.

Tea Supplies.

We have very reason to believe that the Datum Period system (by which we can at present only obtain Teas in proportion to our trade from July 1st. 1915, to June 30th, 1916) will be abolished in the near future; and that a system of rationing of individuals, under which retailers and wholesalers will obtain supplies in accordance with their ascertained requirements, will be substituted.

Pocklington Weekly News, 13th April, 1918

frequently took part in their debates. Colonel Robson was a member of the Yorkshire Law Society. He was a churchman, and for many years a sidesman at the Pocklington Parish Church. At the outbreak of war he was a Captain in the local Territorials (which were then under the command of Colonel Sir Mark Sykes, Bart., M.P.) and joining up immediately, went with his Battalion to France in April, 1915, and directly afterwards he was in action, being slightly wounded in the Battle of St. Julian, and in September, 1916, during the fighting at the front, Captain Robson (as he then was) took command of the Battalion, after Colonel Mortimer. C.M.G. was killed. He was promoted Major, and subsequently Lieutenant-Colonel, on being appointed Commandant of a Divisional School of Instruction overseas, for training Officers and non-commissioned Officers, and on the completion of his work in March 1917, he was appointed to the command of a battalion of Durham Light Infantry, and this position he held up to the time of his death. He was twice mentioned in dispatches for distinguished and gallant services and devotion to duty, and was awarded the D.S.O. Sir Douglas Haig's special mention stated that "Captain F. W. Robson assumed command of the battalion, and carried out his duty with the greatest courage and initiative. He set a splendid example to his men throughout the operations." He was himself unwounded, but his brother. Captain E. M. Robson (then Lieut.) was wounded in four places in the same action. He received the Military Cross, and the two brothers were decorated by His Majesty at Buckingham Palace in December, 1916. Colonel Robson's two younger brothers, Captain E. M. Robson, M.C., and Lieutenant J. Stanley Robson (also wounded) are serving in the Yorkshire Regiment, and have been on active service overseas, since July 1915, Mr. Richard Robson, a member of the firm of Messrs. Bell, Brodrick, and Gray, solicitors, Ormond House, London, E.C., Colonel Robson's eldest brother, died on March 30th last.

20th April, 1918

Local Soldiers Wounded.

News has been received that four more of our local soldiers have been wounded in action. These include Sergt. F.C. Dykes, M.M., Yorkshire Regiment, son of Mr. and Mrs. Dykes, of Market Street, Pocklington who is at present in Portsmouth Hospital, wounded in the arm and leg; he has been previously wounded. Private Wm. Bean, Yorkshire Regt., second son of Mr. Thos. Bean, George Street, has also been wounded in the arm and leg. and has been removed to a Base Hospital: whilst Stretcher-bearer Thomas Henry Skelton, Yorkshire Light Infantry, son of Mr. and Mrs. H. Skelton, Dean's Lane, is at Croydon Hospital, Surrey, having been badly gassed. Private Henry Cains, Northumberland Fusiliers, second son of Mr. and Mrs. F. G. Cains, Canal Head, has been wounded in the arm, and removed to a hospital in France.

ROLL OF HONOUR

The late LIEUT. COLONEL WILLIAM ROBSON. D.S.O. Yorkshire Regiment (Green Howards), attached Durham Light Infantry.

Numerous letters of sympathy have been received by Thomas Robson. solicitor, Pocklington (Colonel Robson's father) from past and present Officers of the Yorkshire Regiment and Durham Light Infantry. An officer of high rank writes:—"Your son was a brilliant Officer, and I foresaw for him a great and noble career; he had enormous ability, command and courage. I have lost a magnificent comrade, England has lost a fine soldier"

A Lieut. Colonel writes: "He was one of the finest type of an Englishman I ever met, and I feel his death very keenly, as will the whole his Battalion; who to a man, trusted and loved him." An Officer of the Battalion of the Durham Light Infantry, which Colonel Robson commanded, writes on behalf of all the Officers : "He died fighting in command of his Battalion (which had then had a week's hard fighting), and no one in the Battalion can praise too highly his conduct, and the example he set, during that battle. He was greatly respected by every officer and man of his Battalion." Another Officer writes: "We have lost not only a most gallant Colonel, but a great personal friend. His memory, and the result of his work and example, will never be forgotten so long as the Battalion exists."

Killed in Action.

Private James Harrison, Highland Light Infantry, eldest son of Private Thomas Harrison and Mrs. Harrison, Church-lane, Pocklington was killed in action on the 24th ult. He was a member of the Wagoners Reserve, was called up in August, 1914, and proceeded on active service a week later. He had been wounded three times and gassed, and recommended for the Military Medal. His father is in Salonika, and a younger brother who has been wounded is now serving in France. He belongs to a family that has provided many men for the Army. Two uncles have completed long service in the Regular Army, and one of his cousins, the son of Mr. Peter Harrison. Pocklington's bellman, is to join up immediately.

Private Thomas Thorpe, Yorkshire Regiment, is officially reported to have died, on April 9th, in the Australian Casualty Clearing Station from wounds received in action. He re-joined the local Territorials on the outbreak of war, and served with the Regiment in France, where he had been twice wounded. Only three weeks ago he was home on leave, and returning to France was attached to the East Yorks. Regiment, with which he was mortally wounded. In civil life he was a stonemason, serving his apprenticeship with Mr. J. Richardson, New Street., and his quiet and genial disposition gained him many friends, who deeply regret his early death at the age of 23 years. He leaves a widow, daughter of Mrs. W. Steels, Chapmangate.

With, deep regret we record the death of Pte. George Gilyead, East Yorkshire Regt., eldest son of Mr. and Mrs. J. W. Gilyead, Meltonby Villas, Pocklington, who was killed in action on March 27th. Previous to enlistment deceased was a much-esteemed clerk with Messrs. English and Son, auctioneers, valuers, and was widely-known and respected in the district. He was a most popular and promising member of the Wesleyan Church, having been a Teacher and Secretary of the Sunday School, and also Secretary of the Wesley Guild. He was a most indefatigable worker for these societies and for anything that would promote the welfare of his church, the members of which will deeply lament his early death at the age of 24 years, and throughout the Pocklington Circuit, sympathy will be extended to Mr. and Mrs. Gilyead in their bereavement.

Private Walter Mizon, Yorkshire Regiment, Church Side, Market Weighton, has fallen in action. He was the fourth son of Mrs. Edward Mizon, of St. Helen's Square, and joined the old Volunteers, and continued to serve when they were transferred to the East Yorkshire Territorial Association. He was only 18 years of age when he first joined the Volunteers, and as he was 35 at the time of his death he had served for 17 years. He was awarded the Volunteer Long Service Medal, his widow resides in Market Weighton.

POCKLINGTON MAN IN PALESTINE

February 28th 1918. To the Editor, "Howdenshire Chronicle"

Dear Sir,--Would you be so kind as to publish this letter to thank the people of Pocklington for their kindness in sending a parcel to me, which I thankfully received on February 27th. I am enjoying one of the good old Woodbines now as I sit writing this letter; it is a great pleasure to have a decent smoke when you know it has come from Blighty. Well, you will no doubt know by now that we are in Egypt at present but for how long I couldn't say. I should very much like to have a look at all my friends again, and hope it won't be long before this is all finished and we get a chance. The climate here at present is colder first thing on a morning to what we had it in ----, but hope it will get warmer in time to come. I shall have to close now, as I have to start work in a few minutes, so again I thank one and all, with all my heart, for their kindness; wishing all God's help and guidance to keep them from all danger. I am, Sir, Yours most respectfully;
S.S. F. BARKER

We learn from another source that Shoeing-smith F. Barker arrived in France last Thursday.

27th April, 1918

POCKLINGTON.

Thanks.

Trooper G. Adamson, (formerly of Burnby); serving with the Australian Forces, sends his best thanks to the ladies of Pocklington for forwarding him such a welcome parcel.

Wounded in Action.

We regret to learn that Private Jas. Geo. King, Notts. and Derby Regt., and formerly of Pocklington, has been severely wounded, having lost his left leg and being severely wounded in the right leg. Writing to his wife at Pocklington, he cheerfully says:— "Do not upset yourself, as I shall soon be better." We trust he will have a speedy recovery.

Killed in Action.

We regret to learn that Sergt.-Major Allan Thompson was killed on the 17th of April by shell-fire. He was transferred to the York. and Lancs. from the Durham Light Infantry on leaving Pocklington for France, where he has been for 18 months.

A Pocklington Soldier.

From an article entitled "East Yorkshire lads in France." which was written by a well-known Yorkshire writer, Mr. J. Fairfax-Blakeborough , and which appeared in the "Hull Times," we cull the following: "There's some of us could slay N.C.O. Windybank, of Pocklington, because he's so cheerful—whistling and singing, and seeming to enjoy the war. Thank God, most of us do make the best of things, even if we aren't quite as successful in the outward and visible signs and sounds of boisterous exuding cheerfulness as he is. He is like a continuous ray of sunshine amongst us all, though I've heard him cautioned more than once.— 'If thoo isn't careful thoo'll blaw thi front teeth out.' That refers to his Yorkshire ploughman's and wagoner's whistle, which one loves to hear in the rural North. May we soon hear it again and may it be as merry as ever it was." - The N.C.O. Windybank referred to is George, second son of Mrs. Windybank, of Waterloo Square, Pocklington, and we sincerely hope that this cheery whistle and song may be heard in the neighbourhood long after the war is over.

Mr. Thomas Robson solicitor, Pocklington, has received official intelligence that his son. Capt. Edward Moore Robson, M.C., Yorkshire Regiment (Green Howards), is reported wounded and missing from April 17th instant. He went out to France in July, 1915, and has twice been previously wounded, once in the thigh and afterwards in four places. The death of his elder brother, Lieut.-Colonel F.W. Robson (killed in action), was chronicled on April 9th, whilst his eldest brother (Mr. Richard Robson, solicitor, London), passed away the same week. It is sincerely hoped that Mr. Thomas Robson, who has been called upon to bear very heavy troubles through the war, may receive before long that his son is alive and cared for.

Thanks!

Bombardier Joseph Atkinson, son of Mrs Atkinson, Union Street, Pocklington, writing from Jubbergore, India says "Will you please thank the people of Pocklington for the parcel which they sent to me and which I received safe, the contents of which I greatly enjoyed. If I had known who to write to I would have written and thanked them myself, but hope they will accept same through the medium of your columns." Driver J. B. Atkinson, A.S.C. Italy, and Gunner G. W. Bell, Army Field Artillery, France, also write similar letters of sincere thanks to the good ladies of Pocklington who sent parcels to them, which they safely received and enjoyed.

A Pocklington Soldier Wounded

Pte. Fred Hotham, Seaforth Highlanders, son of Mr. and Mrs. C. Hotham, Pavement, was wounded in the arm and side during the recent operations in France. He is progressing favourably in the Cheltenham Hospital.

4th May, 1918

ELVINGTON.

Killed in Action

Corporal Alfred Atkin, second son of Mr. and Mrs. R. Atkin. Church-lane, Elvington, near York, has been killed on active service. The deceased was 33 years of age, joined the Army two years ago, up to which time he was in the service of Mrs. Hare, at the Manor Farm, Elvington. An officer of the employment company to which the late Corpl. Atkin was attached has written as follows, to the bereaved parents:— "Your son, was one of the most efficient non-commissioned Officers trusted by his superiors, well liked by his comrades, and could be relied upon at all times. May I be allowed to offer you my deepest sympathy in your affliction and trust that you may derive some small measure of comfort from the fact that his death took place in the performance of his duty, and was absolutely instantaneous." One of the deceased's younger brothers is serving on the Balkans front.

STAMFORD BRIDGE.
Killed in Action.

Mrs. Harry Spaven has received official information that her husband, Gunner H. Spaven, was killed in action. A comrade has written to say that the deceased was killed by the first shell when a bombardment started while warning his comrades in their dug-outs of gas shells. Previous to joining the Army he was employed at the Olympia Oil and Cake Mill, Selby. He was the only son of Mr. and Mrs. Spaven, Stamford Bridge, and leaves a widow and one child.

Pte. Herbert Holmes a Prisoner of War.

Official news has been received that Pte. H. A. Holmes, of the Royal Marines, is a prisoner of War at Parchin, Micklenburg, Germany. Prior to his enlistment he was in the employ of his uncle, Mr. J. Whitehead, printer, Pocklington, and among other duties undertook the delivery of papers and periodicals. He has been at the front over two years and has seen much fighting. We trust he will receive the same kind treatment that the British mete out to German prisoners.

Pocklington Weekly News, 4th May, 1918

11th May, 1918

Pte. Ernest Alvin Wounded

We regret to learn that Private Ernest Alvin, of Pocklington, who is attached to the West Riding Regiment, has been injured by shell-fire. The Germans began shelling and Pte. Alvin and three others took cover in a dug-out. But unfortunately a shell struck the dug-out, killing one man and injuring the other three. Pte. Alvin was injured in the legs and foot, but is in good spirits. They were captured by the Germans, and re-captured by the British, so that he is now in hospital in France. The many friends of young Alvin will wish for him a speedy recovery.

A Deserter

was captured by the civil police at Pocklington on Tuesday, and the man was handed over to a military escort on Wednesday.

On Leave

Our wounded heroes home on leave this week include Sappers T. Flint, son of Mr. and Mrs. T. Flint, Kirkland Street, who has been twice wounded; Pte. Fred Hotham, son of Mr. and Mrs. C. Hotham, Pavement, who was wounded a few weeks ago, and is making favourable progress; Sapper Travis Tinson, London Street, who appears to have at last recovered from the effects of the severe "gassing" which he received several months ago; and Pte. J. E. Atkinson, son of Mr. and Mrs. J. Atkinson, who was wounded some months ago whilst serving in the Tank Corps in France.

Thanks

Corpl. J. Atkinson, R.F.A., son of Mr. and Mrs. J. Atkinson, of Pocklington, who is serving with the Expeditionary Forces in Mesopotamia, wishes to express sincere thanks to the ladies of Pocklington for the parcel which he received in February last, and which he greatly appreciated, and states that the socks came in very useful.

HANGING GRIMSTON.

We are sorry to record that Gunner Geo. Wilfrid Midgley, of Hanging Grimston, has been severely wounded by a gas shell. He was on night duty on the 8th of April when the Germans gassed our artillery. He had been in a dug-out two hours by himself and was picked up next morning and taken to a Hospital in France and thence transferred into Wharncliffe War Hospital, Sheffield. His wife and her brother went to see him last Monday week and were glad to find him on the improve, but still in bed as he had a severe burn on his foot caused by the gas. He was wounded in the leg and in the shoulder in the Battle of the Somme in 1916, and afterwards sent back to France. We wish him a speedy recovery.

18th May, 1918

HAYTON,

A Prisoner of War

Pte. Ben Walker, London Regiment, third son of Ben and Jane Walker, of Hayton is reported missing on the 21st March. His parents have received a card from him stating that he is wounded and a prisoner in Germany, but going on well. He went out to France in 1914 with the Wagoner's Reserve, and transferred to the London Regt. in November 1917. We trust Private Walker will continue to progress satisfactorily.

Soldier Falls in Action.

News has been received that still another soldier from Market Weighton has fallen in action in the recent fighting—Private Hy. R. Rotherburg, of the Royal Welsh Fusiliers, the elder son of Mrs. Rotherburg, of Station Parade. The deceased was only 22 years of age, and previous to enlistment resided in Driffield. After training in England for a short time he was drafted out to France, and about 10 months ago received severe wounds. After treatment in an English hospital for about three months he again returned to France.

HOWDEN.

Soldier Released From Germany.

Sergt.-Major F. Levitt, of Howden, has received a letter from his brother, Lance-Corpl. A. E. Levitt, K.R.R.C, who after being for nearly two years a prisoner of war in Germany, has just arrived in England, and is at present in King George's Hospital, London. Lce.-Corpl. Levitt, who has had pieces of bone taken from his leg, was wounded by an explosive bullet and was on the field two days before being picked up by the Germans, after the second Somme battle. His injured leg is quite two inches shorter than the other. He gives a vivid description of the treatment meted out to our unfortunate prisoners in. Germany, where, in addition to receiving practically no medical attention, they get very little food, and if it were not for the parcels sent out by relatives and kind friends the majority would succumb through absolute starvation. On crossing the border they were well received by the Dutch, they had a pleasant voyage, and were given a great reception on arrival at Boston.

RATION RHYMES FOR RATION TIMES.

Mary had a little lamb
Before the Rations—yes.
But I'm afraid, I really am,
Mary will now have less!

Little Jack Horner
Sat in a corner
Eating a horseflesh pie.
He put in his thumb,
And said, looking glum;
"This it offal!" and started to cry.

Little Miss Muffet
Sat in a buffet
Eating her curds and whey;
In came an Inspector
Who'd hoped to detect her
Evading a Meatless Day.

25th May, 1918

SANCTON.

A Prisoner of War

Mr. and Mrs. Leonard Carr, Sancton, have received official news that, their son, Private Joe Carr, of the Notts and Derby Regiment, has been taken prisoner, and is now in Germany.

SUTTON -ON-DERWENT

Missing.

Private Alfred Foottit, Notts and Derby Regiment, reported missing since March 21st, is the son of Mr. J. Foottit, Woodhouse, Sutton-on-Derwent. He is 20 years of age and joined the West Yorkshire Regiment in December, 1915, At Easter he was drafted to Ireland, and remained there until the early part of 1917, when he was transferred to the Sherwood Foresters, and proceeded on service overseas. After taking part in much heavy fighting he was invalided home in October last, but returned to the front again on January 19th of this year, and has been posted as missing since the date stated. Before joining the Forces he was engaged in agricultural work with Mr. Somerville, of Stamford Bridge.

Awarded the Military Medal

Sergeant T. A. Sapcote, of the Motor Transport Service Corps., an ex-Councillor for Market Weighton and Arras, and a son of ex-Councillor A. F. Sapcote, who served for some considerable time in the South African War, and gave up his licensed business in Driffield to join the Army, he has been awarded the Military Medal.

A POCKLINGTON LAD'S LETTER FROM PALESTINE TORPEDOED

SPLENDID LETTER FROM OUR OFFICE BOY

Private Jas. Wardale, formerly of Pocklington, was one of the finest lads that has ever worked on the staff of the "Pocklington Weekly News" and we are justly proud of him. Under date of March 26th, 1918, he writes, enclosing a photo, but the steamer, being torpedoed, the packet arrived at Pocklington on May 19th, in a somewhat serious condition, the photo being securely stuck to the letter, which runs as follows:—

"Dear Mr. Whitehead.—I know you will be pleased to receive a few lines from me, so as I have half-an-hour or so to spare tonight, I drop you these few lines. Sincerely hoping that you and family are all keeping well, for I am very pleased to say that I am all o.k., and in the pink of condition.

"I do not know whether you received a letter from me or not about 3 months ago; I have concluded, by not receiving a reply thereto, that you did not receive it, and it went along with many more to its doom at the bottom of the sea. The letter business, Mr. Whitehead, is one of the bad things which we fellows in Palestine and Egypt have got to contend with, for when our letters from England do arrive, they are at least a fortnight old, and I have known them six and seven weeks. I will give you another instance, when I was in Port Said in April, 1916, I wrote a letter to Private N. Kendall, of Pocklington, and I did not receive any reply, but last September (18 months later), I got the letter returned to me out here, the envelope being endorsed 'Not Known.'

"Well. Mr. Whitehead, I will say a few words about Egypt and Palestine. I have now been out here over two years, and have during that time travelled about Egypt a great deal. I have had one leave, which was last year, and I went to Cairo. (People say that one has never been to Egypt unless he has been to Cairo.) Well, I must admit that I myself was greatly surprised at the City itself. If it were not for the Egyptian wearing his 'Tarbush' you would think that you were in an English city. The tram service, for one thing, is great, and in the heart of the city, as much traffic prevails as can be witnessed in York, Leeds, and other cities in England. But a word with respect to the campaign out here. I know myself that many people in England thought that the lads out here were practically on a holiday, but they were wrong, and I think that now their minds have changed a lot. Before the Turks were driven out of Egypt into Palestine, the life for an Englishman was very trying. He was in a strange land, and living on a great desert, miles and miles from anywhere, and on this desert, Mr. Whitehead, Tommy has had great trials and difficulties. That was in 1916, and then 'John Turk' was driven back and back, until he was in Palestine, and that's the place where he is today. And there the life is altogether different, civilization, which puts a new heart into the British Tommy. After such a long spell on the great desert, anyone can imagine the leap of joy he gave when he saw fertile soil, fruit plantations galore, and the chief thing, civilians.

"I think the Turk has had a great defeat up here, and I reckon myself he is fed up, but if he cares to carry on, he, will get more than he bargains for. Well, a few words about the situation of the war. When do you think it will be over? I think myself that this year may see the end of hostilities. The Germans have got to receive the punishment they deserve before Peace is declared, and the Allies, given good weather this summer, will administer great blows upon the enemy. We must carry on quietly, and keep our heads together, all pull the same way, and Victory will be ours. Peace at any price is no good. We must have an honourable peace to conclude this war; we have made great sacrifices already to attain it, and if we make peace on any other grounds whatsoever we are traitors to those who have already given their lives for their country. As I say, all must work together, stick it out, keep calm and cool, and in the end we'll win. My brother, Albert, is now in the Army, and is in the O.T.C. in a fashionable town. He is training to be an officer in the Royal Flying Corps, and up to the last mail to reach me he has passed all examinations first class.

"Well, Mr. Whitehead, I do not think I have any more to tell you this time. I enclose you a photo which I had taken a little while ago, and I thought you would like one. You may use it as you like. I will now close, with the kindest regards to all."

Tours sincerely,

J. WARDALE.

[A Photo of Private Jas. Wardale was enclosed in the letter, which was dated March 26th, 1918, was securely adhered to the letter, and on soaking both in luke warm water the photo was found to be in comparatively good condition, and is now on view in Whitehead's window, in Market Square, Pocklington.]—Editor.

1st June, 1918

Wounded in Action.

News has been received that Corporal Ernest William Blissitt has been admitted to hospital in France suffering from severe gunshot wounds in the right leg and chest, his condition causing much anxiety. A letter has been received later stating that the leg had been amputated, and that his condition was a little more favourable. Corporal Blissitt was a gardener at Ivy Hall (now Burnby Hall), and married a daughter of Mr. Wm. Smith, Pocklington. He has been two years and three months on active service, his record including the battles of the Somme, Vimy Ridge, Arras, and St. Julien.

Bar to Military Medal

Our readers will be pleased to know that Rifleman Charles Verney Waites. M.M., King's Royal Rifles, attached Divisional Signalling Company, has been awarded a bar to the Military Medal he gained last year. Rifleman Waite is the son of Mr. and Mrs. J. H. Waite, Baden House, Pocklington. The official notification states:— "I wish to place on record my appreciation of your gallantry and devotion to duty from 25-3-18 to 2-4-18 when all other communications had been cut you delivered important orders under very heavy shell fire. At all times you showed great bravery and set a fine example to other men."

(Signed) General —— "We congratulate Rifleman Waite on his bravery, and hope he may have the luck to return home safe and sound to enjoy the wearing of his well earned rewards."

8th June, 1918

Illegal Use of Petrol

At the Pocklington Police Court, held on Saturday last, before Alderman Fredk. Smith, Mr. C. Proctor, Mr. A. Summerson and Mr. R.W. Newbald, Ethel Hall (married) was charged with unlawful use of petrol on the 19th May.

15th June, 1918

Aeroplane Drops on The Mile.

On Sunday noon, an aeroplane alighted in a seeds field on Mr. T. English's Mile Farm and remained down until about 6-30 p.m. for minor repairs. It was witnessed by a large group of onlookers, many of whom, after partaking of tea, returned to see it ascend, which it did in a graceful and business-like fashion.

Military Cross

A former Primitive Methodist Minister in the Pocklington Circuit, the Rev. E. S. Emmitt, has been awarded the Military Cross for conspicuous gallantry in the field in the recent fighting. The Rev. E.S. Emmitt was for some years Primitive Methodist Minister at Pocklington, Easingwold, Castleford, Glasgow, and Edinburgh, prior to enlisting in the Royal Army Corps as a private in 1916, and in the following September was appointed to a Chaplaincy and proceeded overseas, where he has served with so much distinction.

Died of Wounds

We regret to record the death in the Lord Derby Hospital, Washington, of Sergt.-Major Donald Westlake. Yorks. and Lancs. Regiment, which occurred on Thursday, June 6th, from wounds received in action. He was not a native of Pocklington, but was well-known in the district, being married to a daughter of Mr. and Mrs. W. Allison of Kirkland Street. As a reservist, he was called up at the outbreak of war, and was wounded, shot through the lung, on August 15th., 1915. In the following year he was wounded in the knee; and in the recent advance of the Germans he was again severely wounded, having his right arm blown off close to the shoulder, and both legs badly damaged by shell. He was removed to the above named hospital and appeared to be making favourable progress until the morning of his death. The interment took place at Rotherham, Sheffield, with full military honours, on Tuesday, in the presence of a large concourse of people, which included his fellow employees in the Rotherham Steel Works, who followed the remains a distance of three miles to the cemetery. Amongst the family mourners present were: Mrs. Westlake, widow, and three children; Mrs. Westlake, mother; Mrs. Diggins, Sister; Mrs. Allison, mother-in-law, Pocklington; Mrs. Pickering, sister-in-law, Pocklington; and Mrs. F. Allison, sister-in-law, Everingham.—Deceased was a typical British soldier, of fine physique, and sterling character, and was a notable Army boxer, having won several competitions. He was only 29 years of age, and his early death is regretted by a large circle of friends, with whom he was exceedingly popular.

29th June, 1918

HIGH CATTON.

Killed in Action.

Mr. and Mrs. Patterson, High Catton, have received official intelligence that their son, Private G. Patterson, was killed in action on May 20th. The deceased soldier, who was 22 years of age, was attached to East Kent Regiment; he joined the Army three years ago, up to which time he was in the employment of Messrs. Rowntree. An officer of the battalion in which Pte. Patterson served has written as follows to the parents: "Your son's death occurred late in the evening of May 20th. Although he had been with the battalion only a short time he was immensely popular with everyone in his company, and his loss will be felt by all his comrades. His death was instantaneous. On behalf of all ranks please accept our sincere sympathy in your loss, which I know is a hard one to bear."

6th July, 1918

German Prisoners in the East Riding.

Mr. G. W. Jameson writes very strongly against German prisoners being housed in Pocklington, and supports in no half-hearted manner the stand taken by Mr. Geo. Johnson, of Cot Nab. against employing undesirable Germans on his farm. Such men as Mr. Johnson, he maintains, are more likely to win the war than a lot of weak-kneed pacifists.

Local Casualties

Official intimation has been received that Signaller Thomas Ross Skinner, eldest son of Mr. and Mrs. Skinner, Wold View, Pocklington, has been missing since May 27th. He has been in France over two years, and previous to enlisting was on the reporting staff of a well-known Northern Daily Paper. His brother Frank is at present in Leeds Hospital, his leg having been amputated below the knee, owing so wounds received early in the war. Similar official news has been received that Corpl. Frank Allison, M.M., son of Mr. and Mrs. Allison, of Kirkland Street, has also been, missing since the operations in the latter part of May.

Official notice has also been received by Mrs. T. Scaife, Chapmangate, Pocklington, that her eldest son. Pte. Chris. Scaife, is missing since the latter part of May. Only a short time before he was home on sick leave, recovering from illness contracted in France. His brother Sydney has been killed in the war, and two other brothers, Reg. and Bert, have been wounded.—

Mrs. T. Harrison. Church Lane, Pocklington, has also received notice that her second son, Pte. Redvers Harrison, is missing since May 27th. His elder brother was killed in action some time ago, and his father is at present serving in Salonika.

Mr. and Mrs. J.E. Fielder, London Street, Pocklington, have also been notified that their youngest son, Pte. Cecil Fielder, is in the Australian Hospital in France, having been wounded in the face. Both signaller T. Skinner and Pte. C. Fielder were formerly engaged on the staff of this paper.—We sincerely hope the families of these soldiers may receive more comforting news of their heroes welfare.

Presentation

Arthur Turner, employed as Branch Manager by the Pocklington Co-operative Society, joined the Army on Wednesday last, and in common with 10 other employees who have joined the Forces, he was not allowed to leave without some mark of appreciation being shown by his fellow employees. 35 members of the Staff subscribed to the fund for obtaining the presents, which included the following :- A Luminous Wristlet Watch and Guard, Safety Razor, Silver Cigarette Case, Silver Cigarette Holder, Leather Wallet, and a Purse. —Mr. Haw, on behalf of the Staff made the presentation on Tuesday evening last, and briefly referred to the recipient's career, who at an early stage had been appointed Branch Manager at Bishop Wilton, being subsequently promoted to Stamford Bridge, and had managed both branches with conspicuous success.— They wished him every success in his new life, and a speedy return at the conclusion of hostilities.—Arthur feelingly replied and thanked them for their generosity, and hoped to resume his old vocation in the near future. He thanked Mr. Haw for his kind remarks, and said his success was due in a large measure to his training in the early years of his apprenticeship and the kindly interest Mr. Haw had always shown in his career, and was glad to learn that he had given satisfaction when entrusted with a responsible post. Private Arthur Turner is now training at Rugeley, Staffs.

YAPHAM.

Two Brothers Wounded

We regret to learn that Pte. Herbert Haywood, who is attached to the Northumberland Fusiliers, is now in Leicester Hospital, suffering from heart strain, where he has been for the last five weeks. He has spent three years in France and has seen much fighting. Pte. G. W. Haywood, of the York and Lancaster Regiment, is at present in a Red Cross Hospital at Ipswich, suffering from shrapnel wounds in the left arm having spent two and a half years in France. He has been four times wounded, and we are pleased to learn that he is progressing favourably. They are both the soldier sons of Mr. and Mrs. W. Haywood, of Yapham Mill, who lost a son in the war about two years ago.

13th July, 1918

A Prisoner of War

Mrs. Brewer, of Union Street, Pocklington, received a letter on Sunday morning last from her husband, Lance-Corp. Richard Brewer, M.G.C, attached Seaforth Highlanders, who had been posted as missing since March 21st, stating that he is a prisoner of war in Germany, and that he is quite well. The letter was dated April 2nd. and bore the address of Parchin, the same place where Private Herbert Holmes, formerly of Pocklington, was detained.

STAMFORD BRIDGE.

A Prisoner of War

Mr. F. Ward, of Stamford Bridge, has received official notification that his second son, Private Paul Ward, R.M.L.I., is a prisoner of war in Germany; he had been reported missing since March 24th. He is 24 years of age, joined up on January 3rd, 1915, and served in Gallipoli nearly six months before being transferred to the Western front. Signaller Dick Ward, Gordon Highlanders, brother of Pte. Ward, was killed in action on June 15th, 1917.

Wounded In Action

Pte. Walter Thompson, Lancashire Fusiliers, eldest son of Mrs. Thompson, Chapmangate, Pocklington, was wounded in the lefts side and arm in the fighting of July 3rd, in France; and is now in the military hospital, Warrington. He had served in France over a year; his brother, Wilfred, was killed nearly two years ago, and another brother, Ernest, has served in France nearly three years.

MILITARY MEDAL FOR A GATE HELMSLEY SOLDIER.

LOCAL ATHLETE'S MANY SUCCESSES IN FRANCE

Lance-Corporal J. Swales, of Gate Helmsley, was awarded the Military Medal on June 2nd, for conspicuous service on the battlefield from April 25th to 27th. He joined the forces on the day that war was declared, went out with the Expeditionary Force, and wears the Mons ribbon. He was wounded at the first battle of Ypres, and on recovery was engaged in transport work until drafted to the front again in August of last year, and lost his speech for a period of six weeks. Before being called up he was postman from Stamford Bridge to Kirby Underdale and has been employed in the York Post Office. Lance-Corporal Swales is a well known athlete he has won seventeen first prizes at regimental sports in France, and also carried off many prizes at sports meetings held, around York.

13th July, 1918

AMERICAN TROOPS VISIT YORK

ENTERTAINED BY LORD MAYOR.

… York was en fete on Wednesday, the occasion being a reception and entertainment of American troops by the Lord Mayor (Sir W.A. Forster Todd J.P.) The streets were gaily decorated with American, British, and other flags, bunting and streamers of many hues. The archway entrance to the Guildhall was effectively adorned with a large American flag, floating side by side with a massive Union Jack, the two being surmounted by the City Arms and the flags of the Allies. In Rougier-street every house had its flag, the whole presenting a pretty appearance. The American personnel of eight Officers and 400 other ranks— arrived in detachments from Yorkshire camps between 1-48 p.m. and 2-15 p.m., and at 2-20 p.m. formed up in column of route outside the railway station. Large crowds of citizens gathered and gave rousing cheers for the men of the United States. Hundreds of people watched the arrival and departure of the troops from the embrasures of the ancient city walls overlooking the Station Square, and it must have been a novel sight to the Americans to notice these eager and friendly faces peering from the walls which speak of an old world….

Old York and New York.

The Lord Mayor, in welcoming the American personnel an behalf of the city, said: "Officers and men of the American Army,—According to an eminent Yorkshire clergyman there are 110 Yorks in the world, but I think you will not dispute there are only two that really count—New York, the pride of the United States, and Old York, the Roman Citadel in which you meet to-day. The best elements of the Old World and the New World are merged together now in the greatest fight that man has ever been recorded in the world's history, and you are representative of some of the finest fighting material that either the Old World or the New has produced. (Applause.) We, the people of this ancient city, and all our fellow countrymen are proud of you. On the battlefields of France your comrades have already shown the foe the mettle of which you are made, and they will continue to do so until the victory is won. (Cheers). Meanwhile it is our duty—and an extremely pleasurable one—to make your stay in this country interesting, and on behalf of every man, woman, and child in this city I bid you welcome to-day. (Applause.) The American race has always possessed the true spirit of independence. …

20th July, 1918

HOLME

Local Soldier Missing

Mr. and Mrs. F. Stephenson, Station Farm, Home-On-Spalding Moor, have received official intimation that their second son, Sergt. O. Stephenson, East Yorkshire Regiment, has been wounded and missing since May 28th.

27th July, 1918

MARKET WEIGHTON

Wounded in Action

A chaplain at the front has written to Mrs. G. Dixon, York-road, that one of her six soldier and sailor sons. Private Leonard Dixon, Black Watch, had been wounded in the ankle and is in one of the base hospitals.

An Exhibition in the Air.

A daring young officer flew over Pocklington on Thursday and Friday, and gave a fine exhibition of looping the loop and other thrilling feats.

10th August, 1918

Died of Wounds.

News has been received that Corporal John William Smith, Yorkshire Regiment, youngest son of Mrs. Smith, School House, New Street, Pocklington, who was officially posted wounded and missing on the 30th March last, is now reported "died from the effects of wounds in the arms, whilst a prisoner of war in Germany." His death took place a fortnight after being captured. He was a well-built and popular young man, 27 years of age, and an athlete of considerable ability. Much sympathy is extended to Mrs. Smith and family in their sad loss.

Missing

Corpl. Frank Allison, M.M.. Yorkshire. Regt., son of Mr. and Mrs Allison, Kirkland Street, Pocklington, who has been missing since May, is now officially reported a Prisoner of War in Germany, camp unknown.

17th August, 1918

Sergt. Charlie Spivey.

We are pleased to learn that Corpl. Charlie Spivey, of the Yorkshire Regiment, has been promoted on the field to the rank of Sergeant. He has also gained the D.C.M and bar. Pocklington men have achieved a record of which any place of its size may be justly proud, may we congratulate Sergt. Spivey on his promotion and merit decorations.

Cycle Trick Riding.

One of the most exciting and thrilling sights in Pocklington of late is to watch a group of smart youths in their marvellous feats of trick cycling in the Market Square. These performances are given free almost nightly, and should greatly interest our boys on their return from the front. It is a pity the antics of these youthful cyclists was not included in the Bank Holiday Sports Programme, but they may have a place there on some future occasion.

Prisoners of War

Mrs. W. S. Lamb. of Railway Street, Pocklington, has received a letter from her nephew, Pte. Nicholas Kendall. Yorks., Regt., who is a prisoner of war in Germany, stating that he is well; and Mrs. Priestley (Mrs. Lamb's sister, who resides with her), has also, received a letter from her son, Cpl. T. Priestley, West Yorks., who has been missing since May 27th, stating he is a wounded prisoner of war and is progressing favourably.

RAIDS OVER GERMANY.

NINETY-SIX BRITISH ATTACKS ON ENEMY TOWNS DURING JULY.

During the month of July no fewer than 100 raids were carried out by the Independent Force, Royal Air Force, of which 96 were into Germany itself. In all 81 tons of bombs were dropped upon important military objectives during these raids.

Notwithstanding the frequent periods of bad weather, the month's work constitutes a record both as regards the number of raids undertaken and the weight of bombs dropped. The previous best month was June last, when 74 raids were made into German territory and 61¼ tons of bombs dropped.

These figures cover the work of the R.A.F. Independent Force; altogether from the immense weight of bombs dropped by the Royal Air Force airmen throughout the Western front and upon such coastal objectives as Ostend, Zebrugge, Bruges etc.; or the formidable work of the French Air Service.

24th August, 1918

Wounded in Action

After over three years service in France with the West Riding Artillery, Gunner J. Toyne, son of Mr. and Mrs. Toyne, West Green, Pocklington has been wounded in the right hand. Eleven of his comrades were wounded at the same time.

FRIDAYTHORPE

Killed in Action.

Great regret will be felt in the Pocklington district by the announcement of the death of Lieut.-Colonel Bernard Barton, of the Worcestershire Regiment, who was killed in action on the 11th of August. The deceased officer, who was 38 years of age was the youngest son of the late Rev. T. H. Barton, for many years vicar of Fridaythorpe. Educated at St. Peter's School, York, he afterwards served with the Yeomanry in the South African War. Proceeding to Canada, he devoted several successful years to the study of fruit growing, in which he became an adept. Joining the Army at the outbreak of war, he had an exceedingly brilliant career, being quickly promoted Captain, subsequently Major, and recently Lieut.-Colonel. He was most popular with all ranks under his command, and his high character and fine disposition endeared him to a large circle of friends. He leaves a widow, and son, aged two years.

MELBOURNE.
Sergt. W. Walker gains the Military Medal.
Our readers will be delighted to learn that Sergt. Wm. Walker, 043305 A.S.C., formerly of Melbourne, eldest son of Mr.

SERGT. W. WALKER, M.M.
Richard Walker, Park Farm, Melbourne, and son-in-law of the late Mr. G. H. Ogle, of Yapham Mill, has gained the Military Medal for bravery on the field.

Pocklington Weekly News, 24th Aug. 1918

31st August, 1918

Promotion of Pocklington Tradesmen.

We understand that Mr. S. H. Everingham has recently been passed out of an O.T.C. with a very high percentage of marks and has been gazetted 2nd Lieut, and posted to the King's Shropshire Light Infantry. He has served in the Army since Xmas, 1916, and for most of this time has acted as Instructor in musketry and bombing. Lieut. W. G. Everingham, R.N.V.R., attached R.N.A.S., has been transferred to the R.A.F., with the rank of Captain, and has been recently appointed officer in charge of an important new technical branch of that arm of the service.

Wounded In Action.

Pte. A. Buttle, Australian Imperial Forces, who visited his home in Pocklington a short time ago, was badly wounded by shrapnel in the right ankle, on Friday, August 23rd. He was examined under the X-rays and the shrapnel removed same day, and is now in hospital at Rouen.

Military Medal.

Drv. M. Davison, of the 1st Cavalry Division, son of Mr. and Mrs. F. Davison, Little Grange, Pocklington, and grandson of the late Mr. J. Davison, Bridlington, has been awarded the Military Medal for saving the lives of four of his comrades, and for coolness and bravery during a bombing raid on August 11th. Driver Davison is 20 years of age, and holds the Mons Ribbon, having been in France since the outbreak of War. He went out with Sir Mark Sykes' Wagoners Reserves, and took part in the great retreat from Mons.

Driver R. B. DAVISON, 9th Cavalry Fld. Ambulance, 1st Cav. Div., British Expeditionary Force. He has been in France 15 months. He is 18 years of age, not been wounded, is quite well, and says they are very comfortable in winter billets.

Pock Weekly News Dec 11 1915

On Leave.

During this week local heroes on home leave include Corpl. H. Flint, son of Mr. and Mrs. C. Flint, and Lce.-Corpl. J. Pratt, son of Mrs. Pratt, of Grape Lane; and Driver W. Thompson, son of Mrs. Thompson, Chapmangate. All three have been wounded and are now progressing favourably. Chief Petty Officer W. Andrews, Royal Navy, of George Street, and Engineer T. Brook, R.N., son of Councillor Brook, Pavement, have also enjoyed brief home visit. Driver Harry Elliott, Pocklington is also home on leave, and Trooper Wilfred Ottley, East Riding Yeomanry, son of Mrs. Otley, Chapmangate, Pocklington, late of Warter, is also enjoying a brief visit home after three years service abroad.

7th September, 1918

MILITARY SITUATION.

THE ENEMY'S RETREAT.

110,000 PRISONERS.

On Monday last, September 2nd, (says the Press Association) what may be described as one of the successful operations of the war took place on a front, of eight miles south of the Scarpe. Divisions of the Canadian Corps, with the 4th. Division on the left and the 17th Corps on the right, attacked, forestalling a contemplated German offensive. In the 17th Corps were the 52nd (Lowland Territorial) Division, famous for its magnificent advance last October from along the coast after the battle of Gaza almost to the gates of Jerusalem, the 63rd (Naval) Division, the West Lancashire, and the London Territorial Divisions. The attack resulted in the complete penetration of the Drocourt-Qucant switch and the withdrawal of the enemy with heavy loss back to the Canal du Nord. Apart from the large number of prisoners and other material secured the moral effect on the enemy must be considerable. It may be pointed out that the Canal du Nord forms an exceptionally efficient obstacle against tank attacks even more so perhaps in its dry condition than if it were full of water, but we have already obtained a footing in places across it.

In the Lys salient a steady withdrawal of the enemy has been going on which is still continuing, closely followed by British and American troops. In general, however, the enemy may claim that in this case withdrawal has taken place according to plan. On the French front a steady withdrawal back to the line of the Somme-Oise Canal has taken place under pressure accompanied by heavy fighting. Here, again, the French have obtained a footing on the east side in the neighbourhood of Noyon, which on Wednesday they used as a jumping off place in the further advance towards the Somme. Farther south, heavy fighting has been going on North of Soissons between the Aisne and the Ailette, particularity in the neighbourhood of Juvigny and Terny Sorny where American troops have been operating, and a considerable advance been made. Possibly as the result of this the enemy has commenced to withdraw from the line of the Vesle across the Aisne, thus shortening his line to a small extent and obtaining a certain respite.

The number of prisoners taken by the British since August 1st now amounts approximately to 70,000, whilst the French and Americans are believed to have taken in the same period about 40,000. Without going into actual figures it may be said that the feature of the operations has been the extraordinarily small losses. In the case of the British these do not greatly exceed the numbers of prisoners taken. To a certain extent this may be attributed to temporary lowering in the fighting value of the German Army, the result of being over fought and of the disorganisation inevitable from retreat on a large scale, undertaken under relentless pressure. When these factors are removed we may expect an improvement in the enemy morale.

Generally speaking there is no evidence that the German High Command has not so far kept the situation in hand, although, of course, it has made demands on the troops which cannot be continued indefinitely without grave risk. The front has generally been maintained intact and the withdrawal to a selected line, even if hasty, has been carried out methodically, although with the loss of an enormous amount of material of every description.

14th September, 1918

MARKET WEIGHTON.

Local Officer Missing.

At St. Mary's Roman Catholic Church the Rev. Father Wright said that the residents had been grieved to hear that Flight Lieut. Ian Hickes, of the Royal Flying Corps, was missing. He was sure every member of St. Mary's extended to the anxious parents their fullest sympathies. Mrs. Hickes, as commandant of the local branch of the Red Cross Society, had throughout the past four years striven to bring comfort and healing to other mothers' sons and other wives' husbands, and now her turn for grievous suspense had come. He begged the prayers of the congregation for Mr and Mrs. Hickes in their trial.

SAND HUTTON,

Soldiers Wounded

Information has been received that Private W. Hairsine, Yorkshire Regiment, was wounded by shrapnel in the leg during recent fighting and is now in hospital at Southampton. Private Hairsine is the son of Mr. and Mrs. G. Hairsine of Low Moor Farm, Sand Hutton, and joined the Forces about a year ago.– Cpl. F. O. Sykes, of Sand Hutton, has recently been wounded in the right foot and has been removed to a hospital at Keighley. Corporal Sykes was originally in the transport section of the Yorkshire Regiment, was mobilised at the commencement of the war, and had been overseas since about April, 1915, until the time of his casualty.

Charges Under the Petrol Order

Tom Houfe, farmer, Low Catton, was fined 5s. under the Defence of the Realm Act for withholdings information as to the use of petrol. Sergt. Long said that on the 8th of August he saw defendant riding a motor cycle, and asked him for what purpose he was using his cycle. He refused to give witness any information. Mr. Powell, who appeared for defendant, said that the latter thought he had a right to refuse to state his business to the police, and was prepared to give information to Beverley if required to do so. He admitted, on behalf of his client, a technical offence, and asked the Bench to deal leniently with him. Wm. Fredk. Eugene Todd, of Pocklington, for the unlawful use of petrol on the 4th of August, was fined £1. P.C. Wiles deposed that defendant was riding his cycle at Barmby Moor, and when asked the following day (Monday) what business he was on, said he was on pleasure. The superintendent said that defendant had got the motor cycle out unknown to his father. He had been previously summoned for a similar offence. Harold Archibald Mennell, of Malton, was charged with similar offence. Sergt. Long said that he saw defendant, accompanied by a lady, driving a motor car at Full Sutton on the 8th of August. Asked for what purpose he was using the car, defendant said he had been measuring timber at Stamford Bridge Station, and he called on his journey to see Mr. Leo. Mennell. Mr. Newbald Kay, York, who appeared, for defendant, said that defendant was on his way back to Malton and had gone a short distance out of his way to call on his uncle. He was engaged on Government work, and the lady was assisting him. The case was dismissed, the defendant bearing out council's statement.

BURNBY.
Lieut. G W. Highmore Wounded.

We regret to learn that Lieut. G. W. Highmore,— Batt. West Yorks. Regt., attached to the—Batt. in France has been wounded in both shoulders and face and right hand on September 2nd, near Cambrai and was taken to a hospital at Rouen, and then to the Prince of Wales' Hospital. Marylebone, N.W. We are pleased to say that he is progressing favourably.

21st September, 1918

Military.

Official intimation has been received that Pte. Redvers Harrison, son of Pte. T. and Mrs. Harrison, Church Lane, Pocklington, who has been missing since May 27th, is a prisoner of war in Germany, His brother, James, was killed in March last and his father is serving in the Balkans.— Pte. F. Skinner, son of Mr. and Mrs. Skinner, Wold View, who was wounded early in the war after several operations, recently had his leg amputated below the knee, arrived home this week. His elder brother, Tom, is at present among the missing.

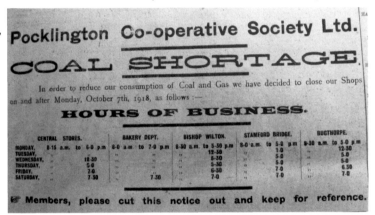

Pocklington Weekly News, 28th Sep. 1918

On leave this week we welcome Gunner M. Sowersby, son of Mrs. Sowersby, London Street, who has served abroad since war began. He has been twice wounded and is now recovering from severe gas effects. Stretcher-bearer Thomas Henry Skelton, son of Mr. and Mrs H. Skelton, Dean's Lane, Pocklington, is also enjoying home leave, he has been twice wounded; and Private George Brown, of the Tank Corps., son of Mr. and Mrs. Brown, Victoria Terrace, is also enjoying a welcome rest at home after recent strenuous and exciting service with the Tanks.

28th September, 1918

Prisoner of War.

Mr. and Mrs. W. Johnson, Kirkland St. have received a photograph from their nephew, Norris A. Leeming, who is a prisoner of war in Germany. He will be well remembered by many of our readers as the grandson of the late Mrs. Agnew, Waterloo Hotel, Pocklington. After leaving Pocklington, he resided with his mother, Mrs. Leeming, at Bolton, Lancashire, when he enlisted in the Lancashire Fusiliers, and after being wounded has now been a prisoner of war for some months. He is 21 years of age, and was for some time with Mr. D. Richardson at the Albion Engineering Works at Pocklington.

BIELBY.

Killed in Action.

Mr. and Mrs. Holdridge, of Bielby, have received official intelligence that their eldest son, Corporal George Wilson Holdridge, was killed in action on August 27th. The deceased was 25 years of age. He joined the East Riding Yeomanry in October, 1914 and was later transferred to the King's Own Yorkshire Light Infantry. Only a few days previous to the first announcement of his death his parents were expecting him home on leave with a view to obtaining his commission. He was educated at Pocklington Grammar School, and for some years was engaged on his father's farm at Bielby Fields. At the outbreak of war he was employed in the firm of MacLeod and Co., Wholesale Tea Dealers, London. He was a communicant of the Church of England, of fine physique, manly and robust, of kindly disposition, and unblemished character. His parents have received many letters of sympathy from a large circle of friends in their bereavement. He died in the noblest of causes, and his King and country will ever be grateful to all their heroic sons who have sacrificed their lives for freedom and justice. A Memorial Service will be held at the Parish Church, Hayton, on Sunday, October 6th, at 6-30 p-m.

MARKET WEIGHTON.
Shrapnel Stopped by Watch.

Residents will regret to learn that Mr. Rd. Kneeshaw, White House, has received official intimation that his youngest of six soldier sons, Lance Corporal Fred Kneeshaw, D.L.I., who only went overseas a few weeks ago, has been somewhat severely wounded and has arrived at the Lincoln Military Hospital suffering from three wounds in the left arm, one in the chest, and one in the left leg. At the time he was wounded he was carrying his wristlet watch in his trousers pocket and this saved him from another wound, a piece of shrapnel penetrated his clothing but was stopped by the watch which was damaged beyond repair.
News has also been received that Gunner Mark Stellings, R.F.A., son of Mr. and Mrs. R. Stellings, has been wounded and is in one of the base hospitals. Before enlistment he was employed at the Hull City Asylum at Willerby.

MELBOURNE.
Killed In Action.

Mr. and Mrs, J. Kidd of Melbourne have received official intelligence that their youngest son, Private J. C. Kidd, was killed in action on September 2nd. The deceased was 20 years of age and was in the York and Lancaster Regiment; he had served at the front for 16 months, and before joining the Army assisted his father who, up to a few years ago, was well-known as a carrier between Melbourne and York. The chaplain attached to the unit in which the deceased served, in a letter of sympathy to the parents, writes:—"The battalion was called upon to take its part in a battle on September 2nd and did magnificent service. But unhappily during the course of the fight your boy was hit and killed. We very much regret to report this. He will be much missed, for he was a brave lad and did his duty faithfully and nobly."

Gunner Ralph Kidd, brother of the deceased, is in the Royal Garrison Artillery, which he joined in October 1915, and is at present doing duty on a Mediterranean front. He is 23 years of age, and up to the time of enlistment assisted on farms in the East Riding.

5th October, 1918
On Leave.

We were delighted to see a few more local lads home on leave looking in the pink of health. Amongst them was Lance-Corpl. Eddie Siddall, of the Duke of Wellington Transport Section, who joined the Territorials on the 5th March, 1910, and went out to France in April, 1915. He is now enjoying his third leave and returns to France on Monday next, having seen much fighting and has, so far, escaped injury. Driver Chas. Smith, of the Machine Gun Corps, joined up in 1912, and returned to the front a few days ago. Both these young fellows went out with the 5th Yorks., and were duly transferred to other regiments. Bombardier Fred Southcoat, R.N.D. is also over from France where he had spent over two years, and their many friends are delighted to see them looking so well.

12th October, 1918

Local Casualties

Pte. Christopher Scaife, the son of Mrs. Scaife Chapmangate, and Signaller T. R. Skinner, the son of Mr. and Mrs. A. Skinner, Wold View, Pocklington, are reported prisoners of war. They are quite well. Trooper Wilfrid Ottley, the son of Mrs. Ottley, Chapmangate, has been wounded in the face, and is in hospital in Sheffield. Sapper Travis Tinson, London Street, has been severely wounded by a shell, and is also in a Sheffield hospital. Sapper Thomas Flint, the son of Mr. and Mrs. T. Flint, Kirkland street is seriously wounded, and is in Woking Hospital, where his mother has visited him. Tinson and Flint, who happily are both improving were wounded by the same shell, which killed two and wounded eight men of the section.

In the Honours List.

Our readers will be delighted to read the following paragraph, which appeared in the "Yorkshire Post." on Monday, under the Honours List :—

"A Pocklington man Corpl. C. Spivey, Yorkshire Regiment, has been awarded a bar to the D.C.M. for a gallant act, which is thus recorded in the "Gazette": "When the enemy, having captured a village, were making some progress, and the situation had become involved, this, N.C.O. volunteered to go forward and ascertain what was actually taking place. He went forward three times through a very intense barrage of gas and high explosive shells, and collected very valuable information as to the position of the enemy and the neighbouring troops. By his gallant action he rendered most excellent service in clearing up a difficult situation."

Regt. Sergt.-Major J.B. MacCartney of Kimberley, South Africa, son of the Rev. T. J. MacCartney, of Pocklington, has been awarded the 'Military Medal' said the French 'Medaille Militaire' for his services in the German South-West Campaign.

BARMBY MOOR

Wounded in Action.

The Rev. W. D. Wood Rees, vicar of Barmby Moor, has received word that his youngest son, Lieut. F. L. F. (Eric) Rees, M.C., has been wounded and is now in Hospital in France.

MARKET WEIGHTON

Local Soldier Wounded

Mr. & Mrs. Henry Arnott, Dalton Rose, have received information that their youngest of four soldier sons, Private Maurice Arnott, Loyal Lancashire Regiment, has been wounded and admitted to the Alexandra Military Hospital, Cosham, Hants.

On Leave.

Shoeing-Smith F. Barker is this week home on leave for the first time, after serving nearly three years abroad, and we are please to see him looking fit and well. He has served on several fronts, including Mesopotamia (twice), Egypt, and France, and has also spent some time in India. Whilst journeying from

Egypt to France their boat was torpedoed, but fortunately he escaped with nothing more serious than the loss of his belongings.

He had some interesting stories to tell of their doings in the East, and brought home several souvenirs, including a dagger-knife, which he and a comrade took from a captured Turk. Shoeing-Smith Barker, who has so far come through without injury, although having some narrow escapes, returns to France next Saturday, and we wish him the best of luck.

2nd November, 1918

LOCAL HEROES DIE OF WOUNDS

We deeply regret to record the death of two local heroes who have nobly laid down their lives in the defence of home and country.

PRIVATE HERBERT H. HOLMES.

Official intimation has been received that Private Herbert Henry Holmes, Cheshire Regiment, only son of Mr and Mrs George Holmes, of York Terrace, Pocklington, was severely wounded in action on October 14th and died the following day in a casualty clearing station. The deceased possessed one of the most pleasant dispositions it was possible to meet with and his death will be much regretted by his many friends. After leaving school he was for some time employed in the butchering trade in Market-place, Pocklington (along with Corporal R. Brewer who is now a prisoner of war); but enlisted in the Army Service Corps eight years ago, in which he attained the rank of Corporal.

He served with the Expeditionary Force on the outbreak of war, and after three years service abroad was badly wounded. Last March he returned to France attached to the Cheshire Regiment and has now made the great sacrifice. He was 28 years of age, and is brother of Nurse Holmes who is so highly esteemed in the district for the care and attention she devotes to her patients. Much sympathy is extended to the family in their bereavement.

SERGT. ARTHUR ROWNTREE.

The sad news has been received that Sergt. Arthur Rowntree, West Yorkshire Regiment, youngest son of Mrs. Rowntree, of New-street, Pocklington, was severely wounded in the back and right leg in the fighting on October 23rd, and died the same day. The unfortunate youth, who was only 20 years of age, was a well conducted and widely respected youth who will be well remembered as being in the employment of Mr. J. H. Hatfield, hairdresser, Market-place, (who is now serving in the Army) where he was a general favourite amongst the patrons of the establishment. He afterwards became an esteemed member of the Pocklington Co-operative Society's working staff, from which he enlisted on attaining Military age. Attached to the West Yorks. Regiment he went to France a year ago, where by intelligent attention to his duties he quickly gained promotion to Sergeant. When over on leave some time ago he expressed himself as pleased with the military training (apart from the war aspect) which had improved his health considerably. His brother, Corpl. Alfred Rowntree, gained the Military Medal for conspicuous gallantry in the field, whilst another brother, Pte. Thomas Rowntree, is at present serving in France.

LATE SERGT. ARTHUR ROWNTREE, OF POCKLINGTON.

Pocklington Weekly News, 9th Nov. 1918

9th November, 1918

BOLTON.

We regret to record that Gunner John Henry Husband, R.F.A., of Bolton, died at a Canadian Hospital in France on the 10th July, from wounds received in action and pneumonia. Deceased was 27 years of age, and the beloved son of Mr. and Mrs. John Husband.

BISHOP WILTON.

Obituary.

Much sympathy is expressed for the parents and grandparents on the death of Jas., Fuguel, of Bishop Wilton.

Memorial to a Gallant Officer

In the S. Edith's Church, Bishop Wilton, on Saturday last; a Memorial Tablet was unveiled by the Bishop of Hull, erected to the memory of the late Sec. Lieut. Gerard Peters, of the Gloucestershire Regt. Lieut. Peters, who was well known in Pocklington, where he served his articles with Mr. H. S. Powell, solicitor, was the youngest, son of the Rev and Mrs Ed. Peters, of Bishop Wilton Vicarage, and died in action near Chaulnes, in France, on the 24th February, 1917.

16th November, 1918

POCKLINGTON.

On the receipt of the news that peace had been proclaimed, the bells of All Saints were rung, and the inhabitants put out flags in honour of the occasion, although there were no demonstrations of any kind. The bells were heard clearly in Coldwold. One impression was that Pocklington had not risen to the occasion, but it would have been better to have had a spontaneous outburst of rejoicing on the eventual day. An impromptu dance, in honour of the occasion, was well attended, dancing being carried on until nearly one a.m.

Telegrams, although sadly delayed, were received at the "News" Office from friends in London, bearing the good tidings, and a thanksgiving service was held in the Parish Church on Wednesday evening.

POCKLINGTON PARISH CHURCH

"To commemorate the signing of the Peace Armistice and the Victory of the Allies, a reverent service of thanksgiving was impressively rendered at the Pocklington Parish Church on Wednesday, in the presence of a large congregation in which all denominations were represented. For the first time for four years the bells rang out their joyous notes of welcome for evening service, whilst the church was lighted as in pre-war days. The service, which was conducted by the vicar, Rev. A.T. Fisher, commenced with the singing of "O God Our Help in ages past," as processional hymn." …

REPATRIATED PRISONERS EXPECTED TO ARRIVE ON SATURDAY

The British repatriated prisoners of war had not left Holland on Thursday, and the arrangements made for their reception at Hull had to be postponed. It is expected that the first ships will arrive today (Saturday). Special trains are already drawn up on the Riverside Quay, and it is understood that the men will be taken to the military clearing station at Ripon. When the ships enter the Humber they will be met by aeroplanes and escorted up the river.

23rd November, 1918

LETTER PROM A POCKLINGTON MAN

Mrs. T. Harrison, Church Lane, Pocklington, has received the following letter from her son, Redvers Harrison, who is a prisoner of war at Cassel, Germany:-- 15-9-18

Dear Mother and all at home,—

Just a line, hoping to find you well, as it leaves me at present, but still waiting for a letter from home. Remember me to all my friends, and tell the girls I shall be home for Christmas, so we shall have a good old spree up. Has P. Walker or H. Cains, or any of the boys been home lately? Mother, do not bother about me, but please thank all in the old place who give to the Red Cross or Prisoner of War Fund, as they will be surprised to hear I get a very nice parcel and a box of biscuits every week. I was surprised to see such a fine parcel, so please tell them they do not a little for nothing; and I once more wish to thank them all, and if you hear anyone when they are gathering for such funds say: "What are they doing with the money ?" you can tell them what, I say, as I am not the only one here to receive these welcome parcels. There are thousands given out every week in this Camp alone. Well, mother, remember me to dad when you write to him, and tell him I am in the best of health and hope to be home soon. We are just going to have a nice concert, but I hope you will all be going to church, as I cannot get there. Well, mother, I think this is all this time. May God keep you all safe till I come home.

From your ever-loving son, REDVERS.

HOWDEN
Several Deaths from Influenza.

Mr. Ibbetson presided at a meeting of the Rural District Council. The Medical Officer reported that influenza was very prevalent in the district and there had been several deaths. Mr. J. G. Thirkell was elected a member of the Food Control Committee in place of Mr. J. W. Blyth, resigned.

OBITUARY

Rev. Fred Seaton-Smith. G.F., B.A., died on November 15th at Boulogne from influenza, after a few days illness. Nearly all of his short ministerial life was spent in the diocese of Ripon, from 1913 to 1915 at St. John's, Bradford, and from 1915 to 1917 at All Souls', Leeds. Before his ordination he had spent some years in the estate office of the North-Eastern Railway, entering this work at the completion of his school course at St. Peter's, York. The war broke out during his curacy in Leeds, and he went to Egypt to serve in the Y.M.C.A. hut. Afterwards for several months he was actively engaged in the Western Front as chaplain, sometimes in the trenches, and sometimes at an advanced base. Mr. Seaton-Smith leaves a widow and two young children. The deceased young man was a brilliant lawn tennis player, and took the premier prize at Pocklington tournament a few years ago. He was a particularly nice fellow, and much sympathy is expressed for his young widow and family.

STAMFORD BRIDGE.

Death of a Local Soldier

Private Edwin Eustace Dresser, who died on November 15th of bronchial pneumonia, at the 5th General Hospital, Rouen, was the youngest son of Mr. and Mrs. T. Dresser, Stamford Bridge. He joined the Army in November, 1915, entering the 2nd Battalion Grenadier Guards. He was once wounded by a German sniper on the Arras front. The deceased was formerly a cashier and clerk in Messrs. Barclay's bank at York, Kirbymoorside, Malton, and Driffield.

POCKLINGTON.

Central Cinema.

Owing to the prevailing epidemic, the Central Cinema has been CLOSED this week, and the Pictures WILL NOT BE SHOWN TODAY.

21st December, 1918

Repatriated Prisoners.

At the outset of this paragraph we wish to say how proud we are of all the local lads who have joined his Majesty's forces during the Great War, for Pocklington has a record of distinctions which many towns of larger size might envy.

Our representative had an interesting chat with Private Redvers Harrison, eldest surviving son of Private and Mrs. T. Harrison, of Church Lane, Pocklington, which our readers will read with intense interest. Redvers joined up in 1916, at the age of 16 years, and was attached to the Northumberland Fusiliers. After a course of training at Ipswich and Doncaster, he was drafted to France on the 6th February last being only 17 years of age at the time, but a big, fine lad for his age. He fought at Cambrai, Champagne, and Bullecourt, being wounded and taken prisoner from the latter place on the 27th May last. Forty of them were fastened in an enclosed truck, and remained there without food or water for fourteen days, without even their wounds being attended, to. Eventually a German Red Cross Nurse appeared on the scene and on being asked for water, she fetched them a bucketful of salt and water. Some the men had lost a limb, and died in the truck, whilst most of the wounds were "walking with maggots." The Germans alleged the prisoners had been forgotten, and they were then taken to barracks, where their wounds were roughly attended to, but received the more careful attention of two American doctors shortly afterwards, and their condition improved. Over 1,500 prisoners were put into one camp and caught dysentery. For five weeks in camp he had nothing to eat from the Germans except a few cabbages pinched through the wires. When he got better he was sent into an aluminium factory. His clothing and boots had been taken from him to give to German soldiers, and in spite of the fact that he and twenty-two other Britishers and eighty Italians had to work along with German girls the only clothing he had on was a pair of pants. They had not enough to eat, and one girl took pity on him, and secretly gave him a cabbage occasionally, which he cut up into slices and ate raw as he worked. About the 13th August British Red Cross parcels started to arrive and things improved, and they were liberated on the 13th November. They were about twenty miles from Holland, and the twenty-three of them decided to walk it. Just after crossing the frontier they were met by two "Daily Mirror" men and a Scotch officer, who took them to have a bath and some good food. After remaining at that convalescent Camp about a fortnight they went on to Rotterdam, where they were supplied with new clothing, and sailed for Blighty. He brought with him a pair of wooden clogs, made out of solid wood, and in which he was photographed by the "Daily Mirror" representative, a capital photo appearing in their issue of 9th December. Germans would offer as much as 15s. for a quarter of a pound of tea, and they used Michaelmas daisies for a tea substitute. Four Germans were rationed with one white herring for a week, and the prisoners worked from 5.30 a.m, to near 9 p.m.,

Redvers Harrison in his clogs walking back to Holland from his prisoner of war camp in Germany. As taken by a "Daily Mirror" photographer

for 9d. a week. If they wanted payment they had to walk a distance of seven miles for it. They did walk for it until their parcels arrived, when they let their wages slide. Pte. Harrison was wounded in the heel and thigh by shrapnel, and he regrets to find that some ignorant girls in Pocklington jeer at his lameness, by shouting him in the street "hopperty-click." Such conduct is deserving of severe censure, and we feel deeply grieved to have to make such a statement.

Redvers Harrison in the 1930's

Two more, of our repatriated Prisoners of War arrived home this week after being in the, hands of the Germans for several months, these being Pte. R. T. Manners, son of Mr, and Mrs. R. Manners, George Street, Pocklington, who was captured on the 9th April, and who has been working since then behind enemy lines in farming, ammunition transport and other work during which he was often exposed to the danger from British Aircraft bombs and shell fire. He was registered as being in Gardelegen Camp, but states that he was never in Germany. After the Armistice he travelled to Liege, where he was extremely well-treated by the Belgians, who did everything possible to restore him to his normal health after his very trying experiences. Pte. Nicholas Kendall, nephew of Mrs. W. S. Lamb, jeweller, Railway-Street, is the other arrival. He was captured in April and subjected to similar treatment to Pte. Manners, whom he met with at Loos. Cpl. T. Priestley, son of Mrs. Priestley, and nephew of Mrs. Lamb, is also visiting Pocklington. He was wounded, and along with sixty four other wounded British soldiers was captured in a field hospital before they could be got away. He speaks well of the doctor who attended his wounds, but received similar treatment to the others when able to get about again.

18th January, 1919

Back to "Blighty".

Lce. Corpl. Richard Brewer, of Union Street, Pocklington, arrived home on Thursday night, after being a prisoner of war in Germany since last March, and we were pleased to see him looking fit and well. "Dick" was a Machine Gunner, attached to the Seaforth Highlanders in the famous 51st Division, and he has some remarkable stories to tell of his experiences in Germany as a prisoner of war, and says the Germans even pinched the ring he was wearing, and that he has several times been hit with the butt end of a German rifle for nothing more serious than getting something to eat after being nearly starved to death. Potato skins were a luxury for the prisoners in the hands of the Huns, and even cigars were not handed out to them, although they were honourable prisoners of war, who had "fought the good fight" fair and square. Lce. Corpl. Brewer brought home with him some German bread, which is coal-black, and says it had to be boiled to soften it before they could eat it. Although their permanent address was "Parchim Camp, Germany." he says that for some time they were not within a hundred miles of that Camp, but were several times placed just behind the German lines which were being shelled by the British artillery. Pte. Herbert Holmes a nephew of Mr. and Mrs. Whitehead is a prisoner of War in Parchim Camp, but Lce.-Corpl. Brewer says he has never heard or seen anything of him.—We hope that other families who are anxiously awaiting news of their heroes may shortly receive the glad tidings that they are safe and well.

Pocklington Church Book of Remembrance
- Men of Pocklington who served in the Great War 1914-1918

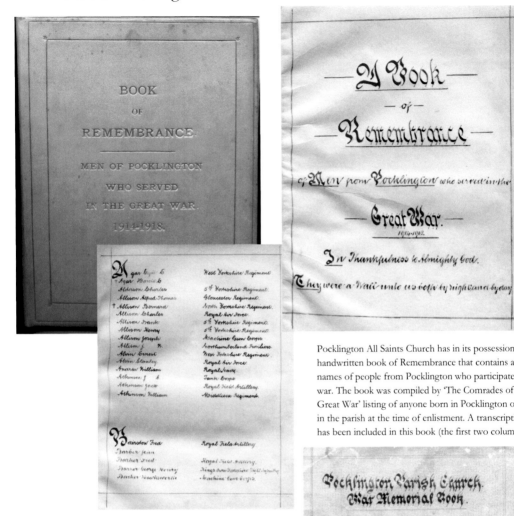

Pocklington All Saints Church has in its possession a handwritten book of Remembrance that contains all the names of people from Pocklington who participated in the war. The book was compiled by 'The Comrades of the Great War' listing of anyone born in Pocklington or living in the parish at the time of enlistment. A transcription of it has been included in this book (the first two columns only).

A Book of Remembrance
of Men in Pocklington who served in the Great War
1914 – 1918

In Thankfulness to Almighty God

They were a wall unto us both by night and by day

Thy Kingdom Come
Let us have faith that right makes might and in that faith let us to the end dare to do our own duty as we understand it.
To love of God the fallen are commended
And lo they passed over and all the trumpets sounded for them on the other side.

They shall not grow old as we that are left grow old age shall not weary them nor the years condemn at the going down of the sun and in the morning we will remember them.

Service Record Key: Enl = Enlisted, L/Corp = Lance Corporal, Corp = Corporal, Sgt = Sergeant, CQMS = Company Quartermaster Sergeant, Dchd = Discharged (Regulars), Post. = Posted, #=Regimental Number, Tfr=Transferred to, Rgt = Regiment, b.=Birth, m.= Married, d. =Death, App.=Apprentice, Bat. = Battalion, Disem.=disembodied (Territorials) , MGC= Machine Gun Corps, DMob=Demobilised, WiA=Wounded in Action RFA= Royal Field Artillery, BEF = British Expeditionary Force

* In September 1940, as the result of a fire caused by an incendiary bomb at the War Office Record Store in Arnside Street, London, approximately two thirds of 6.5 million soldiers' documents for the First World War were destroyed. Because of the lack of a comprehensive data record on each soldier, information provided here may be a best guess and must be treated with caution and checked with other sources. Sources of this information is from Ancestry.co.uk (Anc), www.forces-war-records.co.uk (FWR) and www.findmypast.co.uk (FMP)

Name	Regiment	Service Record* (not from Memorial Book)
Agar Cyril E	West Yorkshire Regiment	88 Rothbury St., Scarboro, Enl. 11/11/14 Scarbro, #15906, 16/1/15 L/Corp, Post. France Corp. 26/8/15, Sgt 19/10/15 CQMS 8/4/17 Dchd 7/7/17. (C001)
Agar Harold E		Harold Edward Agar son of Fred M Agar (Pocklington Station Master in 1921) b. 1891 Lieut. in Princess Patricia's Canadian Light Infantry (Eastern Ontario Regiment) Died 30 Oct 1917 age 26. Buried in Passchendale New British Cemetery. Son of Frederick Matthew Agar and Margaret Annie (née Wetherill) of 28, Fountain St. Anlaby, Hull. (C002)
Alderson Charles	5th Yorkshire Regiment	27 yr Old Groom in 1911, 6 Stathers Yd, Chapmangate Enl. 27/8/14 Darlington #90017, Dchd 11/1/19. (C003)
Allison Alfred Thomas	Gloucester Regiment	24 Regent St., Pock. Bricklayer/Plasterer, #910 Gloucester Reg Army Service Corps MT Tfr Suffolk Rgt #35840 30/5/17, Dchd 1/10/17. After the war joined his brothers to run the family building firm and Pocklington's Cinema in Oak House. (C004)
Allison Bernard †	North Yorkshire Regiment	Plumbers App. In 1911 b. Pock. Disem. 18/4/15 Medal record Corp. 1/5th Yorks Bat. Enl. Scarboro. Corporal. Died in Action in France 10/10/15, #1792. (C005)
Allison Charles	Royal Air Force	Charles Henry Allison baptised in Pocklington in 1873 (mother's last name was Rooks), Charles was a hairdresser who resumed business in Hull after the war. Air Force #23675 Driver (M.T.) Sergeant Mechanic. Joined 25/2/16 Promoted 1/7/17. (C006)
Allison Frank	5th Yorkshire Regiment	In1911 at 25, Kirkland St. Pock (Machine Feeder). Joined Pock Territorials 11/2/09 (5yrs) worked at Harrison & Co. #1488 18/4/15 L/Corp. #33199 Captured 27/5/10 Demob. 12/4/19. Awarded MM. (C007)
Allison Henry	5th Yorkshire Regiment	(C008)
Allison Joseph	Machine Gun Corps	(C009)
Allison J. N.	Northumberland Fusiliers	(C010)
Alvin Ernest	West Yorkshire Regiment	His Father Herbert was Railway Signal Porter in 1911 at the Balk Crossing, Pock. Enl. 29/1/17 2nd W. York. R. #57952 Pte. Dchd. 17/7/17. (C011)

Name	Regiment	Service Record* (not from Memorial Book)
Alvin Stanley	Royal Air Force	Brother of Ernest. b. 10/8/00 enl. 3/7/18 age 18 RAF #264147. (C012)
Andrew William	Royal Navy	(C013)
Atkinson J.A.	Tank Corps	(C014)
Atkinson Jack	Royal Field Artillery	Corp. R.F.A. #60682, L/Serg. R.F.A. #106885 Driver 1918 (C015)
Atkinson William	Middlesex Regiment	b.1887 Enl. @ Beverley 6/3/16 East Yorks Reg. 5, Union St. Pock., Traveller, #41963, Transf. to Middlesex Reg. #G/12996 15/3/16 then to Queens Own (Royal West Kent Reg.G/41963 18/7/19. (C016)
Bairstow Fred	Royal Field Artillery	In 1911, Fred was a Boot Shop Errand boy age 14 in employ of his father who was Manager of Stead & Simpson boot shop in Pock and living at 8 Victoria Terrace, Pock. (C017)
Barber John		(C018)
Barber Fred	Royal Field Artillery	(C019)
Barker George Henry	Kings Own Yorks Lt. Inf.	20 Chapmangate Pocklington, 1911 census a bootmaker Age 52 by 1916 at 37 Union St., Pocklington. (C020)
Barker Hawksworth	Machine Gun Corps	Son of George Henry. 1911 Age 20 a bricklayer. 8/6/15 Enl Scarbro 3/5th Yorks MGC #34330 37 Union St., Pock. 10/10/16 Mesopotamia Exp. Force, WiA 25/3/17, Dmob Port Said 7/2/19, Dchd 13/4/19. (C021)
Barker Walter	Kings Royal Rifles	In 1911 In Sculcoates, b.1877 Pock. Bricklayer Labourer. Son of George Henry. (C022)
Barnet Henry	East Yorkshire Regiment	(C023)
Barnes Leonard	5th Yorkshire Regiment	Francis Leonard Barnes aged 12 in 1911 living at Toft House Farm, Yorks reg #3100 Driver RFA #127304 Disem 18/4/15 Dchd 3/11/15. (C024)
Bean Charles	2nd East Yorks Regiment	In 1911 census a 15yr old Bricklayer George St., Pock #21046 also 7th, 8th & 12th Bat., After war entered Z Class War reserve stood down after 1920. (C025)
Bean William	5th Yorkshire Regiment	Brother of Charles. Grocers Errand Boy Age 14 in 1911. #337 5th West Yorkshire Enl. York, L/Sgt, Wounded France/ Flanders 26/8/15. (C026)
Beckett Richard	5th Yorkshire Regiment	Age 16 in 1911 Richard Wright Webster Beckett, Chemists Labourer, 9 West Green, Pock., #241012 #3084 Cpl, Awarded Military Medal in France 8/4/15 Wounded Left Shoulder by Shell 27/12/17 Disemb. 13/2/19 d. 2/8/64 buried at Allerthorpe. (C027)
Bedford Tom	East Yorkshire Regiment	Pig Dealer, Percy House, 9 London St. Pock in 1911 later St. Helensgate Pock., M. Jessie Louise Bedford, Pock Chapel 6/11/13 enl. Beverley 24/1/17 #52963 & 3rd N. Staffs

Name	Regiment	Service Record* (not from Memorial Book)
		8/12/17 #645768 WiA and became ill transferred home for treatment. (C028)
Bennison Charles	5th Yorkshire Regiment	In 1911 Tailors Apprentice Aged 18 at 20 George Street with father Fred a traction engine driver. #1033 #240070 Sgt. Disemb. (C029)
Bentley Albert Edward	Royal Engineers	In 1911 a border at Mile End House, Pock. Age 19, with John Henry Buttle a Horse Slaughterer Enl. S. Staffs. Regt. #28664. Pte., Royal Engineers. #309527 Sapper #W.R.277066 Royal Eng. (Railways) (C030)
Bentley William B	Kings Own Yorks. Lt. Inf.	Age 12 in 1911 William Bentley was staying with brother Albert E. as a border at Mile End House. #50616 Pte 8th Yorks L.I. #80575 (C031)
Bishop Robert	East Yorkshire Regiment	In 1911 a Grocers Warehouseman living in Barmby Moor Age 30. 1st, 10th. E. York R. Pte #15678 Transferred to Class Z reserve disbanded in 1920's (C032)
Brewer Alfred J	Royal Engineers	Alfred Brewer a painter was living at home in 1911 aged 34 with Father Alfred a Council Labourer (63) at 3 Victoria Terrace, Pock. Father Alf took part in the Boer War in 1900. (C033)
Brewer Richard	Machine Gun Corps	Richard O. Brewer Age 28 in 1911 Butcher in Chapmangate, Pock. Best Guess #59973 From 10/12/15 Private MGC Dischd 21/3/19. (C034)
Brooks John Edward	5th Yorkshire Regiment	John Edmonson Brook in 1911 Census Plumber and Painter Age 22 living at home with parents John Edmonson (Age 55 Plumber & Painter) and Ellen (42) #2088. York Reg. Pte, Tfer #23539. M.G.C. Disemb. 18/2/19. See his war diary on Page 204. (C035)
Brooks Maurice W	Canadian Rifles	Brother of J E Brook. Srce: Canada Library and Archives RG 150, Accession 1992-93/166, Box 1097 - 44 Item 65843 Canadian Expeditionary Force (CEF) M W Brook Lieut. Joined 13/12/14 Unit Supplier Officers. (C036)
Brooks Norman Leslie	West Yorkshire Regiment	Brother of J E Brook. #51332 Pte 4th Res. Btn & 2nd Btn. West Riding Reg, Disch. to "Hill Crest" Pocklington 17/9/19. Defective Vision. (C037)
Brooks Tom	Royal Navy	1901 Thomas Earl Brook (Plumbers Apprentice) Age 17 Living as Visitor at house of Jane Ellen Smith (confectioner) in George Street. Various ships from 11/6/06 Telern, VictoryII, Amythyst, Hawke, Tamar, King Alfred, Crescent, Transferred to Royal Fleet Reserve #B4307 13/5/11 Served from 3/9/11 to 19/11/14 on Victory II, Pathfinder, Alexandria, Galatea as Stoker. From 1/10/15 to 17/2/18 on Galatea, Dolphin, Victory II, Tisgard, Royal Sovereign as Leading Stoker, Became Stoker Petty officer from 1/8/18 to 10/6/22 aboard Royal Sovereign, Victory II, Alexandria, Victoria & Albert d. Portsmouth 15/8/34. (C038)

Name	Regiment	Service Record* (not from Memorial Book)
Broughton Ernest	East Yorkshire Regiment	In 1911 Ernest Arthur Broughton (19) Butchers Journeyman b.1892 living at home with parents Charles Broughton (47) Police Sergeant and Sarah (40) at the Old Police Station George St. Pock. d. Leeds Mar. 1954 #38430 Private East Yorks. Regiment. (C039)
Broughton Stanley	Royal Air Force	Brother of Ernest. b. 23/12/1899 Rillington Joined Royal Airforce age 18 25/1/18 #247789 Civilian occupation: Motor Driver, Father: Charles, 3 Rose Waldon, Barmby Road, Pock. Pocklington Police Sergeant. Tfr to RAF Reserve 13/11/19 Buried Pock Cemetery 1971. (C040)
Brown Alfred	Army Service Corps	In 1901 Living at Canal Head with Parents John W Brown, Engine Driver (Flour Mill) and Alice C Brown. Too many possible linking Army Service Corps records to link up with. (C041)
Brown George	Royal Engineers	1911 No. 1 Victoria Terrace, Pock. George Brown 27 b. abt. 1884 Bricklayers labourer living at home with parents Alexander Richinson Brown (62) Brewers Cooper and Annie (58). #2970647 & #301551 Royal Engineers Road Foreman Age 31. Joined 22/11/15. Posted France Disemb. Le Havre 1/2/18. Sick with Myalia at St. Pol. Tfr. to Army Reserve Demob. 25/2/19. (C042)
Brown Roland †	Kings Royal Rifles	See Page 12. (C043)
Bulmer Arthur	Army Service Corps	1901 Arthur F. Bulmer (36) b. Abt. 1865 Pocklington—A Boarder in Sowerby, Thirsk at the House of Sarah Walker (56) Wid. 1911 Arthur Foster Bulmer Barclay Bank Clerk, still a boarder at same place. #715 Army Service Corps, R.A.S.C. C (HT) 715 Driver. Dis. 16/1/16. d. Dec. 1953 in Thirsk. (C044)
Buttle Francis Charles†	Kings Royal Rifles	See Page 12. (C045)
Buttle George Harold	Kings Royal Rifles	In 1911 George Harold Buttle a joiners apprentice (Age 16) b. abt. 1895 in Pock. Living with parents George Thomas Buttle (46, Tailor) and Dinah (50). 30 London St. Pock. 21st. Bn. K.R. Rif. C. #C/12248 Pte., 1st. Bn. K.R. Rif. C.#C/12248 (C046)
Buttle James		In 1901 Sarah Eliz. Buttle (31) was head of house in Grape Lane a Laundrymaid Wash, James Wm. was 3. In 1911 James W Buttle (age 13) son living with family Thomas B Huck Farmer. Labourer. (age 48) and Sarah E Huck (Age 38) in 23 Grape Lane, Pock. #235716 & #116753 Duke of Wellington's (West Riding Reg. James William Buttle enl. Scarborough 22/2/13 5th Yorks Reg. Served in France Dischd 4/12/18 to Manor House, Chapmangate, Pock. (C047)
Cains Frank	East Yorkshire Regiment	1911 Frank Cains was 13, a Grocers Errand Boy living at Prospect House, Canal Head, Pock, with parents Francis George (40, Law Clerk & Assist. Bailiff of Cty. Court) and Lucy (38). #5744 Pte. & #224175 East Yorkshire Regiment, Labour Corps. (C048)

Name	Regiment	Service Record* (not from Memorial Book)
Cains Henry	Northumberland Fusiliers	Brother of Frank Age 12 in 1911 in above household. d. 1977 Pock. #57996 4th Btn. Northumberland Fusiliers Private Gunshot Wound, shoulder left. Date back to active service 15/4/18. (C049)
Cattle Henry Irving †	East Yorkshire Regiment	See Page 13. (C050)
Cattle Robert Norman	Royal Air Force	In 1911 Robert Norman Cattle b. Pocklington abt. 1894 living at 31 Ambleside Avenue, Bradford as Wool Merchants Clerk with cousin Herbert August Middlebrook (34, a wool merchants manager) and Annie (34). 4 Feb 1916 joined RAF #20311 Civilian occ. Motor Driver. Joined 50 Squadron 14/2/16 Dischd. as unfit 1/3/18 d. Mar 1959 - Southampton, Hampshire. (C051)
Cattle Roland M	Royal Navy	In 1911 Census Ronald M Cattle Age 11 living with parents Henry Ward Cattle (47, Brewer) and Annie (49) in Pocklington. Middle M is for Middlebrook. Military Record not found. (C052)
Copeman Arthur	Royal Air Force	Father is Arthur David Copeman b. Oct 1871 Mutford, Lowestoft m. 1892 Lavinia Gooderson Bosworth. In 1911 was in Hull as a butcher journeyman. Joined Royal Airforce #160876 22/4/18 for duration of war. Person to be informed of casualty Lavina Copeman of Yapham Mill, Pocklington (wife). Tfer to RAF Reserve 8/8/19. (C053)
Crisp Walter J †	South Staffs Regiment	See Page 15. (C054)
Cross John †	Royal Field Artillery	See Page 16. (C055)
Courrell H E		H.E. Corrall, Royal Artillery (Royal Horse Artillery and Royal Field Artillery) #88809 13th Brigade Royal Field Artillery Rank Disemb. 14/10/14 Gunner awarded 1914 star 16/11/21 RGA #203207 Known as Edward. No link found to this area. (C056)
Dales George Nolton	Royal Army Service Corps	Bap. 29/8/00 Pock. In 1911 living at home 25 & 27 Market Street, Pock., age 10, with Parents William James Dales (Age 40,Butcher) and Louisa (30). Likely record #M2/076436 George Dales, 353rd Co., Royal Army Service Corps. Mechanic Staff Sergeant British Forces in Salonika Meritorious Service Medal d. Feb. 1984 Leeds. (C057)
Dawson James	5th Yorkshire Regiment	(C058)
Day John P	East Yorkshire Regiment	1911 John Peacock Day Age 25 b. abt. 1886 Bank Clerk living at Oakdene House, Pock., with Parents John Day (62, Retired Draper) and Elizabeth (54), East Yorks. Reg. #10/1035 Sgt. disemb. 22/12/15 awarded 1915 Star Medal France. After war Class Z resrv. (C059)
Dixon Charles	Royal Field Artillery	1911 Charles Dixon Age 31 b. abt. 1880 Threshing? Machine Feeder m. Sophia (30) in Pocklington, Too many RFA records with Charles Dixon to identify. (C060)

Name	Regiment	Service Record* (not from Memorial Book)
Downham George	5th Yorkshire Regiment	In 1901 George Downham (7) was with parents George Downham (Age 33, Horse Man on Farm) and Susan (28), at Barnby upon Don, Doncaster. In 1911 the family were in New Pavement, Pocklington but George is not there, Brother Lyth is age 14 Errand Boy. #1663 Yorks. Reg, #496505 In France 17/4/15 Labour Corps #4381388 5th Yorkshire. George Downham was wounded in 1916 and treated at No.2 Gen. Hosp., Becketts Park, Leeds and returned to the Btn. (C061)
Downham Lyth	East Riding Yeomanry	Brother to George. #2251 ER Yeomanry #150371 MGC Desemb. 25/5/19. (C062)
Dumville George Ernest - Royal Field Artillery		George Ernest Dumville married Daisy A. Johnson in Pocklington in 3rd Qtr 1913. In 1901 he was Age 12 b. Snape, Yrks. and living at Snape, Bedale with parents James (45, Gardeners Labourer) and Elizabeth (44). He was employed by Mr. D. Richardson at the Albion Foundry, Pocklington. #2904, #756056 Royal Field Artillery. A/Sgt. Corporal and Shoeing Smith. The Distinguished Conduct Medal was second only to the Victoria Cross in prestige. "For conspicuous gallantry and devotion to duty during more than three years of continuous service in the field. During the recent fighting he has on several occasions shown great coolness and skill in leading ammunition wagons to the battery position under heavy shell fire. " (C063)
Dunning William Knapton -Northumberland Fusiliers		In 1911 he was staying at the New Red Lion, Pocklington at the house of Walter H Askham (32, Publican) as a Servant. William K Dunning 29, Ostler b. Pock). 1/4th Northd Fus #4/3651 Pte, 20th Northumberland Fusiliers #37443. (C064)
Durkin Thomas	5th Yorkshire Regiment	In 1911 Age 11 in Chapmangate, Pock. living at home with parents John Durkin (36, Farm labourer) and Jane (31). #14614, Prince of Wales's Own (West Yorkshire) Regiment, #102843 Durham Light Infantry. (C065)
Dykes Albert	Royal Army Service Corps	In 1901 Albert Dykes age 4 (b.1897 Barmby Moor) living with Parents William Dykes (45, Shepherd on Farm) and Susannah (44) in Bridge St. Pock., In 1911 age 14 Mkt St. Pock., Telegraph Messenger RASC #T37189 Driver. Suspected Appendicitis 02/09/1916 Newspaper report (see Arthur) says he joined the Army Service Corps early in the war was sent to Mediterranean, then later in another theatre of war. Before war was in the Post Office Telegraph dept. (C066)
Dykes Arthur	5th Yorkshire Regiment	In 1911 with brother Albert in Mkt. Street, Pock, General Labourer age 16 b. abt 1895 in Cowthorpe. Joined Territorials at Pock. 17/6/13 Under Capt. Scott. #33205 & #1489 AF WR Yks Regt 5/8/14 Pte Exp. Force in France 7/8/16 L/Corp 4/4/17 Corp. 26/6/17 Retained in Army of occupation 1919. Yorkshire Gazette (18/12/17) reports say

Name	Regiment	Service Record* (not from Memorial Book)
		he was in Territorials and went to front with brother Tom. Was awarded Military medal. Led the men foiling a German attack with Bayonets and bombs and captured a German officer. (C067)
Dykes Fred Chapman	5th Yorkshire Regiment	In 1911 at 52 Union St. Pock., Age 22 Farm Labourer Head & Lily Dykes Age 24 Wife #1293 Alexandra, Princess of Wales's Own Yorkshire Regiment Corporal Disembarked 18/4/15 Disembodied 25/1/19 Awarded 1914/15 Star. Newspaper report (see Arthur) says he was in the Territorials sent to front April 1915. Was awarded the Military Medal for bravery going out under heavy shell fire and carrying a wounded officer to safety. Before the war was employed at the Wagon works at Horbury. (C068)
Dykes Thomas James	East Yorkshire Regiment	In 1911, Thomas James Dykes Age 24 (b. Nelson Lancs.) living In Bielby, nr. Pock. As bricklayers labourer on Farm with Wife Miriam (26). In Territorials at start of war. #758, #238066 East Yorkshire Regiment, Lincolnshire Regiment or #T4/086316, #40294 Army Service Corps, East Yorkshire Regiment. Yorkshire Gazette (18/12/17) reports he was wounded by a machine gun bullet in his leg. After the war was a shoe repairer in Pocklington. (C069)
Dykes William H	Royal Navy	In 1891 William H. Dykes Aged 8 (b. Selby in 1883) living at Nolton, Doncaster with parents William H Dykes Age 32 Agricultural Labourer (b. Melbourne) and Susannah (35). Navy Record not found. Yorks. Gazette (above) says he was employed at a Maltkiln in Market Weighton. Took part in the retreat at Mons and in France 16 months. Then joined the Navy as a submarine chaser. (C070)
Eagan Joseph †		See Page 16 (C071)
Easton Fred †	Royal horse Artillery	See Page 17 (C072)
Eastwood James William - 5th Yorkshire Regiment		In 1911 living at 1 Waterloo Terrace, Pock. A Rope and Net Maker Age 27 b. abt. 1884 in Pock., and wife Annie (24), Possibly #205142 Private West Riding Regiment #569928 Private Labour Corps or #309 Sergeant Yorkshire Regiment, #401643 Royal Army Medical Corps or #14774 Pte 9th Yorks L.I., 6th Yorks L.I. (C073)
Elliott James †	Royal Field Artillery	See Page 18 (C074)
Elmer Arthur	South Staffs Regiment	In 1911 Arthur Elmer Age 30 (b. Sutton on Forest abt. 1881) House Painter living at 6Richmond Terrace, Pock., with wife Annie May (31). #28741 South Staffordshire Regiment Enlisted 30/6/16 Discharged 2/12/17 Sick—No longer physically fit for active service. (C075)
English Robert Cecil †	Kings Royal Rifles	See Page 19. (C076)
English Henry Turner	East Riding Yeomanry	In 1911 Harry Turner English Age 20 (b. Pock abt. 1891) Clerk (Corn Merchant) living with parents Richard Massey English

Name	Regiment	Service Record* (not from Memorial Book)
		(61, Corn Merchant & Auctioneer) and Mary (59) at Pocklington. Henry Turner English #50449 Household Cavalry Pte #1690 Sub Unit E.R. Yeomanry Lcrs. Pte Entered Egypt Theatre of War 10/11/15. (C077)
Etherington Thomas	East Yorkshire Regiment	In 1891 Census Thomas Etherington Age 20 b. Elvington living at Woodhouse Sutton on Derwent as Farm Servant on Farm of Richard Beal (42, Farmer). #14565 East Yorkshire Regiment Pte. Theatre of War Balkans 7/10/15. (C078)
Everingham Sydney H	Tank Corps	In 1911 Sydney Herbert Everingham (19, Shop Assistant) was living with parents John Thos. Everingham (53, Master Tailor and Outfitter) and Eleanor (56), Pocklington. Shop was in Railway St., Joined 11th Dec 1915, living at 1, Thorncroft Barmby Row, Pock., Occ. Cycle Motor Dealer & Mechanic, m. Evelyn Ida Steel 1/6/15 #61752 Training Reserve Battalion Tank Corps. Joined Mechanical Transp. Depot Army Service Corps 16/12/16 Joined 85th Training Res. Btn. 29/12/16 Fully trained 20/11/17 Yks Reg. 85 Btn 7/4/17 L.Cpl. Dischg. 12/8/18. (C079)
Everingham Wycliffe G - Royal Air Force		Brother of Sydney. In 1911 Wycliffe Galland Everingham (30 b. Pock., abt. 1881, Electrical Engineer and Manufacturer of electrical instruments) and Kate Nellie (29), in 37 Auckland Rd., Ilford. Royal Naval Air Service Temp. Lieut 8/3/17 Ministry of Munitions, Duties included Magnets Production. (C080)
Ezard Charles	Royal Army Medical Corps	In 1911 Charles Ezard 19, b. abt. 1892 in Pock., a border at 73 Arthur St., Withernsea, Vansman. In 1901 at home with Parents Harry Ezard (33, Millers Wagoner) and Ann (31) in Union St., Pock. #56676 RAMC, Pte. Theatre of War 1/France Date of entry 20/6/15. His Medal was returned 18/11/20 as misspelled as Egzard. Reissued 10/2/21. (C081)
Ezard Herbert	Kings Royal Rifles	Brother of Charles. In 1911 Charles Ezard (14, Newsboy) at 8, London St. Pocklington living at home with parents Harry Ezard (43, Mill Wagoner) and Ann (41). 21st. Bn. K.R. Rif. C. #C/12247 Pte., 7th. Bn. K.R. Rif. C. #C/12247., 9th. Bn. K.R. Rif. C. #C/12247. (C082)
Fairburn Ernest	5th Yorkshire Regiment	In 1911 Ernest Fairburn Age 17 b. abt. 1894 Grocer's Apprentice, living at home in East Crossing (Balk), Pock., with parents Mark Fairburn (62, signalman on railway) and Mary Alice (62), #14716 E J Fairburn Duke of Wellingtons West Riding Reg. 9th btn. On 30/9/17 Admitted to Corps Rest Station for Inflammation of Connective Tissue in Left Knee. (C083)
Fairburn Harry	Royal Engineers	In 1911 Harry Fairburn (24 b. Pock abt. 1887), Asst Shunter NE Ry Co.) living with brother Fred Fairburn (26, asst shunter NE Ry Co.) at 4, Claremont Av., Courtny St. Holderness Rd. Hull. # Wr. 265778 SPR. 21/North'd Fus: #4257., Royal Engineers. #240052. Spr. Sub. Unit Railways (C084)

Name	Regiment	Service Record* (not from Memorial Book)
Ferisy James	6th Yorkshire Regiment	In 1911 James Richard Ferisy age 15 b. abt. 1896 apprentice iron founder living at 4, London St., Pocklington as border with 4 other boarders at house of Joseph Mason (57, blacksmiths striker and widower). In 1901 he was at home in London St. Pocklington with father Richard Ferisy (43, Consumptive) and Emma (39). #20132 6th E. York. R. Pte. Discharged. (C085)
Fielder Cecil	Kings Own Yorks Lt. Inf.	In 1911 Cecil Fielder (12) living at home with parents John Elliott Fielder (52, joiner and wheelwright) and Annie E (52, 15 children born alive!, 4 died) at 1, London St., Pock., #50532 Pte 7th Yorks L.I., 2/5th Yorks L.I., 1/4th Yorks L.I. Joined Z Reserve 22/11/19. (C086)
Fielder John	Royal Air Force	John Elliott was brother of Cecil. In 1911 living at home with parents above. (20 b. abt. 1891, joiner and wheelwrights assistant), Royal Navy b. 30/9/1991 #F48665 Occ. joiner, Pock., Assigned to President II 31/1/18 Crystal Palace (which was initial training establishment for all theRNVR volunteers and also for Officers destined for the RND or RAF. It was also a radio or communications centre. Tfr RAF 16/3/18. After the war was a joiner and funeral director. (C087)
Fisher Arthur Roland	Royal Navy	In 1891 Census Arthur R (6) son of Arthur Thos. Fisher (39, Clerk in Holy Orders, Rector of Skelton) and Dora J. (34), Skelton Rectory, Yorks., Between 1908 and 1921 Arthur Thomas was Vicar of Pocklington Church. (C088)
Fisher Cyril Martin	6th Yorkshire Regiment	Brother of Arthur R. In 1911 was 11 living with parents Arthur Thomas Fisher (59, Clergyman Established Church) and Dora Jane (55), in The Vicarage, Pock., #65002 6/York. R. Pte. Alexandra, Princess of Wales's Own Yorkshire Regiment. Discharged. (C089)
Fisher Thomas Wilfred † - 9th Border Regiment		See Page 20. (C090)
Fletcher Ernest		In 1911 Age 17 (b. abt 1894 at Pickering Marishes) Wagoner working for James Brocklebank Farmer at Mill Farm, Thornton. There was a marriage recorded in Pocklington in 1Qtr 1919 of Ernest Fletcher and Annie Boyes and another recorded 3Qtr of Ernest Fletcher to Frances Pearson both in Pocklington. To the latter marriage is recorded sons Thomas L. Dec. 1920, Stanley Sep. 1923 and daughter Edith E. Dec. 1924. Too many possible Military records to assign. (C091)
Fletcher Oswald		In 1911 Oswald Fletcher b. Pickering Marishes (13) and sister Blanch (9, b. Bishop Wilton) Living in Full Sutton with his mother Mary Fletcher (46 b. Castle Howard, Housekeeper and Widow) to Alfred Oliver (36, Farm Labourer, Single & Head of household). Oswald and Blanch are in the Census as Son & Daughter of Alfred and likely siblings of Ernest. Most likely military record #241767. Pte. 2/5 York & Lanc: Reg., 8th York & Lanc: Reg., 9th York & Lanc: Reg. Z Reserve 13/12/19. (C092)

Name	Regiment	Service Record* (not from Memorial Book)
Flint Charles †	Northumberland Fusiliers	See Page 21. (C093)
Flint Henry	5th Yorkshire Regiment	In 1911, Henry Flint (24, Seller Man in brewery) living at home with brother Charles (26, above a brewer in brewery) and parents Charles Flint (62, Labourer—general) and Elizabeth (60), in 19 Grape Lane, Pocklington. All above mentioned b. Pocklington. 1/5 W. York. R. #6362 Pte., 1st W. York. R. #203007. Entered Z resrv. 19/4/19. After the war became a Chimney Sweep. (C094)
Flint Tom Oswald	Royal Engineers	In 1911 Thomas Oldfield Flint (25, joiner and wheelwright) was living at home with parents Thomas Flint (75, Caretaker and Grave Digger) and Sarah (68), at Cemetery Lodges, Pock., On 24 Nov 1915 was living at 25 Kirkland St., Pock., worked for Stubbs & Son. and joined the Royal Engineers #131256 Sapper. Embarked for France 3/5/15 Wounded 15/6/17 and also 29/9/18. Discharged 8/8/19 Wounded Hand and Thigh. Leg Amputated. A sound recording interview by Alf Peacock exists from the 1980s. York Oral Hist. Soc. (C095)
Forth William Arthur	East Yorkshire Regiment	In 1901, William A. Forth (23 b. Pock. abt. 1878, Stationers Assistant) and wife Ada (23) in Chapmangate, Pock. In 1911, William Alfred Forth (33, Bookseller & Stationers Assistant), and Ada (33) with 3 daughters lily, Mabel & Marian. 20 London St., Pock., m. Ada Todd Jan 1901 Pock., Possible military record #4335443 A Forth. East Yorkshire Regiment. Former no. #55511 Medal for Iraq conflict. Became a Motor Engineer in Pocklington. (C096)
Foster Fred †	Durham Light Infantry	See Page 21. (C097)
Foster Harold		1911 census has Harold Foster (21 b. Pock., Packer in Flour Mill) living at home with parents John Allen Foster (60 b. Pock., Bootmaker dealer) and Grace (57) at Wells House, Burnby Lane, Pock. Difficult to assign Military record with no given Regiment in the Church Remembrance Book. (C098)
Fowler Donald Fawcett	- South Staffs Regiment	In 1911, Donald Fawcett Fowler (11 b. 1900 Pock., at school) living at home with parents George Henry Fowler (38 b. Pock., Linen and Woollen Draper) and Annie (34) at The Briars, Burnby lane, Pock. d. Jun. 1972 at Pocklington. Cannot find Military record. (C099)
Fox Ted	5th Yorkshire Regiment	In 1911 Edward Fox (16, Fish Dealers assistant) adopted son of John J. Magee (47, single, Fish Dealer) both living at 6, Poor House Yard, London Street, Pocklington. Cannot assign Military Record. (C100)
Francis Jack O'Neil	5th Yorkshire Regiment	In 1911 John McNeil Francis (20 (b. Lincoln's, Bicker), Drapers Assistant) Boarder staying at house of Mary Newsome (65 , Widow) in 68 George St., Pocklington. #2657 John McNeil Francis Alexandra, Princess of Wales's

Name	Regiment	Service Record* (not from Memorial Book)
		Own Yorkshire Regiment, Corporal Disembarked 1/11/15 Disembodied 15/10/19 Awarded Military Medal 23/08/16 awarded to J M Francis for acts of gallantry and devotion to duty under fire or for individual or associated acts of bravery which were insufficient to merit the Distinguished Conduct Medal. Sergeant. (C101)
Giles George	Royal Garrison Artillery	In 1911, George Giles (20 b. abt. 1891 in Pock., Butcher (journeyman)) boarder at the house of George Johnson (62, joiner (Master)) at 27 St, Pauls Rd., Shipley. In 1901 George (10) living with parents James Giles (39, bricklayer born USA British sub.) and Hannah M (33) at 35 Union St. Pock. Cannot assign Military Record. (C102)
Giles Jim †	West Yorkshire Regiment	See page 22. (C103)
Gilyead George †	East Yorkshire Regiment	See page 23. (C104)
Grainger George Henry † - 6th Yorkshire Regiment		See page 23. (C105)
Grainger Jonathon	Green Howards	In 1911 Johnathon Grainger (39 b. Pock abt. 1872, Labourer) with wife Hannah (38) and 7 children at Smithy Hill, Pocklington. Cannot assign Military Record. (C106)
Gray Richard Duckwith - Royal Engineers		In 1911, Richard Duckwith Gray (24, Pianist) was living at home with parents Richard Gray (63 b. Pock., Saddler and Harness Maker) and Alice (63, b. Bishop Wilton) in Colenso House, 4 Peters Sq., Pocklington. When he enlisted at Beverley 13/12/16 his profession was Harness Maker at 4 Alexandre Place, Pock., with wife Mable Lewes Gray neè Steel m. 15/6/14. #216675 Royal Engineers Army Ordnance Dept. 440th Cheshire Field Company Btn. Sapper. Discharged 25/4/19. After the war was a saddler in St. Peter's Square, Pocklington. (C107)
Gray Sydney	Kings Royal Rifles	In 1901 Sydney Gray (10, b. abt. 1891, Pock.) living at home with parents William Gray (45, Taylor and Clothier) and Ann E (34), in Lambs Yd., Railway St. Pocklington. In 1911 Sidney Gray still living at home with parents age 20 and a Rural Ancillary Postman in 20 Railway St. Pock., #C/12591 Pte. Kings Royal Rifles. (C108)
Green James		In 1911 James Green (50 b. Abt 1861 Burcott, Bucks, Farm Labourer) One of 16 Boarders in the Lodging House of Richardson Towse (69, widower) in 23 Union St., Pock. (C109)
Greig John George	East Yorkshire Regiment	In 1911 John George Greig (30 b. abt. 1881 in Pock., Clerk in Brewery) with wife Edith Mary (26) in 33 Chapmangate, Pock. (C110)
Greig William Allan	5th Yorkshire Regiment	In 1911 William Allen Greig (23 b. abt. 1888 in Mkt. Weighton, Mineral Water Manufacturer) living with mother Mary Greig (63, Widow and Innkeeper and Licenced Victualler) in Half Moon Hotel, Market Weighton. #1289 5th Battalion Yorkshire Regiment joined from Territorials joined 7 May 1912. A mineral water manufacturer in Waterloo Sq.

Name	Regiment	Service Record* (not from Memorial Book)
		Pock., Appointed L/Cprl 30/4/13 Embodied 5/8/14 Medically Unfit 10/9/14 and again 11/9/16. (C111)
Hall Stanley †	5th Yorkshire Regiment	See Page 24. (C112)
Hardy William Herbert	Army Service Corps	1911 Census William Hardy (18, b. abt. 1893 in Southburgh, Norfolk. (which is in parish of Hingham), Farm Work) living with parents Peregrine Hardy (40, Farm Labourer) and Martha (42) living the Churchyard, Hingham, Norfolk. Joined the Wolds Wagoners #WG713. Attested at Pocklington 17/1/14 from Farm Service. Pte. BEF France awarded 1914 Star. Discharged 16/1/16. (C113)
Harrison Frank	Lincoln Regiment	In 1891 Frank Harrison was 2 (b. 1889 in Pock.) living with parents Michael (50 (b. 1841 in Ireland), Agricultural Labourer) and Mary (44, Hawker) in Market Place, Pocklington. #588541 Lincolnshire Regiment gives address as 3 Deanes lane, Pock., Active Service 25/6/15 Some time spent in India (Fort William, Calcutta) in 1915. Damaged hand by accident in 1916. Invalided and transferred to Labour Corps in England 18/5/18 21 days detention for AWOL 19/9/18 to 9/10/18 absent from Farm Work, released from detention 31/10/18 Demob. 23/1/19. (C114)
Harrison George	5th Yorkshire Regiment	Most likely in 1911 Census George Harrison (11, b. Pocklington) living at home with parents James Harrison (35 b. Pocklington, Farm Labourer) and Mary Ann (34, b. Pocklington) living in 45 Jackson St. York. Too many possible military records for a George Harrison. (C115)
Harrison John George	5th Yorkshire Regiment	In 1901 Census John Harrison (1,b. abt. 1900 Pock.,) and parents George Harrison (26, Brewers Labourer) and Kate (22) in Chapmangate, Pocklington. Cannot link military records for a John George Harrison. 1911 Jack Harrison (11) with parent (George Edward Harrison 35, Farm Labourer) in Chapmangate, Pock. Too many possible military records for a John George Harrison. (C116)
Harrison James †	London Scottish Regiment	See Page 25. (C117)
Harrison Martin	2nd East Yorks. Regiment	1891 Census Martin Harrison (7 b. abt. 1884 Pock., scholar) with parents Michael Harrison (50, Agricultural Labourer) and Mary (44, Hawker) in Market Place, Pocklington. In 1901 Martin Harrison (18, Groom not domestic) at the Common Lodging House, Dean's Lane, Pock., with parents Michael Harrison (60, Lodging House Keeper, and Mary (56, Licensed Hawker). Cannot find Military record. (C118)
Harrison Norman	Royal Air Force	In 1901 Norman M Harrison (9 b. Abt. 1892) living at home with parents (Mansfield Harrison (58 b. Foston, Manager & Groom at Broomfield Stud) and Eliza(45) at St. Pancras London. In 1911 Norman Mansfield Harrison (19 b. abt. 1892 Highgate London, engineers fitter) was a boarder with Fred Dowman (43, joiner) at 11Tooley Street, Gainsboro, Lincs., In 1913 & 1921 Kelly's Directories, father Mansfield

Name	Regiment	Service Record* (not from Memorial Book)
		Harrison was at Brunswick House, Brunswick Place, Pocklington which was next to Albion Foundry. 26/8/18 Norman Mansfield Harrison of Brunswick House, Pocklington joined the RAF #21 Squadron in France. 20/11/18 qualified as pilot 2nd/Lt. Unemployed 2/6/19. Service nos. #1416, #110910. In Dec 1924 Norman Harrison married Kathleen Ablitt in Pocklington. d.1967 Wharfedale, W. Yorks. (FMP) (C119)
Harrison Richard	Royal Air Force	In 1901 Richard (7, b. St. Pancras, London) and brother of Norman, In 1911 father Mansfield Harrison (67, Gentleman of Private Means) with wife Mary H (62, Private Means) was at Brunswick House, Pocklington. Richard Harrison was born in St. Pancras, London in 1893 and was educated at High Gate School, Scarborough College and after became a Student of Engineering in Sheffield University. He joined the Army in July 1916 as a 2nd Lieutenant in the Hampshire Regiment and transferred to the Royal Flying Corps in April 1917 as a Lieutenant Flying Officer. Promoted to acting Captain he was awarded the Croix de Guerre by the French government in Sept. 1918, followed by the Distinguished Flying Cross for low altitude reconnaissance flying in October 1918. He remained in the RAF until 1946 retiring as Air Vice Marshall Richard Harrison, CB, CBE, DFC, AFC. (C120)
Harrison Redvers	Highland Light Infantry	In 1901 Census Redvers Harrison (11m, b. Pock.) son of Thomas Harrison (25 b. Pock. abt. 1876, Labourer on Farm) and Sarah (24 b. Scarboro) at Waterloo Terrace, Pock., In 1911 Redvers Harrison (10, school) with parents T W Harrison (37, Farm Labourer) and S Harrison (35) at 12 Chapmangate, Pock. Military: Redvers T. #TR/5/83169 51st Kings Own Yorks. Lt. Infantry #30854 Gordons Highlanders Pte. Tfr. to 6th Northumberland Fusiliers Entered France 27/5/15 He fought at Cambrai, Champagne and Bullecourt, being wounded and taken prisoner from the latter place on the 27th May 1918 captured by Germans he was photographed and appeared in the Daily Mirror on 9th December 1918 with the clogs he wore to walk back through Holland from Germany. Redvers d. April 1944. (C121)
Harrison William	2nd East Yorkshire Reg.	Thomas William Harrison was father of Redvers and James (see Census above). Thomas William enlisted as Private Thomas William Harrison and was shipped out to the Balkans and fought in Salonika. The 2nd Battalion arrived in Alexandria, Egypt 22/11/15 and on 4/1/16 went to Salonika they were in action during the occupation of Mazirko and the capture of Barakli Jum'a. In 1917 they captured Ferdie and Essex trenches (near Barakli Jum'a) and then the capture of Barakli and Kumli. In Mid 1918 some units returned to France and the remainder were in the Battle of Doiran to capture the Strumica valley. They later moved to Gallipoli and occupied the Dardanelles Forts. (C122)

Name	Regiment	Service Record* (not from Memorial Book)
Harvey Bert	5th Yorkshire Regiment	In 1901 Herbert Harvey (12 b. Pock.) with parents John Harvey (46 b. Pock., Road Mender) and Sarah (46) in 1 Alma Terrace, Pock. In 1911 Herbert Harvey (21 abt. 1890 b. Pock., Wagoner on farm) on the farm of John Johnson (49, Farmer) at Burnby, Nunburnholme Station. Cannot find Military Record. (C123)
Hatfield John Henry	Royal Garrison Artillery	In 1911 John Henry Hatfield (33 b. abt. 1878 Mkt Weighton, Hairdresser) with wife Mary (33) at 36 Market Place, Pock., #151179 Royal Garrison Artillery attested 7/12/15 m. Mary Nicholson in Pock., Wesleyan Chapel 4/6/08. Gunner. Injury to Shoulder 27/8/17 preparing a gun position to receive a gun. He applied for a war pension after the war because of his injury. The official report stated "The man was in no way to blame for the injury which he received it was due to the water logged conditions". Demob. 01/28/19. (Anc)(C124)
Hayton Clifford †	Canadian Regiment	See page 26. (C125)
Hayton Thomas		In 1911 Thomas Hayton (56 Widower b. Beswick, Labourer (Gas Works)). Visitor at house of Ralph Spivey (45, Gas Manager) at Gas Works, Pocklington also possibly Thomas Hayton (47, Flour Miller Foreman with wife Lillian (47) & son Thomas Hayton age 8 in 65 Chapmangate, Pocklington). Difficult to identify the individual. (C126)
Hinde Ernest	5th Yorkshire Regiment	In 1911 Census Ernest Hinde (16 b. Leeds abt. 1895, Roper) living at home with mother Jane Hinde (56, Charwoman & Widow) and brother Frederick George (10 b. Leeds) at Alma Terrace, 9 Kirkland St., Pocklington. (C127)
Hinde Fred	Durham Light Infantry	In 1901 Frederick G. Hinde (10m b. Leeds) living with mother Jane Hinde (46 b. Birkenhead, Cheshire) at 1, Wansford Road, Driffield and brothers including Robert. (12, b. Leeds, Errand Boy Port.). In 1911 Frederick George (10, b. Leeds) see brother Ernest above. After the war was a painter. (C128)
Hinde Robert	Royal Field Artillery	1901 Robert (12, b. Leeds abt. 1889) and 1911census see brothers Fred & Ernest above. #36392 Robert Hinde Gunner Disembarked 20/7/15 or #115397 Robert Hinde Gunner. (C129)
Hindwell Harry	5th Yorkshire Regiment	In 1911 Harry Hindwell (26 b. Pock abt. 1885., Tailor) with wife Sarah (24, b. Leeds) living at 15, Grape Lane, Pocklington. #235555 5th Batt. Yorkshire Reg. 5/11/13 crossed out and E. Lancs inserted Tfr to E. Lancs 2/4 Batt. #1541 L/Cpl. Theatre France. 16/10/17. Also served earlier for 2nd Batt. East Yorks Reg. Tailor for Everinghams. Casualty in active service 3/3/18 Invalided to Eng. 10/3/18 16/4/18 promoted to Corporal. Transfer home 16/1/19. Demob. 13/2/19. After the war became the towns gas lighter and fire brigade 'knocker up'. First captain of the rugby team, reformed in 1920. (C130)

Name	Regiment	Service Record* (not from Memorial Book)
Hindwell William		In 1911, William Hindwell (12 b. Pock. abt. 1899) living with Uncle William Hindwell (49,Shepherd on Farm) at 21 Grape Lane, Pock. (C131)
Holmes Henry †		See page 27. (C132)
Holmes Herbert †		See page 27. (C133)
Hopper Alfred †	5th Yorkshire Regiment	See page 29. (C134)
Hotham Albert	7th East Yorkshire Reg.	In 1911, Richard Albert Hotham (11, b. Pock abt. 1900) Brother of Charles (17 b. abt. 1894, Butcher) and Frederick (13 b. abt. 1898, School) and Harry (see Harry), living at home with parents Charles Hotham (51, Butcher) and Cecilius May (39, Assistant in Shop), at 11 Pavement, Pocklington. #40013 East Yorkshire Regiment Pte. Richard A Hotham. b. 3/9/1889 Pocklington, d. 2nd Qtr. 1983 at York. (C135)
Hotham Charles †	5th Yorkshire Regiment	See Page 30. (C136)
Hotham Fred	Seaforth Highlanders	For 1911, see Albert. #s/13383 Pte. Seaforth Highlanders 9/ Btn & 7/Btn horse. (Anc) Fredk Hotham - Enlisted 10/12/15 Wounded in Action. Discharge 14/4/19 (FMP) with Silver War Badge (issued to service personnel honourably discharged due to wounds or sickness). (FWR) (C137)
Hotham Harry	10th Royal Hussars	1911 Henry Ullathorne Hotham (19 b. abt. 1892 Pock., Butcher) AKA 'Harry'. Harry Hotham #43531 Durham Light Infantry (FMP) Pte. #28804 Pte. Harry Hotham 10th Hussars. Enl. 19/9/14 Joined Class Z Res. 7/2/19. (Anc) (C138)
Hotham John William	East Yorkshire Regiment	1911 Census John William Hotham (30 b. abt. 1881 Pock., Joiner) with wife Jane (30) at 2 South Parade, Pocklington. Cannot assign Military Record. (C139)
Hunter Albert	5th Yorkshire Regiment	1911 Census Albert Hunter (14 b. Abt. 1897 Pock., Ironmonger's Errand Boy), living at home with parents John Thomas Hunter (47 b. abt. 1864 Seaton Ross, Chargeman on NE Railway) and Hannah Hunter (43, Pock.) and brother George (20 abt. 1891 Pock., Bricklayers Labourer) and brother Tom (16, Apprentice Tailor) at 1 Railway Crossing, Burnby Lane, Pocklington. Possibly #240192 Pte. Alexandra, Princess of Wales's Own Yorks. Reg. 1st Btn. (C140)
Hunter George	Royal Engineers	1911 see brother Albert. Cannot assign military record. (C141)
Hunter J H	5th Yorkshire Regiment	Cannot find. Possibly is the father John Thomas. (C142)
Hunter Thomas	5th Yorkshire Regiment	1911 see brother Albert. Cannot assign military record. Lost five toes with trench foot. Despite this became a prolific goal kicker of Pocklington rugby club and captained the cup winning side of 1923. (C143)
Irwin H G N	Royal Army Service Corps	#??2/222644, #??MT/782 1st ISC Army Service Corps, 1st ISC Army Service Corps J H G Irwin [John H G Irwin] Date of Entry 17/8/14 (Anc). Connection to Pocklington & Census entry not found. (C144)

Name	Regiment	Service Record* (not from Memorial Book)
Javerley George H †	5th Yorkshire Regiment	See Page 31. (C145)
Javerley Henry	East Yorkshire Regiment	1911 Census Harry Javerley (35 b. abt. 1876 Bishop Wilton, Farm Labourer) with wife Kate (37 b. Essex), at 3 Georges Place (Yard), George St., Pocklington. Cannot find military record of any Javerley serving in the East Yorkshire Regiment. He joined the West Yorkshire Regiment 3 Btn. #3542 on 1 Jun 1898 at age 22y 7m in York and resided at Chapmangate with mother Emma. Served in S. Africa 2nd Boer war 7/3/00 Discharged 3/4/01. 1914 joined Royal Field Artillery #L/19403 Gunner discharged in 1920. (FMP) (C146)
Jebson Frederick	Scots Greys Regiment	1911 Census Frederic Jebson (22 b. Bishop Wilton abt. 1889, Bank Clerk), living at home with Parents William Henry Jebson (51 b. Bishop Wilton abt. 1860, Veterinary Surgeon and Farmer) and Flora (50) at Wilton House, Pocklington. #D/15348 Frederic Jebson Household Cavalry and Cavalry of the Line (Corps of Dragoons) D/15348. 2nd Dragoons Royal Scots Greys. Pte. (C147)
Jennings Thomas †	5th Yorkshire Regiment	See Page 32. (C148)
Jessop Arthur †	Northumberland Fusiliers	See Page 33. (C149)
Jessop Herbert †	3rd East Yorkshire	See page 33. (C150)
Johnson Alfred	Royal Engineers	In 1911 Alfred Johnson (28 b. Pock. Abt. 1883, Bricklayer), living at home with parents William Johnson (57 b. Pock. Abt. 1854, Bricklayer) and Annie (50 b. Strensall abt. 1861) at 27 Kirkland Street, Pocklington. Possible military record Alfred Johnson #179414 Royal Engineers Sapper (but other Alfred Johnson's were in the Royal Engineers). (C151)
Johnson Arthur	5th Yorkshire Regiment	In 1911 Arthur Johnson (25 b. Pock. Abt. 1886, Shunter N E Railway Co.) and wife Ada (19 b. Market Weighton abt. 1892) in 12 Chiltern St. Hull. Too many possible military records. (C152)
Johnson Enzor	5th Yorkshire Regiment	1911 Census John Enzor Johnson (12, b. Pock, abt. 1899, School Newsboy) living at home with mother Edith Jane Johnson (37 b. Pock. Abt. 1874, Widow) at 46, Union Street, Pocklington. Enzor Johnson 1/5th Yorks. R. #3433 Pte, 5/6th R. Scots #202731, 1/9th High. L.I. #350699 Emb. 4/7/15 Expid. Force France 7/11/15 to 30/3/17 Ret. to France 1918 Wounded in Left Buttock Discharged 3/3/19 (Anc). d. Dec. 1975 in York. Lived with a piece of shrapnel in his leg until it worked it's way out in the 1960's. Worked for the Co-op after the war. (C153)
Johnson Fred	Machine Gun Corps	Too many Frederick Johnson's in MGC. After the war was a rope maker in New Street, Pocklington. (C154)
Johnson Gilbert	5th Yorkshire Regiment	In 1911 Gilbert Johnson (19 b. Pock., abt, 1892, Bricklayers labourer) living at home with mother Harriet Johnson (55 Widow, Laundress) at 46 Market St. Pock., Too many possible military records. (C155)

Name	Regiment	Service Record* (not from Memorial Book)
Johnson Harold †	5th Yorkshire Regiment	See Page 34 (C156)
Johnson Henry †	Royal Garrison Artillery	See Page 35. (C157)
Johnson John		John Johnson**, Engineman b. 29 Jan 1871 in Pocklington in Royal Naval Reserve, Killed or died as a direct result of enemy action #1042.E.S. (Ch) died 17/2/17 aboard H.M.S. Trawler Hawk Body not recovered for burial. Wife: Maude, 2 Andoe Road, Clapham Junction, SW. **This may not be the John Johnson referred to in the Church Remembrance book, but the Pocklington link for this Navy man should be recorded here. Too many John Johnson's to accurately link to.
Johnson Robert	Army Ordnance Corps	Too many possible records to accurately assign. (C159)
Judson Albert	East Yorkshire Regiment	In 1911 Albert O Judson (23 b. Pock., Dec. 1887, House Painter) boarder at the house of Mary Crusher (59 b. Goodmanham, Private Means) in 36 Chapmangate, Pocklington. #32250 Albert Octavius Judson Pte. South Staffordshire Reg. , #607646 Labour Corps. (C160)
Kemp George †	5th Yorkshire Regiment	See Page 35. (C161)
Kendall Nicholas	5th Yorkshire Regiment	1911 Census Nicholas Harvey Kendall (15 b. Cardiff abt. 1896, Watchmaker and Jewellers Apprentice) nephew of Susannah Lundy (76 b. Pock., Widow, Watchmaker & Jeweller (dealer) living at 18 Railway Street, Pocklington. Military: 5/York. R. #1312 Pte., 5/York. R. #240143, 4/York. R. #240143. Date of Embarkation 18/4/15 Theatre of war (1) France. Disembodied 4/4/19. (Anc). (C162)
King George	East Yorkshire Regiment	Not Found. (4 possible Military records for George King). (C163)
Kirby Edwin † (D.C.M.)	5th Yorkshire Regiment	See Page 36. (C164)
Laister Ernest James	Royal Air Force	In 1911 Ernest James Laister (26 b. abt 1885 Pock., Assistant to Draper) visitor of Henry Crawford Walker (61, b. Hendon, Middx., Commercial Traveller (Woollen Goods)) in 9 Allison Rd., Hern Lane, Acton, Middx. In 1901 Ernest J. Laister (16 b. Pock., Drapers Assistant) in York Guildhall., In 1891 Ernest J Laister (6, b. Pock.) with parents James W. Laister (30 b. Pock., abt. 1861, Rope Maker) and Emily (28 b. York) in Market Place, Pocklington. #42701 Royal Airforce Ernest James Laister ~~Draper~~ Rope Maker. Birth 1883. Marriage 22/8/11 at Acton. Living at 13, Oakland Road, E.Sheen?, Surrey, Enlisted 3/8/16 Embarked to France. B.A.S.D Paris. Villa Compley 17/9/16 I.A.D. Rein Park 31/1/1 transfer to RAF Reserve 6/3/19. Discharged 30/4/20. (C165)
Laister Horace Septimus	Tank Corps	1911 Census Horace Septimus Laister (17 b. Pock, abt. 1894, Grocer's Assistant) living with parents James William Laister (50 b. Pock, abt 1861, Rope and Twine Manufacturer) and

Name	Regiment	Service Record* (not from Memorial Book)
		Emily (48) at The Grove, Pocklington. #42885 Royal Tank Corps Theatre of War: France entered 5/3/18 Lieutenant. Became a Captain in WW2 in the Royal Tank Regiment. (C166)
Laister Lambert	Royal Field Artillery	In 1911 son of James William above, Lambert Laister (23 b. Pock., abt. 1888, Clerk Cocoa Chocolate & Confectionery Manufacturer) living at home at the Grove Pocklington. Base Dtls. Royal Garrison Artillery. #167212 Gunner 199 Btn. Became Gunner Signaller 22/8/1 Enlisted at Age 28 on 11/12/15 Posted 8/6/17. Address 68 Chestnut Grove, New Earswick, York, Mercantile Clerk. Married Margaret Amy Allanson of Farnworth Bolton Lancs 8/9/15. Transferred to Z Class Army Reserve 8/2/19. (C167)
Laister Roland	Royal Engineers	1911 Census Roland Laister son of James William (above) (crossed Out) Actually living at Etton, Beverley as an apprentice Blacksmith Age 18, b. Pocklington Dec. 1892 at the house of Charles Cooper (28, Blacksmith). Military: Roland J Laister Army Ordnance Corps #O38720 Pte. Entered Z Reserve 3/3/20. (C168)
Laister Wilfred	Royal Army Medical Corps	In 1911 son of James William above, Wilfred Laister (22 b. Pock. Abt. 1889, Draper and Outfitter) living at home at the Grove, Pocklington. Cannot find Military Record. Possibly Wilfred Lester. (C169)
Laughton Leonard	East Yorkshire Regiment	1911 Census has Leonard Laughton (15 b. Brantingham abt. 1896, At Home), living with parents William Laughton (55 b. Burringham, Lincs. Abt. 1856, Farmer) and Jane (52 b. Hull abt. 1859) at Kimberley House, Union Street, Pocklington. There is a picture of his marriage on the Pocklington History Website. Cannot find military record. After the war was a farmer in Union St. and later on Yapham Rd. (C170)
Lee John	2nd Northants Regiment	See Page 37. (C171)
Lister Robert	Lincs Regiment	1911 Census Robert Cecil Lister (19, b. Pock. Abt. 1892, Grocer) living at home with father Robert Jackson Lister (46 b. Pock., abt. 1865, Hairdresser and Widowed) at 20 / 22 Pavement, Pocklington. Married Adelaide Howse (30) on 10/10/16 at Hawley in Southampton. #49961 82nd Reserve Battalion Home address 74 George Street, Pocklington. Private. Age on enlistment 24, 11/12/15 Casualty on active service and transferred to Labour Corps 7/8/17 (Anc Pension Record). (C172)
Lister William	East Yorkshire Regiment	1911 Census William Lister (30 b. Pock. Abt. 1881, assistant cow-keeper), living with father Thomas Lister (63 b. Pock, abt. 1848, Cow-keeper) at 15 Kirkland Street, Pocklington. #202807 East Yorkshire Regiment 4th Battn. Enlisted 24/8/16 Date of Discharge 13/8/17. (C173)
Lockerbie John Currie	Royal Garrison Artillery	Married Widow Elizabeth Alice Spink (dau. of Ralph J. Scaife (Auctioneer and Valuer) in Pocklington Jun 1906. His

Name	Regiment	Service Record* (not from Memorial Book)
		gravestone is in Pocklington Cemetery at it reads "In loving Memory of Elizabeth Alice beloved wife of J. Lockerbie who died Aug. 11th 1933. Aged 60 years. "At Rest" Also of the said John Lockerbie Died 5th Sept. 1956 aged 78. Also Muriel. Died 3rd Feb. 1977." #96072 Royal Garrison Artillery Gunner , #520331 Labour Corps. (C174)
Longhorn John	East Yorkshire Regiment	In 1911 John Longhorn (42 b. Pock., abt. 1869, Bricklayer) living at 18, Stathers Yard, Chapmangate, Pocklington. #3404 Pte. 5th Btn. Yorkshire Regiment. Disembarked France 1/10/15 #184361 Pte. Labour Corps. Dismissed 21/2/19. (Anc). (C175)
MacMillan A L	Royal Navy	In June 1871 Andrew Macmillan married Fanny Vokes in Pocklington. In 1881 Andrew MacMillan (32 b. Hull abt. 1849, Shipwright Boat Builder) and Fanny (31 b. Pock. Abt. 1850) at 33 Eton Street, Hull. Son Andrew MacMillan (1 b. Hull abt. 1880). In 1891 Andrew MacMillan (11 b. Hull 1880) with parents Andrew (42, b. Hull, Foreman Shipwright) and Fanny (41). In Dec 1896 Muriel E. Macmillan died in Pocklington age (0). In 1911 Andrew McMillan (31, b. Hull 1880, General Labourer) and wife Edith Annie (20 b. Hull). Nov. 13th 1923 issued with RN Long Service Medal Eng S Lt Rnr A Macmillan (Anc). (C176)
Manners Robert T	Durham Light Infantry	In 1911 Census Robert Tindale Manners (11 b. Pock. Abt. 1900, School Boy) living at home with parents Robert Manners (54 b. Pock. Abt. 1857, Joiner & Cabinet Maker) and Elizabeth (52 b. Eckington, Lincs., Business Assistant) in 33 Grape Lane, Manners Yard, Pocklington. #81130 3rd btn. Durham Light Infantry Pte. Joined 3/7/17 Captured April 1918. POW in Germany. Repatriated 14/12/18. (C177)
Meynall George William - Royal Garrison Artillery		In 1911 George William Mennell (25 b. Wykeham abt. 1886, Gardner) living at home with parents George Mennell (57 b. Norton, Malton abt. 1854, Gamekeeper) and Elizabeth (57) at The Lodge, Kilnwick Percy, Pocklington. George William Mennell #185605 Royal Garrison Artillery Gunner. (C178)
Moore Percy	East Riding Yeomanry	Percy Moore married Marriet E Brigham in Mar 1916 in Pocklington. Birth in Sep. 1919 of Percy G R Moore in Pocklington. Followed James Campbell as the farmer of Clayfield Farm. (C179)
Morris Frank W	Royal Air Force	1911 Census Francis William Morris (20 b. Pock. Abt. 1891, Cycle & Motor Assistant) living at home with parents Henry Morris (46 b. Frodingham abt. 1865, Grocer & Provision Merchant) and Mary (48, b. Warter) at 8, Chapmangate, Pocklington. #23707 Francis William Morris Enlisted 25/2/16 Trans. RAF 1/4/18 139 Sqdrn. 9/10/18 Methodist. b 1890 Civillian Occupation Mechanic for Fred Lee Market Sq. Pocklington. Married Ivy Alberta "Jolly Sailor" Inn, Cawood. Discharged 30/4/20. (FMP) (C180)

Name	Regiment	Service Record* (not from Memorial Book)
Morris Harry	Kings Royal Rifles	Brother of Francis William above. In 1911 Harry Morris (18 b. Pock. Abt. 1893, Apprentice to Stationer & Smallwares) at 8 Chapmangate, Pock. 2nd Bn. K.R. Rif. C. #3017 Pte., 3rd Bn. K.R. Rif. C. #3017 Joined 15/9/14. (C181)
Morris Herbert	Kings Royal Rifles	Brother of Francis William above. In 1911 Herbert Morris (16 b. Pock. Abt. 1895, Apprentice to Ironmonger & Tin Smith) at 8 Chapmangate, Pocklington. Herbert Morris b. 1894 in Pocklington #49311 joined RAF 15/11/15 at age 21. Civilian occupation Ironmonger. Joined 233 Sqn. 18/10/19 Transferred to RAFG Reserve 5/3/19. (C182)
Mutimer Chester	Royal Field Artillery	Census record not found. Married Amy A S Grainger in Sep 1913 in Pocklington. #81132 Chester Mutimer Royal Field Artillery Gunner Date of entry: 25/9/15 #640839 Labour Corps. Corporal. Entered Z Reserve 11/2/19. (C183)
Moor Wilfred	5th Yorkshire Regiment	In 1911 Wilfred Moor (25 b. Pock., abt. 1886, Bricklayer) living at home with parents John Moor (64 b. Market Weighton abt. 1847, Tailor) and Sarah (61, b. Pock.) in 82 Chapmangate, Pocklington. #2087 Pte 1/5th & 2/5th Yorkshire Regiment Discharged 15/3/16 for enlistment in R.F.C. in Farnborough 6/3/16 #G/21709 Royal Flying Corps 18/10/16 Disch. as not physically fit for war service. (C184)
Nelson Arthur George	Royal Marine Light Infantry	In 1911 Arthur George Nelson (35, b. Pock. Abt. 1876) living with mother Hannah (71 b. Pock. Abt. 1840, Boot Dealer) in 39, 41-42 Market Place, Pocklington. #3321 Royal marine Light Infantry: Chatham Division Short Service. Enlisted 1/10/18 Date of Birth: 10th Oct. 1875. Boot Repairer. Wife Ethel Anne. Discharged 15/3/19. (C185)
Newsome Fred	Royal Engineers	1911 Census Fred Newsome (23 b. York abt. 1888, Joiner (House)) married to Nora (22, b. Pock.) at 18, New Street, Pocklington. #170461 Royal Engineers Sapper. (C186)
Nicholson Rex H	Royal Engineers	Rex Harper Nicholson b. 3rd Qtr. 1895 in Driffield. Rex H Nicholson married Laura E. Green in Pocklington district Apr Qtr 1920. 1901 Census Rex Harper Nicholson (5, b. Kilham) a boarder at the Post Office in Bolton Percy, in the house of David Swepson (48, Postman) two census entries away from John Ripley Nicholson (51 b. Bilton, Gardener domestic) and Margaret H. (45, b. Snape, Suffolk). #126458 Rex H Nicholson Royal Engineers Rank Pioneer. (C187)
Nicholson William	Royal Air Force	In 1891 William Nicholson (3, b. Pock., abt. 1888) living at home with parents John Nicholson (43 b. Langtoft abt. 1848) and Elizabeth (44 b. Pock.) at Northfield Farm, Sherbutt Gate. In 1911 William Nicholson (23, b. Pock., abt. 1888, Tea Merchant) a boarder at the house of James Poole (23, Grocers Assistant) at Pear Tree Cottage, South Elmswell. #24361 William Nicholson Royal Air Force b. 1888 Wesleyan next of kin John (father) North Field Farm, Pocklington. Grocers Traveller. Enlisted Royal Flying Corps 2/3/16 Royal

Name	Regiment	Service Record* (not from Memorial Book)
		Air Force 1/4/18 Pool Pilots Range in 112 Sqdn. at RAF Halton. Moved to Blandford 26/6/19. Became Corporal 1/9/17. Appointed Sgt. 1/1/18. Tfrd as Sgt. Mech. 1/4/18. Became dangerously ill with Influenza. Disability tfr. from France to England 16/2/19. (FMP). (C188)
Oliver Reginald A	Northumberland Fusiliers	In 1911 Census, Reginald Arthur Oliver (14 b. Pock., abt. 1897, School) living at home with parents Arthur John Oliver (b. Leicester abt. 1868, Solicitor's Clerk) and Jessie (41 b. Edinburgh) at 2 Richmond Terrace, Pocklington. In 1918 Electoral Role were at Thumby Villa, Garths End, Pock. 2 possible records : #69796 Arthur Oliver Northumberland Fusiliers Pte., #61702 Gordon Highlanders. The other is #29777 Arthur Oliver Northumberland Fusiliers Pte. #7/5735 North. Fus. Pte., #291848 North. Fus. Pte. (Anc) (C189)
Ottley Wilfred C	East Yorkshire Regiment	Wilfred Clement Ottley b. Pocklington Jun 1890. 1891 Census Wilfred Ottley (11mths b. Warter) with parents Alfred Ottley (37 b. Brid., Saddler, Grocer & Post Master) and Letitia (44 b. N. Dalton, Grocer) in the Post Office, Warter. In 1901, Wilfred C Ottley (10, Scholar) with Alfred Ottley & Letitia in Warter Post Office. In 1911, Letitia Ottley (64, b. N.Dalton, Sub Postmistress) at Warter Post Office. Date of Entry: 27/10/15 #1368 1st E. Rid. Yorks. Yeo. Pte., #M/410670 Army Service Corps 25/11/18 , #150198 Machine Gun Corps. Discharged 26/3/19. (C190)
Pearson William	Royal Garrison Artillery	In 1911 William Pearson (10 b. Meltonby abt. 1901, School) with parents Thomas Pearson (46 b. Meltonby abt. 1865, Farmer) and Susannah (44 b. Walton Carr) at Northfield House, Pock. Cannot assign the Military record. (C191)
Pratt John	5th Yorkshire Regiment	Brother of Robert killed in the war. In 1911 John Pratt (16 b. Pock. Abt. 1895, General Farm Labourer) with parents Robert Pratt (74 b. Seaton Ross abt. 1837, Rabbit Catcher) and Hannah (47, b. Barmby Moor) and brother Robert (20 b. Pock., Rabbit Catcher) at 3, Grape Lane, Pocklington. Cannot assign military record. (C192)
Pratt Robert †	5th Yorkshire Regiment	See Page 38. (C193)
Priestley Tom	Machine Gun Corps	Thomas Victor Priestley b. Pocklington Jun 1887. In 1901 Thomas Victor Priestley (13 b. Mkt. Weighton, Clerk Ship Yard) with parents Thomas Henry Priestley (54 b. Stainland abt. 1847, Railway Engine Driver) and Emma (51 b. Knaresborough) in Selby St. James. In 1911 Thomas Victor Priestley (23 b. Mkt. Weighton abt. 1888, Manufacturers Clerk) with wife Millicent Mary (22, b. Riccall) at Barff View, Green Lane, Selby. #3504. W York R. Pte. Date of entry 25/12/15, #136465. MGC. Dischd. 7/12/18. (C194)
Prowle William		In 2nd Qtr 1904 a Marriage between William Prole and Alice Rowley in Pocklington. William Prole #3034 Yorkshire Regiment Pte. Disembarked 1/11/15 Theatre of War (1) France became Sgt. #265550 Disembodied 21/5/19. (C195)

Name	Regiment	Service Record* (not from Memorial Book)
Rippon Arthur	5th Yorkshire Regiment	Arthur Rippon b. Pocklington Sep. 1882. In 1911, Arthur Rippon (29, Lamplighter for Urban Council) living at home with parents John Cundy Rippon (68 b. Beverley abt. 1843, Cordwainer and Lamp Lighter for Urban Council) and Mary Ann (65 b. Pock.) in 9 Church Lane, Pocklington. (C196)
Rippon Frank	Machine Gun Corps	Frank Rippon b. Sep 1876 in Pocklington. On Dec. 26th 1900 married Alice Robinson in Bishop Wilton. In 1911, Frank Rippon (34 b. Pock., Wholesale Clothiers Presser) and wife Alice (34 b. Fencehouses, Durham) living at 73 Crossflats Parade, Beeston, Leeds. In 1891 was living with father John C. in London St. Pock. Joined 5th Yorks, 7th Corps 4/9/14 #2553 (& #2765) was living at 8 Liddon Terrace, College Road, Leeds working for Epworth's Tailors. Private. #8748 4th Yorks. Regt. Sent to France 18/8/15. Transferred to Class W 19/Dec. 1916. Became injured or sick 18/7/16 sent home to parents at 14 Victoria Terrace, Pocklington. Awarded pension for 20% disability 22/1/19. Discharged 24/1/19. (Anc) (C197)
Rippon Thomas William † - Kings Royal Rifles		See Page 39. Thomas Wilfred Rippon and in Machine Gun Corps in Mesopotamia. Died of wounds. (Anc). (C198)
Rix Ernest Frederick	Royal Field Artillery	Ernest Rix attested on 15 May 1915 at Beverley. 23, Grape Lane, Pocklington, 26 yrs 7 months b. abt. 1889, Farm Servant, East Yorkshire Regiment #81133 Royal Field Artillery. Next of Kin: William Rix, Hadleigh, Suffolk. Posted 22/6/15, Driver 27/10/15, Completed Agricultural Furlough 12/11/17, Posted BEF France 5/4/18, Demob. 31/3/20, Received Medals 2/11/1920 to 23, Grape Lane Pocklington. Ernest Rex m. Margaret E Boyes in Pock. 4th Qtr. 1921. (Anc) (C199) [n.b. Redaction in original]
Robinson Thomas		1901 Census Thomas Robinson (10 b. Brough abt. 1891) living at home with parents Thomas Robinson (52 b. Holme abt. 1849, General Labourer) and Sarah (46 b. Holme) in Chapmangate, Pocklington. Too many possible military records. (C200)
Robinson Percy		Son of John Robinson and Harriot Hamlyn farmers of High Warrendale, Kilnwick Percy and trawler owners in Hull. Married Clara Leaf in Millington 4th Qtr. 1917. d. 26 Sep. 1943 aged 47. b. abt. 1896. Farmed at Oak Farm, Algarth, Pock. Cpl. 10th Royal Hussars and wounded in France. Gravestone in Pock. Cemetery. (C201)
Robson Edward M † (M.C.) - 5th Yorkshire Regiment		See Page 40. (C202)
Robson Frederick W † - 5th Yorkshire Regiment (D.S.O)		See Page 41. (C203)
Robson John Stanley	5th Yorkshire Regiment	In 1911 John Stanley Robson (17 b. Pock. Abt. 1894, Music Student) living at home with father Thomas Robson (55 b. Full Sutton abt. 1856, Solicitor) and brothers Frederick William Robson (23 b. Pock, Solicitor) and Edward Moore

Name	Regiment	Service Record* (not from Memorial Book)
		Robson (21 b. Pock. Solicitors Articled Clerk) , at Pembroke Lodge, 49 Chapmangate, Pocklington. Both his brothers died in Action. (see above). John Stanley Robson 4th & 5th Battalion Yorks. Regiment 2nd Lieut., 4th Battalion Yorks. Regiment Captain. Theatre of War: France July 1915. Awarded 1914-15 Star. (C204)
Rooks Lyth	5th Yorkshire Regiment	1911 Census Lyth Rooks (26 b. Pock abt. 1885, Gardener) living at home with parents Lyth Rooks (71 b. Pock. Abt 1840, Labourer (Agricultural and Horticultural)) and Mary Ann (69 b. Pock.) living at 15 Tute Hill, Pocklington. [Thomas Rooks (brother of Lyth) Attested at Bradford 30/11/14 Discharged 5/1/15 because of Civil conviction offence before enlistment.– Drunk & Disorderly with time in Hull Prison] #1288 Lyth Rooks 24th Provisional Battalion (became the 18th Yorkshire Regiment). Private. Enlisted 17/5/12 Discharged 26/2/16 due to Sickness and Pain. (C205)
Rowntree Alfred	Royal Field Artillery	In 1901 Census Alfred Rowntree (6, b. Stamford Bridge abt. 1895) and Arthur Rowntree (2, b. Stamford Bridge abt. 1899) living with parents John Rowntree (40 b. Cottingham*, abt. 1861, Agricultural Labourer) and Elizabeth (33 b. Stamford Bridge) at Fangfoss. In 1911 Father John Rowntree was at 20 New Street Pocklington with Thomas (20) and brother Arthur (12). Alfred (17) was Third Lad on Farm of Mark Beal (64, Farmer) at Loaningdale, Warter. #755659 Royal Horse Artillery and Royal Field Artillery Battalion C/251 Brigade. Awarded Military Medal for gallantry in action. (Anc) (C206)
Rowntree Arthur †	East Yorkshire Regiment	See page 43 (C207)
Rowntree T E	Royal Garrison Artillery	1911 Census Thomas Rowntree (20 b. Stamford Bridge abt. 1891, Labourer General) living with parents John Rowntree (46 b. Wilberfoss* abt. 1865) and Elizabeth (43 b. Stamford Bridge) and brother Arthur (12, b. Stamford Bridge) at 20 New Street, Pocklington. Thomas E Rowntree #2085 Royal Garrison Artillery Sapper, #250171 Royal Engineers Sapper, #297627 Royal Garrison Artillery Sapper. Thomas Edward Rowntree Territorial force attested at Pocklington 5th Btn. APWO Yorks 8/2/12 (Anc). * n.b. John gives a different age and place of birth in 1901 and 1911. (C208)
Rowley Frederick	5th Yorkshire Regiment	In 1911 Fredrick Rowley (28 b. Pock., abt. 1883, Bootmaker) with wife Elizabeth (23 b. Millington) in East Stamford Bridge. #T/4/061616 Frederick Rowley 5th Btn. Yorks. Marriage with Elizabeth Suggitt at Millington 25/11/08 Children Nora, Mary & Edna. Joined at Bradford 2/3/15 Insurance Agent and Enlisted as Driver. Embarked Southampton 6/5/16 Disemb. Le Havre 7/5/16 Posted to BHTD. Discharged 21/6/19 to 7 Victoria Terrace, Pocklington. (Anc). (C209)

Name	Regiment	Service Record* (not from Memorial Book)
Rowley Harry	East Yorkshire Regiment	1901 Census Harry Rowley (15 b. Pock., abt. 1886, Joiners Apprentice) living with parents William Rowley (59 b. Allerthorpe, abt. 1842, Wheelwright) and Hannah E (48 b. York) in Chapmangate, Pocklington. In 1911 Census Harry Rowley in 2nd Batter East York Regt Age 25 b. abt. 1886 in Pocklington stationed in India. Harry Rowley #8410 Theatre of War: France (1) 1st and 2nd East Yorkshire Regiment Sergeant 22/6/15. Awarded the Distinguished Conduct Medal 26/7/17 presented by Brigadier General J.G. Chaplin DSO for gallantry, distinguished conduct, and devotion to duty in the trenches. He displayed great courage and resource in putting out barbed wire in front of our trenches, under very heavy hostile fire. (C210)
Rowley William Snr.	5th Yorkshire Regiment	In the 1911 Census William Rowley (34 b. Pock. Abt. 1877, Tailor) and wife Annie Elizabeth (34 b. Pock) and son William (13 b. Pock. Abt. 1898, School Greengrocer's Errand Boy) at 13 Alma Terrace, Pocklington. William Rowley #240026 Yorkshire Regiment Sgt. Enlisted 4/8/08 Discharged 3/10/17 No longer Physically fit for war service. (C211)
Rowley William Jnr.	5th Yorkshire Regiment	For 1911 see father William Snr. William Rowley #29178 Yorkshire Regiment. Entered Z Reserve. (C212)
Ruder Charles	Grenadiers	Marriage in 6th Feb. 1907 in Pocklington George Ruder to Florence Foster. In 1911 Charles Ruder (28 b. Settrington abt. 1883, Grocers Drayman) and wife Florence (26 b. Pock., Dressmaker) at Mitel Yard, London Street Pocklington. Charles Ruder #27610 Grenadier Guards Guardsman 4 GGds Pension Record: Charles Ruder next of Kin Florence Ruder 90 Bridge St. Pocklington. Children Ernest & Charles William. Last employer C. Proctor, Market Place, Pock. Drayman. Attested 8/12/15 Posted 2/11/16 Discharged 27/3/19. (Anc) (C213)
Savage Herbert †	Life Guards	See page 44. (C214)
Scaife Bert	East Yorkshire Regiment	1891 Census Herbert Scaife (10 b. Everingham abt. 1881, Scholar) living at home with parents Thomas Scaife (46 b. Brafferton, abt. 1845, Joiner) and wife Martha Hannah (44 b. Shipton abt. 1847) at Everingham. In 1901 Herbert Scaife (20 b. Everingham, Joiner/Carpenters apprentice living with John Cattley (35, Joiner/Carpenter) at Escrick. In 1911 Herbert Scaife (30 b. Everingham, Joiner) and wife Mary Josephine (31 b. Shiptonthorpe abt. 1880) at Escrick, York. Bertie Scaife #3310 Yorkshire Regiment Private #241092 Yorkshire Regiment. Disembodied. (Anc). Territorial Attestation: #3309 Bertie Scaife 5th Reserve Battn. Yorks. Reg. 52 Chapmangate, Pocklington. Plate Layer. June 1915. Private. Appointed L/Cprl 16/8/15 reverted to Private 27/8/15 at own request. 11/2/16 Exp.Force to France. 13/7/16 to 11/8/16 in hospital with 'Trench Fever'. At Rouen 4/1/17 & Etaples 16/1/17. Posted 13/7/16. Wounded in Action 28/10/17. Appointed L/Cprl 6/11/17 "Taken on Strength". 15/6/18 Admitted to Hornsea Hospital. E.Yorks

Name	Regiment	Service Record* (not from Memorial Book)
		with Influenza. Appointed Act/Cprl 13/7/18. Medals received 30/10/21. (FMP) (C215)
Scaife Christopher	5th Yorkshire Regiment	In 1901 Christopher T. Scaife (13 b. Pock., abt. 1888) living at home with parents Thomas Scaife (37 b. Pock abt. 1864, Cab Proprietor Stable) with wife Eliza (37 b. Pock.) and brother Sydney (10, b. Pock.) in Chapmangate and brother Reginald (6 b. Pock.). In 1911 Chris. Scaife (23 b. Pock. Abt. 1888, working Cab Proprietor) living at home with Thomas (49 b. Pock., Cab Proprietor) and wife Eliza (47) in 52Chapmangate, Pocklington and brother Reginald (16 b. Pock., Gardener (Market)) In 1911 brother Sydney (20 b. Pock., Wagoner on Farm) is Servant to James Wm. Blyth (30 b. Huggate, Farmer) at Burnby, Nunburnholme Station. (C216)
Scaife George	5th Yorkshire Regiment	In 1911 George Scaife (20 b. Pock, Labourer) was living at home with his Grandfather Christopher Scaife (63 b. Pock., Labourer) and Grandmother Mary (60 b. York) at Alma Terrace, Kirkland St. Pocklington. George Scaife was in the 2nd Btn. Life Guards #2436. (Anc)George landed with the 2nd Life Guards at Zebrugge, Belgium on 8 Oct. 1914 and was converted into Machine gun battalion in March 1918. They fought in the first battle of Ypres. (C217)
Scaife Reginald	5th Yorkshire Regiment	For Census see brother Christopher above. #1294 Sergeant. 5th Yorks. Reg. #35065 10th Btn. King's Own Yorkshire Light Infantry. Serg. Territorial Force Medal. Disem. 11/1/19. (C218)
Scaife Sydney †	5th Yorkshire Regiment	See Page 45. For Census see brother Christopher Scaife. (C219)
Scott George Jefferson † - 5th Yorkshire Regiment		See page 46. (C220)
Sellers John	East Yorkshire Regiment	1891 Census John Sellers (3 b. Pock., abt. 1888) with parents Thomas Sellers (44 b. Pock., Wheelwright) and wife Ann (37 b. Market Weighton) in London St., Pocklington. In 1901 'Jack' Sellers (13 b. Pock abt. 1888) living with parents Thomas Sellers (55 b. Pock., Joiner Carpenter) and wife Ann (49 b. Market Weighton) at London St. Pocklington. In 1911 Jack Sellers (22, b. Pock., abt. 1889, Stone Mason) living at home with parents Thomas Sellers (64, House Joiner) and Ann (58) at 6, London Street, Pocklington. Jack Sellers #10884 East Yorkshire Regiment Private. Theatre of war (2B) Balkans. (Anc) (C221)
Siddall Thomas Edward - 5th Yorkshire Regiment		Thomas Edward Siddill. Born Q4 1893 in the Pocklington District. Thomas Edward Siddill (18 b. Pock., Rulleyman Grocers) living at home with parents Thomas Siddill (43 b. Pock. Abt. 1862, Joiner & Cabinet Maker) and Annie (50, b. Bishop Wilton abt. 1861) in St. John's Terrace, Pocklington. #1031 Yorks. Reg. Territorial Force Attestation: Thomas Edward Siddall age 17 in Mar 1910. #TD3592 & #235699 Duke of Wellington's (West Riding) Regiment. Corporal. Living at George St., Pock. Re-enlisted into the 5th Territorial Force Green Howards 16/10/20. Promoted to Sgt. 3/9/21. (Anc) (C222)

Name	Regiment	Service Record* (not from Memorial Book)
Silburn Henry	Colonel Enslins Horse Reg.	In 1891 Henry Silburn (8 b. Pocklington abt. 1883) living at home with parents Henry Silburn (51 b. Pock. abt. 1840, Butcher & Farmer) and wife Marina (40 b. Nailsea, Somersetshire) at Market St., Pocklington. In 1901, Henry Silburn (18, b. Pock., abt. 1883, Bank Clerk) living at home with parents Henry Silburn (61, Butcher Shopkeeper & Farmer) and wife Marina (50) and brother Reginald (15 b. Pock., abt. 1886) and brother Lionel B. (16 b. Pock., abt. 1885) at Market St., Pocklington. He departed to South Africa with Brother John. In South Africa he was a trooper in *Colonel Enslin's* Horse. That unit was engaged in suppressing the Boer revolt, which began in August 1914 as a protest against South African support for the British war effort. (C223)
Silburn Lionel	East Yorkshire Regiment	Brother of Henry & Reginald. See Henry for Census. Lionel Burnell Silburn (16 Sep 1884 - 6 Mar 1963). He married Hilda May Moore of White House Farm, Hayton in 1929 and the 1939 register shows him described as a farmer and cattle dealer. The Silburn family oral history is that Lionel was gassed in WW1 and could never work again. Lionel Silburn #23151 East Yorkshire Regiment. Private. Discharged to Class Z AR (Army Reserve). After the war was a cattle dealer. (C224)
Silburn Reginald	Royal Field Artillery	In 1911 Reginald Singleton Silburn (25, b Pock., Shop Assistant) staying as a Boarder at 9A Margaret Street, St. Marylebone, London. Brother of Henry and Lionel above. Reginald Singleton Silburn #180849 Badge no. B224057. Royal Artillery (Royal Horse Artillery and Royal Field Artillery). Gunner. Enlisted 14/12/16. Discharged 4/6/19 due to Sickness. Awarded Silver War Badge. (C225)
Simpson Arthur	Royal Air Force	In 1911 Arthur Simpson (24, b. Fridaythorpe abt. 1887, Wagoner on Farm) Boarder on the farm of John Robinson (42, b. Wharram, Hind & Farm Foreman) at Duggleby, Wharram. #282883 RAF Service Record b. 25th April 1886, Fridaythorpe. Motor Driver. Next of Kin: Mary Jane Simpson, 14 George St. Pocklington. Married 27/11/12 in Pocklington. Active Service from 20/8/18 Disch.30/4/20. (FMP) (C226)
Simpson Herbert	East Yorkshire Regiment	In 1911 Herbert Simpson (26 b. Spittle abt. 1885, Farmers Son Working on Farm) with wife Margaret (29 b. Londesborough) at Dolman Cottage, Railway Street, Pocklington. Herbert Simpson #26998 East Yorkshire Regiment. Private. (C227)
Skelton George †	5th Yorkshire Regiment	See Page 47. (C228)
Skelton Henry	5th Yorkshire Regiment	In 1911 Census, Henry Skelton (42 b. Pock. Abt. 1869, Labourer) with wife Martha (36 b. Pock.) and son John Henry Skelton (13 b. Pock., School) at 5 Church Lane, Pocklington. (C229)

Name	Regiment	Service Record* (not from Memorial Book)
Skelton John Henry	Kings Own Yorks. Light Inf.	Census see father Henry. (C230)
Skinner Frank	5th Yorkshire Regiment	Frank Skinner (16 b. Pock abt. 1895, Chemist's Apprentice) living at home with parents Atkinson Skinner (51 b. Scotter, Lincoln abt. 1860, Teacher Elementary School) and Minnie (46 b. Stillington abt. 1865) at Wold View, Pocklington. Brother of Thomas Ross who died in a POW camp. From a newspaper report Frank was wounded on 26th April 1915, and after several operations had his leg amputated below the knee, and arrived home for recuperation. Frank Skinner 5th Yorks Regt. Private. #240589. Awarded Silver War Badge #214485. Enlisted 9/9/14 Discharged 13/3/17 with wounds. (Anc) (C231)
Skinner Thomas Ross †	4th - East Yorkshire Reg.	See Page 47. (C232)
Smith Ernest	Royal Air Force	In 1911, Ernest Smith (22 b. Pock. Abt. 1889, Cabinet Maker and Joiner) living at home with mother Margaret Smith (54 b. Pock. Abt 1857, Widowed) at 19, New Street, Pocklington. #44130 Royal Air Force record—b. 28/10/1887 CofE Entered R.F.C. 18/8/16 R.A.F. 1/4/18. Joiner. Next of Kin: Annie Alice Smith (Wife), 37 Kirkland St., Pocklington. Promoted Corporal 1/9/17. Appointed Sgt. 1/3/18. Tfer, to RAF as mechanic 1/4/18. (FMP)(C233)
Smith Fred Seaton †	York and Lancs Regiment	See Page 49. (C234)
Smith Harry		1911 Census, Harry Smith (30 b. Bishop Wilton abt. 1881, Railway Porter) with wife Mary (28 b. Hull abt. 1883) at 7 West Green, Pock. Pension Record: #39806 3rd Northumberland Fusiliers. Private. Harry West, 7 West Green, Pocklington. Railway Porter. Attested Beverley 9/12/15. Next of Kin Mrs Mary Smith wife 7, West Green, Pock. 2 children Lucy Georgina, James Wilfred. Posted to Italy 40 days 5/12/17. Discharged as not physically fit with Tuberculosis contracted in active service in France 15/2/18. "Character Good. A steady and sober man". (C235)
Smith John William †	5th Yorkshire Regiment	See Page 48. (C236)
Snow John		John Snow b. 1881 Pocklington Married Charlotte Harrison at Bishop Wilton 28/10/1922. Engine Driver. Father (John William Snow—Engine Driver). Wife Father (Frederick Harrison— Police Constable). 1891 Census at South Newbald age 10 and states N.Newbald is birthplace. Cannot find Military Record. (C237)
Sowden Robert	London Rifle Brigade	Robert F Sowden Married Edith S Sugden in Pocklington 2nd Qtr 1919. Record of Service: Frederick Robert Sawdon #44246 Yorkshire Regiment 17 Eastgate Beverley, Cooper, 20/11/16 Next of kin Joshua Sowdon in Goole (brother) Enlisted 2/3/16 Called up 20/11/16. Private. Transfer: First to Durham Light Infantry 31/7/17 then Frederick R. Sawdon #860644 33rd London Regiment. b. 1873. (Anc). (C238)

Name	Regiment	Service Record* (not from Memorial Book)
Spence Archie	Coldstream Guards	See Page 50. (C239)
Spivey Charles (D.C.M.) -	5th Yorkshire Regiment	1911 Charles Spivey (15 b. Liversedge abt. 1896, Grocer's Apprentice) living at home withparents and 11 siblings, Ralph Spivey (45 b. Heckmondwike abt. 1866, Gas Manager) and Clara (43 b. Liversedge) at Cemetery Lane (Gas Works), Pocklington. Charles Spivey #1280 Alexandra, Princess of Wales's Own Yorkshire Regiment. Private. C . Spivey 5th York R (Territorial Forces) #240129. Charles Spivey awarded the D.C.M. 17/4/18 Yorkshire Regiment #240129 Corporal. *"For conspicuous gallantry and devotion to duty. When the enemy raided our line under intense barrage he volunteered to carry a message to battalion headquarters. Though wounded he showed splendid courage and determination. For conspicuous gallantry and devotion to duty. When the enemy, having captured a village, were making some progress and the situation had become involved, this NCO volunteered to go forward and ascertain what was actually taking place. He went forward three times through a very intense barrage of gas and high explosive shells and collected very valuable information as to the position of the enemy and neighbouring troops. By his gallant action he rendered most excellent service in clearing up a difficult situation. 3/10/10 BAR"* (C240)
Stather Charles Cyril	6th Northants Regiment	In 1901, Charles C Stather (4 b. Pock. Abt 1897) at home with parents Charles Stather (36 b. Goodmanham abt. 1865, Draper & Shopkeeper) and his wife Amy J (36 b. Selby) at Market Place, Pocklington. In 1911 Charles Cyril Stather (14 b. Pock. Abt. 1897, Boarder at Elmfield College, Malton Road, York.). Charles Cyril Stather 11th East Yorks. #21837 Pte. #TR5/25332 Durham Light Infantry Training Reserve. Granted commission Northamptonshire Regiment 25/4/17 #TR/5/25332 Retired 15/1/24. Holmlea, Pocklington, York. (C241)
Stabler George	Royal Army Service Corps	George Stabler Married Lily Coulson in Mar 1915 in Pocklington Reg. Dist. George Stabler #T4/249630 Army Service Corps S/Sgt. Previous Units: W.R.D. T&S Col. AS (TF) T/277 Sergeant. Transfer to regular RASC 1/9/16. Attestation: George Stabler West Riding Reg. Address Brandesby nr Stillington Wife Lily Stables 23 New Street, Pocklington. Address for pay: 34 New Street, Pock., Theatre of war: France. Born 1889. Became injured with dislocated shoulder due to a fall from a ladder on 5/10/15. Home April 1919. (C242)
Steel Francis H	Royal Engineers	In 1901 Fred Steel (9, b. Hull) with parents William Gordon Steel (40 b. Pock., abt. 1861, Bricklayer) and Clara Annie (30, Thixendale) and brother Walter (2, b. Pock) in George Street, Pocklington. In 1911 Fred Steel (19, b. Hull abt. 1892, Bricklayers Apprentice) at home with Mother Clara Connie Steel (40 b. Riggs, Charwoman and Widow) and brother Walter (12 b. Pock. Abt. 1899) at 25 Chapmangate,

Name	Regiment	Service Record* (not from Memorial Book)
		Pocklington. Territorial Attestation Fred Steel b. 1892 Born Hull, reg. no. ??9 (record burnt), attested in 1909 for Territorial force 5 Btn. Yorks Reg. 10/2/13 Pack on the back test with Pte. Allison #690, Pte. Hunter #817, Pte Steel #689. #3035 & #241013 5th Btn. Yorks. March 1915. No. 4 Union St. Pock. 4th Res. Btn. Fred Steel of 25 Chapmangate Works for Joseph Steel in Pock. 25/5/18. Wounded in Action, tfr. to England, Hornsea Hospital. (C243)
Steel Walter	5th Yorkshire Regiment	For census, see brother Fred (Francis H). Walter Steel born Sep. 1898 in Pocklington. 5/York. R. #3435 Pte., 9/York. R. #241174, 8/York. R. #241174. Disembodied. 13/2/20. (C244)
Stephenson Oscar		Oscar Francis Stephenson bap. At Huggate 14 Nov. 1888. Mother Louisa Susannah Stephenson. 1891 Census Oscar F. Stephenson (2, b. Huggate) with parents Francis Stephenson (39 b. Tibthorpe abt. 1852, Shoemaker) and Louisa S. (31 b. Holme Spalding Moor) at Huggate. 1901 Census Oscar Stephenson (12 b. Huggate) living with parents Francis Stephenson (49 b. Tibthorpe, Farm Carrier and Farmer) and Louisa S (41 b. Holme on Spalding Moor) and brother Robert P (7 b. Huggate abt. 1894) at Huggate. d. 28/5/18 1st Btn. East Yorkshire Regiment #225043 Killed in Action repulsing the German offensive at Aisne on the Somme.. Will: Oscar Francis of Station Farm Home on Spalding Moor Yorkshire Sergeant East Yorkshire Regiment died on or since 28 May 1918 in France Administration (with will) York 28 April to Louisa Stephenson (wife of Francis Stephenson) Effects £259 18s 3d. He is commemorated on the Soissons Memorial. (C245)
Stephenson R P	Royal Army Medical Corps	Brother of Oscar (see 1901 census for Oscar). 1911 Census Roberts Phillips Stephenson (17 b. Huggate abt. 1894, Apprentice to the Drapery) living with parents Francis Stephenson (59 b. Tibthorpe, Farmer) and Louisa Susannah (51 b. Holme on Spalding Moor) at Yapham, Pock. Possible Robert Stephenson #32598 RAMC Sgt. (C246)
Stewart Percy Marlborough - Royal Fusiliers		In 1901 was an Assistant Master at Pocklington school. Percy Marlborough Stewart (29 b. Stokesley, Hampshire 1871, Single). Percy married heiress Katherine Priestman in 1901. In 1904 the couple purchased Ivy Hall (later called Burnby Hall). They transformed the gardens by building a lake and installed water lilies for which the gardens became world renowned. Between 1906 and 1925 they travelled the world collecting mementos from wherever they travelled or hunted. In 1899 Percy joined the East Yrks. Volunteers and became Captain, but left in 1902. In WW1 Percy was in the 4th public schools and Universities Training Reserve Battalion and in Jan. 1917 was Major. Manpower shortages in 1917 meant he was sent to France with the Royal Fusiliers in Jan 1918. For a full account of their lives see "The Stewarts of Burnby Hall & the People of Pocklington"

Name	Regiment	Service Record* (not from Memorial Book)
		by Jim & Margaret Ainscough. (C247)
Stubbs Henry	Royal Air Force	In 1911 Henry Stubbs (18 b. Pock. Abt. 1893 Joiner (House & Coach)) living at home with parents John Tinson Stubbs (49 b. Pock. Abt. 1862, Joiner (House & Coach)) and Margaret Emma (47 b. Pock.) at 10 Deans Lane, Pocklington. #212042 Royal Air Force Henry Stubbs b. 11 Mar 1893 Pocklington, joined R.N.A.S. 16/2/16 joined R.A.F 1/4/18. Joiner. Air Mech II (G) 16/2/16. Air Mech I (RH) 15/12/16. Act A.M. 1 (RHC) 2/11/17. Trans RAF A.M. 2. 1/4/18. Tfer to RAF res. 12/4/19. (C248)
Stubbs Louis	King's Own Yorks Lt. Inf.	1911 Census Louis Arthur Julian Stubbs (10 b. Malton, abt. 1901, School) and brother Richard Mark Stubbs (14 b. Malton, At school) and brother Reginald Mervyn Stubbs (12 b. Malton, School) living with parents Walter Stubbs (41 b. Malton, Poor Law Relieving Officer) and Lucy Maria (40 b. Bromsgrove, Worc. Abt. 1871) at Aston Villa, Union Street, Pocklington. Louis Arthur Julian Stubbs #TR/5/223444 Kings Own Yorkshire Light Infantry 53rd Battalion Called up for service 11/10/18 Posted 12/10/18. L/Cpl 17/2/19 Cpl 22/9/19. Demob. To join Z Class reserves 13/12/19. (FMP) (C249)
Stubbs Reginald Mervyn - Life Guards		For Census see brother Louis Stubbs. b. Malton 4th Qtr 1898. Will: Reginald Mervyn Stubbs Maxwell-Road Pocklington died 9 May 1954 Admin (Ltd) York 4 Dec. to Louis Arthur Julian Stubbs bank manager and Walter Carlton Stubbs bank cashier, Effects £4606 7s 2d. Cannot find military record. (C250)
Stubbs Richard M †	Northumberland Fusiliers	See Page 51. (C251)
Suggitt Arthur		In 1901 Arthur Suggitt (11 b. Warter, abt. 1890) with parents Richard Suggitt (43 b. Warter, Shepherd on Farm) and Annie (37 b. Pock.) at Millington Road, Millington with Little Givendale. In 1911 Arthur Suggitt (21 b. Warter abt. 1890, Wagoner (farm)) Servant of Richard Hardy (47 b. Elmswell, Farmer) at Elmswell, Driffield. 11 Mar 1916 m. Gertrude Emily Annie Webb in Driffield. Arthur Suggitt d. 11 Nov 1976 in Pocklington. Arthur Suggitt #69298 Prince of Wales's Own (West Yorkshire) Regiment. Private. Enlisted 3/1/17. Discharged 7/5/19. No longer physically fit for war service. (C252)
Sugden George	5th Yorkshire Regiment	b. 4 April 1882 in Pocklington. In 1891, George H Sugden (9 b. Pock., Scholar) living with mother Maria Sugden (45 b. Pock., Chapel Caretaker) in Kirkland Street. In 1911 George Herbert Sugden (29 b. Pock. , Tailor (Maker) Boarder In 650 Bolton Road, Bradford. Territorial Attestation: 20 May 1912 Age 30yrs 2mths George Herbert Sugden 10, Victoria Terrace, Pocklington Tailor for Mr. Charles Rowley. Born 1881. #1291 2nd V.B. East Yorks Reg. Transferred from 5th Yorkshire Regiment to 23rd Provisional Btn. in March 1915.

Name	Regiment	Service Record* (not from Memorial Book)
		Transferred to 73rd Protection Company Royal Defence Corps in 1916. #38771. Disemb. 15/3/19. Rank Sergeant. No Overseas Service. Family: Mrs A Sugden, Shields Farm, Bishop Wilton 2 daughters & 1 son. 1919. Address for pay GH Sugden Sgt., 29 Kirklands St., Pocklington. (Anc) (C253)
Sunley John William	Northumberland Fusiliers	In 1911 John Wm Sunley (31 b. Helmsley abt. 1880, Farm Labourer) living with parents Thomas V Sunley (57 b. Helmsley abt. 1854, Farm Manager) and Mary J Sunley (53 b. Helmsley) at Yapham Mill, Pocklington. John W Sunley #4582 Northumberland Fusiliers Private #387523 Labour Corps. (Anc) (C254)
Swaby Louis		Louis Swaby b. Pocklington Sep. 1884. 1891 Census Louis Swaby (6 b. Pock.) with parents Thomas Swaby (59 b. Beverley abt. 1832, General Labourer) and Elizabeth (53 b. Allerthorpe) at Canal Head, Pocklington. In 1901, Louis Swaby (16 b. Pock. , Cattleman on Farm) Boarder on Simpson's Farm for Martha A Harper (59 b. Earswick, Widow & Housekeeper Domestic). In 1911, Louis Swaby (25 b. Canal Head, Pock., Farm Labourer) with wife Martha Victoria (23 b. Hull) at Canal Head, Pocklington. Louis Swaby #T4/124006 Royal Army Service Corps. Driver. Theatre of War: 1 France. Entered Z Reserve 29/4/19. (Anc) (C255)
Shaw James Edwin	Royal Field Artillery	James Edwin Shaw b. 2nd Oct. 1882, Pocklington. In 1891 Census James Wm Shaw (b. Pock.) with parents John Robert Shaw (31 b. Pock, Railway Signalman) and Sarah Jane (30 b. Pock.) at Kirkham, Whitwell, Malton. 1901 Census James Edwin Shaw (19 b. Pocklington, Footman domestic) at Fencote Hall, Kirkby Fleetham, Bedale. In 1911 James Shaw (29 b. Pock., Publican) and wife Mary Shaw (28 b. Hexham, Business Assistant) at Black Bull Inn, Matfen, Corbridge on Tyne, Northumberland. James Shaw #32334 Northumberland Fusiliers Private. Rank of Private (32334) in the 1st Battalion of the Northumberland Fusiliers. Killed in action on 6th Dec 1916. The grave / memorial (I.G.5) to James William is in the Euston Rd Cemetery in Colincamps which is in the Somme. (C256)
Tate Herbert L	Royal Field Artillery	b. abt. 1897 m. Winifred Pinkney at Driffield in Dec. 1929 d. Pocklington Sep. 1933. 1901 Census Herb Leach Tate (4 b. Knottingley abt. 1897) living with parents James Wm Tate (32 b. Carlton abt. 1869, Blacksmith) and Emily (33 b. Hook) at No.2 Victoria Terrace, Pocklington. In 1911, Herbert Leach Tate (14 b. Knottingley, Grocers Errand Boy) living with Grandmother Betsy Leach (69 b. Airmyn abt. 1842, Widowed) at 128 Jackson Street, Goole. Cannot find Military Record. (C257)
Tayleure Arthur J †	Lincs Regiment	See Page 52. (C258)

Name	Regiment	Service Record* (not from Memorial Book)
Theakstone Robert Henry - Royal Garrison Artillery		Possible birth Robert William James Theakstone 3rd Qtr 1861 Pocklington District. Possible 1891 Census Robert W J Theakstone (29 b. Burnby abt. 1862, Living on own means) with two sisters Jane (32, b. Burnby) & Mary (21 Burnby) living in Chapmangate, Pocklington. Robert Henry Theakstone #294312 Royal Garrison Artillery. Gunner. Prev. Units: Base Details RGA 3769 Gunner. (Anc) (C259)
Thompson Ernest William - Royal Garrison Artillery		Ernest William Thompson b. Jul 1892 in Pocklington. Attestation: Ernest Thompson age 22 in 1914 #312195 Royal Garrison Artillery. Driver. 3 Skins Yard, Chapmangate, Pocklington. Farm Labourer. 10th Dec. 1914. Next of Kin Clara Thompson of 3 Skins Yard, Pocklington. Demob. 26/1/21. Pneumonia & Bronchitis. Served in France. (C260)
Thompson John Wilfred - 5th Yorkshire Reg.		See Page 53. (C261)
Thompson John William		1911 John William Thompson (40 b. Pock. Abt. 1871, Chimney Sweep) living on his own at Wilkinson's Yard, Church Lane, Pocklington. In 1901 same as 1911. In 1891 John W. Thompson (20 b. Pocklington, Sweep) a boarder with Benjamin Lockwood (49 b. Almondbury, Sweep) at Black Swan Yard, Pocklington. A picture of Benjamin Lockwood is on the www.pocklingtonhistory.com website Black Swan page. Too many possible military records without a regiment to narrow it down. (C262)
Thorpe Frank	Royal Air Force	In 1911 Frank Thorpe (26 b. Pock., abt. 1885, Ironmonger's Manager) with wife Hilda Louisa (23 b. Kirbymoorside) at 18 George Street, Pocklington. Frank Thorpe #24851 Royal Air Force b. 27/11/1883 CofE Pocklington. Ironmonger & Tinsmith. R.F.C. 11/3/16 R.A.F. 1/4/18 Mechanic. Married Hilda Louisa 11/8/09 in Pocklington they live at 18 George St., Pocklington. Tfer to RAF reserve 30/4/20. (C263)
Thorpe Fred	Royal Air Force	1911 Census Fred Thorpe (31 b. Pock., abt. 1880, Tailor) with wife Anne (25 b. Pock.) at 4 South Parade, Pocklington. Attestation 5/1/17 at Age 36. Fred Thorpe. B. 1880. Journeyman Tailor. #53499 Married in Thornton 11 Jul 1907 to A J with 6 children Louisa Madge, Richard Ellis, Ronald, Mollie, Fred, Margaret. Address: 4 South Parade, Pocklington. Air Mech. 3rd Class 5/1/17 A.M. 2nd Class 1/6/17 Pte 1/4/18. (C264)
Thorpe Thomas Richard † - 5th Yorkshire Reg.		See Page 54. (C265)
Timbs Alfred		Alfred Timbs b. 20 Apr. 1892 in Yapham, Pocklington. Alfred S. Timbs m. Ida Hebden in Pocklington in 1921. Alfred Timbs d. Sep. 1978 in York. In 1901 Census Alfred Timbs (8 b. Yapham abt. 1893) at home with parents William Timbs (45 b. Nash, Bucks abt. 1856, Beastman on Farm) and Harriet (33 b. York) at Yapham-cum-Meltonby. Alfred Timbs #241165 Alexandra, Princess of Wales's Own Yorkshire Regiment Previous Units: 5/York. R. #3423 Pte., 9/York. R. #241165.

Name	Regiment	Service Record* (not from Memorial Book)
		Disembarked 7/11/15. Theatre of War: (1) France. Disembodied 13/3/19 Medals Reissued 13/1/20. (Anc)(C266)
Timbs Richard James †		See Page 54. (C267)
Tinson George	Northumberland Fusiliers	In 1891 George Tinson (15, b. Pock., abt. 1876, Farm Servant) living as Servant to John Rook (60 b. Seaton Ross, Farmer & Provision Dealer) at South End, Seaton Ross. In 1911 George Tinson (35 b. Pock. Abt. 1876, Bricklayer Labourer) living on won in Union Street, Pocklington. George Tinson #202639, #577020, #GS/104023 Northumberland Fusiliers, Labour Corps, Royal Fusiliers. (Anc) (C268)
Tinson Travis	Royal Engineers	In 1891 Travis Tinson (6, b. Pock. Abt. 1885) with parents William Tinson (34 b. Pock., abt. 1857, Bricklayer) and Fanny S. (32 b. Hovingham) at St. Helensgate, Pocklington. In 1911 Travis Tinson (26 b. Pocklington abt. 1885, Bricklayer) and wife Jessie (b. Shipton abt.1887) at 32 London St., Pocklington. Travice Tinson #171007 Royal Engineers. Sapper. (C269)
Todd Arthur Henry	5th Yorkshire Regiment	In 1911 Arthur Henry Todd (16 b. Pock., abt. 1895, Grocer's Apprentice) with parents George Todd (41 b. Yapham, Grocer) and Ada (36, b. Pock.) at Sherbutt House, Pock. #265239 5/York. R. #1797 Private. Attestation Record: Arthur Henry Todd b. abt. 1893 Age 21 in 14th Aug. 1914 Sherbutt Cottage, Pock. #1797 Yorks. Regiment. 5th Btn. Later 24th Btn. 29/5/15. Awarded Good Conduct badge 4/9/16. Exped. Force France 18/4/15 to 20/9/16. Home then until 30/1/19. Discharged. Brother of Charles. He was a Grocer on Pavement, breeder of racing pigeons (supplying carrier pigeons to the Military in the war) and skilled wood carver. (C270)
Todd Charles R	5th Yorkshire Regiment	In 1901 Charles R Todd (6 b. Pock. Abt. 1879) with parents (George Todd (53, b. Yapham abt. 1870, Grocer & Shopkeeper) and Ada (48 b. Pock. abt. 1876) at 4 York View, Barmby Moor parish (but Pocklington). George Todd #200952 Alexandra, Princess of Wales's Own Yorkshire Regiment Previous: 4/York. R. #3423 Cpl. Disemb. 2/9/15 Discharged 23/1/19. Brother of Arthur Henry. One of the country's fastest runners who was a professional sprinter and also played professional rugby. (C271)
Todd Neville H M	Durham Light Infantry	Neville Hector M Todd b. April 1900 in Pocklington. In 1901 Neville H M Todd (10mths b. Pock) with parents William E. (32 b. Pock., abt. 1869, Tailor & Shop Keeper) and Margaret (32 b. Mansergh, Westmorland) at Market Place, Pocklington. Neville Hector Milburn Todd #172387 Durham Light Infantry. Vaccinated at Oakland House Pocklington 18/6/18. 52nd Unit D.L.I. First joined 12/6/18 at Hull when 19. Private. #114242. Called up for service. Punished for dirty rifle 31/10/18. Disembarked Dunkirk 5/3/19. (Anc) (C272)

Name	Regiment	Service Record* (not from Memorial Book)
Topham Ernest	Machine Gun Corps	In 1911 Ernest Topham (10, b. Pock. Abt. 1901) living with parents Henry Topham (38 b. Pock., abt. 1873, Labourer) and Sarah Ann (39 b. Pock., abt. 1872) and brother Frank (15 b. Pock., abt. 1896, Apprentice Draper) at 54, Chapmangate, Pocklington). Ernest Topham #172003 Machine Gun Corps. Private. Entered Class z Reserve. 9/2/19. (C273)
Topham Frank	5th Yorkshire Regiment	See Ernest for Census. Possibly Frank Topham #76618 Prince of Wales's Own (West Yorkshire) Regiment 8th W. York. R. #76618. Private. Entered Z Reserve 25/2/19. Unsure of military Record. (C274)
Topham Henry		Richard Henry Topham in 1901 Census was in Pem Lane, Pock. aged 13 (b. 1887 in Pock.) son of John G Topham (40 Kilham, Butler) and Mary A (49, b. Durham). Richard Henry Topham #F8001 Royal Navy first service date Aug 1915 aboard the "President" (Training area?). At Felixstowe. Naval record had DOB as 15 Oct 1887. Occupation Cabinet Maker. Record states Engineer sent to R.A.F. #208001 Enlisted RAF 01/11/17 as Carpenter Sergeant Mechanic. (Anc, FMP) (C275)
Toyne James		In 1911 Jim Toyne (18 b. Nunburnholme abt. 1893, Wagoner (farm)) with parents Tom Ellis Toyne (43 b. Middleton abt. 1868, Farm Labourer) and Ada (43 b. Rudstone) at White Mill, Pocklington. James Toyne #312196 Royal Garrison Artillery West Riding Heavy Battery. [RGA - (TF)] Previous Units: R.G.A. (T.F.) #312196 Gunner. Disembarked 17/4/15. (C276)
Trout Mills C		1891 Census Charles M Trout (8 b. Brazil abt. 1883, Scholar & Boarder) with William Gelder (50 b. Lindley, Schoolmaster) at Clarenden House, Knaresborough. Charles George Holland Mills (outfitter & hosier) living at 78 Dragon Av. Harrogate Bilton. Married Gertrude Clegg at Bilton with Harrogate on 18 Aug 1908. Charles Mills Trout #305294 London Regiment, 5th (City of London) Battalion (London Rifle Brigade). Rifleman. Prev Units: 5/Lond. R. Rfn. #305294, 8/Rif. Brig. Enlisted 9/12/15. Discharched 12/11/18 with Wounds. Awarded Silver War Badge. Will: TROUT Charles George Holland Mills of Berry Hook 97 St. Winifreds Rd. Harrogate. Died 7 Feb 1949 at Raglan Street, Harrogate. Probate London 20 Apr to Gertrude Mills Trout Widow. Effects £1840 11s 3d. Cannot find Pocklington link. (C277)
Turner Arthur	Durham Light Infantry	In 1911, Arthur Turner (10 b. Pock. Abt. 1901, School) with parents Harry Turner (55 b. Pock. Abt. 1855, Coal Carter) and Mary (55 b. Barmby Moor) at 55 George St., Pocklington. Too many possible Military Records. (C278)
Turner William	Royal Army Service Corps	In 1911, William Turner (10 b. Pock. Abt. 1901, School) with parents Charles Turner (42, b. Pock. Abt. 1869, Tailor Master) and Jane Elizabeth (35 b. Kirby Grindalythe) at 9 Market Place, Pocklington. Too many possible Military Records. (C279)

Name	Regiment	Service Record* (not from Memorial Book)
Unwin Daniel	Royal Army Service Corps	Marriage of Daniel M Unwin to Ethel Anderson in Pocklington Mar. 1920. Daniel Unwin Cat. "C" HT324 Army Service Corps R.A.S.C. C (HT) #324 Driver. (C280)
Waite Charles Vernon	Kings Royal Rifles	b. Pocklington Oct. 1896. In 1901 Charles V Waite (5 b. Pock. Abt. 1896) at home with parents John H Waite (29 b. Pock. Abt. 1872, Cabinet Maker) and Ada (23 b. Heslington) living at Chapmangate, Pocklington. Charles V Waite #C/12243 King's Royal Rifle Corps Prev. Units 21st. Bn. K.R. Rif. C. C/12243 Pte., 21st. Bn. K.R. Rif. C. #C/12243 Awarded the Military Medal + Bar. London Gazette: C/12243 Pte. C. V. Waite, M.M., K.R.R.C. (Pocklington). (M.M's gazetted 12th December, 1917.) (Anc & FMP) (C281)
Walker Ben	Royal Engineers	1901 Census, Ben Walker (5 b. Pock., abt. 1896) at home with parents Ben Walker (33 b. Cliffe, Shepherd on Farm) and Jane (35, b. Wheldrake) and brother John (7, b. Pock. Abt. 1894) at Hayton. 1911 Census, Ben Walker (15 b. Pock. Abt. 1896, Beastman) Servant for Joseph Thomas (55, b. Everingham, Farmer) at Blamise Farm, Everingham. M. Urenle Rhodes in 4th Qtr 1919 at Pocklington. Ben Walker #224599 Royal Engineers Previous Units: Royal Engineers #224599., Midd'x. Rgt. #61135. Pte., Royal Engineers #224599. Sapper. (C282)
Walker John	East Yorkshire Regiment	1901 see Brother Ben. In 1911 John Walker (18 b. Pock., abt. 1893, Private in 1 Btn. East Yorks. Regiment) at Salamanca Barracks (Part Area 11C), Wellington Lines, Aldershot. Military record: Too many possible records. (C283)
Walker Percy	Sherwood Foresters	In 1911, Percy Walker (12 b. Wilberfoss abt. 1899, School) with parents Robert Walker (50 b. Wilberfoss abt. 1861, Labourer General) and Mary Jane (40 b. Bolton abt. 1871) living at 7 Church Lane, Pocklington. Military record: Too many possible records. (C284)
Walker William † (M.C.) - Durham Light Infantry		See Page 55. (C285)
Ward Heneage C	East Yorkshire Regiment	In 1911, Heneage Cyril Ward (17 b. Darlington abt. 1894, Apprentice Ironmongery) with parents Frederick Heneage Ward (50 b. Beverley, Manager Wine & Spirit Dealer) and Annie (49 b. Bridlington) at 103 Holderness Road, Hull. Married Evelyn Gray (from Pocklington dau. of William Gray, Tailor at 20 Railway St. Pock. and sister of Sydney Gray) in Mar 1918 in Sculcoates. Military: Heneage C Ward #11/778 East Yorks. Regiment Previous Units:11th E. York Reg. Cpl. 11/778 Disch. to E.Y.R. Class Z res. (Anc)(C286)
Warrior George	Durham Light Infantry	In 1911, George Warrior (15 b. Leeds abt. 1896, Butcher) living with parents George Warrior (37 b. Melmerby abt. 1874, Railway Rulleyman) and Mary Ann (37 b. Melmerby abt. 1874) living at the Balk, Pocklington. George Warrior #45246 Durham Light Infantry. Private. Previous Units: 14th. Durh. L.I. #45246 Pte., 1/7th. Durh. L.I. #45246. (C287)

Name	Regiment	Service Record* (not from Memorial Book)
Warters Jim	5th Yorkshire Regiment	In 1911 Census, James Warters (11 b. Pock. Abt.1900, School) living with parents Thomas Warters (39 b. Pock., abt. 1872, Labourer) and Margaret (31 b. Pock. Abt. 1880) at 6 Church Lane Pocklington. James Warters #146630 Machine Gun Corps. Private. Disembodied 10/3/19. (C288)
Warters Joseph	5th Yorkshire Regiment	In 1911, Joseph Warters (29 b. Pock., abt. 1882, Tailor) with wife Jessie (27 b. Pock., abt. 1884) at 32 George St. Pocklington. Joseph Warters #1292 Yorkshire Regiment. Private. Enlisted 20/5/12. Disch. 3/3/16. No longer Physically fit for war service. Silver War Badge. (C289)
Warters William	Royal Army Service Corps.	In 1911, William Warters (30 b. Pock., abt. 1881, Blacksmith) and wifeHarriett Warters (29 b. South Cave abt. 1882) living at 49 George St., Pocklington. William Warters #TS/9323 Army Service Corps. Staff Sergeant. Previous Units: R.A.S.C. TS/9323 S/Sergeant. (Anc) Awarded Military Cross for his service in Salonika, Bulgaria, Serbia, Turkey Austria and Russia and presented by the King of Hellenes Ref. HC&PWN. (C290)
Wilson James B	East Yorkshire Regiment	In 1901, James B Wilson (6, b. Pock. Abt. 1895) with parents James Wilson (27 b. Barmby Moor, Chemists Traveller) and Mary (32 b. Ireland) living at 1 Kirkland St., Pocklington. Military record: Too many possible records. (C291)
Wilson John T	Royal Air Force	In 1891, John T Wilson (5 b. Pock., abt. 1886) with parents Joseph Wilson (41 b. Badsworth, abt. 1850, Butcher) and Martha (39, b. Pock.) living at New Pavement. John Tonkinson Wilson #198895 Royal Air Force. b. 12/10/1885. Pocklington. Joined RAF 16/6/18 at age 32 8/12. Butcher. Marriage 17/4/11 at Barmby Moor. Next of kin: Amy Adelaide Wilson, 11 Victoria Terrace, Pocklington. Wife. Transferred to RAF Reserve 24/4/19. After the war was a builder in New Pavement, Pocklington. (C292)
Windebank George E	Royal Field Artillery	In 1901 George Windebank (3, b. Pock.) with parents Henry Windebank (50 b. Horndean, Hampshire, Groom Domestic) and Mary (29 b. Painsthorpe) at Waterloo Terrace, Pocklington and brother Henry Windebank (7, b. Pock.). In 1911 George Edward Windebank (13 b. Pock., Errand Boy with mother Mary Windebank (39, b. Painsthorpe, Char Woman & Widow) at 5 Waterloo Terrace, Pocklington. Geo Edward Windebank #765557 Royal Artillery (Royal Horse Artillery and Royal Field Artillery) sub unit: Royal Field Artillery. Territorial Force. Previous Units: RFA. T. 2555. Bdr. Rank: Acting Corporal. (C293)
Windebank Henry	Royal Navy	Brother of George E. See his Census. Henry Windebank #K14621 Royal Navy. b. 25 Dec 1893 in Pocklington. First Service date 6/4/12, First Ship: Excellent. Stoker II. Last Service date: 29/7/21 Last Ship: Victory II. Became a coal merchant at Canal Head. (C294)

Name	Regiment	Service Record* (not from Memorial Book)
Witty Alfred		In 1901 Census, Alfred Witty (5 b. Driffield abt. 1896) with parents Thomas Witty (28 b. Fridaythorpe, Shepherd on Farm) and Ada (26 b. Driffield) at Fridaythorpe. In 1911 Alfred Witty (16 b. Driffield, Horseman) boarder with James Witty (34 b. Fridaythorpe, Farm Foreman) at Holmfield, Wetwang. Alfred Witty#WG157 Wolds Wagoner Reserve Attested 4/3/13 at Duggleby at Age 18. Had a family fish & chip van. (C295)
Wood Roy	Royal Air Force	In 1911 Census, Roland Wood (11 b. Huntington, Yks abt. 1900, School) living with parents Joseph E. Wood (39, b. Goathland abt. 1872, Inn Keeper—Old Red Lion, Regent St., Pock.) and wife Sarah (43 b. Flaxton abt. 1868, Assisting in the business) Joined RAF #96661 14/9/17 at age 18. Transferred to RAF Reserve 21/11/19. (C296)
Wreghitt Alfred	Northumberland Fusiliers	(C297)
Wright George	Army Ordnance Corps	(C298)
Wyatt Louis		(C299)

The Women and Children Did Their Part

The proud volunteers who joined up for King and Country

A cadet award ceremony at Pocklington School

Other names not included in Memorial Book or the War Memorial who took part or fell in the Great War:

N.B. Where this says "b. Pocklington", means the birth could have been in the Registration District of Pocklington which includes Allerthorpe, Barmby Moor, Bielby, Bishop Wilton including (Belthorpe), Bolton, Bugthorpe, Burnby, Catton, Cottingwith, East Cottingwith, East Stamford Bridge, Everingham, Fangfoss, Fridaythorpe, Full Sutton, Goodmanham, Great Givendale with Grimthorpe, Harswell, Hayton, High Catton, Huggate, Kilnwick Percy, Kirby Underdale, Londesborough including (Esthorpe), Low Catton, Market Weighton (including Arras), Melbourne, Millington (including Little Givendale), Newton upon Derwent, Ousethorpe, Pocklington, Sanction (including Houghton), Scrayingham, Seaton Ross, Shipton, Skirpenbeck, South Cliffe, Stamford Bridge, Storwood, Sutton upon Derwent, Thixendale, Thornton, Thorpe le Street, Waplington, Warter, Wilberfoss, Yapham cum Meltonby, Youlthorpe with Gowthorpe. Many of the following records are from the Ancestry.com database "UK, Soldiers Died in the Great War, 1914-1919"

Name	Regiment	Service Record
Andrews John †	5th Btn. Yorkshire Reg.	2772 Cpl John Andrews. Enlisted at Pocklington, Yorks. Killed In action on 19th July 1917. Commemorated at Heninel Communal Cemetery Extension. (X01)
Balmford David Claude	East Yorkshire Regiment	A native of York, Mr. Balmford won the Military Cross on the Somme in 1916 when holding the rank of Sergeant Major with the East Yorkshire Regiment. After the war he went to reside in Pocklington, where he took an active interest in the Legion of Frontiersmen, in which he held the rank of Lieutenant. For Several years he was employed as an inspector on the Everingham bus service. D.C. Balmford married in Pocklington in 1918 to Poppy Doretta Watson b.1900 de. 1974. D C Balmford d. in Pocklington aged 49. (X02)
Bell Harold †	Army Service Corps	Enlisted at Pocklington. #T4/040043 Army Service Corps. Driver. Died of Wounds 28 Sep 1918. (X03)
Binge Thomas †	East Yorkshire Regiment	b. Pocklington. In 1891 family lived at Stathers Yard, Chapmangate. His father George b. Leavening moved to Wetherby by 1911. Thomas Binge #28852 8th Btn. East Yorkshire Regiment. Private. Died in France/Flanders 27 Sep 1917. Killed in Action aged 35. (Anc). Brother of Mrs Gladys Boakes , Rushworth St. Newtown, Leeds. Buried in Tyne Cot Memorial, West-Vlaanderen, Belgium (X04)
Boulton Alfred Edward	5th Highland Light Infantry	Born in Hunslet Leeds and went to Glasgow when 12. Before the war he worked in the returns dept. of "Thompson's Weekly News". The first day of the war he was with 5th Highland Light Infantry City of Glasgow Battalion. After training in Stirling in June 1915he was sent to the Dardanelles and from there to Egypt. About Christmas time a bullet passed through his spine. This paralysed his lower body and became crippled for life. He was sent back to England for recuperation. Whilst in hospital he fell in love with his Nurse and married her. He moved to Pocklington and from his electric wheelchair he became an active member of the community. (X05)
Burks Fred †	Yorkshire Hussars	b. Millington, Pocklington. Yorkshire Hussars (Alexandra, Princes of Wales' Own) 2nd Btn. #8391. Enlisted Malton. Killed in action. Western European Theatre. (X06)

Name	Regiment	Service Record
Byass Bernard †	Household Cavalry	Bernard Byass b. Warter, Pock. Lived at Warter. Died 14 Nov 1917 in Palestine. Rank A L Corporal. #50081 Regiment: Household Cavalry of the line. Battalion 1st East Riding of Yorks. Yeomanry (Anc) Buried at Ramleh War Cemetery, Israel & Palestine (inc. Gaza), (CWGC) (X07)
Chapman Thomas †	Northumberland Fusiliers	b. Seaton Ross. Enl. Pocklington. Northumberland Fusiliers 1st 5th Battalion (Territorial) #242341. Private. Killed in Action. 14 Nov 1916. France/Flanders. (X08)
Cliff Herbert Theodore † - Prince of Wales Own (West Yorkshire Regiment)		b. Leeds 1875. Son of William Dewhurst Cliff a wealthy Collier owning family and his uncles Stephen and Walter were steel masters in Leeds. Herbert moved to Barmby Moor Manor House after his marriage in 1912. After prior military service in South Africa, in 1914 Herbert joined the West Yorkshire Regiment 3rd Btn. In rank of Major. He was fighting in the Battle of Aisne and was wounded on the morning 13th Oct 1914, fought on, and was killed by a shell in the afternoon. He was acting Lt. Colonel at the time of his death at age 39 and is buried at Outtersteene Communal Cemetery Extension at Bailleul, France. An impressive monument to him is in Barmby Moor Church. *(Val Hewetson & monument picture)* (X09)

Conmy Arthur †	East Yorkshire Regiment	b. Pocklington abt. 1893, Residence: Market Weighton. Enlisted Beverley East Yorkshire Regiment. 8th Battalion. Private. #28501. Formerly #1393 E.Riding Yeomanry. Killed in Action France/Flanders 3 May 1917. Commemorated at Arras Memorial. Bay 4 and 5. In 1911 Arthur Conmy (18 b. Pock., Joiners Apprentice) staying with Uncle Joseph William Conwy (4, b. Mkt Weighton, General Dealer and mail contractor) and mother Lillian Wilson Conwy (44 b. Mkt Weighton, House Keeper and Sister in Law of Joseph W) in North Gate, Market Weighton. (X10)
Conmy Robert †	West Yorks. Regiment	Robert Conmy. b. Pocklington Died 4th Jul 1916 in France & Flanders #23588 Prince of Wales's Own (West Yorkshire) Regiment 2nd Battalion. Died of Wounds 4/7/16.Robert Owen Conmy Aged 16. Son of Margaret Maude Conmy of 20 Carmelite St., Hungate, York. Buried at Daours Communal Cemetery Extension, Somme, France. (X11)
Cook Robert †	Essex Regiment	On Bishop Wilton War Memorial d.1915. b. Bishop Wilton. Residence Cape Town, South Africa.Enl. Cape Town. Essex Regiment 2nd Btn. L.Corporal. #15812. Killed in Action 2nd May 1915 Age. 35. Ypres (Menin Gate) Memorial (X12)
Cook Robert †	Northumberland Fusiliers	b. Warter in 1883. Enl. Beverley. Northumberland Fusiliers. A coal miner and son of George Cook (b. Warter in 1860, a Dewer In Stone Quarry) in 1911 was in Worksop. 1st /7th Battalion (Territorials) #4394 Killed in action 15th Sep. 1916 In France/Flanders. (X13)

Name	Regiment	Service Record
Cooper Joseph †	Military Police Corps	b. Barmby Moor Enl. London in the Military Provost Staff Corps #W/1716 This unit looked after Military Prisoners of War. He served in France Mar 1915 to Mar 1916 and made a Sergeant. He died Age 33 on 31/03/18 of Heart Disease and is buried in Barmby Moor Churchyard. (X14)
Coulthirst Gordon †	West Yorkshire Regiment (Prince of Wales Own)	b. Redcar in 1892. Gordon was the second son of John William and Jane Coulthirst. William was a Grocer in Hinderwell but by 1911 he had retired to the Close at Allerthorpe, and Gordon was a farmer. Gordon joined up in September 1914 and was posted to A Company, 12th Battalion of The Prince of Wales Own West Yorkshire Regiment. The company went to France on 10th September 1915 as part of the 21st Division. According to "The Long, Long Trail" the experience of the 21st Division was "truly appalling. Having been in France only a few days, lengthy forced marches brought them into the reserve for the British assault on Loos. GHQ left it too far behind to be a useful reinforcement on the first day but it was sent into action on 26th September, whereupon it suffered 3,800 casualties for very little gain". Gordon was one of those killed and whose bodies were never identified. He is commemorated on the Loos Memorial, Pas de Calais. He was aged 22. (*Research by Val Hewetson*) (X15)
Craven Alfred †	Yorkshire Light Infantry (King's Own)	b. Newton-on-Derwent. Enl. Pocklington. King's Own 1st Btn. #59034 Formerly #61068, Yorks Regt. Killed in Action. 8 Dec 1918. France/Flanders. (X16)
Cundall John †	Yorkshire Hussars	b. Howe Enl. Scarborough Disembarked in France 18/4/1915 Killed in action 25/04/1915. Death recorded on Bishop Wilton War Memorial. (X17)
Dales William Ripley †	Durham Light Infantry	b. Melbourne. Enl. Pocklington. Durham Light Infantry 1/5th Battalion #200723 Formerly #26540, K.R.R.C. Died of wounds. 16th Feb. 1917. France/Flanders. (X18)
Dawson Fred †	Northumberland Fusiliers	b. Huggate, 1897. Enlisted in Hull. Fred Dawson Northumberland Fusiliers 1st Battalion #9460. Died of Wounds on 7 Dec 1914. Buried at Boulogne Eastern Cemetery, Pas de Calais, France. In 1911 Fred Dawson (14 b. Huggate, Farm Horseman) Servant at Manor House Farm at Huggate. (X19)
Eastwood George †	Durham Light Infantry	b. Pocklington. Residence: Easingwold. Enlisted in Richmond. George Eastwood #7257 Durham Light Infantry 1st 9th Battalion formerly #28639 York Regt. Killed in Action 5 Nov 1916 in France/Flanders. In 1911 George Eastwood (13 b. Pock., School) living with father Isaac Eastwood (37 b. Wrexham, Wales, Farm Labourer) and widower at Walbut Mill, Thornton. (X20)

Name	Regiment	Service Record
Flower Charles Ernest † - Royal Army Medical Corps		b. Warter. Royal Army Medical Corps #113918 Private. Enl. 24/6/16 Disch. 24/8/17 Sick. Admitted to No.6 General Hosp. on 21/3/18, Rouen. Died on March 15 1919 Age 41. Youngest son of Isaac Flower of Warter and Mrs. Flower of Chapmangate. Ernest left a wife and 4 children. Ref. HC&PWN 22/3/19. (X21)
Flower Henry Bernard† - Northumberland Fusiliers		b. Warter. In 1911 census Henry Flower (b. 1894 at Warter, Game Keepers Helper) with parents John Flower (b. 1864, North Cliff, Woodman on Estate) & Mary Flower (b. 1864 in Bishop Wilton) living at Woodmans Lodge, Warter. At the time of Bernards death in 1916 John & Mary were in The Green, Rawcliffe, Goole, Yorks. Bernard Enlisted at Pocklington. #22591 13th Btn. Northumberland Fusiliers Lce. Cpl. Killed in Action on 28th Sept. 1916 at age 22. (X22)
Foster William †	East Yorkshire Regiment	b. Selby. Enl. Pocklington. East Yorkshire Regiment 7th Battalion. Private. #8761. Killed in action. 31st Mar. 1918. France and Flanders. (X23)
Futcher Arthur †	Household Cavalry	b. Allerthorpe abt. 1885. Enlisted Beverley. Rank: Sergeant. Arthur Futcher #128 Household Cavalry and Cavalry of the Line. Battalion 10th (Prince of Wales Own Royal) Hussars. Killed in Action 25 Mar 1918 in France/Flanders and awarded the D.C.M. Commemorated at Pozieres memorial, Somme, France. DCM Citation read "*For gallant conduct on many occasions in conveying messages under heavy fire, and for the zeal and coolness displayed in the performance of his duties*". In 1911 age 26 with the Tenth Hussars in India. In 1891 Arthur Futcher (7 b. Allerthorpe, Scholar) with father James (38 b. Upper Wallop, Hants., Ag. Lab.) and Harriet (39, b. Bielby) at Current tree Cottage, Allerthorpe. (X24)
Gospel Fred †	Prince of Wales's Own (West Yorkshire) Reg.	b. Allerthorpe, Pock. Fred Gospel #3/9621 Prince of Wales's Own (West Yorkshire) Reg. 1st Battalion. Enlisted at Harrogate 12/11/14. Died at home 31 July 1916. In 1901 Fred Gospel (14 b. Allerthorpe, Office Boy) with parents William Gospell (44 b. Allerthorpe, Railway Drayman) and Margaret (41 b. Beverley) at 68 Kitson St. Leeds. In 1911 Fred Gospel (24 b. Allerthorpe abt. 1887, Railway Porter) Boarder at Nidd Bridge, Ripley. Buried in Beckett St. Cemetery, Leeds. (X25)
Gospel Henry (Harry)† - Leicestershire Regiment		Harry (as known in family) b. Bugthorpe 15th May 1877. In 1901 he married Sarah Mary Tindale in Bugthorpe. Sarah was born in Yapham. Harry lived at Bishop Wilton as a builder. Harry was serving, because of his construction expertise, with the 11th Pioneer Battalion of the Leicestershire Regiment #46650 and Formerly #179397, R.E.. On 23 Oct 1917, he and a colleague were loading shells onto a transporter during the battle of Passchendaele when one exploded killing them both instantly. He is buried in the Menin Road South Military Cemetery, Belgium. (X26)

Name	Regiment	Service Record
Haith John Robert †	Coldstream Guards	b. Warter in 1882. Husband of Gertrude Mary Haith, of 6, Butt Lane, Queensgate Rd., Beverley, Yorks. Served in the South African Campaign. Enl. Burnley. Coldstream Guards 3rd Btn. #18499. Killed in action 13th Nov. 1916 Age 34 in France/Flanders. Commemorated at Theipval Memorial, Somme, France. (X27)
Harrison Albert †	Northumberland Fusiliers	b. Nunburnholme. Son of John Brigham Harrison and Mary Elizabeth Harrison of Rose Cottage, Nunburnholme. n.b. No known connection to William ("Bills Book") Harrison. Enl. Pocklington. Northumberland Fusiliers. 1st 4th Battalion (Territorials). #66522 Private. Died 12 Sep 1918 France and Flanders. Buried Chauny Communal Cemetery British Extension 5. D. 2. (X28)
Harrison George Wilfred † - 5th Yorkshire Regiment		b. Howden. Enl. Scarborough, Son of Frederick (Policeman of Bishop Wilton 1900-08) and Fanny Harrison. 5th Yorkshire Regiment #2316. Died 9 Jan 1915 in Newcastle. Buried at Bishop Wilton. Frederick had four sons in the war, 2 of which died and 2 daughters. A newspaper report said the Military Funeral was perhaps the first the village had seen. (X29)
Harrison Reginald †	Household Cavalry	b. Howden. Enl. Derby. Brother of Wilfred & Harold. Household Cavalry of the Line and 5th Reserve Reg. #17524. Died 19th Dec 1917. Buried in Bishop Wilton. (X30)
Hawes Abraham †	King's Own (Yorkshire Light Infantry)	b. Sprowston, Norwich & moved to E.Yorks just after 1901. Abraham joined Hull Police in 1907 after his marriage to Annie Fox of Market Weighton. Annie died in 1911 after giving birth to James and Gladys Mary. He married Annie's younger sister Elizabeth in 1912. Abraham became a platelayer to NER and lived at Barmby Moor. He entered the war in Sept 1914 in the 2nd Btn. KOYLI #8501 and taken prisoner of war after being reported missing in Sept 1914. He died in Germany age 31 on 19/05/18. Buried in Berlin SW Cemetery. He is recorded in Memorials in Barmby Moor, Market Weighton and St John Sepulchre, Norwich. (X31)
Hayton Harry †	Household Cavalry and Cavalry of the Line	b. Pocklington. Residence in Leeds. Enlisted Beverley. Harry Hayton Cavalry of the Line #4968 Household Cavalry and Cavalry of the Line Battalion: 18th (Queen Marys Own Royal) Hussars. L Corporal. Killed in Action 8 Feb 1916. Cannot find birth record, nearest is Walkington. (Ref. Anc*). (X32)
Hayton William Ward † - East Yorkshire Regiment		b. Pocklington. Enlisted Hull. William Ward Hayton #32958 East Yorkshire Regiment 10th Battalion. Killed in Action in France/Flanders 25 Mar 1918. (Ref: *Anc—"Soldiers who died in the Great War") (X33)

Name	Regiment	Service Record
Haywood Reginald Bernard Rands † - York and Lancs.Regiment		Son of W. and E. Haywood, of Yapham Mill, Pocklington; husband of Ivy Hinde (formerly Haywood), of 43, Union St., Pocklington, Yorks. York and Lancaster Regiment 10th Btn. #16511 Died 26/09/1915 Age 23 (CWGC). b. 1892 Tickhill, Doncaster Enl. Sheffield. Private. Killed in Action in France/ Flanders. The regimental diary reports orders were received to attack the HULLOCH-LENS road. They took the road but then had to attack square wood. After severe resistance the wood was taken but beyond the wood were concealed machine guns. The Germans were in force N.E. of BENIFONTAINE with guns raking the road. The 10th Btn. pulled back after casualties. Captain Foster suggested a rally to retake the wood. Four gallant attempts were made but the machine gun fire was just too powerful. The push was abandoned and the diary reported 13 Officers wounded or missing and 400 men unaccounted for on this 25/26 Sep. 1915 engagement. On the Loos Memorial, France. (X34)
Hillerby Alfred †	Royal Fusiliers	b. Holme on Spalding Moor in 1886. His father John was a farm worker at Barmby Grange. He moved to Coxhoe, Durham to be with his brother George where he worked as a furnace charger at a Magnesian Limestone Quarry. Alfred enlisted in the Roral Field Artillery in Sunderland in 1915 but transferred to 11th Btn. Royal Fusiliers by Aug. 1918. He was killed in action "by a machine gun bullet" during an attack on 30th Aug. 1918 aged 35 and commemorated on Artois Memorial, Pas De Calais, France. (X35)
Husband John Henry † - Royal Field Artillery		b. Kirby Underdale. Son of John and Annie Husband of Bolton, he grew up in Youlthorpe. In 1911 he was a wagoner at Robert Wilson's farm in Youlthorpe. He enlisted in 1916 as a gunner with D Battery, 296th Brigade of the Royal Artillery. He died of wounds at Terlincthun Base Hospital, Boulogne on 10th July 1918. He was buried in the British Cemetery there aged 28. He is commemorated on the Bishop Wilton Memorial. (X36)
Ibson Edward Henry † - Machine Gun Corps		b. Hovingham in 1899. John was a Railway worker in 1911 living in two Railway Cottages down Keldspring Lane, Barmby Moor. Enl. Easingwold. 1st/4th Btn. Territorial Force Yorkshire Regiment in 1916 #203897. Transferred to the Machine Gun Corps. Private. #103740. He was killed 27/03/18 aged 18 and buried at Vendresse Cemetery, Aisne, France. (X37)
Ireland Harold †	Yorkshire Light Infantry (King's Own)	Was the son of Frederick William Ireland of Weaverthorpe and his wife Letitia (nee Craven). In 1898, the year Harold was born, Frederick died. By 1911 the younger members of the family were living with Harold's mother and step-father at Tank Cottage, Waplington. Harold was a farm servant, described as a yard boy, at Hallgarth Farm, Thornton and going to school part-time. He enlisted in the 10th Service Battalion of the King's Own Yorkshire Light Infantry in

Name	Regiment	Service Record
		September 1914. Like Gordon Coulthirst, Harold's Battalion was part of the 21st Division which arrived in the Reserve just in time for the battle of Loos. Harold was killed on the 27th September (the parish magazine records his death as Sunday 26th September 1915) aged 17. He is commemorated on the Loos Memorial. (*Val Hewetson research*) (X38)
Jackson Herbert †	East Yorkshire Regiment	b. Barmby Moor in 1890. Third son of George Jackson of Red House Barmby Moor. He was a Farm Worker. Herbert Joined The East Yorkshire Regiment 8th Btn. in April 1915. In 1916 it was part of the 3rd Division and part of all the major battles of the Somme. He was killed in the push to clear Delville Wood of German Forces on 18th August 1916 and commemorated on the Thiepval Memorial. (X39)
James Kirby Easingwood † - Army Ordnance Corps		b. Pocklington Mar 1868. Kirby Easingwood James #06950 Army Ordnance Corps. Private. Enlisted Portsmouth. Died in Mesopotamia 5 Dec 1915. In 1911 was a builders clerk in Southampton. In 1881 Kirby E James (13 b. Pocklington, Scholar) with parents Kirby James (43 b. Walkington, Chemist & Druggist Maker) and Dinah(30 b. Everingham) at North Bar Within, Beverley. (X40)
Johnson Edward Wills † - East Yorkshire Regiment		b. Rotherham. Lived at Warter most of his life with his Grandparents Mark & Elizabeth. Son of Elizabeth Bennett (formerly Johnson), of 61, Tudor Rd., Cardiff, and the late Mr. C. Johnson. East Yorkshire Regiment 11th Battalion #11/1176 Private. Killed in action 3rd June 1916 in France/Flanders. (X41)
Johnson Robert †	Royal Horse Artillery & Royal Field Artillery	1911 Census Robert Johnson (13 b. Pock., abt. 1878, School) living with parents John Thomas Johnson (38 b. Pock. Abt. 1873, joiner for NER) and Eliza Ann (35, b. Pock. Abt. 1876) at 5 Riseholme Av., Wheeler St., Hull. Robert Johnson #27933 Royal Horse Artillery and Royal Field Art. Gunner. Enlisted Hull. Killed in Action 4th Nov. 1916 in Fr./Flanders. (Ref. Anc—"Soldiers who Died in Gt. War") (X42)
Kidd John Charles †	Yorkshire & Lancs. Regiment	b. Melbourne in 1897 the second son of John James and Elizabeth Kidd. He worked on his father's farm until he was called up in January 1917. He was allocated to the 80th Territorial Reserve Battalion for training and sent to France in May 1917. He then joined the 2nd Hallamshire Territorial Force Battalion of the Yorkshire & Lancashire Regiment. He was killed in the assault on Vraucourt Copse on 2nd September 1918 aged 20. He is buried in the Vraucourt Copse Cemetery. (*Val Hewetson research*) (X43)
Loft Albert James †	East Yorkshire Regiment	b. Bishop Wilton. Residence Bishop Wilton. Son of George and Margaret Loft, of Bishop Wilton. Enl. Pocklington. East Yorkshire Regiment. 1st Btn. #16854 Private. Died of Wounds. 6 Dec 1915 Age 26. France/Flanders. Left £50 to John Robert Loft labourer in will (X44)

Name	Regiment	Service Record
Lunt Oswald †	Royal Garrison Artillery	b. Everingham. Enl. Pocklington. Royal Garrison Artillery #158108 Gunner. Killed in action 21st March 1918. France & Flanders (X45)
Messenger Thomas †	West Yorkshire Regiment	b. Market Weighton. Enl. Harrogate. Residence Bramham. Prince of Wales's Own (West Yorkshire) Regiment. 9th Battalion. Private #47218. Killed in Action 29 Apr 1917 in France/Flanders. (X46)
Nicholson George †	Royal Garrison Artillery	b. Pocklington. George Nicholson #312402 Royal Garrison Artillery. Battalion West Riding Heavy Battery. [RGA—(TF)]. Gunner. Enlisted York. Died in Africa 25th Sept. 1917. In 1901 George Nicholson (17 b. Pock., Farmer's Son) with parents John Nicholson (53, b. Langtoft, Farmer) and Elizabeth (54 b. Pock.) at North Field Farm, Pock. (X47)
Nicholson George Robert † - Manchester Regiment		Native of Bielby m. Amy Nicholson of Primrose Cottages, Church Lane, Bramham., Enl. Pocklington Manchester Regiment 18th Btn. #40286 and #165832 Royal Field Artillery. Killed in action 01/08/17 buried at Buried at Lijssenthoek Military Cemetery , Belgium. (CWG) (X48)
Nicholson Leonard R. † - Seaforth Highlanders		b. Warter, Pocklington. Leonard R. Nicholson #S/6302 Seaforth Highlanders. 8th Battalion. L Sergeant. Killed in Action 25th Sept. 1915 in France/Flanders. In 1911 Leonard Nicholson (20 b. Warter, Footman) Servant at The Hall, Kibworth Harcourt, Leicester for Col. J.W. Chaplin V.C. In 1901, Leonard R. Nicholson (10 b. Warter) with parents Leonard Nicholson (40 b. Frodingham, Police Sergeant) and Sarah A. (42 b. Walkington) at Northgate, Market Weighton. (X49)
Oliver Harold †	Duke of Wellington's (West Yorkshire Regiment)	b. Spittle in 1899. Younger brother of Robert. Joined in 1916 aged 17 and posted to 10th Btn. West Riding Regiment (part of the 23rd Division) #269073. He was killed in action engaged in the Battle of the Menin Road (part of the 3rd Ypres Campaign often known as Passchendaele) on 20th Sep. 1917 age 19 and commemorated on the Tyne Cot Memorial. (X50)
Oliver Robert Arthur † Scots Guards		b. Spittle in 1894. 3rd son of 11 of John and Martha Oliver a farmer and Carrier, In 1911 Robert was a horseman at Manor House Warter under Robert Byass. Enl. Scots Guards in late 1913/early 1914 and posted to the 2nd Btn. #8792 In Aug. 1914 they were at the Tower of London and merged with the 7th Division and entered Belgium on 7th Oct. 1914. He was killed in action on 19th April 1916 age 21 and commemorated on the Menin Gate. (X51)
Pearson Francis Frederick - Labour Corps		b. Warter Wold. Family were at Field House, Fangfoss by 1898. In 1911 was a shepherd on the family farm. He was called up 5th June 1916 to the East Yorks, Regiment but served in the 16th (Labour) Btn. Of the Yorkshire Regiment. He was posted to France 11th July 1916 on road and rail

Name	Regiment	Service Record
		building. He was transferred to the newly formed Labour Corps from 12th May 1917. He remained in France until 23rd June 1918 when he returned to Aldershot sick. He was discharged medically unfit 9th Sep. 1918. He is recorded on the roll of honour as having died in the Great War and died around 1920. His grave in Yapham Churchyard is listed as a Commonwealth War Grave and maintained as such though died ten months after the war officially ended (X52)
Peters Gerard †	Gloucestershire Regiment	b. Airmyn vicarage Goole, Gloucestershire Regiment 6th Battalion (Territorial) Second Lieutenant PETERS was the son of the Rev. Edward Peters and Ada Annie Peters, of The Vicarage, Bishop Wilton, York. Born at Airmyn Vicarage, Goole. A Solicitor. Educated at St. Peter's School, York. Honours man in Final Law Exam. Died aged 25 on 24th February 1917. Buried at Fouquescourt British Cemetery, Somme, France. Recorded on BW War Memorial. (X53)
Rawlings William †	King's Royal Rifle Corps	b. Warter. Residence Hull. Enlisted Sheffield. In 1911 he was in Hull working for the N.E. Railway co. with wife Rose and 3 sons age 3 and 2 month old twin boys. King's Royal Rifle Corps 2nd Battalion #2457 RFN. (L Corporal) Killed in action 1st July 1916 in France/Flanders. (X54)
Richmond William †	Prince of Wales's Own (West Yorkshire) Reg.	William Arthur Richmond b. Pocklington Jan 1885. William Richmond #9538 Prince of Wales's Own (West Yorkshire) Regiment 2nd Battalion. Private. Enlisted Hull. Died 19th Dec. 1914 in France/Flanders. 1901 Census William A Richmond (16 b. Fangfoss abt. 1885, Engineers Apprentice) with Uncle William T. Richmond (25 b. Fangfoss abt. 1876, Railway Guard) & Aunt Jane H (25 b. Cloughton) at 11 Albert Av., Hull. (X55)
Rushton John Hawcroft † - Yorkshire Hussars		b. Pocklington. Residence Pocklington. John Hawcroft Rushton #1801 Yorkshire Hussars (Alexandra, Princes of Wales' Own) 5th battalion. Private. Enlisted Scarborough. Killed in Action 17 Sep 1916 in France/ Flanders. (Ref: *Anc—"Soldiers who died in the Great War") (X56)
Sanderson Arthur †	Duke of Cambridge's Own	b. Pocklington. Residence Scarborough. Arthur (Middlesex) Regiment Sanderson #G/52278 Duke of Cambridge (Middlesex) Regiment 23rd Battalion. Enlisted at Richmond. Killed in Action on 22nd Sept. 1917 in France and Flanders. In 1911 Arthur Sanderson (27 b. Allerthorpe, Butchers Manager) and wife Florence (26 b. Shrewsbury, Shropshire) at 14 Aberdeen Terrace, Scarborough.(*Anc)(X57)
Scaife John †	King's Own Yorks. Lt. Inf.	b. Pocklington. John Scaife #3/1355 King's Own Yorkshire Light Infantry 8th Battalion. Private. Enlisted at Wakefield. Died of Wounds 14 Dec 1917. in France / Flanders. In 1901 John Scaife (5 b. Pock.) with parents Charles Scaife (33 b. Pock., Railway Platelayer) and Mary (26 b. Lichfield) at Back Street, Sutton Without, Hull. In 1911 John Anthony Scaife (15 b. Pock. Abt 1896, Pit Fop Labourer) with parents

Name	Regiment	Service Record
		Charles Scaife (43 b. Pock., Labourer Agriculture) and Mary Sophia Scaife (37 b. Leckonfield) at Green End, Carlton, Wakefield. (*Anc) (X58)
Shearsmith Thomas †	East Yorkshire Regiment	b. Pocklington. Thomas Shearsmith #13/1318 East Yorkshire Regiment 13th Battalion. Enlisted at Hull. Private. Killed in Action 4th Aug. 1916 in France / Flanders. In 1911 Thomas Shearsmith (30 b. Pocklington abt. 1881, General Labourer) and wife Annie Shearsmith (31 b. Hull) at 11 Buckingham Terr., Buckingham St., Holderness Rd., Hull. (*Anc) (X59)
Simpson Albert †	Prince of Wales's Own (West Yorkshire) Regiment	b. Melbourne, Pocklington. Albert Simpson #15317 Prince of Wales's Own (West Yorkshire) Regiment 9th Battalion. Private. Enlisted at York. Residence: Riccall, York. Killed in Action on 22nd August 1915. (Ref: *Anc—"Soldiers who died in the Great War") (X60)
Simpson Joseph Sydney † - Northumberland Fusiliers		b. Allerthorpe in 1892. Eldest son of Joseph and Jane Simpson. Joseph was a Farm Bailiff living at Walbut Mill in 1901. In 1911 he was a farm servant at Thornton but when he enlisted he reported himself as a Railway Porter in York living at 84 Sutherland St. He was called up in August of 1916 and allocated to the 32nd Northumberland Fusiliers and was sent to France on 29th August. On 13th September 1916 he was transferred to D Company of the 5th Battalion of the Yorkshire and Lancashire Regiment who were part of the 49th West Yorkshire Division and was thrust into the Somme Battlefield. He was wounded on the 19th October and died the following day. The day he was mortally wounded was his 24th birthday. (*Val Hewetson research*) (X61)
Slater Hartley †	Duke of Wellington's (West Riding Regt.)	b. Bishop Wilton. Hartley Slater son of William and Elizabeth Slater, of Bishop Wilton; husband of Agnes Slater, of Church St., Huggate, York. Duke of Wellington's (West Riding Regt.) 2nd Btn. #24346 Killed in Action 7 Oct 1917. Buried Tyne Cot Memorial, Zonnebeke, West-Vlaanderen, Belgium. (X62)
Smith James †	King's Own Royal Lancaster Regiment	b. Pocklington. James Smith #6156 King's Own Royal Lancaster Regiment 1st Battalion. Private. Enlisted: Manchester. Killed in Action 26th Aug. 1914 in France and Flanders. (*Anc) In 1911 James Smith (30 b. Pocklington abt. 1881, Superintendent Of Mew) Servant in Workhouse in Ancoats Manchester. (X63)
Smith Phillip St. George - Lincolnshire Regiment		b. Whiseley, Yorks. Resident Pocklington. Enlisted Richmond. Lincolnshire Regiment 2nd, Btn. Private. #41495. Formerly #35712, S. Staffs Regt. Died. 1 September 1917 in France/Flanders. (X64)
Snowden George Fred † - East Yorkshire Regiment		b. Pocklington. George Fred Snowden #19605 East Yorkshire Regiment. 1st 4th Battalion. Private. Enlisted at York. Killed in Action on 26th March 1918 in France/Flanders. Attestation: George Fred Snowden, b. 3 June

Name	Regiment	Service Record

1897 in Pocklington. Labourer. At Beverley for East Yorkshire Regiment 6/7/15. Next of kin: Father and mother William and Ann Snowden of 6 Dale St., Nunnery Lane. York. Sister Agnes aged 26. The Regimental diary for 26th March "*Withdrew under orders, at about 11am, under heavy machine gun fire, to a position across the ROSIERES - VRELY road, where the battalion dug in. The enemy attacked about 10pm. It was repulsed. Lt.Col. Wilkinson was wounded and taken down. Heavy enemy shelling & one of our batteries shelled us for about 2 hrs.*" (X65)

Spaven Harry † — Royal Horse Artillery and Royal Field Artillery

b. Pocklington. Harry Spaven #231857 Royal Horse Artillery Gunner. Enlisted at Selby. Killed in Action 21st March 1918 in France and Flanders. In 1911 Harry Spaven (21, b. Fangfoss abt. 1890, Groom Domestic) and wife Emily (27 b. Thornton) at Bulmers Yard, Gowthorpe, Selby. (X66)

Stairs Frederick William † - Royal Horse Artillery

b. Waplington in 1884. In 1911, Fred was in his own premises at Allerthorpe and working as a blacksmith and iron founder. Frederick William Stairs #96672 Royal Horse Artillery and Royal Field Artillery. Driver. Enlisted at York. Disembarked 2/12/14. Died at Home 15th April 1916. He died of an infection resulting from his war service in Huddersfield War Hospital on 15th April 1916 and was given a military burial at Allerthorpe on 18th April 1916 (X67)

Steels Herbert William — 83rd Overseas Btn. Canadian Exp. Force

Born in Pocklington and emigrated to Canada. The Steels family were grandchildren of William While who was Independent Minister in Pocklington for many years and a cousin of the Silburn family and several of the Steels siblings, together with some Silburns emigrated to Johannesburg to the gold mines & gold rush in the 1890's & 1900's. (X68)

Steward Robert Edward † - Yorkshire Regiment

b. Hayton. Enl. Pocklington. Alexandra, Princess of Wales's Own (Yorkshire Regiment) 6th Battalion #241169. Killed in Action 27 Sep 1917 in France/Flanders. (X69)

Story Walter † — Army Service Corps

Enlisted at Pocklington in Dec 1914. b. 1887 in York. Walter Story #T4/040069 Army Service Corps, Driver. 4th Aux. HorseTransport Coy. Taken to Marseilles hospital from kick in the abdomen by a horse. Died on 8 Jan 1917 Age 29. Next of Kin James Beckett Story, 45 Farrar St. York. 1 brother and 6 sisters. Buried at Mazargues War Cemetery, Bouches-du-Rone, Marseilles, France. (X70)

Thorington Frank † — Northumberland Fusiliers

b. In Kent in 1893. Enl. York. He married Blanche Ellen Chapman in Pocklington in 1914. Frank seems to have had no connection with Allerthorpe prior to his marriage, and his residence in 1917 is given as York. He may well have been a Railway employee in civilian life. He was conscripted into the Army in 1916 and posted to the Northumberland Fusiliers. 1st /4th Battalion (Territorials). #44624. Killed in Action 26 Oct 1917 in France/Flanders. The Second Battle of Passchendaele (part of the Third Battle of Ypres) began on

Name	Regiment	Service Record
		26th October 1917, the very day Private Thorington was killed. He is commemorated on the Tyne Cot Memorial in Flanders. (*Research by Val Hewetson*) (X71)
Vilain Alphonse	Belgian Army	Alphonse Vilain was the son of a family of Belgian Refugees housed and supported by the parish of Thornton. Mr Joseph Vilain was an upholsterer from Ostend and he and his wife and family of one son and two daughters arrived in the village on 11th November 1914. Joseph died in March 1915 and his son Alphonse who had been born in 1894 and joined the Belgian Army on 17th July 1915. He died in Chorley Lancashire in 1964. He appears in the Belgian Golden Book which gives details of all who subscribed to the book after the war. He is listed as a soldier (Private in the 1e Svarte Artillerie). The Belgian Army was less than 60,000 strong at the end of 1914. King Albert 1 commanded it through the succeeding four years for most of which it played a purely defensive role. The Belgian Army defended a line from Nieuwpoort to Ypres. During the course of the war, evaders and Belgian refugees like Alphonse joined the Army so that by September 1918 it was about 170,000 strong and took part in the last allied offensive which led to the Armistice. (*Written by Val Hewetson*) (X72)
Wales Robert †	East Yorkshire Regiment	b. Sutton-on-Derwent Resident at Bishop Wilton. Enl. Pocklington. East Yorkshire Regiment 1st Btn. #21764. Private. Killed in Action 23 Jul 1916 in France/Flanders. (X73)
Walker John Thomas†	Yorkshire Hussars	b. Kilnwick Percy, Pocklington Jan 1887. In 1911 at Foston, Flaxton, York a farm lab. with parents William (55) and Hannah (55). d. 2 Apr 1917 in France/Flanders #29014 Yorkshire Hussars 2nd Btn. Killed in Action. (X74)
Walker William Ernest†	East Yorkshire Regiment	Mr and Mrs Ben Walker of Ousethorpe Manor and farm manager of Captain Whitworth were parents of William Ernest Walker b. Hayton who died in Flanders on 14th July of 1915 during battle. #16021 Private 2nd Btn. East Yorkshire Regiment (X75)
Walkington John Cooper † -	Durham Light Infantry	Bishop Wilton war memorial d. 1918. Son of William and Annie Walkington of Bishop Wilton. Enl. Crook, Co. Durham. Durham Light Infantry 22nd Btn. Private. #22/911. Died of Wounds 20th Feb 1918 at A.D.S. Somme Redoubt (France). Left a widow Annie who remarried Alf Gowland (Goulden?) in Sep 1920 in Auckland district to live in Crook, Durham.(X76)
Ward Albert †	Royal Garrison Artillery	b. Slingsby, Yorks. Enl. Pocklington. Royal Garrison Artillery Battalion Durham. [RGA - (TF)] #338283 Gunner. Killed in Action 14 Jul 1917 in France/Flanders. (X77)
Ward John William †	York and Lancaster Regiment	b. Barton-Le-Street, Yorks. Enl. Pocklington. York and Lancaster Regiment Battalion: 10th (Service) Battalion #38278 Private. Died 14 Mar 1917 in France/Flanders. (X78)

Name	Regiment	Service Record
Ward Thomas †	Northumberland Fusiliers	b. Warter. Enl. Pocklington. Northumberland Fusiliers Battalion: 1/5th Battalion (Territorial) #263025 Private. Died 26 Oct 1917 in France/Flanders. (X79)
Watson William †	Duke of Wellington's	b. Kilnwick Percy, Pocklington Mar 1895. Enlisted Keighley 1st & 6th West Riding Regiment btn. West Riding Reg. #265114 d. 13 Oct 1918 Died of Wounds age 24. (Anc). Son of Mrs. Hannah Watson, of 50, Pitt St., Keighley, Yorks. Buried at Naves Communal Cemetery Ext. in Nord, Fr. (X80)
Webster Harry †	Royal Marine Light Infantry	b. Burton Agnes in 1893. Private Harry Webster Service Number PO/258(S) Portsmouth Bn. R.N. Div Royal Marine Light Infantry Son of George (a gardener) and Mary J. Webster, of North Lodge, Bolton Hall, Wilberfoss, York. (Ref. CWGC). On the 29th April Portsmouth Battalion arrived at Kaba Tepe Anzac beachhead at Gallipoli and were ordered to land to relieve the Australians. They occupied the trenches during the following night and over the next few days attempted to advance, only to be repulsed with heavy casualties. The heaviest casualties were incurred on 6th 1915 when Portsmouth Battalion were amongst those ordered to charge Razor Back Hill in the Monash Valley. Here Private Webster was killed at age 21 but his body was never recovered. He is commemorated on the Helles Memorial at Gallipoli and also on Bishop Wilton War Memorial (X81)
Willis George †	Yorkshire Regiment	3883 Pte George Willis. Born at Pocklington. Home at Old Eston, N Yorks. Enlisted Middlesbrough. He had suffered wounds on 15th Sept 1916 and died of these on the 21st. He is buried at Heilly Stn. Cemetery Mericourt-L'Abby. (X82)
Wilson Thomas †	Coldstream Guards	b. Driffield. Residence Pocklington. Enl. Driffield. Coldstream Guards #16200. Died of Wounds 31 Jul 1917 in France/Flanders. (X83)
Wilson Thomas Arthur † - King's Own (Yorkshire Light Infantry)		b. Barmby Moor 1895. Enl. Pocklington. King's Own (Yorkshire Light Infantry) 10th Battalion. #34731 Formerly #2481, Yorks Regt. Step brother of Joseph Cooper. Killed in Action 25 Sep 1916 age 21 in the Battle of Morvil on the Somme. Recorded on the Thiepval Memorial. (X84)
Whiteley John Appleby† - Prince of Wales's Own (West Yorkshire) Reg.		b. Pocklington 1895, John Appleby Whiteley #9920 West Yorks. Reg. 2nd Btn. Enlisted in York. Private. Died in France/Flanders 22 Apr 1915. Killed in Action Aged 19. The CWGC site records him as Son of Richard & Louisa Whiteley of South Duffield, Selby. The 1901 census records him as their nephew John Appleby, with Louisa born at Barmby Moor. Buried at Rue-David Military Cemetery, Fleurbaix, Pas de Calais. (X85)

Wood Harry Blanshard V.C.   Scot's Guards

Harry Wood was born in Newton upon Derwent in June 1882, and his birth was registered at Pocklington, the head of the registration district, which erroneously led to some sources publishing Pocklington as his birthplace. He was from a Newton upon Derwent farming family, both his grandfathers farmed locally and his middle name, Blanshard, came from a local farmer great grandfather, but he became a professional soldier, serving with the Scots Guards. He had a quite unexceptional military career; before all that changed in the final weeks of the war when he was awarded the Military Medal for his courageous actions in the trenches in August 1918, and followed up by winning the Victoria Cross, the country's highest award for bravery, just two months later. He returned home a hero, and was chosen as one of Britain's 100 bravest men to form the guard of honour at the burial of the Unknown Warrior in Westminster Abbey in 1920. But his remarkable story had a bizarre and tragic ending in 1924, when his wife was involved in a minor traffic incident and he collapsed with shock, never recovered and died a few days later. (X86)

Unidentified soldiers with a Pocklington connection

Left: The photograph was sent by Jan Robertson and is kept at the Royal Canadian Legion. Branch 94 in Quesnel, British Columbia, Canada. 'Slights Pocklington' is written in pencil on the cardboard backing. The cap badge is for the Lincolnshire Regiment.

Right: Possibly William Tayleure father of Arthur John Tayleure who was only 17 when he died and is on the Pocklington WW1 memorial. (see p.52).

Left: Found in an old photograph album sold at a local auction. In the album was a death card of Edward Barker of Bishop Wilton who died 17 Dec. 1888 aged 64.
Right: Found in an album with origins in Warter.

Pocklington and District Local History Group

Where the Pocklington Memorial war dead families lived*
(© Crown Copyright 1910)

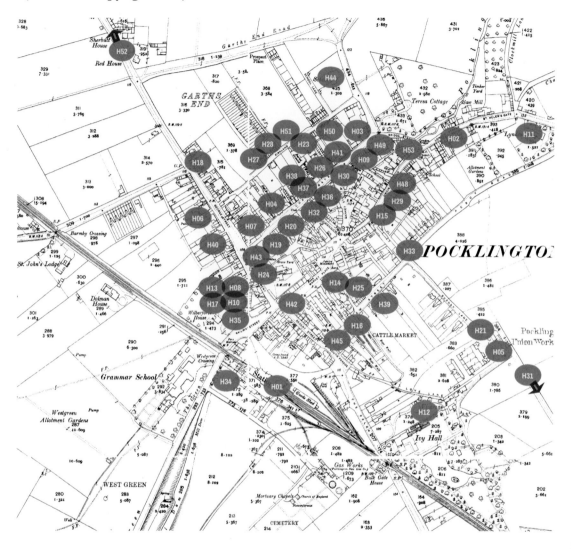

[*Please note this is only an approximate location]

Surname Index

Numbering convention

The 'Heroes' on the Pocklington War Memorial are numbered H01 - H53

The Church Memorial Book Soldiers are numbered C001 - C299

The Others or 'Extra' Soldiers found in records or in the local District are numbered X01 - X86

Eastwood, George (X20) p.230

Eastwood, James William (C073) p.196

Elliott, James (C074) p.196 (H10) p.18

Elmer, Arthur (C075) p.196

English, Robert Cecil (C076) p.196 (H11) p.19

English, Henry Turner (C077) p.196

Etherington, Thomas (C078) p.197

Everingham, Sydney H (C079) p.197

Everingham, Wycliffe G (C080) p.197

Ezard, Charles (C081) p.197

Ezard, Herbert (C082) p.197

Fairburn, Ernest (C083) p.197

Fairburn, Harry (C084) p.197

Ferisy, James (C085) p.198

Fielder, Cecil (C086) p.198

Fielder, John (C087) p.198

Fisher, Arthur Roland (C088) p.198

Fisher, Cyril Martin (C089) p.198

Fisher, Thomas Wilfred (C090) p.198 (H12) p.20

Fletcher, Ernest (C091) p.198

Fletcher, Oswald (C092) p.198

Flint, Charles (C093) p.199 (H13) p. 21

Flint, Henry (C094) p.199

Flint, Tom Oswald (C095) p.199

Flower, Charles Ernest (X21) p.231

Flower, Henry Bernard (X22) p.231

Forth, William Arthur (C096) p.199

Foster, Fred (C097) p.199 (H14) p.21

Foster, Harold (C098) p.199

Foster, William (X23) p.231

Fowler, Donald Fawcett (C099) p.199

Fox, Ted (C100) p.199

Francis, Jack O'Neil (C101) p.199

Futcher, Arthur (X24) p.231

Giles, George (C102) p.200

Giles, Jim (C103) p.200 (H15) p. 22

Gilyead, George (C104) p.200 (H16) p.23

Gospel, Fred (X25) p.231

Gospel, Henry (Harry) (X26) p.231

Grainger, George Henry (C105) p.200 (H17) p.23

Grainger, Jonathon (C106) p.200

Gray, Richard Duckwith (C107) p.200

Gray, Sydney (C108) p.200

Green, James (C109) p.200

Greig, John George (C110) p.200

Greig, William Allan (C111) p.200

Haith, John Robert (X27) p.232

Hall, Stanley (C112) p.201 (H18) p.24

Hardy, William Herbert (C113) p.201

Harrison, Albert (X28) p.232

Harrison, Frank (C114) p.201

Harrison, George (C115) p.201

Harrison, George Wilfred (X29) p.232

Harrison, James (C117) p.201 (H19) p.25

Harrison, John George (C116) p.201

Harrison, Martin (C118) p.201

Harrison, Norman (C119) p.201

Harrison, Redvers (C121) p.202

Harrison, Reginald (X30) p.232

Harrison, Richard (C120) p.202

Harrison, William (C122) p.202

Harvey, Bert (C123) p.203

Hatfield, John Henry (C124) p.203

Hawes, Abraham (X31) p.232

Hayton, Clifford (C125) p.203 (H20) p.26

Hayton, Harry (X32) p.232

Hayton, Thomas (126) p.203

Hayton, William Ward (X33) p.232

Haywood, Reginald Bernard Rands (X34) p.233

Hillerby, Alfred (X35) p.233

Hinde, Ernest (C127) p.203

Hinde, Fred (C128) p.203

Hinde, Robert (C129) p.203

Hindwell, Harry (C130) p.203

Hindwell, William (C131) p.204

Holmes, Henry (C132) p.203 (H21) p.27

Holmes, Herbert (C133) p.203 (H22) p.28

Hopper, Alfred (C134) p.203 (H23) p.29

Hotham, Albert (C135) p.204

Hotham, Charles (C136) p.204 (H24) p.30

Hotham, Fred (C137) p.204

Hotham, Harry (C138) p.204

Hotham, John William (C139) p.204

Hunter, Albert (C140) p.204

Hunter, George (C141) p.204

Hunter, J H (C142) p.204

Hunter, Thomas (C143) p.204

Husband, John Henry (X36) p.233

Ibson, Edward Henry (X37) p.233

Ireland, Harold (X38) p.233

Irwin, H G N (C144) p.204

Jackson, Herbert (X39) p.234

James, Kirby Easingwood (X40) p.234

Javerley, George H (C145) p.205 (H25) p.31

Javerley, Henry (C146) p.205

Jebson, Frederick (C147) p.205

Jennings, Thomas (C148) p.205 (H26) p.32

Jessop, Arthur (C149) p.205 (H27) p.33

Jessop, Herbert (C150) p.205 (H28) p.33

Johnson, Alfred (C151) p.205

Johnson, Arthur (C152) p.205

Johnson, Edward Wills (X41) p.234

Johnson, Enzor (C153) p.205

Johnson, Fred (C154) p.205